THE WANING OF EMANCIPATION

Guy Miron

The Waning of EMANCIPATION

Jewish History, Memory, and the Rise of Fascism in Germany, France, and Hungary

WAYNE STATE UNIVERSITY PRESS   DETROIT

15 14 13 12 11   5 4 3 2 1

Library of Congress Cataloging-in-Publication Data

Miron, Gai.
The waning of emancipation : Jewish history, memory, and the rise of fascism in Germany,
France, and Hungary / Guy Miron.
p. cm.
Includes bibliographical references and index.
ISBN 978-0-8143-3470-6 (cloth : alk. paper)
1. Jews—Germany—History—1800–1933. 2. Jews—France—History—20th century.
3. Jews—Hungary—History—20th century. 4. Jews—Identity—Germany—History—20th
century. 5. Jews—Identity—France—History—20th century. 6. Jews—Identity—Hungary—
History—20th century. 7. Germany—Ethnic relations. 8. France—Ethnic relations.
9. Hungary—Ethnic relations. I. Title.
DS134.25M57 2011
305.892'40409043—dc22
2011012874

Typeset by Maya Rhodes
Composed in Adobe Garamond and Serlio LH

CONTENTS

ACKNOWLEDGMENTS

My work on this book began in the academic year 2000–2001 with the generous support of the Warburg Post-Doctorate Fellowship at the Mandel Institute of Jewish Studies in the Hebrew University of Jerusalem. During this year I initiated a systematic search for the German sources related to the project primarily at the Yad Vashem Library as well as in the National Library of Israel in Jerusalem. Subsequently I began the study of the Hungarian language with the kind and dedicated guidance of Dr. Anna Szalai. Dr. Szalai shared and still continues to share with me her rich knowledge of Hungarian Jewish culture, and our cooperation led, in addition to the third part of this book, to other projects.

From January to May 2002 I was a visiting professor at the Allen and Joan Bildner Center for the Study of Jewish Life at Rutgers University, under the directorship of Professor Yael Zerubavel. This period proved to be important for the deepening of my knowledge and understanding of the Hungarian national historical discourse as well as for addressing certain methodological problems that concern the project as a whole. On my trip from Israel to the United States I stopped for a few days in Budapest, Hungary, where I located a variety of valuable sources in the National Széchényi Library and the library of the local Jewish Theological Seminary–University of Jewish Studies.

During the fall semester of 2002–3, I was a fellow at the International Institute for Holocaust Research at Yad Vashem, under the directorship of Dr. Tikva Fatal-Knaani and the late Professor David Bankier. This generous grant enabled me to focus on the Hungarian part of the project. As a result of the seminar at Yad Vashem, which was led by professors Bankier and Dan Michman, I decided to expand the scope of the research to the French case and turned to studying French and Yiddish. I have continued to make use of the library at Yad Vashem for the location of primary sources and literature vital for conducting the research for this book. Chapter 5 in this book is partly based on my article: Guy Miron, "History, Remembrance, and a 'Useful Past' in the Public Thought of Hungarian Jewry, 1938–1939," *Yad*

Vashem Studies 32 (2004): 131–70. I thank Yad Vashem for the permission to publish it here in a new form.

A research grant that I received for the academic year 2004–5 from the Leonid Nevzlin Research Center—which focuses on the study of the history, culture, and traditions of Russian and East European Jewry—at the Hebrew University enabled me to spend a few more days in Budapest and locate additional sources there.

The Schechter Institute of Jewish Studies in Jerusalem, which has been my academic home since the fall of 2003, was the academic institute under whose auspices this book was written. I express here my gratitude to my colleagues and friends at the institute—scholars, teachers, and students—for providing a fruitful and pleasant working environment throughout these years. The completion of the book was delayed by my appointment as dean of the institute for three years (2005–8), during which time I was privileged to work closely with and receive the support of Rabbi Professor David Golinkin, the president of Schechter Institute. This period, however, helped me to be more reflective about the project and thus to improve its quality. In addition, the research grant from the Schechter Institute was a crucial source of financial support for the English translation of this book.

The Leo Baeck Institute in Jerusalem served throughout my work on the project as the central source for any issue concerning the German Jewish aspects of this research. Shlomo Mayer, the director until 2009, was always kind and hospitable. The scholarship of Professor Shmuel Feiner, head of the institute, about the construction of a Jewish usable past during the Enlightenment era served as an illuminating model for the reconstruction of the ways in which Jewish intellectuals came to terms with their history and created a usable past in the much less optimistic time of the 1930s–40s.

I completed work on this book at the library of the Van Leer Jerusalem Institute during my sabbatical from the Schechter Institute. The library as well as various research groups at the Van Leer Jerusalem Institute served as an ideal and fruitful working environment and contributed to a deeper understanding of the theoretical dimensions of my research.

During the process of writing this book, I presented parts of the research in various venues. An especially important presentation took place at the Young Scholars Forum for History of the Jewish People and Israel Studies at the Chaim Weizmann Institute for the Study of Zionism and Israel, Tel Aviv University, which is headed by Professor Anita Shapira and directed by Dr. Orit Rozin. The discussion that developed following my lecture and especially the illuminating remarks of Professor Shulamit Volkov were very helpful for my reflection on the entire project. I would also like to thank my colleague Dr. Avi Bareli, editor of *Iyunim Bitkumat Israel: Studies in Zionism, the Yishuv and the State of Israel,* whose critical remarks on the article that I submitted following the Tel Aviv workshop were very valuable.

Throughout the process of working on this book I received the help of friends, teachers, and colleagues. Two of them were especially devoted throughout my work on the project. Dr. Havi Dreifuss (Ben-Sasson) was kind enough to read the entire draft of the book (in its original Hebrew version) more than one time. Her critical remarks and friendly support were important in the improvement of the text. The support of Professor Jay Berkovitz proved to be crucial for the publication of this book in English. Professor Berkovitz helped me to make the first contact with Wayne State University Press. Later he was kind enough to go through the entire English draft of the book, which was based on my translation. He suggested revisions and improved the language significantly. The publication of this book in a language that is not my native tongue would not have been possible without his support.

In addition, Dr. Anna Szalai, whom I have already mentioned, as well as Professor Attila Pok, Professor Gábor Gyáni, Professor Paul A. Hanebrink, Professor Árpád von Klimó, and Dr. Kinga Frojimovics, with whom I had fascinating talks concerning Hungarian and Hungarian Jewish history, helped me considerably in entering a new field and sharpening my thesis. Professor David Weinberg and Dr. Shmuel Bunim were also helpful in sharing their knowledge of French Jewish history. In addition, I would like to thank Professor Richard Cohen, Dr. Nathan Cohen, Professor Adi Gordon, Professor Alexandra Garbarini, Professor Moshe Sluhovsky, and Dr. Anja Siegemund for their friendly support in different stages of the project. I wish to thank my friends Dr. Shulamit Laderman for her recommendation for the image for the book's cover as well as Ido Carmel for his support during the last stages of the project. I would also like to thank Kathryn Wildfong, the acquisitions manager at Wayne State University Press, and Kristin Harpster Lawrence the editorial, design, and production Manager for their very pleasant cooperation throughout the whole process, as well as M. Yvonne Ramsey for her devoted copyediting of the book.

The book is dedicated lovingly to my parents, Yaacov and Carmela Miron, as well as to my children, Shira, Noa, Itamar, and Neta. Each was very supportive in his or her way.

INTRODUCTION

This is not the place to write this history. However, a sketch of it is still vital here, because in order to understand the future of a human group, as well as of an individual, and especially in order to understand the future of an idea, it is important to know where it originated. . . . Concepts such as assimilation, emancipation and dissimilation need examination if we want to reach a truthful understanding of what happened to the Centralverein since 1933 and to the goal to which it aspires.

—Alfred Hirschberg, "Der Centralverein deutscher
Staatsbürger jüdischen Glaubens"

These words, from a 1935 programmatic article by Alfred Hirschberg, one of the leaders of the Centralverein deutscher Staatsbürger jüdischen Glaubens (Central Union of the German Citizens of the Jewish Faith [CV]), concerned not just his own organization, which was the largest among German Jewry.[1] This was an expression of a wider tendency that motivated German Jews from other political groups to also reexamine the emancipation period and come to terms with its fundamental principles during what seemed to be its decline. Moreover, the distress experienced in the 1930s by members of European Jewish communities outside Germany inspired their spokespeople as well to reexamine their pasts in light of the challenges of the present.

The rise of Fascist regimes in Europe and primarily the rise of the Nazi Party to power in Germany compelled European Jews to grapple with the

1

severe crisis. Jews in Germany and eastern Europe and also, to a growing extent, in western Europe were forced to cope with the unending erosion of their civil and social status, increasing daily difficulties, and dark future on the horizon. Even before this crisis developed into a tangible threat to Jewish life, it deeply damaged the self-confidence of Jews in their various countries of residence. Members of Jewish communities whose self-consciousness had been shaped for generations by the emancipation experience now had to come to terms with either its impending collapse, as in Germany, or the threat of its abrogation, as in other countries.

Aside from the struggles for political and economic survival, Jewish intellectuals and publicists from various ideological camps assessed the long-term significance of the collapse of emancipation by turning to Jewish history and memory. They endeavored to find meaning in contemporary events and to predict future developments. They also used the past in order to understand their present political struggles; in other instances they invoked history to calm and comfort their readers.

This book deals with the ways in which Jewish spokespeople from three European communities—Germany, France, and Hungary—confronted these challenges and examines how representations of the past reflected various Jewish political ideologies. A central topic is the question of continuity versus change. The book seeks to assess the extent to which spokespeople of the various Jewish political camps continued to hold on to historical perceptions that materialized during the emancipation era and how the new ominous reality brought about the decline of these earlier perceptions and the emergence of new views.

The German, French, and Hungarian Jewish communities are presented in the pages that follow as case studies of three different paradigms of emancipation Jewry. French Jews won their civic equality during the French Revolution, and this new status was further consolidated in the first decades of the nineteenth century.[2] The roots of Jewish integration in Germany can be found in the Enlightenment discourse of the late eighteenth century, but German Jewish emancipation materialized very slowly, often along a twisted path, during the nineteenth century.[3] In Hungary, the political discourse regarding the emancipation began to mature in the 1840s. However, the Jews were granted full emancipation only in the last third of the nineteenth century, when Hungary became an autonomous nation-state within the Habsburg Empire.[4]

Since the 1980s, several scholarly projects have examined the varieties of the European Jewish experience of modernization, enlightenment, and emancipation in different countries. These projects were based on the cooperative efforts of historians who focused on different national settings and drew conclusions that reflected a comparative perspective.[5] Accordingly, it is clear that from the beginning Jewish modernization did not constitute a single process, not even in western and Central Europe. One should therefore refer to various paths of emancipation (as the title of one of those volumes suggests) or perhaps, even better, to emancipations rather than emancipation. Furthermore, it is noteworthy that the term "emancipation" has a complex history of its own. Reinhart Koselleck, who presented the history of the concept of emancipation from its Latin sources up to the political discourse in the nineteenth century, has asserted that we can speak of emancipation not only as "the singular act of the state granting equal rights" but also as a "long-term process designed to achieve equal rights through adaptation, habituation, or self-emancipation."[6]

Germany, France, and Hungary thus represent three interesting case studies because of the divergence of the starting points of Jewish emancipation in each instance and, moreover, on account of the different discourses that developed in the post–World War I period. As we shall see, the circumstances in which emancipation developed in each of these countries were very different: each one had a unique and complex political culture during the golden age of emancipation as well as in the years of its decline. In Germany, France, and Hungary, the relationship between church and state as well as between the various non-Jewish religious groups also differed in important ways.

Jewish emancipation in France was founded on a radical, secular, and revolutionary ethos, and the status of French Jews as citizens continued to depend, even in the 1930s, on the relative strength of this French ethos vis-à-vis the Catholic conservative ethos. In Germany, Jewish emancipation was achieved through a graduated reform process that was fundamentally rooted in nationalist and liberal values. Significantly, the Germans have never developed a deep-rooted secular political tradition, as have the French. German Jewish emancipation had to develop in a society and a state that were essentially Christian even in their most liberal stages. In Hungary, the national political culture was more profoundly and explicitly influenced by its Christian roots, especially during the interwar period. The status of Hungarian Jews, who were primarily associated with local national liberalism, was therefore largely determined by the orientation of the Christian conservative elite (mostly but not only Catholic) and its strength vis-à-vis the rising Fascist power.

The preemancipation Jewish experiences in these three countries were also diverse, a fact that is important to take into account when focusing on the politics of Jewish memory. As we shall see, there were also major variations in the internal structure of these three Jewish communities, particularly with respect to institutional life, the relationship among different Jewish religious streams, and the relationship between native and immigrant Jews. All of this naturally had major implications for the development of Jewish historical perceptions with which we shall deal in this book.

The history of emancipated Jewry in France and Germany has been extensively treated in Jewish historiography and also from a comparative perspective. The centrality of these two cases can be explained by both the trajectory of modern European Jewish history and the close interaction between these two Jewries, dating from the period of the French Revolution and the Napoleonic reforms. For example, Jacob Katz's classic book *Out of the Ghetto,* which depicts the background of European Jewish emancipation, can be viewed as a primarily German-French portrait.[7] A recent study was devoted to a more systematic comparison between just these two cases.[8]

This book follows the German-French comparison but also expands it by introducing Hungary into a study of western and Central European Jewry and contributing to the integration of Hungarian Jewish history, which for many years has been treated historiographically as an enclave, into the overall history of European Jewry. The problem of integrating Hungarian Jewish history into the overall history of European originated already with the very beginning of moden Jewish historiography during the nineteenth century. Heinrich Graetz, for example, held that "the role of the Hungarian Jews in general Jewish history is very marginal if they had a role at all."[9] A local Jewish historiography did in fact develop in Hungary, mostly from the late nineteenth century, but the fact that it was written in Hungarian made it inaccessible to the vast majority of Jewish scholars abroad, thereby leaving it on the margins of European Jewish historical discourse. After the Holocaust as Jewish historiography became more international, the Hungarian language obstacle continued to prevent historians who sought to write a comprehensive European Jewish history from including the Hungarian Jewish case in their writings. Even Salo Baron, the great American Jewish historian, admitted that his lack of command in Hungarian limited him in his efforts to integrate the events in Hungary into his research on Jews in 1848.[10]

But the isolation of the Hungarian Jewish case was a product of not just the language problem. It also had to do with the lack of clarity as to whether Hungarian Jewry belonged to the eastern or the western element of European Jewry. "East," "west," and "central" are not just geographical terms. They are also concepts in Jewish history. Thus, since the east European

Jewish type is usually identified with a traditional Yiddish-speaking culture and later on with modern ethnic Jewish politics in Slavic surroundings and is identified much less with emancipation and assimilation, Hungarian Jewry could not be considered a natural part of east European Jewry. On the other hand, in spite of the fact that Hungary's Jews were emancipated and at least partly assimilated, Hungary's geographic location and the presence there of a very strong Orthodox sector made it look unfit to be considered a part of west European Jewry. Furthermore, the fact that Hungary was part of the Eastern Communist bloc for more than four decades also isolated the development of Hungarian Jewish historiography from the discourse of west and Central European Jewish historiography. By including the Hungarian Jewish case, this book will demonstrate that in many respects, the internal development of Hungarian Jewry and the forms of Jewish identification in its public discourse should be conceptualized more in the context of the west and Central European emancipated Jewries.[11] Furthermore, the uniqueness of the Hungarian Jewish setting in the 1930s as well as the fact that its communal structures and public discourse continued to develop until the spring of 1944 makes it quite valuable in expanding and enriching the German-French picture of emancipated Jewry in its waning years.

Of course, German, French, and Hungarian Jewries were not the only emancipated Jewish communities in Europe. Still, the profound impact that emancipation exerted on these Jewries and their diverse forms of integration into the surrounding societies make them especially fruitful case studies. In countries such as Poland, Czechoslovakia, and Lithuania, Jews did not have the same sort of multigenerational tradition of emancipation in their newly founded nation-states.[12] Jews were also emancipated in smaller communities in Europe, but the German, French, and Hungarian Jewish communities, which were relatively large (in the 1930s there were several hundred thousands Jews in each of these countries), were more internally diverse in their social composition and communal structure. In fact, during the interwar period they consisted of established liberal integrated Jews, Zionist and national Jewish movements, and Orthodox Jewish communities as well as various political and communal organizations of Jewish immigrants from eastern Europe. Each of these groups reacted to the crisis of the 1930s from its own unique perspective. The fact that Jews in Germany, France, and Hungary experienced the rise of Fascism and the waning of emancipation in a variety of ways and on different levels of severity also makes these three locations interesting loci for the discussion of the problems raised in this study.

The long multigenerational development of emancipation in Germany, France, and Hungary fostered a major Jewish orientation in all three countries that was identified with this formative experience. By the end of the nineteenth century, an intensive process of acculturation had transformed the Jewish populations of France and Germany. These modern, mostly bourgeois, Jews became patriotic citizens of their new homelands and were usually associated with the local version of the national liberal political culture. In the late nineteenth century, a parallel Jewish type became common in Hungary. Although this Jewish type did not clearly become the mainstream camp of Hungarian Jewry, as in Germany and France, it did develop a class identity, a self-consciousness, and a historical discourse fundamentally similar to the French and German examples.

No less significant was the impact that the acculturation and acceptance of modern liberal political culture in these three Jewish communities exerted on other Jewish sectors. Modern Orthodox communities developed in Germany and Hungary, and the religious split between Orthodox and liberals eventually became institutionalized. Members of these Orthodox communities associated themselves with the ideals of emancipation and were deeply influenced by the process of acculturation, even if their spokespeople interpreted the new reality in a different manner from the liberals. Even spokespeople of the Zionist minorities, which appeared in these communities around the turn of the twentieth century, were in most cases associated with the values of emancipation despite their disapproval of the way that most Jews became assimilated into the surrounding society.

The shaping of Jewish public memory in the emancipated communities did not take place in a vacuum. National historiographical traditions and cultures of memory in Europe emerged in the nineteenth century and gained popularity, primarily in the last decades of the century, within the emerging modern mass culture. Figures, symbols, and events from the past, such as the French Revolution (1789), the unification of Germany (1870), and the Hungarian national liberation struggle (1848–49), were incorporated within national historical narratives and were disseminated by means of literature, the press, and state education systems. Museums were established, monuments were erected, and national memorial days were declared.

Scholarly research on nationalism has typically taken one of two positions with respect to the historical roots of nineteenth-century nationalism. Prominent scholars such as Eric Hobsbawm and Benedict Anderson have characterized the development of such national cultures of memory as "invented tradition" (Hobsbawm) or as part of the construction of "imagined communities" (Anderson).[13] Whereas Hobsbawm and Anderson doubt or even deny the very authenticity of national memory and some like-minded historians go so far as to portray it as a product of manipulation, other his-

6

torians assert that even if nationalism itself is a modern phenomena, ethnic premodern sources of modern national culture and memory cannot be denied.[14]

Aside from these theoretical discussions, extensive research literature in the last two decades has portrayed the diversity of each of the European national memory cultures and the different—and occasionally even opposing—voices that can be found in each of them in relation to all major topics of modern nationalism. A national memory culture, which was shaped and portrayed as a uniting factor, was consistently and predominantly, especially in times of crisis, a matter of dispute among competing religious, social, and political cultures. Each political culture developed its own version of the national past.[15]

German, French, and Hungarian Jews were influenced by the national historical discourse in their countries and endeavored to take part in it. Along with their acceptance of formal civil equality and their social and cultural integration into their surroundings, these Jews viewed themselves as part of the national culture within which they were living. However, since they had been considered aliens in their countries of residence prior to their emancipation and because many Jews had also arrived in these countries as immigrants, it became necessary to invent or imagine (in Hobsbawm's and Anderson's terms) or to redevelop (according to Anthony D. Smith) a usable past to help them become members of their respective nations, both in their own eyes and in the eyes of their fellow countrymen. The culture of memory that they developed and disseminated during the nineteenth century was therefore meant to provide them with "homemaking myths," a term that was suggested in the research literature to characterize the attempts of immigrants to create and even invent historical links to their new homeland.[16]

Jewish spokespeople therefore tried to integrate the history of their own communities within the national histories of their European homelands. They dealt extensively with the history of emancipation and clung to historical figures such as Wilhelm von Humboldt (Germany), Abbé Henri Grégoire (France), and József Eötvös (Hungary). They also pointed to deeper roots, often as far back as the medieval era, of Jewish settlement in their particular European homeland. In each instance, the turn to the past and the restructuring of their historical narrative were crucial for the development of an orientation that would inform their present condition and future horizons.[17]

This reconstruction of the Jewish past was founded predominantly on the faith of modern Jews in the fundamental liberal values of emancipation as well as in the rational course of history and the idea of progress. The readiness of Jews to accept the ethos of historicism that had become increasingly dominant in the shaping of national identity, especially in Central Europe, in the nineteenth century led to secularization and a profound transformation of the premodern Jewish cultural memory that was founded on an entirely different worldview.[18]

Of the three Jewish communities with which this book deals, Germany has been the subject of the most extensive research regarding the formation of modern Jewish history and memory. Already in the late eighteenth century, German Jewish intellectuals began to create a usable past and developed modern, rational Jewish historical thought. They also presented a pantheon of historical heroes who supported the values of the Enlightenment movement.[19] In the nineteenth century, German Jews witnessed the emergence of the modern science of Judaism (*Wissenschaft des Judentums*), which provided them with new images of the past. The science of Judaism helped them integrate into the liberal political culture of the German bourgeoisie, reform their religious tradition, and redefine their collective identity in a way that would suit their integration into the surrounding society.[20] It is important to note that these initiatives, which also reflected the growing religious diversity of modern German Jewry, were not shared by just a narrow group of scholars and intellectuals. From the mid-nineteenth century, a growing number of German Jewish writers, publicists, and communal activists were vigorous in the dissemination of the new culture of memory by means of historical novels, popular essays in the Jewish press, and the formation of Jewish reading associations.[21] A recent study has also shown that the attempts by German Jews to develop a homemaking myth that would strengthen their roots in the local motherland (*Heimat*) and depict an association of many centuries to their place of settlement were especially prominent among the spokespeople of small and medium-sized local Jewish communities.[22]

The modern Franco-Jewish culture of memory, which crystallized during the nineteenth century, naturally focused on the French Revolution. Toward the mid-nineteenth century, the mainstream of emancipated French Jewry adopted an ethos that has been termed in recent research "Republican Judaism" or "Jewish Republicanism." This ethos grasped the events of the French Revolution and the bestowal of citizenship to the Jews as a messianic phenomenon that fundamentally changed the nature of relations between Jews and non-Jews. The two major French Jewish organizations—the Consistoire Central des Israélite de France (Central Consistory of the Jews of France), the communal establishment that was founded during the Napoleonic era, and the Alliance Israélite Universelle, founded in 1860—had clear liberal orientations and were deeply committed, each in its own way, to the so-called values of 1789.

The adoption of this view of the Revolution by French Jews and its dissemination throughout their educational system and religious life made it a very powerful homemaking myth. Jewish Republicanism became the basis of the modern Franco-Jewish collective consciousness and was the backbone of French Jews' newly developed historiography.[23] French Jews were among the most enthusiastic supporters of the Third Republic, and in this spirit July 14, which was proclaimed in the early 1880s as the French national holiday, also became a central symbol in the memory culture of French Jews.

Most Hungarian Jews—both in the Neolog Judaism (liberal) stream, which was led by the Pest community, and in the Western modern Orthodox stream (but not the more traditional Eastern Orthodoxy)—underwent an accelerated process of Hungarian acculturation in the last decades of the nineteenth century.[24] Similar to Germany and France although somewhat later, the experience of emancipation and integration within the Hungarian nation became the basis for the formation of a homemaking myth that was embraced by a major part of Hungarian Jewry. Hungarian Jewish spokespeople nurtured this myth by adopting key events in Hungarian national history. First and foremost was the 1848–49 Liberation Struggle against the Habsburgs, which was marked every year on March 15. The Hungarian national tradition was portrayed as distinctively tolerant toward the Jews, major Hungarian kings and statesmen were presented as pro-Jewish cultural heroes, and the deep Jewish roots and loyalty to Hungary across generations was emphasized. Nathaniel Katzburg, who carefully set forth the features of modern Hungarian Jewish historiography, asserted that this was a major tool in the struggle for emancipation and integration in the Hungarian nation. The prevailing impression was that historically, anti-Semitism was fundamentally far removed from and foreign to the Hungarian nation.[25]

The German, French, and Hungarian Jewish communities are presented here as parallel cases. In all three countries we find shared values and common characteristics relating to the representation of the local Jewish past before the rise of Fascism threatened the future of emancipation. Of course, as we shall see in the three parts of this study, a variety of orientations exist among Jewish spokespeople in each of these communities. Nevertheless, most tended to identify with the liberal factions of the national movement in their respective homelands, conceptualized the history of the nation in this spirit, and attempted to integrate the Jewish narrative of their communities accordingly. Since their historical view was rational and based on the idea of progress, spokespeople for Jewish establishments in these communities were naturally inclined toward a teleological view of the history of their homeland: they viewed its entire premodern and prenational past as preparation for its national realization in their day. The integration of the Jews in this historical narrative was therefore based on representations of the history of German, French, and Hungarian Jews as leading to their full integration within these nations. This integration was deeply rooted in the past and rested on the universal values of emancipation.

In each of the three countries, we also find that the late nineteenth-century crisis of European liberalism had a decisive impact on the national political culture. Jews in Germany, France, and Hungary had to cope with the growing power of conservative forces that defined the local national identity in Christian religious terms (Catholic or Protestant), a definition that implicitly and sometimes even explicitly excluded the Jews from the nation. The strengthening of the conservative orientation in German nationalism, the decline of the idea of progress, and the rise of organic ideals of blood and soil created in German-speaking Central Europe a conducive atmosphere for the rejection of Jewish emancipation and the rise of anti-Semitism. Furthermore, this process shaped German nationalism in a very different way from the liberal form that emancipated Jews associated with and internalized.[26] Although the historical dynamics of the development of French nationalism in this period were different, France also experienced a certain conservative revival. In the late nineteenth century, new powers in France rejected the legacy of the Revolution as well as the idea of progress and Jewish emancipation, a phenomenon that was clearly expressed during the Dreyfus Affair.[27] In Hungary as well, where the national movement at this time was struggling primarily with the problem of the large minorities living within its territory, powerful voices expressed reservations concerning the national, secular, liberal orientation in general and Jewish emancipation in particular.[28]

Emancipated German Jews and, to a lesser extent, French and Hungarian Jews were therefore threatened as early as the late nineteenth century by the weakening of the liberal political culture.[29] As a result, their political and communal history were shaped by this challenge. In Germany, the structure of the Jewish political system was transformed fundamentally in the last decade of the nineteenth century. In 1893 the CV was founded as the first Jewish organization to represent German Jews in a national struggle against anti-Semitism. In a few years the CV became the central political association of mainstream liberal German Jews. Four years later the German Zionist Union was also founded. Although a minority group, the German Zionist

Union had a growing influence on the Jews' internal political discourse in Germany.[30]

In France, where the Dreyfus Affair concluded with Dreyfus's exoneration and the victory of the supporters of the French Republic, there was no political development comparable to what occurred in Germany.[31] French Jews had fundamentally more confidence in emancipation, and the vast majority of their spokespeople therefore felt comfortable emphasizing the fact that major forces from the general French political arena acted in defense of Dreyfus. The final outcome of the Dreyfus Affair, which was seen by the Jews as a victory for the values of the republic and of "true France," held back the development of a distinctive Jewish political activity and historical self-awareness among the mainstream integrated French Jews. The relative frailty of the specific French Jewish historical awareness was also due to the fact that the French national consciousness, with which the Jews tended to associate, was founded primarily on secular and universal values. Jews could easily identify with French republican values since they were not associated with Christianity, and their need to develop their own political organizations and ethos was therefore less prominent than in Germany. Still, even among French Jews of that time there were certain voices—of Zionists and non-Zionists—that raised doubts about the total devotion of Jews to the republican ethos. This laid the foundation for the development of a distinctive French Jewish historical self-consciousness.[32]

As in the French case, in late nineteenth-century and early twentieth-century Hungary, anti-Semitism did not lead to a deep transformation of the local Jewish political culture. However, the new challenge resulted in the institutionalization of the public struggle of the integrating Jews. The weekly *Egyenlőség* (Equality), which was founded in 1882, became the chief political journal of Hungarian Jewish Neolog liberal politics. Interestingly, the political positions of the spokespeople of the modern Orthodox stream regarding Jewish emancipation and political integration were basically similar to those of the Neologs, despite the deep religious schism between them. Other positions, mostly of Jewish nationalist spokespeople, began to be articulated in Hungary prior to World War I, but they were quite marginal.[33]

All in all, it can be said that in the decades preceding World War I, liberal political values were diminishing in all three countries. Germany turned more and more to aggressive and exclusive nationalism. Hungary turned to liberalism, which reached its peak in the mid-1890s and then began to decline. And in France conservative Catholic forces challenged the legacy of 1789. Still, despite this antiliberal wave and despite the rise of anti-Semitism as a political power during this period, in none of these cases did the transformation become a tangible threat to Jewish emancipation. The vast majority of German, French, and Hungarian Jews therefore continued to adhere to their belief in emancipation as well as to their homemaking myths and the rational, optimistic, historical view of progress. In confronting anti-Semitism, they made more intensive political use of past images, and this emerged as a major tool in their struggle against those who challenged their position as equal citizens.[34]

The results of World War I transformed the political culture in Germany and Hungary significantly. As members of the defeated Central Powers, these two countries were forced to sign peace agreements under very harsh terms. In the Treaty of Versailles and the Treaty of Trianon, respectively, the German and Hungarian governments were compelled to surrender extensive territories and agree to conditions that were viewed by their populations as unjustified and humiliating. The political culture that prevailed in both countries during the trauma of the postwar period, which was accompanied by the experience of collective humiliation, is best described as a "culture of defeat."[35] In both countries the defeat at the hands of a foreign external enemy resulted in the disintegration of the traditional political system and in a radical and violent political polarization that concluded with elements of civil war. The deep collective longing to understand the meaning of the defeat and to learn its lessons motivated many to interpret it primarily as a consequence of an internal decline that had preceded the external defeat. Invariably the humiliating experience of the defeat, which was accompanied by a deep economic and political crisis, produced the rise of a pessimistic public mood. At the same time, however, many also had faith in a possible national revival that would eventually restore national dignity and reverse the results of the war. In both countries this public discourse was largely founded on the perceptions and images of the national past. Many historians and publicists who took an active part in this discourse tended, under the new circumstances, to embrace irrational and even mythological ideas—much more so than in the prewar era—and came to deny the liberal idea of progress.[36]

These transformations in the political and cultural mood had a major impact on the status of the Jews in Germany and Hungary and on the future of emancipation. The internal national decline, which was grasped in the postwar years as the root cause of the military defeat, was linked in each instance to the nineteenth-century liberal political culture that was responsible for the emancipation of the Jews, among others things. The much-desired national revival was therefore imagined as having to redefine the national identity either in conservative and religious (Christian) terms or in Volkist and racial terms.[37] In both cases, such a transformation entailed the exclusion of the

Jews from the nation's core, that is, the partial or even total abrogation of their emancipation. In Hungary, the political realization of this vision, in its conservative version, started with the formation of Miklós Horthy's regency regime and the enactment of the *numerus clausus* law in 1920 and continued in the late 1930s and early 1940s with the gradual abolition of Jewish emancipation.[38] In Germany, the transformation was fulfilled in its racial version with the rise of the Nazis to power in 1933, which had immediate repercussions for the emancipation of the Jews.

France may have been one of the victorious Allies in World War I, but the public mood that prevailed in French society in the postwar era, especially in the 1930s, was decisively influenced by the trauma of the war. The relative proportion of fallen soldiers in France was larger than in any other European country and engendered among the French profound anxiety about the threat of another war. Postwar French society also suffered from a severe demographic decline that encouraged, especially in the 1930s, a growing sense of inferiority vis-à-vis the rising German power. In the 1930s France also encountered an acute economic crisis and the severe problems caused by the mass influx of immigrants and refugees. The republican ethos and the legacy of the Revolution, which were also the foundation of the Jewish emancipation, became the core of intensive disputes that polarized French society and politics, especially since 1934. Under these new circumstances, the French public mood grew melancholic, pessimistic, and sometimes even irrational, and the voices that fundamentally challenged the 1789 legacy, including the Jewish emancipation, became much stronger.[39]

The Jews of Central and western Europe were therefore compelled to cope in the 1930s with the repercussions of the rise of an antiliberal political culture and with the growing fragility (in France), decline (in Hungary), and even total nullification (in Germany) of their emancipation. This book will analyze the politics and culture of memory that informed attempts by Jewish historians, publicists, and community activists in Germany, France, and Hungary to manage and ascribe meaning to the waning of the emancipation. It will also consider the various reactions of Jewish interpreters to the undermining of the homemaking myths that bound them to the European countries in which they resided.

As they had done during the golden era of emancipation, Jewish spokespeople related even during its period of decline both to the Jewish past and to the national history of their European homelands. Many—predominantly those who were associated with the liberal integrationist camp in each of the three communities—continued, even under the pressure of the new circumstances, to cleave to the optimistic historical narratives that were shaped in the nineteenth century. Some of them did so in a simplistic and dogmatic manner; others adapted the old narratives to the new gloomier reality. Others—first and foremost Zionist and national Jewish spokespeople but occasionally also Orthodox and liberal spokespeople—harshly criticized the historical consciousness of emancipated Jewry, breaking from this tradition and attempting to offer an alternative. In their attempts to present a usable past to the Jewish public, Jewish writers reacted to the national historical discourse in their country and, at the same time, were also influenced by it in the way that they described the Jewish past. While attempting to maintain their faith in the rational progress of history and in the liberal legacy, Jewish spokespeople were inevitably drawn to more pessimistic positions and were influenced by intensifying irrational trends.

The Jewish historical discourse that will be portrayed and analyzed in this book is primarily based, as the organization of the chapters shows, on the national perspective. However, this discourse also has transnational dimensions insofar as national borders did not exclusively define Jewish polemics in these years. German Jews understandably dealt first and foremost with questions concerning the nature of German nationalism and the rise and fall of emancipation. Nevertheless, as we shall see, some of their prominent spokespeople also evaluated the past and reflected on the future of Jewish emancipation in other countries. It is interesting to note that in the early years of the Nazi regime, this transnational tendency was more characteristic of Zionist spokespeople (most prominent among whom was Joachim Prinz), as will be evident in chapter 1. However, as the question of emigration became increasingly central to the agenda of German Jewry, non-Zionist publicists also turned to transnational writing, as we will see in chapter 2.

In France, the tendency toward transnational discourse can be traced first in the way French Jewish spokespeople came to terms with the rise of the Nazi regime in Germany and later on with the *Anschluss,* the occupation and annexation of Austria into Nazi Germany in March 1938. Furthermore, the fact that one of the two major sectors of French Jewry, the Yiddish-speaking immigrants, conducted its political and historical discourse in an international Jewish language and was in fact an integral part of an international Yiddish republic of letters fundamentally shaped its discourse as transnational, as will we seen in the discussion about the return-to-the-ghetto debate (chapter 4). In Hungary, the Jewish historical discourse was relatively more self-centered, especially in the 1930s. Nevertheless, even in Hungary transnational tendencies, primarily among national Jewish writers, can be identified. Such tendencies became more prominent in the early 1940s, as is evident in the discussion about Ernő Marton in chapter 6. Taken as a whole, the transnational perspective is important to this book, for it permits more fruitful comparisons among writers in various countries and supports the thesis that we have here a single Jewish historical discourse, even though it was conducted in a variety of countries, languages, and settings.[40]

The primary sources on which research for this book is based include articles and essays that appeared in Jewish journals and periodicals in Germany, France, and Hungary as well as historical literature, mostly popular, that was published by Jewish publishing houses. The historical narratives and images of the past that were delineated and circulated by Jewish publicists in this period are based on a wide variety of publications: some are ideological and programmatic, while others are more scientific or descriptive. Many statements and interpretations regarding historical themes were incorporated in the news and political reportage found in Jewish journals as well as in book reviews. They were also used by Jewish activists in their struggles to defend the status of the Jews, sometimes in direct confrontation with hostile anti-Semitic perceptions of the past. Jewish writers also turned to the past in order to encourage and comfort their readers, and these writers used the past in conducting the ideological polemics in which they engaged with spokespeople of rival Jewish streams. Numerous descriptions and interpretations regarding the Jewish past, often also with clear connotations for the present, appeared in publications that marked a variety of commemorative events. This was the case, for example, in January 1936, which was the 150th anniversary of Moses Mendelssohn's death; in late 1937, the seventieth anniversary of the emancipation of Hungarian Jewry; and in the spring and summer of 1939, the 150th anniversary of the French Revolution.

Based on diverse sources written by Jewish historians, publicists, and public activists espousing a range of ideological and political views, this book focuses on the role of history and the use of past images in contemporary Jewish public discourse.[41] Are these sources, however, truly representative of the wider Jewish public opinion in this period? In a recent review article, the historian Henry Wassermann asserted that the Jewish press of the postemancipation era was a marginal source of information for a Jewish public whose political and cultural life was focused elsewhere. The methodological challenge for historians who utilize this journalism, Wassermann added, is to recognize the fact that in such publications, Jewish writers represented—especially when they dealt with questions of Jewish identity—only their narrow perspective as communal activists and not necessarily the wider perspective of their constituencies.[42]

This critical perspective requires careful consideration with regard to the representation of the ideas and interpretations that will be presented in this book. It is likely that in the golden era of emancipation, Jewish public thought, as it was expressed in the communal press, reflected primarily the views of relatively small Jewish groups. Furthermore, the writings of those intellectuals, publicists, and communal activists who published their ideas in the Jewish press during or after the decline of emancipation (i.e., in the 1930s and in Hungary also in early 1940s) did not represent the entire variety of ideas present among the Jews of Germany, France, and Hungary. In fact, Jewish community journals did not articulate the voices of assimilated Jews who had dissociated themselves from any contact with the Jewish political and literary community or the voices of others who, for various reasons, did not express themselves in these publications. Nevertheless, it is not at all apparent that the Jewish communal press remained marginal in this period.

In the waning years of emancipation as Jews were excluded from the general public arena, many of them felt alienated by the national press. This was of course most evident in Nazi Germany beginning in 1933 but occurred also in Hungary and much less so in France. The circulation of communal Jewish journals therefore increased significantly, and accordingly so did their impact within the Jewish community. The process of the transformation of the Jewish press from a secondary to a primary source of information for its readers was especially conspicuous in Germany.[43] Of course, the fact that the Jewish press and literature published in Germany beginning in 1933 was under the scrutiny of the Nazi censor cannot be ignored. Nevertheless, it seems that with regard to the topics treated in this book, which are not explicitly political, the impact of censorship was not very extensive. In Hungary too, the decline of the status of Jews and their intensifying social isolation, especially beginning in the late 1930s, brought the communal Jewish press, Neolog and Orthodox alike, to a much more central position in the Jewish public.[44] The French Jewish situation is more complicated in this context because of the fact that the Jewish community in France was divided into two approximately equal groups: the local French-speaking Jews and the east European Yiddish-speaking immigrants. As Jewish emancipation in France remained in force until 1940, local French Jews did in fact continue to read primarily the general French press throughout the 1930s, and the communal Jewish press was for them only supplementary. This can be clearly demonstrated by the agenda of the communal Jewish press: communal journals, first and foremost *L'Univers Israélite,* covered primarily Jewish topics, leaving the national and international news to the general press. For immigrants, however, the Yiddish press printed in France, which was in part a daily press, was not secondary but instead served as their main source of national and international news during the tumultuous decade of the 1930s.

The fundamental orientation of this book is comparative and focuses on similarities and dissimilarities in the ways that Jews from these three countries came to terms with the challenge of shaping Jewish identity and Jewish memory during the rise of Fascism. Nevertheless, the focus of each discussion within the particular setting and in the wider context of past representations in each of the three non-Jewish societies in France, Germany, and Hungary requires a separate discussion in each of the cases. The book is therefore divided into three parts: the first deals with Germany, the second deals with France, and the third deals with Hungary. Each part consists of two chapters that examine how each of the three communities came to terms with the crisis in relation to the internal diversity and the political splits within the particular community.

The discussion in the German case begins with the late Weimar period and focuses mainly on the first years of the Nazi regime until late 1938, when the Jewish journals and periodicals were almost entirely closed down by the Nazis. Concerning France, the discussion begins with the ways that Jewish spokespeople reacted to the political turning point in 1933 in Germany and concludes by relating to the last voices heard in the Jewish press in the spring of 1940, on the eve of the military defeat of the French Republic. The third part deals with Hungary from the early 1930s until the spring of 1944, the time of the conquest of Hungary by the Nazis and the beginning of the mass murder of its Jews. Insofar as this book is based on the analysis of primary sources from each of the three countries, it differs from more partial comparative efforts that are based on the thorough study of sources from a particular Jewish community, with cases of other communities most often resting on the existing secondary literature.[45]

In the past, mostly in the days of the so-called Jerusalem school, Jewish and primarily Israeli historiography tended to paint a generalized picture of Jewish history in various countries.[46] This tendency, which stemmed largely from a national Jewish worldview, sometimes hindered detailed analyses of the social and political processes in individual communities. As a result, an understanding of the unique circumstances of each community was very difficult to attain.[47] In the last several decades, on the other hand, Jewish historiography in the Diaspora and later also in Israel has engaged in deeper and more detailed research of individual communities. This tendency, which is related to the growing liberation from the national ideological thought of the Jerusalem school, was also motivated by the aspiration to write more professional and scientific Jewish history with a significant connection to the general national historiography of each country. Analytically, however, this tendency has sometimes led to the fragmentation of the study of Jewish communities into subdisciplines and has thwarted the ability to examine key historical problems from a general Jewish perspective and to reach more sweeping generalizations. By its use of the comparative method, this book hopes to strike a balance between the two foregoing tendencies.[48] Comparisons of past perceptions and images in pre-Holocaust Germany, France, and Hungary will enable us to address the wider questions that concern Jewish identity and self-consciousness and the cultural memory of Jewish emancipation during the rise of Fascism without forfeiting a comprehensive examination of each community in its unique context.

The historical views, insights, and interpretations that are discussed in this book were articulated by a variety of individuals, the vast majority of whom were associated with certain Jewish political or communal streams or organizations. I have made an effort to include basic biographical details about these writers, but it is important to emphasize that such information was not always available. As the reader will see, biographical information was more available for German Jews than for French and Hungarian Jews.

PART 1

GERMANY
1929—38

1

IN SEARCH OF THE MEANING
OF THE MISFORTUNE

During the Weimar Republic in the 1920s and early 1930s, German Jews found themselves in a very confusing situation. By 1919 Germany had become a democratic republic. On the one hand, it seemed that the new regime had fulfilled, for the first time, its promise of complete emancipation. Many of the institutional frameworks such as the civil service and academia, which had previously barred admittance to Jews, now accepted them. The change in the regime, however, required the Jews to adapt themselves to a new style of German politics. While this time period had become more free and democratic, it was also more violent and polarized.[1] Furthermore, the Weimar era—in the first years of the republic until its relative consolidation in 1924 and then in the last years before its fall—was characterized by an escalation in the scope and brutality of German anti-Semitism. Naturally, this had a major impact on the German Jewish public discourse.[2]

Most of the approximately 550,000 Jews living in Germany during the Weimar Republic identified with a liberal political orientation. These Jews strove for integration into the German state and society. This line was represented primarily by the Centralverein deutscher Staatsbürger jüdischen Glaubens (Central Union of the German Citizens of the Jewish Faith [CV]). Since its founding in 1893, the CV acted to defend the civil rights of Jews. During the Weimar years the CV increased its public and political activities.[3] In addition to the CV, there was a Zionist movement that represented an active minority among German Jewry. One section of the Zionist movement focused its efforts on developing the Jewish national home project in Palestine. The other part focused on *Gegenwartsarbit,* the development of Jewish community life in Germany as an active national community (*Volksgemeinde*).[4] Another minority group that developed into its own subculture within Germany Jewry during this period was the Orthodox group. This group combined its religious obligation to observe Jewish law with its political aspiration to become integrated as equal citizens.[5]

German Jewry also included east European Jews, who represented 10–20 percent of the German Jewry population. However, politically the members of this group did not voice views that were distinct from those of the major political groups among German Jews and did not form a significant separate political organization. In this context the east European Jews in Germany were different from the much larger population (in relative numbers) of east European Jews in France who were more leftist oriented. These Jews who would come later will be discussed in the second part of this book.[6]

The fall of the Weimar Republic and the rise of the Nazis to power came as a great shock to German Jews and was a turning point in their history. In September 1933 most of the Jewish organizations joined together to form the new Reichsvertretung der deutschen Juden (Reich Representation of German Jews). At the same time, their activities as separate associations within the internal Jewish political landscape and the ideological tensions among them intensified in the first years of the new regime.[7]

The members of the central liberal camp seem to have experienced the most difficult crisis. Until 1933 they believed in Jewish integration in Germany and held a fundamentally optimistic view about the future of emancipation. The political upheaval caused by the rise of Nazism seriously undermined the beliefs of these German Jews, especially the young. Unable to continue the political confrontation against the Nazis, the spokespeople for the CV now devoted a great amount of effort to ascribing meaning to the new situation, redefining their goals, and preserving their heritage.[8]

In contrast to the ideological confusion of the Jewish liberals, there was a sharp rise in the influence of the Zionists. Their more skeptical position regarding the German Jewish integration as well as their vision of a Jewish national revival became more attractive, especially for the young. However, the Zionists also had to cope with the political crisis and face the fact that the solutions they suggested for the Jewish plight were not applicable for most German Jews.[9] Orthodox spokespeople in their communities offered solutions in the spirit of their traditional positions.[10]

Discussions about ways to confront the crisis were conducted predominantly in the German Jewish press. Finding the best strategy to adapt to the new political climate assumed a central role in Jewish public life as well as in popular books and public lectures.[11] This chapter begins by presenting the fundamental features of the public discourse on Germany's past, especially as reflected in the changing positions of German historians vis-à-vis the crisis of German liberalism and the decline of the Weimar Republic. Then by examining historical topics, narratives, and perceptions of the past, the chapter portrays and analyzes the attempts by major German Jewish spokespeople and representatives of their various organizations to employ historical memory in order to conceptualize the tragic turning point in the position of the Jews in Germany. This discussion will consider how they interpreted the decline of German liberalism, whether they viewed the decline as a German phenomenon or the beginning of a general European or even global chain of events, and how they reevaluated the path of German Jewry to modernity and their long years of struggle for emancipation. Representatives of the three major factions of German Jewry—liberals, Zionists, and Orthodox—utilized different modes of historical interpretation in order to grant meaning to the agonies of the present and outline the right path for the future. The chapter will focus on the last years of the Weimar Republic and the first years of the Nazi regime until early 1935.

German Representation of Past Images in the Transition from the Weimar Republic to the Nazi Era

In his comprehensive study of German historical consciousness, Bernd Faulenbach has stressed the importance of historical representations in the social and cultural life of the Weimar Republic. Faulenbach described the period between the last decades of the German Empire to the Third Reich as peak years in terms of the intensity with which professionals dealt with history. During this period the number of academic historians who were members of the professional guild increased, and their involvement in public life and in popular writing grew significantly. These historians played a key role in the formation of the notion of German official nationalism during the imperial era. They were very aware of the connection between the way they conceptualized and presented the past and the political problems of the present. Their contribution was therefore important in shaping both the public image of the present and expectations for the future.[12]

Despite the fact that there was continuity in the way that modern German history was represented, just as there was continued involvement of historians in the public discourse, the post–World War I crisis left its own clear impact. Most German historians in the Weimar period identified with the conservative legacy of the imperial era and therefore belonged to the antirepublican camp. Even those who supported the establishment of the republic did so, in most cases, as a consequence of their rational recognition of the lack of alternatives, not out of any fundamental identification with republican values. Thus, they presented themselves as *Vernunftrepublikaner* (republicans of reason).[13]

The polarized political discourse of the Weimar Republic also changed the way that historical narratives were constructed. Different political camps and social milieus employed past images in order to legitimize their divergent worldviews.[14] The deepening split in the historical discourse and the political use to which it was increasingly put heightened the need to find contemporary relevance rather than pure historical research. Aside from national German historians—most prominent among them Friedrich Meinecke—who in spite of the overwhelming trends tried to preserve the scientific core of German historiography, there was a popular German tendency to transform historical writing from science to a source of myth. This position was associated with *Antihistorismus* (antihistoricism) and was part of the so-called crisis of historicism that intensified the political crisis of the Weimar Republic.[15] Thus, out of this emerged a relativist attitude that claimed that history cannot be presented impartially and should be conceptualized and narrated from the context and values of contemporary society.[16]

The crisis of the Weimar Republic therefore left its imprint on the decline of rational forms of historical interpretation and also resulted in a growing rejection of the idea of progress. Whereas the economic and political success of the Second Reich had influenced the emergence of an optimistic teleological historical narrative—a national German history progressing toward Otto von Bismarck's unification—the defeat in World War I and the fragile political reality of the Weimar Republic produced the rise of pessimistic approaches and stressed more and more the inevitable repetition of catastrophes throughout history. As the awareness of the crisis facing the republic increased, the historical discourse, which rejected the liberal idea of progress in favor of a deterministic cyclical view of history, became more dominant. This new historical discourse, characterized by Faulenbach as "eternal ups and downs of the events" (*ewigen Auf und Ab des Geschehens*) and by Dietmar Schirmer as "archaic-mythic," supplied Germans with a reason to believe in a possible revival from a seemingly lost situation.[17] This discourse was popular in the circles of the conservative and nationalistic Right but also infiltrated the republican and Socialist milieus.

The shock and rapid transformation experienced by many Germans during the first months of the Nazi regime reinforced their tendency to invoke past images and to reevaluate their history vis-à-vis the present. The new regime's powerful influence during the *Gleichschaltung* (the process by which the Nazis established a system of tight coordination over politics, society, and commerce) accounts for this change in historical outlook among new and veteran supporters of the Nazi Party, including many who had dissociated themselves from the party until 1933. Many German historians, who until 1932 tended to support the old conservative elites, chose under the new circumstances to grant their support to Adolf Hitler. During the first months of the new regime, it became common among German historians to speak not only about the fall of the republic but also about the end of an era more than 150 years old and the decline of the liberal bourgeois values associated with that era. Some of them even developed a new historical view according to which the Nazis—and only the Nazis—were destined to redeem Germany from its degeneration and lead it to a national revival.[18]

The Nazi movement itself did not hold an official historical worldview and was not successful in imposing a Nazi historical worldview on German historians. Even so, the new atmosphere in Germany triggered the rise of a historical interpretation that negated the heritage of enlightenment, rationalism, and liberalism. Jewish emancipation, considered one of modernity's maladies, was also targeted.[19]

Facing the Decline of Liberalism: The Jewish Historical Discourse in the Last Years of the Weimar Republic

During the last years of the Weimar Republic, German Jewish spokespeople increasingly turned their attention to history in hopes of understanding the meaning of the events they were experiencing. Prominent Jewish historians such as Ismar Elbogen (b. 1874), Selma Stern-Täubler (b. 1890), and Ismar Freund (b. 1876) published, in addition to their research, articles in Jewish popular journals, primarily in the *Central Verein Zeitung* in which publicists and public activists addressed historical topics. The publication of the Jewish historical journal *Zeitschrift für die Geschichte der Juden in Deutschland,* which had closed in 1892, was reopened in 1929.[20] The monthly magazine *Der Morgen,* founded in 1925 by the CV, contained many historical discussions, including some with implications for contemporary events.[21] Zionists and Orthodox intellectuals and publicists also referred to historical topics in their journals. This trend can be seen in popular publications that offered comprehensive histories of the Jewish people. Popular books, such as those published by Josef Kastein and Joachim Prinz, were based on a Jewish national worldview and were therefore criticized by liberal Jewish spokespeople.[22]

Many contemporary Jewish spokespeople continued to struggle for emancipation, believing, as had their nineteenth-century predecessors, in Germany's future as an enlightened liberal country. However, even they were aware of the changes in their surroundings. Therefore, their attempts to present past images based on liberal values can be seen as part of the broader struggle for the future of German society.[23] Other Jewish spokespeople—predominantly Zionists but also a growing number of liberals—began to grasp the decline of liberalism as an inevitable fact that the Jews should accept and interpret. Some of them even began reevaluating modern German and German Jewish history, a process that can be seen as foreshadowing the German Jewish discourse under the Nazi regime.[24]

On March 16, 1929, Bruno Weil, the deputy chairman of the CV, delivered a lecture titled "The Path of German Jews." Speaking in Frankfurt to a crowd of more than one thousand Jews and non-Jews, Weil rejected the "new nationalism" that regarded German identity as being based on a deterministic foundation of blood and race.[25] He presented German nationalism as an open liberal collective united under the principles of the social contract by personal commitment and cultural inclination. The position taken by Weil, whose interpretation of the collapse of emancipation will be discussed later in this chapter, reflected a common tendency among liberal Jewish spokespeople to represent Germanness as a pluralistic liberal heritage based on Enlightenment values. This depiction of Germanness was a key element in the homemaking myth that helped link German Jews to their homeland.

In the last years of the Weimar Republic, Jewish commentators similarly represented the heritage of the 1848 revolution in a positive light, trying to use it as a source of inspiration for the declining German liberalism and even as a source for its revival. Efforts were also made to present key figures in German history, such as the great Prussian reformer Karl Freiherr von Stein, as symbols of liberalism and even democracy.[26] Liberal Jewish spokespeople were most likely aware that they loaded these historical symbols with a very different meaning than what was portrayed in mainstream German historical discourse. Non-Jewish commentators, on the other hand, depicted the German bourgeoisie as helpless during the 1848 revolution and depicted Stein as an antirevolutionary Prussian conservative.[27] The way in which the liberal and Orthodox spokespeople received the renewed *Zeitschrift für die Geschichte der Juden in Deutschland* demonstrated how aware German Jewish spokespeople were of the political importance of the discourse about past representations in the last years of the Weimar Republic.[28]

Jewish spokespeople who spoke and wrote about history in the last years of the republic worked to advance the integration of Jewish and German history. In May 1929 the historian Selma Stern-Täubler argued that the goal of historical integration as a means for political and social integration must be a central objective of any future German Jewish research.[29] In September 1932 when the Nazi threat to the future of German Jewry became tangible, the young publicist Fritz Friedländer (b. 1901) claimed that a reliable presentation of an integrated German and Jewish history may provide "good testimony" and discredit Nazi attempts to portray the Jews as an alien element in German history.[30]

The belief in progress and the clear distinction between the dark ghetto age and the light of Enlightenment and emancipation era still epitomized the shared historical perspective of most spokespeople of liberal German Jews during these years. This worldview was plainly expressed by many publicists in 1929, when German Jewry marked the two hundredth anniversary of the birth of Gotthold Ephraim Lessing (in January) and Moses Mendelssohn (in September). Mendelssohn's and Lessing's friendship was for many a symbol of progress and enlightenment.[31] However, due to the political circumstances of 1929, certain writers—mostly Zionist or Orthodox but also some members of the liberal camp—related much more critically to the Mendelssohn myth and especially to the validity of the values that it represented than their predecessors had during the 1829 and 1879 anniversaries. Thus, there were voices that associated Mendelssohn's legacy, primarily through his offspring and disciples, with the danger of assimilation; others stated that he should be evaluated only in the context of his era, which was fundamentally different from the present.[32]

Another aspect of the historical awareness of German Jewry at that time was the image of the Middle Ages. German Jews whose orientation was liberal tended to link their belief in progress with a denunciation of what they saw as the ghetto era, a dark age that the Enlightenment era had brought to an end.[33] They presented Nazism as a movement whose struggle against modernity aimed to return the darkness of the Middle Ages.[34] Other liberals, who also subscribed to the idea of progress, presented a different, more positive attitude to the ghetto era. For them the historical legacy of medieval German Jewry and its centuries-old bond to their motherland (*Mutterland, deutschen Heimatboden*) served as an additional source—older and more rooted than the age of emancipation—of the bond of German Jews to their Germany.[35]

In Jewish writings dealing with representations of the past during these crisis years there exists a clear awareness of the range of historical interpretation advanced by prominent non-Jewish thinkers, characterized above as archaic-mythic or cyclical. In a review article published in the summer of 1930 in the *Central Verein Zeitung*, Judge Jacques Stern, a prominent member of the organization, turned against the Volkist historical view. This attempt to depict the rules of world history as a wavy structure of ups and downs (*Auf und Ab*) and as a manifestation of *Antihistorismus* was presented by Stern as unfounded and arbitrary.[36] He not only criticized the anti-Jewish positions that were raised by the Volkists but also defended the dignity of history as an honest academic discipline, in contrast with the way it was misused by right-wing political powers in Germany.[37]

Alongside those who drew upon the evidence of history in order to support the values of liberalism and emancipation, other writers, also associated with the liberal camp, accepted the historical decline of these values as a fact that should be acknowledged. Only then could its meaning be understood. In a series of articles dealing with German nationalism published in the *Central Verein Zeitung* in late 1931, some of these writers distinguished between a nationalism that was based on voluntary cultural foundations and leaned toward democracy and the new Romantic-Volkist movement that shaped an antidemocratic version of German nationalism.[38]

A sharper perspective on the crisis in Germany was advanced in April 1932 by the liberal journalist and public activist Arno Herzberg.[39] The current historical reality, Herzberg asserted, brought about the rise of an antirationalist atmosphere that fundamentally contradicted the liberal legacy of the nineteenth-century bourgeoisie. Furthermore, he claimed, the bourgeoisie associated itself with this atmosphere, abandoning its original commitment to the value of the individual. Recognizing that the old era leading up to the civil emancipation to the Jews was gone for good, Herzberg called on German Jews to find an alternative to the bourgeois legacy. He explicitly opposed Jewish nationalism because it had absorbed too many irrational elements. Instead, he encouraged a deeper integration of German Jews around the members of their ethnic origin (*Stamm*), a solution that did not in his estimation mean self-ghettoization. Such a view did not fundamentally reject the values of liberalism that were bequeathed by the nineteenth century; rather, this view acknowledged their decline and called for a reorganization of Jewish life in Germany. This can be seen as having foreshadowed the discussion about new emancipation, which stood at the center of the CV agenda in the wake of the Nazi rise to power.

Zionist spokespeople in the later years of the Weimar Republic also addressed themselves to the decline of German liberalism and to the profound change in the character of German nationalism. More skeptical than the liberals concerning the ideals of progress and emancipation, they sought alternatives to the goal of social and political integration among other nations. With the escalation of German anti-Semitism in the early 1930s, German Zionists could not continue their policy of remaining at a distance from the German political discourse and concentrating exclusively on the development of Jewish settlement in Palestine.[40] This change was clearly expressed when Kurt Blumenfeld (b. 1885), the leader of the German Zionist movement, admitted in September 1932 that the Nazi threat to the Jews was new and unique and that it constituted an essential change in the nature of German nationalism.[41] Responding two months earlier to the German voices demanding a return to the Middle Ages, an anonymous Zionist writer argued that the Jews too must return to the collective forces they possessed before the age of liberalism and materialism of the nineteenth century.[42]

An especially radical reaction to the decline of German liberalism and the rise of Nazism was articulated in an essay by Zionist writer Gustav Krojanker (b. 1891) about the new German nationalism.[43] In Krojanker's view, liberalism tended to ignore the very existence of an organic national entity. German Jews internalized this position so thoroughly that it became a part of the religion of emancipated Jewry.[44] This position was portrayed as fundamentally contradictory to national ideologies, including Zionism, because they all rested on the belief in organic bonds of blood and fate. For many Jewish readers, including Zionists, Korjanker's view was problematic because he seemed to recognize the authenticity of the Nazi Party's ideals even though he did not make explicit reference to Nazism but instead referred to it as the "new German nationalism." In the context of our discussion, it should be pointed out that if successful, Krojanker's appeal to his readers to accept the demise of the liberal era—not only in Germany but also in other countries—would inevitably lead to the dissolution of liberal Jewry and the rise of Jewish nationalism.[45] In spite of his essentially nonliberal view of Jewish nationalism, Krojanker recognized the importance of its liberal background. He asserted that Zionism would always have an ambiguous relation to the liberal legacy. Zionism was, in fact, indebted to liberalism and therefore would have to find the right balance between its liberal roots and its aspiration to develop organic postliberal Jewish nationalism.[46]

Krojanker's essay evoked many reactions within the Jewish public in Germany. His position, and especially his partial acceptance of the new features of German nationalism, clearly seems to have been rejected by both liberal and most Zionist spokespeople.[47] However, his clear call to German Jewry to accept the demise of liberalism and to adapt itself to the postliberal collectivist era while also recognizing its liberal roots foreshadowed positions that other Zionist and even certain liberal spokespeople expressed in the Jewish press after the Nazi rise to power. Krojanker left Germany for Palestine in 1932.

The Turn to Jewish History in the First Months of the Nazi Regime

The rise of the Nazis to power and the first anti-Semitic measures of the new regime—the economic boycott and the beginning of anti-Jewish legislation—naturally created a strong mood of crisis among German Jews. Their growing need to reevaluate their situation as well as their inability to articulate their political views openly under the new political circumstances increased the intensity of their turn to the past. This turn occurred either in order to seek historical lessons or sometimes primarily for comfort and in certain cases also functioned as a way of veiling political critiques of the National Socialist regime and its anti-Jewish policy.

In the first weeks following January 30, 1933, the liberal Jewish press continued to publish articles that disputed the views of Nazism. On March 16 the *Central Verein Zeitung* commented on declarations by Nazi officials that portrayed the Jews as foreign nationals. One anonymous writer responded by articulating the traditional liberal German Jewish view of the German nation as a pluralistic collective nation composed of a variety of races and ethnic groups united by common history, territory, and culture.[48] German Jews, he emphasized, do not estrange themselves from their ethnic origin, but at the same time they will oppose any attempt to be presented as foreigners in their homeland. The fact that "Jews have lived on German soil for more than a thousand years" was evidence of their being an integral part of the German nation.[49] Such arguments, however, could neither change the fact that the new masters of Germany refused to see the Jews as part of the German nation nor cope with the total collapse of the liberal worldview in German society and politics.

Other spokespeople of the liberal camp, who recognized that the traditional positions were becoming no longer effective or relevant, turned now to Jewish history for a different perspective. Instead of seeking support for the declining liberal views, they tried to draw strength and inspiration from the past in order to encourage German Jews. This attitude appeared in February 1933 in an article written by the Berlin rabbi Max Eschelbacher (b. 1880) in *Der Morgen*. German Jews should face the current harsh attacks against them by leaning on the lessons of the Jewish past, Eschelbacher asserted. Jewish history was founded not only on the individual but also on the family and community. Eschelbacher presented Jewish history as representing social and communal solidarity, values that would be at the center of the German Jewish public agenda in the coming years.[50]

Eschelbacher's article reveals an internal conflict between his liberal propensity to rely on law and emancipation and his awareness of the need to seek an alternative moral foundation for the struggle of German Jews. He therefore felt it necessary to turn to a more distant historical horizon. "For fourteen years," he wrote, "we have been conducting the struggle for our rights on the foundation of the Weimar constitution . . . [according to which] all Germans are equal before the law."[51] Indeed, there seemed to be no reason to stop relying on that constitution. But in the final lines of his article, Eschelbacher touched on the possibility that a turning point in Jewish history was beginning to unfold. He consequently suggested a fresh response to changed circumstances:

> Constitutions can change. If the upheavals of history will lead to the unbelievable and the National-Socialist program will be realized, and if a new constitution determines that a Jew can no longer be a citizen, then we will no longer be able to rely on the constitution. In such a case, however, we will not give up our rights, but rather derive them from a deep, eternal foundation. Our ancient Jewish past and our history of almost two thousand years in Germany bear powerful witness to God's will . . . [and] we will finally lead our struggle for full civil rights in Germany as German Jews, on the basis of God's will.[52]

Rabbi Eschelbacher tied his proposed solution to both religious destiny and a more remote historical horizon. The possibility of the Weimar Republic's collapse (which had already become a reality by the time his article was published) took him much further back than the beginnings of the emancipation period to the real or invented starting point of almost two thousand years of Jewish life in Germany. This historical continuum, which Eschelbacher presented as an expression of Divine Will, served as a deeply rooted durable moral foundation for the future of Germany's Jews. Eschelbacher left Germany for England a few years later after his arrest by the Nazis in the wake of the November 1938 pogrom.

A somewhat different claim regarding the return to history and its lessons was articulated by Fabius Schach in an article that was published in mid-March 1933 in the independent journal *Israelitisches Familienblatt*. Schach viewed the return to history as a basic need of the Jews, that is, as a return to the source of life. However, he chose to focus not on the preemancipation era but instead on the mid-nineteenth century. The assimilation of the Jews into their surroundings at that time, claimed Schach, was external insofar as it did not diminish their core Jewish identity. This form of Jewish life as presented by Schach was the key to the struggle in the present crisis of German Jews in the 1930s: "The past is talking to us today, calling us to approach it. It is not dead; it still has a lot to offer us. . . . In times when the ruling direction will create its more supreme powers from the old, we the Jews should not feel uncomfortable about getting back to our own history."[53]

Similar to Eschelbacher but with a different emphasis, Schach's position gave voice to the struggle of many German Jews. They were torn between adhering to German culture and the legacy of the emancipation on the one hand and their understanding of the change that Germany was undergoing on the other hand and thus were looking to Jewish history in order to cope with it.

Jewish journals at the time provide ample evidence of the turn to Jewish history as a source of comfort for the misery of the present.[54] In an essay published to mark the Jewish holiday of Shavuot,[55] Caesar Seligmann (b. 1860), the retired liberal rabbi of Frankfurt, argued that the image of Jewish history as a chain of persecutions and humiliation, to which the events of post-January 1993 in Germany (i.e., the beginning of the persecution of German Jews) were attached, is only an outcome of peering in from the outside.[56] Even in difficult times before the emancipation, he added, our ancestors were glad to be Jewish and were proud of their history and culture despite the brutal forces that oppressed them (Edom, Rome, and later on medieval Europe). From this standpoint Seligmann developed a critical discussion about the era of emancipation and the consequences of its demise, presenting a view that became common among quite a few publicists at that time. The opening of the ghetto walls in the late eighteenth century had intoxicated the Jews and had motivated them to relinquish their traditional cultural treasures for the sake of the new culture. Nowadays, "in this time of emergency when fate is turning us its iron fist," Seligmann stated, German Jews should return to their sources and reevaluate their history and heritage. "We should become aware of the fact . . . that we did not enter European culture as beggars." Only a reevaluation of Jewish heritage of this type, which provides a radically different view from that of the emancipation era, grants back to the Jews their self-respect and even the joy of being Jewish.

Recognizing the crisis in the first months of the Nazi regime motivated some spokespeople of the central liberal camp of German Jewry to speak openly about the end of the emancipation era—at that point 120, 150, or even 180 years old—and to discuss the meaning of this turning point. "The past weeks have freed German Jewry from its illusions," wrote CV activist Alfred Hirschberg (b. 1901) in July 1933. "At the end of a Jewish development in Germany which lasted one hundred and twenty years and was founded on the ambiguous concept of emancipation, we stand today before a situation more difficult in many respects than was the starting point."[57]

Hirschberg rejected the view of certain Jewish publicists who claimed that the Jews would be able to integrate into the so-called German national revolution. German Jewish youths, he insisted, were being called upon to undertake tasks in the new era that were comparable to those of Mendelssohn and Gabriel Riesser in the old era.[58] Nothing could be more fallacious, Hirschberg continued, than to say that German Jews were again beginning a process of emancipation from the same starting point as a century and a half earlier. Men such as Mendelssohn and Riesser would continue to serve as models for German Jews, but the present era had entirely new requirements. While Jewish emancipation had meant an improvement in the Jews' political standing, there was no denying that the process at play now was one of political decline. Moreover, the bourgeois ideals of *Bildung* (a unique German concept that refers to education and culture as well as inner development of the individual) and *Besitz* (property ownership), which had served as the bases of German Jewry's economic and cultural achievements, had themselves declined in the general German set of values.

Hirschberg's article reflected an early stage in the liberal Jewish internalization of the new German reality. However, despite his plea for a new strategem for Jewish life in Germany and for a "new emancipation," he continued to speak in the name of integrative values associated with the "old emancipation" espoused by liberals. It is noteworthy that Hirschberg's article provoked a great deal of criticism, primarily from readers who were not willing to accept what they understood to be his renunciation of the old emancipation. Two weeks later in response to these criticisms, he made it clear that he had not meant that German Jews should give up on reemancipation (*Wiederemanzipazion*); rather, he was calling for the formation of a new synthesis between Germanness and Judaism, one more in tune with the new reality.[59]

In the following months, appeals to renew the strategy for Jewish integration within Germany continued to appear in the *Central Verein Zeitung*. In some articles, especially those written by younger contributors, the appeals were accompanied by attempts to explain the decline of the old emancipation.[60] In an article directed at German Jewish youths, Robert Wohlheim attributed the failure of the emancipatory project to the lack of strong Jewish attachment.[61] The new emancipation that would enable most German Jews to remain in their homeland, he implied, would be possible only if the Jews had a stronger Jewish foundation before they built a bridge to the non-Jewish world. Even more powerfully, Heinz Warschauer, another liberal writer, stressed the need to break free from the "rubble of the old assimilatory Jewish shadow-life" in order to form a new German Jewish type. The goal was not, he stressed, to return to ghetto life but rather to open up new horizons for Jewish consciousness.[62]

The Zionist Challenge

Zionist publicists naturally criticized the emancipation period more than Jewish liberal spokespeople did, even attributing blame to it for the current situation in Germany in order to validate their worldview.[63] A few Zionists went even further by criticizing certain positive aspects of the historical events that had caused the decline of nineteenth-century values. In May 1933 in the journal *Jüdische Rundschau,* one of the commentators called the period of the late nineteenth and early twentieth centuries "the anarchic-individualistic era" and expressed his hope for a new dawn that would rise after the twilight.[64]

A central topic concerning Zionist commentators was, as they characterized it, the historically mistaken path that German Jews had taken in the early emancipation era. Zionist educator Hugo Rosenthal (b. 1887) argued that the Jews should have rejected the very idea of assimilation as a condition for emancipation. They should have understood, he asserted, that their citizenship would have been meaningful only if their ethnic uniqueness had been recognized. Their misunderstanding, Rosenthal claimed, was the cause of the Jews' current distress.[65] Still, it is worth noting that in the next part of his article Rosenthal refrained from completely rejecting the emancipation era and would not deny its relevance for the future of German Jews. He insisted that one hundred years of emancipation represented a rather short period in all of Jewish history, yet the German Jews had created in this period a very important Jewish legacy. Emancipation would leave a positive imprint on Judaism if the Jews integrated using the proper proportions instead of distorting the Jewish self-perception.[66] Rosenthal served as the director of a Jewish agricultural school in Herrlingen (southern Germany) during 1933–39 before immigrating to Palestine.

In May 1933 an anonymous Zionist publicist provided a noteworthy suggestion about the misunderstanding on which the emancipation was founded. When the Jews became Europeans, he claimed, they should have understood that they were being accepted, at the very best, like salt in soup.

The extent of European society's willingness to absorb them was therefore a matter of good taste and proportion.[67] But most Jews either refused to admit this fact or did not even understand it. Instead, they grasped at every opportunity for outward advancement without taking sufficient note of the reluctance of general society to accept them until that reluctance became forcefully evident in the Nazi period. Thus, the solution to their predicament had to be based on the admission of past failures and on a realistic recognition that there was no place for assimilation. Rather, Jews had to seek a return to Jewish history. Despite all this, the publicist added, only a few non-Zionist spokespeople made provisional attempts since January 1933 to come to terms with the meaning of these failures. They continued to believe in the restoration of liberalism after a short interruption.[68]

In early August 1933 Zionist activist Elfride Bergel-Gronemann (b. 1883) published an article that provides an interesting attempt to grant meaning to the tragic turning point in the position of German Jews. Bergel-Gronemann's discussion of this topic heralds the shift of certain German Jewish spokespeople—Zionists and, to a lesser extent, liberals—to the kind of historical discourse that Dietmar Schirmer called "archaic-mythic." This discourse integrated a deep historical regularity that directs events. German Jews, claimed Bergel-Gronemann, denied the existence of the "inescapable Jewish fate" (*unentrinnbare Judenschicksal*) or at least felt that they had found a way out of it until the historical turn of the 1930s: "In the midst of the daylight of our civilization this absurdity took place: The metaphysical rule of our existence was revealed again and proved its validity."[69]

Bergel-Gronemann described a fundamental Jewish otherness (*Anderssein*), an otherness that German Jews had tried to forget but that was unavoidable due to recent events. The unique law of Jewish existence determines, she asserted, that the Jewish people cannot ever totally assimilate. Occasionally this leads to the reemergence of anti-Semitism—as it took place in medieval Spain and was taking place in both Germany and eastern Europe—as a factor that rebinds Jews to their heritage and reunites them against the dissolution that threatens them. Bergel-Gronemann immigrated to Palestine in 1937.

During 1933–34, the young liberal Berlin rabbi Joachim Prinz (b. 1902), a Zionist activist, held a series of lectures that filled the halls with hundreds of Jewish listeners. These public lectures represented the most radical and systematic Zionist challenge to the basic tenets that had emerged from the German Jewish emancipation and sought to reevaluate how the ghetto era was interpreted in German Jewish history.[70] Prinz's historical analysis and lectures were the foundation of his book *Wir Juden* (We Jews). He was active in Nazi Germany until his immigration in 1937 to the United States, where he became a prominent rabbi in New Jersey and vice chairman of the World Jewish Congress.

The exodus of European Jews out of the ghetto had been extremely abrupt, Prinz argued. The ghetto Jews, who had lived peacefully in a traditional society, were like prisoners whose cell bars had suddenly been removed.[71] The Jewish generation nurtured a naive faith in enlightenment and French revolutionary ideas and showed little reflective propensity in the speedy abandonment of its traditional surroundings.

Within the ghetto, Prinz continued, Jews had enjoyed freedom in their inner lives. As a result of emancipation, their names and origins become only sources of distress. Prinz rehabilitated the image of the ghetto life, claiming that in spite of the oppression and agony that Jews had experienced there, life in the ghetto should be associated with Jewish cultural wealth. The ghetto should not necessarily be associated with beggary and humiliation; rather, it had brought dignity to the Jews and enabled them to find value and meaning in their Judaism.[72] In sharp contrast to his positive evaluation of the Ghetto, Prinz described emancipation as an enduring attempt to escape not only their tradition but also themselves: "In this way emancipated Jews lived on the margins. They took a wide detour around their Judaism and missed the path to a true life."[73]

Unlike moderate liberals who called for a German Jewish critical reassessment of the emancipation era and unlike most other Zionist spokespeople who likewise directed their more moderate critique at German Jewry, Prinz challenged the entire course of events that had led German Jews out of the ghetto and presented it as problematic from its very beginning. He directed his criticism against Mendelssohn, the icon of modern German Jewry. "Humpback Moses, the son of the biblical copyist from Dessau," as well as "Solomon Maimon, the Polish Jewish youth," heard the voices of the storm outside the ghetto and became attracted to them.[74] Prinz was unimpressed by Mendelssohn's cultural achievements and his loyalty to Judaism. Instead, Prinz focused his discussion on the price of Mendelssohn's legacy and on the opposition that his path had aroused among other Jews: "His relatives who remained in the ghetto, like thousands of other Jews loyal to the Torah [Jewish law], cursed the Bible translation of the rebel from Berlin."[75]

If the curses of Mendelssohn's traditional relatives, who had stayed behind in the ghetto, exemplified for Prinz the cost of Jewish integration in Germany, Prinz presented the conversion of Mendelssohn's children to Christianity as the ultimate proof of the failure of his vision: "Moses the son of Menachem from Dessau was a religious person. . . . The fate of his children is the fate of German Jewry in the nineteenth century. Only his son Joseph remained Jewish."[76]

Prinz painted a harsh picture of humiliation: "Hunchback Mendelssohn is knocking on the doors of Berlin walls, asking to enter the Prussian capital as a beggar asking for mercy" (a very unfavorable metaphor for the entrance of the Jews to German society). This depiction of the most prominent icon of German Jewish emancipation as a beggar stood in stark contrast to the inner pride of the ghetto Jews, as reflected in the heroism of biblical Samson as he broke the doors of the Philistine city.[77]

Prinz's critique of emancipated Jewry reverberates with the language of the contemporary *völkisch* ("radical ethnic-nationalistic") critique of modernity and liberalism: "We the Jews are nothing but players (and even subplayers) in the grand European tragedy called liberalism."[78] The alienation of emancipated Jewry to their history and people was, he claimed, only an extreme expression of the general process in which liberal freedom had brought about the disintegration of traditional bonds of alienation.

The principle, encapsulated in Count Stanislas de Clermont-Tonnerre's statement in the French revolutionary National Assembly that "the Jews should be denied everything as a nation, but granted everything as individuals," had led Western Jews to disintegration and deadlock.[79] For Prinz, this quote demonstrated the tragedy of modern Jews, who accepted the terms of the deal that the modern liberal state offered to them. It was a solution (*Lösung*) to the Jewish question but at the price of disintegration (*Auflösung*) and the absolute renunciation of all manifestations of Jewish exclusiveness.[80] Prinz argued that the acceptance of this deal, which was based on the false belief that progress and equality would provide the solution to every problem, led many Jews to self-alienation. This introduced a "disease" to the development of Jewish history during the emancipation age: "One cannot fully delineate the history of the Jews since the French Revolution in historical terms. In major parts it is a psychopathology of complex and repression. . . . Jewish history in the last one and a half centuries is in many aspects a history of a disease."[81]

The self-alienation of Western Jews had an impact not only on their political choices but also on various social aspects of their lives. In an argument that invoked the mythic glorification of agriculture and country life in the general German discourse of the time, Prinz asserted that while many non-Jews continued to live in rural areas as farmers, the vast majority of Jews had migrated to the big cities to work in bourgeois professions. They became a people working and living on city asphalt and among libraries, offices, and department stores. They were completely cut off from the power of the soil and from the primeval process of production (*Urproduktion*). The liberal emancipation had defined the modern Jews as a displaced group with no peasant class and had installed them in an anonymous ghetto that was far more oppressive than the old ghetto. At least in the original ghetto the Jews had maintained their self-respect and inner confidence.[82]

Prinz's positions embody the shift of the German Jewish representation of the past to archaic-mythic forms. He not only rejected the ideals of progress and liberalism but implied that there was a deterministic and unavoidable character to the anti-Jewish outburst: "The essence of anti-Semitism . . . lies deep inside the [non-Jewish] peoples [*Völkern*], [and] it ultimately cannot be uprooted, cannot be struggled. It is rooted in spheres to which reason and enlightenment cannot approach."[83] Furthermore, he sympathized with the idea of a deep secret in Jewish history, a secret that always pulled the Jews out of periods of decline.[84] This perception, which implied the existence of a cyclical regularity that directs Jewish history, is conveyed by Prinz's use of the concept of fate as the major power that determines Jewish history. This was a very typical concept in the archaic-mythic discourse.[85]

Prinz's deterministic historical interpretation led him to anticipate a deep crisis in the position of Jews in other countries:

> When the Jewish fate will attend to the Jews in France, England and the United States; when its mighty fist—which has shaken the Jews of Eastern Europe already for several generations and begins now to shake the German Jews—will shake them as well; when the shadows, the gigantic frightful shadows of the eternal Jew will be thrown on them in the midst of sunny days; then their arrogance will come to its end.[86]

The historical narrative presented in Prinz's works, its cyclical regularity as well as the future anticipations that arise from it, are linked to his Zionist message. Not surprisingly, he identified with the teachings of Theodor Herzl and mentions the development of the Jewish settlement in Palestine as a foundation for a better Jewish future.[87] However, the power of his message seems not to have originated primarily from the Zionist solution but instead originated from the way it had granted meaning to the deep crisis that his listeners and readers were experiencing.

Non-Zionist Responses

Prinz's lectures, which were attended by many people, and his book naturally aroused responses from liberal spokespeople. Their comments, published primarily in the *Central Verein Zeitung,* defended the liberal Jewish legacy. According to Karl-Heinz Flietzer of Berlin, Prinz's views were not founded on fact, and his thesis that anti-Semitism was a counterreaction to the Jews' overuse of the rights provided by the emancipation period was totally baseless. Flietzer deeply objected to the suggestion that Jews should "return to the ghetto," which he saw as Prinz's principal message.[88] Other liberal commentators claimed that Prinz's positions were very simplistic and presented Jewish history in Germany in terms of black and white. While Prinz accepted and even wanted a regression in the course of history as well as a total renunciation of the integration between Jewish fate and German identity, these liberal commentators continued to believe in the validity of this integration. They saw the developments of the Nazi era as no more than a temporary crisis.[89]

Rabbi Manfred Swarsensky (b. 1906), a young Berlin liberal, responded to Prinz in the *Central Verein Zeitung* with a different and much more complicated comment. Like Prinz, Swarsensky was a member of the group of young rabbis who became the most influential religious leaders of the liberal community at the time.[90] Swarsensky defended the era of emancipation but accepted its decline as a historical fact. The Jewish question, he asserted, was not, as the Zionists said, an inevitable outcome of the basic living conditions of the Jews in exile (i.e., since the destruction of the Jewish Temple in Jerusalem). Rather, the roots of Jewish abnormality are even deeper and originate from the very nature of Jewish history:

> Our history is characterized by eternal ups and downs. Ages of external success, which were almost always times of "assimilation," are followed by ages of distress. Both are crucial and eventually also fruitful. The ages of assimilation provide the Jews new and valuable momentum, even if they must pay for it in a certain loss. Then, after action of the centrifugal forces come the ages of "dissimilation," and the centripetal forces rise again.[91]

Unlike the previous critiques that rejected Prinz based on the traditional liberal views, first and foremost the idea of progress, Swarsensky accepted the cyclical historical view. Like Prinz, Swarsensky integrated concepts such as "eternal" and "fate" into his view of the course of Jewish history. He even presented "the metaphysical law of life" as the reason for the tragedy that German Jews were experiencing in 1933. In spite of the fact that his positions on the nature of Jewish history were fundamentally different from those of Prinz, Swarsensky's article reflected not a rational historical discourse based on the belief in progress but instead the archaic-mythic discourse similar to Prinz's discourse. Swarsensky genuinely defended the basic values and legacy of the liberal era while striving to help his readers recognize and accept what he perceived as the Jewish fate, a recognition and acceptance that were for him beyond any particular Jewish political ideology.[92] Swarsensky continued his activity as a liberal rabbi in Berlin until the November 1938 pogrom. After a few weeks in the concentration camp of Sachsenhausen, he left Germany in 1939 for the United States, where he became a reform rabbi in Madison, Wisconsin.

Bruno Weil's public lectures, articles, and book provided the most systematic response of CV spokespeople to Prinz's positions.[93] Born in 1883, Weil, a member of a generation older than that of Prinz and Swarsensky, offered his listeners and readers his own version of the cyclical narrative of German Jewish history. A glance at the fate of the Jews living on German soil (Weil also used the word "fate" extensively) reveals that their history had been characterized from its very beginning "by large wavy lines with steep heights and horrible abysses."[94]

Weil emphasized the antiquity of the Jewish settlement in Germany, dating at least from Roman times (sixty generations of Jewish life on German soil), and described the first one thousand years of Jewish life in Germany as a peaceful era of coexistence, a kind of "ancient emancipation." The turn for the worse came, he continued, only toward the end of the first millennium AD. Marked by the violent anti-Jewish riots of 1096, the events heralded the annexation of the Christian order in Germany and the final break with the tolerant legacy of antiquity. Weil describes this transformation in a way that clearly hints at the position of the German Jews in the 1930s:

> After a thousand years of common life with the other Germans, the position [of the Jews] deteriorated very quickly. Legally, socially and economically . . . the efforts to prevent [a] joint life of Jews and Christians became more and more vigorous. The Jews have settled in the ghetto. What was initially a voluntary separation has become, since the thirteenth century, compulsory. . . . [T]he historical observation and the decree of a thousand years of joint life in Germany did not provide a defense against anti-Semitism. After a millennium of peace and relative tran-

quility came half a millennium of anguish. The wavy line of
Jewish fate!^{95}

After a few centuries, this oscillating design turned in the Jews' favor during the modern era as Jewish life began to rise again, reaching its peak when
Jews were granted civil equality. Weil did not portray the development of the
status of the Jews in Germany since the Enlightenment era as a continuous
process of progress that was cut off only in 1933 but instead claimed that
the modern era was also curvilinear. Thus, he illustrated the modern history
of Prussian Jews as an "oscillating character of the Jewish fate" and demonstrated the importance of the changing nature of this oscillation. "In the new
era," he explained, "the waves do not need a time frame of a few centuries
to reverse and flow from the mountain to the valley. The pace of events con-
stantly increases. . . . The life circle and the experiences of the individual and
the community gyrates faster and faster."^{96}

Weil's concepts, which he called "the Jewish law of development," depicted the intensive wavy development of the Jewish emancipation in Prussia
in the course of 120 years, from the Prussian Emancipation Edict of 1812 to
the rise of the Nazis to power in 1933. He did not deny the fact that none
of these ups and downs had undermined the foundations of Jewish equality in the way the events of 1933 had, yet he still called upon his readers to
avoid despair and continue to hope by understanding the course of Jewish
history.^{97}

Weil not only presented a different form of historical regularity than
Prinz had but also challenged Prinz directly. The Zionist historical interpretation is based, so Weil claimed, on the image of emancipation as doomed
to fail from its very formation. This attitude is the reason why spokespeople
such as Prinz tended to present the ghetto and the medieval form of Jewish
life as heroic and even called for a reversion to Jewish isolation from the
general surroundings.^{98} Contrasting these positions, Weil reemphasized the
misery and humiliation of Jewish life in the ghetto and Mendelsshon as the
important hero of the early emancipation era.^{99}

Similarly to Prinz, Weil considered historical rules as being very important not only as the basis for understanding and evaluating the events taking place in Germany but also as the key to anticipating the future of Jews
in other countries. Thus, he responded to Prinz, as well as to certain Nazi
spokespeople, who argued that the events taking place in Germany were part
of a greater global trend, that is, that the decline of political liberalism and
Jewish emancipation would take place in other Western countries as well.
In a lecture in Berlin in late 1934, Weil discussed the topic of immigration,

concentrating on the question of the future of emancipation elsewhere.[100] He imposed the cyclical wavy model on the development of emancipation in countries such as Spain, England, and France. In none of these countries was emancipation, in his view, a simple process; in fact, there had been in each case developments that impeded progress toward emancipation. Understanding the historical dynamics of emancipation, he said, requires a perspective of more than one thousand years. This demonstrates how the oscillation of a development always depends on the spirit of the time (*Zeitgeist*) in each culture. In spite of the Nazis' efforts to create a worldwide racial ideology, the real situation, claimed Weil, was that in no other country in the world except Germany, not even in Fascist Italy, had there been a political system founded on race, and therefore there was no reason to expect a global collapse of Jewish emancipation. Weil left Nazi Germany for France in 1935 and fled to the United States in 1940.

In 1934 Hans Joachim Schoeps (b. 1907) joined the Prinz-Weil debate, adding a perspective from the margins of the German Jewish communal political system. Schoeps was the leader of a small Jewish student movement called *Deutscher Vortrupp* (German Vanguard) that was founded in February 1933 and aspired to integrate German radical nationalism and loyalty into the Jewish religion. He published the book *Wir deutschen Juden* (We German Jews) in which he challenged Prinz's ideas and offered a different historical narrative from that of liberal spokespeople.[101] Throughout history, Schoeps wrote, Jews were integrated into the nations among whom they lived. Jews had become fully Hellenist, Spanish, Russian, and German in the national-secular sense, but this did not harm their Jewishness, which was based on origin and religious belief. This dual consciousness of belonging, which represents, according to Schoeps, an integral union—much more integral than the German Jewish ideal of the CV—was for Schoeps the real Jewish destiny. For him, the Zionist ideals of Prinz embodied a sharp deviation from this original Jewish destiny.[102]

Schoeps sharply criticized the nineteenth-century historical path of integration of the Jews in Germany as much too rapid. In this era, "the age of false assimilation," the Jews had abandoned their unique traditions in order to integrate into German society, a process that Schoeps characterized by the Nazi term *Gleichschaltung* (the Nazi policy of forcible coordination). Interestingly, he accused these same German Jews during "the first emancipation" of not assimilating sufficiently into German society (*unzureichenden Assimilation*), as they had not become attached enough to the traditions of the German national entity (*Volkskörper*).[103]

A critic of Schoeps argued that the accusations that Schoeps tendered against several groups within Germany Jewry did not form a coherent historical narrative that offered a new direction of thinking.[104] Still, it is noteworthy that even Schoeps, who was the spokesman for a marginal Jewish group, criticized assimilation and sought an alternative historical narrative that would explain the failure of the emancipation era. Schoeps fled from Nazi Germany to Sweden in 1938 and returned to Germany in 1946.

Jewish history was not used only in the internal Jewish debates. Fritz Friedländer used it in a polemic against certain Nazi spokespeople. More than other publicists, Friedländer presented his readers a theory regarding the questions of representations of the past and the relationship between past and present. Friedländer, a communal activist and publicist, had an in-depth education in history. During the Weimar Republic he had written about various historical figures, primarily Riesser, using their memory to encourage German Jews to defend their rights against their enemies.[105] In 1932 as representations of the past were still being used by Jewish spokespeople as part of their efforts to block the rising Nazi Party, Friedländer called on the Jewish education system to directly confront the Nazi attempt to portray the Jews as foreigners in German history.[106] Later on during the first years of the Nazi regime, he was a central figure in the liberal Jewish education system, primarily in the Berlin area.[107]

From 1933, Friedländer published, mostly in the *Central Verein Zeitung*, quite a few articles that addressed history and its public uses. In May 1934 he discussed the challenge of teaching history in Jewish schools, which had to operate according to the Nazi state regulations but were obliged to meet their students' needs.[108] A few months later when he examined the role of Jewish historical research vis-à-vis the escalating crisis in Jewish life, he explicitly implored the need to develop a usable past. Current historical writing, he asserted, should be based on the needs of the Jewish public more so than had been the case in previous historical writing. These writings were necessary to help the liberal Jew cope with the ideological confusion caused by the events in Germany as well as help grant new meaning to the question of the Jewish-Gentile relationship.[109]

When defending the liberal values of the CV and the historical memory of Jewish integration in Germany, Friedländer not only confronted the contentions of certain Zionist spokespeople but also challenged the various Nazi commentators who declared that the collapse of Jewish emancipation and assimilation were evidence of a historically ill-directed path. In an August 1934 article—the last contribution to a seven-article series about German Jewish history—Friedländer strove to grant a positive meaning to the concept of assimilation.[110] Assimilation, he asserted, was a general human process that did not concern only Jews; it was an inevitable development whose historical roots reached back much earlier than the nineteenth century. Friedländer described in universal terms the price that the Jews had paid for the process of assimilation, the very price about which Zionist interpreters were so critical. Assimilation, Friedländer asserted, had certain tragic implications. It must lead to the disappearance of certain noble and valuable elements for the sake of a higher unity. This was the case in the assimilation of the Germanic Franks in France, and this was also the case for the German Jews.

To this review of assimilation Friedländer added a more fundamental argument against those who were using the present events (the abolition of emancipation by the Nazis) to disqualify the legacy of the past (the era of Jewish integration in Germany in the nineteenth century). Relating to Leopold von Ranke's famous saying that "Every generation is equidistant from God," Friedländer stated that all the ages in history are equally close to God. Therefore, each age should be evaluated by its own unique values and not by those that are dominant in the present time.[111] A scientific discussion about the history of the emancipation and the age of assimilation, which would portray this age "as it has actually been" in an unbiased manner according to Ranke's ideal, should therefore be conducted on the values of this age itself. This referred to the liberal values even though it seemed that in contemporary Germany they were no longer valid. Ignoring the fact that the decline of German liberalism had already started in the late nineteenth century, Friedländer stated that any historical assessment of the nineteenth century must not be founded on the present postliberal values. Such assessments, which had become a common practice, were, according to Friedländer, totally unscientific, and historians must therefore not be influenced by them.[112]

In a brave confrontation with a Nazi spokesman, Friedländer reemphasized these points more profoundly. The young German historian Wilhelm Grau, who dealt with the history of the Jewish question in the Nazi-founded Reichsinstitut für Geschichte des neuen Deutschlands (Reich Institute for History of the New Germany), published a book in 1935 about Wilhelm von Humboldt and the Jewish question. In his work Grau warned that Humboldt's positive attitude toward the integration of the Jews in Germany was evidence of his defective German national commitment and that this defect damaged the German people. Grau also sharply criticized what he called the liberal and assimilating Jewry.[113]

In a review article about Grau's book, Friedländer not only contested Grau's historical interpretations but also lambasted the positive reception by certain Zionists who utilized Grau's work to undermine Jewish liberal positions.[114] Friedländer did not plea for a restoration of liberal values in politics, a goal that he recognized as unrealistic in late 1935, but instead tried to keep the dignity of the liberal heritage. Thus he asserted against Grau's position that just as Napoleon's defeat at Waterloo should not make us forget his great victory at Austerlitz, it would be wrong to forget or diminish the historical significance of Jewish emancipation, notwithstanding the present defeat of the emancipatory ideals.

It is noteworthy that in an atmosphere where open political struggle on behalf of the liberal values and against the Nazi policy had become impossible, Friedländer openly criticized Grau's perceptions about the past. Recognizing the present political circumstances, Friedländer defended the memory and dignity of the liberal past and presented the ideals of the Enlightenment and the emancipation as suitable for at least their own time. Thus, he emphasized that the century of assimilation that had just ended—which was also partly productive, as in the legacies of the nineteenth-century pioneer Jewish scholars Leopold Zunz and Isaac Marcus Jost and the Jewish liberal politician Riesser—was not in vain, a statement that was aimed at giving moral support to the German Jews in the wake of the Nuremberg Laws.

Beyond his specific interests in the Jewish past, Friedländer argued more generally for the public value of history while criticizing the growing impatience with the scientific approach. His statements contained obvious implications about the crisis of historicism and the interest in the archaic-mythic discourse and also reflected the public mood in Nazi Germany. Against this background Friedländer depicted the German historian Friedrich Meinecke as a cultural hero, the representative of the heroic resistance of the historical consciousness against the new irrational trends.[115] Friedländer left Germany for Shanghai in 1939 and settled in Australia in 1946.

Between Theology and History: The Orthodox Discourse on the Past

Parallel to the historical discourse conducted by liberals and Zionists and corresponding to their attempts to elucidate the crisis of German Jews in a way that would fit their worldview prior to the crisis, discussions about the meaning of Jewish history were also conducted within the Orthodox circles of German Jewry. Orthodox spokespeople, mostly those who published articles in *Der Israelit,* related to positions espoused by liberals and Zionists. However, their discourse was quite closed. Only a few publicists took part in it (sometimes anonymously), and their participation did not evoke significant reactions from the spokespeople of the other German Jewish groups.

In the summer and autumn of 1932, *Der Israelit* published a three-part article titled "The End of an Illusion."[116] The writer, Markus Elias (b. 1886), was the director of the Orthodox school in Frankfurt am Main from 1928 until his immigration to the United States in 1939. He outlined the reasons for and implications of the decline of the liberal era. The nineteenth century, he asserted, had put the Jews in a situation of fata morgana, an illusion, that encouraged them to abandon their historic destiny for the sake of the present narrow horizons of *Zeitlichkeit* ("temporality"). This path of assimilation, which was founded on liberal politics, was now in 1932 collapsing. Many Jews had broken free from the illusion and were trying to reassess the past while pointing to a new path for the future. Elias mentioned Krojanker's views—primarily his call to surrender the liberal path and to embrace anew Jewish fate and nationalism—but claimed that Krojanker had missed the crucial point. Whereas for Krojanker the basic sin of Jewish liberalism was its estrangement from the national element in Judaism and its attempt to re-create it as a pure religion, Elias pointed to the weakening of Jewish religious commitment in the Enlightenment age as the real root of the false path taken. Krojanker saw a fundamental similarity between the liberal and Orthodox legacies that had originated in nineteenth-century Germany, and he therefore tried to present Zionism as an alternative for both. Elias, on the other hand, viewed Orthodoxy as the only alternative to the declining liberalism.

From this perspective it is clear why Elias emphasized the Orthodox struggle against nineteenth-century liberalism much more than Krojanker did. This struggle, Elias claimed, was not only about the religious laws; it was also motivated by political considerations, that is, to preserve the religious uniqueness of the Jews as a nation. Zionism, as depicted by Elias, was nothing more than a new version of the old liberalism and in fact offered the Jews no more than a new form of assimilation. Only the Orthodox, whose disagreement with liberal Judaism was much more fundamental, he concluded, could present a viable alternative to the Jewish existence following the decay of liberalism.

Despite his characterization of the nineteenth-century liberal era as an age of illusion, Elias did not reject the modernization process of German Jewry in toto and certainly did not call for a return to the ghetto. He expressed the traditional position of German Jewish Orthodoxy, which associated itself with the legacy of its nineteenth-century founding father Samson Rafael Hirsch, and thus offered a more balanced path for modernization than did the liberal path.[117]

In the wake of the Nazi rise to power, Orthodox spokespeople understood the ideological crisis of German Jews as having primarily affected the liberals. They also referred to the rivalry between Orthodoxy and Zionism for the support of those liberals, mostly young Jews, who under the new circumstances were motivated to reassess their fundamental positions.[118] In an editorial that was published in *Der Israelit* following the anti-Jewish economic boycott and the beginning of the anti-Jewish legislation in early April 1933, the writer turned to the German people in the name of the Orthodox Jews, implying that their ethos could be the foundation for a more realistic integration of the Jews in Germany.[119] The Orthodox, he claimed, accepted emancipation as a blessing because they knew how to preserve their traditional values and keep their distance from the power centers of Germany. Their integration in Prussia, which according to this writer had been based on their gratitude to its sovereigns (Bismarck and later Emperor Wilhelm), is presented as a more restrained and respected form of emancipation that could serve as a model for the future of all German Jews under the Nazi regime. Attempting to draw upon Jewish history in Germany as the basis for a theological argumentation, he added that the very fact that Jews had lived in Germany for many generations proved that God had designated for them a destiny in Germany. Of this, he argued, the German people must be made aware.

Other Orthodox writers tried to link the waning of the emancipation to a historical neglect of the Jewish religion.[120] The Orthodox too, wrote Rabbi Moses Auerbach (b. 1881), a lecturer at the Orthodox rabbinical seminary in Berlin, have to reassess their historical path over the past one hundred years. Auerbach did not doubt the principles of Samson Rafael Hirsch's legacy but claimed that its implementation in daily life was deficient. In the education system, which had been established on a firm basis in Hirsch's age, there had since been an intensive decline in the study of the Torah: "Nowadays one cannot speak anymore about 'Torah im Derech Erez' [Hirsch's historical slogan for combining Jewish tradition and Jewish law with the modern world] but, at the most, about 'Derech Erez im Torah.'"[121] The need of the present difficult hour, he stated, was therefore the return to the study of the Torah. In 1934 Auerbach left Germany for Palestine, where he continued to be active in the field of Orthodox education.

On March 23, 1933, the Orthodox journal *Der Israelit* published an article under the pseudonym Nechunia.[122] In an introductory comment the editors noted that they had decided to publish the article due to its call for repentance (*teshuva*), although they were not in agreement with all of the author's ideas. The article expressed an extremely radical approach in its interpretation of the emancipation period and in its explanation of the emancipation's collapse. Liberals, Zionists, and even some sections of the Orthodox were characterized by Nechunia as sinners because of the path they had chosen during the emancipation era. His conclusion was clear: German Jews must recognize and confess their sin. A great wave of repentance must now flood German Jewry.

Nechunia was the pseudonym employed by the young rabbi Simon Schwab (b. 1908). Born in Frankfurt, Schwab had studied for a few years in east European *yeshivot* (traditional Talmudical academies). In 1933 he was nominated as the rabbi of Ichenhausen in Bavaria, where he served until he immigrated to the United States in 1936. There he became a leading Orthodox rabbi in Baltimore and New York City. The young Schwab expressed his ideas more systematically and without using a pseudonym in the book *Return to Judaism,* which appeared in 1934.[123] The key concept that he used to describe and analyze Jewish history was exile (*Golustum*) or exile existence (*Golusexistenz*), which he presented as the standard pattern of Jewish existence since the first century CE following the destruction of the Jewish Temple in Jerusalem. The emancipation period was thus no more than a temporary hiatus in that situation: "For more than a century German Jews felt the cold wind of exile only from a distance and did not really experience it. Merciful God, Who directs our fate, provided the German Jews approximately a hundred years ago with a respite in order to examine their loyalty to his Torah outside of the ghetto. This respite has come now to an end. German Jewry has hardly passed the test, [and] major sections have failed."[124]

It was the weariness from the existence of exile (*Golusmüdigkeit*), Schwab asserted, that had motivated German Jews to choose the path of assimilation in the nineteenth century and break down the barriers between them and their environment. They thus surrendered the totality of the Judaism (*totale Volljudentum*) that was characteristic of ghetto life. The poison of assimilation, which was most clearly expressed by religious liberalism—that is, Sabbath desecration—and intermarriage had even penetrated the ranks of German Jewish Orthodoxy, whose majority, according to Schwab, had turned to the path of "partial assimilation" (*partielle Assimilation*).[125]

Schwab's position, which was radical even within the Orthodox camp, can be most clearly seen in his view of Mendelssohn. Various Orthodox spokespeople, he claimed, tended to appreciate Mendelssohn highly and to see his legacy as a symbol of a successful synthesis between the Jewish world and the German environment. These spokespeople forgot the position of the great rabbinical figures of Mendelssohn's time—Rabbi Ezekiel Landau of Prague, Rabbi Raphael Cohen of Hamburg, and Rabbi Phinehas Levi

Horowitz of Frankfurt—who had realized that Mendelssohn's cultural desire for knowledge presented an unprecedented threat to traditional Jewish existence. Mendelssohn did not deviate personally from the traditional Jewish law (*Halacha*), but the integration that he created between German culture and Jewish identity was considered by Schwab as "Orthoprax assimilation." This paved the way for much more serious deviations from the Jewish laws.[126] Zionism was, for Schwab, nothing more than a new form of such deviations, and he thus stated that "Mendelssohn's twisted path has led directly to Herzl."[127]

Schwab's thoroughgoing rejection of the German Jewish emancipation path was even expressed in his reassessment of Hirsch's "Torah im Derech Erez" legacy. Like other Orthodox spokespeople, Schwab described Hirsch as the great hero of the nineteenth century. On the other hand, Schwab claimed that Hirsch's legacy of building bridges between observant Jews and the modern world was valid only for the nineteenth-century age of the pause of exile (*Goluspause*) and therefore lost its validity as the storm of exile erupted once again.[128]

Schwab's view of Jewish history and his eventual rejection of all possible paths that German Jews might take to modernity led him, more so than for any other German Jewish spokesperson including Prinz, to turn back to the Middle Ages: "We are knocking on the doors of the heroic Jewish Middle Ages, stretching out our hands to our ancestors, fathers and mothers, to know: How could you overcome this abyss, the alienation, the excommunication and the isolation? Where did you draw the strength to suffer and carry all this with such a modesty and pride?"[129]

The lesson that German Jews in the 1930s could learn from the history of the exile, Schwab contended, was the recognition of the need to carry on and be persistent. Schwab praised the efforts of German Jews to change their professional structure and to emigrate as a return to models of earlier periods. However, the foundation of his historical view was the return to the Torah and the renewed seclusion of the Jews in the ghetto:

> The ghetto in which our forefathers were confined in the Middle Ages has been disgraceful, but life within it was a triumph full of light. Thus the Torah of the ghetto prevailed over the ghetto and the sun shone in the gloomiest corner of Earth. . . . Good night *Menchenkultur* [human culture,] . . . we are stepping back, retreating into the motherland of Torah that was foolishly and rashly betrayed a hundred and fifty years ago, into the place of *Urjudentum* [ancient Judaism].[130]

Schwab's sweeping rejection of the legacy of emancipation and his call to return to the ghetto were, by any measure, extreme as compared to the position of most other Orthodox spokespeople, who continued to cling to Hirsch's legacy. Thus, for example, it was stated in *Der Israelit* in early 1934 that the undeniable political failure of the emancipation should not make the Jews forget the cultural achievements that the emancipation had brought them, achievements that were not always accompanied by Jewish self-denial.[131] Another article, which was published in *Der Israelit* in the summer of 1934 by an anonymous writer, described the close bond that German Jews felt toward their homeland, a bond that was rooted in one thousand years of life on German soil. The bond to German culture rested on an "active assimilation power," and a clear distinction was drawn between it and the other kind of assimilation that is based on a mere imitation of the environment and endangered the very substance and continuity of Judaism. The anonymous Orthodox writer did not raise any substantive doubt concerning Hirsch's legacy, but had rather presented it as a genuine expression of the active power of assimilation.[132]

Markus Elias, a member of the older generation, challenged Schwab's historical views more directly. In the spirit of his aforementioned 1932 article, in early 1935 Elias also related to the guilt of nineteenth-century German Jewry who had given up the natural association to the Jewish tradition. The disillusionment from the naive belief in progress and the recognition that the Jews had lost what they had gained in the nineteenth century had become, according to Elias, a matter of consensus after two years of Nazi rule. Representatives of the CV were now proclaiming the need for a new emancipation—a more respectable form of Jewish integration—that would permit a more prominent place for Jewish tradition alongside the association with Germany. Even the Zionists, he added, were now calling for spiritual regeneration.[133] Even so, Elias contended, it is impossible to accept Schwab's call to return to the preemancipation period, cut almost all links to the surrounding culture, and concentrate solely on study of the Torah:

> We cannot accept this. It is true that we also see the previous century as a disaster for Judaism, a dead end from which we must get out. But can we ignore the fact that these hundred years are now behind us? . . . Can we close our eyes to the fact that our environment did not stand still? The social, economic and cultural relations, as well as modes of transportation and technology, have changed in the last century more than in the

whole millennium before. Can I just state now that I will live as people used to live a thousand years ago?[134]

The irreversible change that in Elias's view required acceptance concerned not only technology and economy but also the cultural transformation that modern German Jews had undergone as well. This attitude clearly contradicted Schwab's thesis that all the forces necessary for the rehabilitation of post-1933 German Jewry could be found in the pre-Mendelssohn era. Furthermore, Elias expressed his concern that Schwab's position might lead to the complete isolation of the Orthodox minority from the rest of German Jewry:

> The vast majority of those Jews to whom we are linked by our blood and fate . . . are not ready to add a cultural ghetto to the social ghetto. The borderline between Jewish and non-Jewish culture passes today within us. Can we return today to the pre-Mendelssohn era? If we do, we should build for ourselves *a ghetto within a ghetto,* a *fortified wall* around our own children. . . . We cannot close our eyes to the objective changes that have taken place in the world in order to step back into Mendelssohn's path and return from Berlin to Dessau. Even Dessau has changed in the meanwhile.[135]

Using this metaphor, Elias clearly articulated the position of the Jewish Orthodox establishment in Germany, which rejected Schwab's extremist line. In spite of the sharp criticism of Orthodox spokespeople on the historical course of emancipation in the nineteenth century, most of them still felt that they were part of it. They therefore called to repair it from its foundations but not to eliminate it. This historical view was epitomized in their attitude toward Mendelssohn: Orthodox spokespeople such as Elias did not alienate themselves from his legacy but instead preferred to criticize it moderately, in the spirit of Hirsch.

Conclusion

In 1935 the Nazi security services produced a report concerning new trends in contemporary Jewish literature in Germany. Two fundamental themes were identified.[136] The first was the plea to return to the ghetto voluntarily. The Nazi authors cited Schwab and Prinz as examples. Each one in his own way held emancipation responsible for the decline of Judaism, and each depicted ghetto life as heroic. The second theme, as identified in the report, was the Jews' continued adherence to German nationalism, based on the belief that the Jews had integrated into German history in an irreversible way. The Nazi report speculated on the possible implications of these two tendencies regarding the future of German Jewry and on the potential dangers that each of them posed for the Nazi regime. The first ran the risk of promoting unfounded arrogance that might encourage anti-Nazi resistance; the second could result in Jewish adherence to the German Volk, thus damaging the Nazi policy of excluding the Jews from German society and culture.

At the center of the various Jewish perceptions about the past was a growing acknowledgment among representatives of all major German Jewish parties that the liberal political culture, including the Jewish emancipation, was in decline. The recognition that this decline was an undeniable fact, at least for the foreseeable future, therefore served as the point of departure for those who endeavored to understand its meaning. As we have seen, it was easier for Zionist and Orthodox spokespeople to link this decline primarily to crucial historical mistakes of mainstream German Jews in the period of emancipation; that is, they put the blame mostly on the liberals. Nevertheless, I have also presented the development of a critical historical narrative advanced by several Jewish liberal writers. They conceded that there were certain Jewish failings in the emancipation (mostly in the nineteenth century) and even hinted at possible ways to remedy the situation.

The acceptance of the waning of liberalism as well as the surrender of the belief in the inevitable progress of history motivated various Jewish spokespeople to change their basic attitude about Jewish history. Under the impact of the crisis of German historicism and the increasing blurring of the distinction between the scientific nature of history and its use as a source of myths, Jewish writers assembled a number of historical rules that were intended to grant meaning to the new situation. Thus, the Orthodox spokesman Schwab developed a narrative that placed Divine providence as well as Jewish sin and punishment at the center; Prinz, the Zionist, suggested a dramatic narrative of national Jewish decline and revival; and Weil, the liberal, outlined the wavy path of German Jewish history. All of these attempts, which intertwined such concepts as fate, eternity, and recurrence in their historical narratives, expressed the growing influence of the archaic-mythic forms in the German Jewish public discourse.

Nevertheless, it is important to emphasize that the ideas of the writers discussed in this chapter did not necessarily represent those of the Jewish party for which they spoke. This was especially true for Schwab, whose radical positions were rejected, as we saw, by most established Orthodox spokespeople. It was also true for Prinz. Most of the other Zionist spokespeople did not share his sweeping disapproval of the emancipation era. Weil's positions, however, seem to have represented a more central line in his own Jewish party—the CV and the liberals—even though they also did not produce a consensus.

Programmatic books and essays such as those discussed in this chapter were not the only way German Jewish spokespeople grappled with the meaning of the Jewish past during the first years of the Nazi regime. As we shall see in the following chapter, which will address the way German Jews marked historical anniversaries and honored their historical heroes, many other Jewish spokespeople, including professional historians, found more ways to turn to the Jewish past and utilize it without necessarily drawing radical conclusions. Still, one can understand the choice of the composers of the 1935 Nazi report to focus on more programmatic writing. They wanted to present the dynamic trends in Jewish society, trends that were interested in advancing an agenda and pointing to new directions: national revival, a religious revolution of repentance, or German Jewish understanding of the wavy nature of the events in anticipation of the next turn of the wheel of history.

2

THE CREATION OF A USABLE PAST

The turn toward Jewish history in the first years of the Nazi regime was reflected not just in the programmatic writings of rabbis and public spokespeople such as Joachim Prinz, Bruno Weil, Fritz Friedländer, and Simon Schwab. Their attempts to identify certain regularities in Jewish history and to link them to contemporary issues were part of a much wider endeavor of German Jewish writers in the 1930s. By delineating an overall structure to the course of Jewish history, they were attempting to create a usable past that could help their readers come to terms with the challenges of the time. This trend had additional, more specific, aspects: German Jewish professional historians and historically minded writers reinterpreted the significance of a variety of major events and figures in the German Jewish past.

By the eve of the Nazi rise to power, professional historians, some of them active scholars and lecturers in central Jewish institutions, were already using popular writing in order to advance their public agenda. In the summer of 1932, Ismar Elbogen, the rector of the Berlin liberal Hochschule für die Wissenschaft des Judentums (high school for Jewish studies) and from 1929 also the editor of the historical journal *Zeitschrift für die Geschichte der Juden in Deutschland*, published an article titled "Jewish Research in Times of Trouble." Historical scholarship for its own sake, Elbogen claimed, is a vital need for every society, but at the same time research is also a necessary tool for preserving the freshness of Judaism. To abandon history, Elbogen suggested, was akin to committing spiritual suicide.[1]

In 1933 Elbogen became a central member of the new Reichsvertretung der deutschen Juden (Reich Representation of German Jews). He was to emerge as one of several Jewish professional historians who turned to popular writing and to the creation and development of a usable Jewish past.[2] Thus, for example, he took part in composing a series of seven articles about the history of the Jews in Germany from the Roman era to the age of emancipation. These were published in the spring and summer of 1934 in the *Central Verein Zeitung*.[3] Then in 1935 Elbogen published a book on German Jewish history, the first comprehensive research work in the field.[4] In Michael Meyer's view, "this work is written with passion and a maximum of engagement" in a style that resembles that of Heinrich Graetz. Meyer suggests that Elbogen's work can be read as a Greek tragedy that struggles to deal with the question of Jewish survival.[5] Elbogen left Germany for the United States in 1938.

Academic historians such as Elbogen tended to focus on certain periods rather than others and from time to time would address theoretical issues that linked the present and the past.[6] However, the Jewish public's growing interest in its own history had more to do with a desire to embrace it in order to invest the present with meaning. Such attempts were articulated in the Jewish communal journals not only by historians but also by community activists and educators.

German Jewish spokespeople—professional historians and communal publicists alike—made efforts to create a usable past in a variety of ways. They responded to various anniversaries marked during the 1930s (the most prominent of which was the 900th anniversary of the establishment of the Worms synagogue) and dealt with various historical figures from the Jewish and German Jewish pantheon of heroes. Looking to the past for answers to the agonies of the present and to the challenges of the future motivated them also primarily in the second half of the 1930s to discuss the meaning of emigration and of exile throughout Jewish history.

Anniversaries and Places of Memory

One of the ways in which the Jewish press in Germany related to the past was the marking of anniversaries. Such events, termed *les lieux de mémoire* ("places of memory") by Pierre Nora, are not necessarily located in any physical space but can be found on the annual calendar.[7]

During the years 1933–34, the German Jewish press commemorated a variety of events that concerned the history of the emancipation. In June 1933 the journal *Israelitisches Familienblatt* marked the 100th anniversary of the Prussian Emancipation Edict in Posen, emphasizing the opportunities that this edict had opened up for Posen Jews primarily in the field of education.[8] A few months later the communal press as well as prominent leaders of the Reichsvertretung der deutschen Juden reflected on the history of German Jewry with the marking of the 125th anniversary of the granting of civil rights and the establishment of the Supreme Council (Oberrat) of Baden Jews.[9] Another historical event that was widely discussed in the Jewish press vis-à-vis the current events was the formative Prussian Emancipation Edict of 1812. Considered by many as the major breakthrough in the legal emancipation of Jews in Germany, this edict resurfaced in the 1930s amid the decline of the emancipation. The edict became part of the discussion concerning the proposal of new legislation to settle the status of German Jews in the postemancipation era.[10]

Aside from marking historical events of the emancipation, various writers identified the Jewish struggle with events and places in a more remote past. Such references deepened the Jewish bond to Germany and helped form a homemaking myth that linked the Jews to their homeland in the preemancipation era.[11] Thus, Elbogen more than once discussed the beginning of Jewish settlement in Germany and stressed the naturalization of the Cologne Jews in the fourth century. Elbogen conceived of the legal status of the Jews in the Roman era, when they were free to engage not only in commerce but also in agriculture, as a clear expression of normalization and perhaps even an ancient version of emancipation.[12] Another historic Jewish community that figured in the public discourse of the 1930s was that of Regensburg in Bavaria, Germany. Various writers focused on its medieval history, primarily the expulsion of its Jews.[13]

The medieval synagogue in Worms is an especially interesting illustration of the public discussion associated with a German Jewish anniversary in the 1930s. Worms, one of the most well-known centers of medieval German Jewry, was intensively used by modern German Jews as a place of memory. Associated with the biblical and Talmudic commentator Rashi, the town had become a major cultural symbol. Worms attracted Jewish tourists and was loaded with new meaning in the emancipation era. In the second half of the nineteenth century as the process of legal emancipation was gradually completed and German Jews were in the midst of intensive urbanization and modernization, the legacy of Worms became an icon symbolizing the entirety of the German Jewish legacy and the blessing of emancipation. Later on in response to the growing anti-Semitic pressures in the Weimar Republic, Jewish spokespeople clung to the memory of Worms as evidence of their deep-rootedness in Germany.[14]

Political use of Worms in service of the ideas of German Jewish integration reached its peak in 1925 when the city of Cologne hosted an exhibition marking one thousand years of German culture in the Rhineland. Jewish spokespeople attached themselves to this German anniversary by presenting the Rhineland as the first area of Jewish settlement in Germany and by relating it as well to the memory of Worms.[15]

The memory of Worms was placed at the center of the German Jewish public agenda once more in the spring of 1934 with the 900th anniversary of the establishment of the medieval synagogue in the town. This anniversary was marked at a central ceremony, and participants included representatives of the German Jewish leadership, headed by Rabbi Leo Baeck. The Reichsvertretung der deutschen Juden published a special greeting to the Worms communal board. The greeting emphasized the historical importance of the anniversary, as it represented the long association of German Jews with the German soil (*Boden*) and spirit (*Geist*) and the long road that led them "from a very meaningful past to the present and the future."[16] At the same time, the local communal board opened a special anniversary volume of the journal *Zeitschrift für die Geschichte der Juden in Deutschland* with a statement that emphasized the uniqueness of the Worms synagogue, the only one in Germany and in all of Europe that had been continuously active since the Middle Ages. Worms exemplified Jewish communal strength and vitality in contrast to the lethargy that resulted from the contemporary situation.[17]

It is clear that the Worms anniversary primarily served the agenda of the Jewish liberal sector, whose spokespeople stressed the deep Jewish roots in Germany. In an editorial that appeared in the special anniversary volume of the *Central Verein Zeitung,* Alfred Hirschberg described the Jews who prayed in the medieval synagogue as citizens who had enjoyed full and equal rights in their town. It is true, he conceded, that their rights were later undermined, but the synagogue continued to exist over the centuries, symbolizing for Jews the integration of homeland and faith (*Glaube*), even in times when their legal status had eroded. Referring to the fate of the Worms Jewish community in the upheavals of German history, Hirschberg stated, in the spirit of Weil, champion of the cyclical perspective, that "history is not a mathematical exercise that proceeds smoothly. . . . *Fortschritt* [progress] and *Rückschritt* [regression] alternate with each other."[18]

The concepts that Hirschberg chose to integrate in his depiction of the medieval Worms community were clearly drawn from the emancipation era. He not only used the term "citizenship" but also the combinations "German Jewish," a phrase that many Zionists rejected and that Nazi authorities later banned, and "faith and motherland" (*Glaube und Heimat*), a well-known phrase used by the Centralverein deutscher Staatsbürger jüdischen Glaubens (Central Union of the German Citizens of the Jewish Faith [CV]).[19]

Hirschberg's perspective would be supported in more scientific articles published by academic historians such as Elbogen. These historians presented Jewish life in early medieval Worms and more generally in Germany as an era of "ancient emancipation," a few centuries during which the Jews enjoyed a variety of civil rights, lived in cultural and linguistic proximity with their neighbors, and even took an active part in military service.[20] In this spirit Offenbach's liberal rabbi Max Dienermann (b. 1875) suggested that the history of the Worms community epitomized the entire history of the Jewish people. That history typified not only Jewish suffering in times of persecution but also Jewish participation in Germany's bourgeois life in better times.[21]

Such descriptions helped create an image of continuity between the Worms Jewish heritage and the modern German Jewish experience. The depiction of the ancient emancipation era as a prologue for modern emancipation also created the impression that the integration of the Jews in Germany was the normative path of history. Thus, their exclusion in the late Middle Ages and implicitly in the Nazi period was no more than a temporary deviation from this path. There was also an unmistakable analogy between the Jews of Worms in the late Middle Ages and the German Jews of the 1930s: both continued to feel bonded to their homeland in spite of the persecutions, and both identified with their citizenship and faith equally, even in eras of crisis and loss of rights.

Zionist writers also referenced the Worms legacy in the journal *Jüdische Rundschau* but from a different perspective. In a *Jüdische Rundschau* editorial, Kurt Loewenstein (b. 1902), a Zionist journalist and youth movement activist, presented Worms as proof of the Jews' unique bond to Germany. This countered the anti-Semitic argument that the Jews had always been unwanted guests and even "phantom" (*Gespenst*) entities.[22] The city's Jews had been restricted in various realms, he conceded, but they had also shared various public responsibilities with non-Jews; hence, they should not be seen as guests but instead as a resident minority. It seems that Loewenstein consciously chose not to use the term "equal citizens," preferring to describe the Jews in medieval Worms as a "minority," a concept that better reflected Zionist aspirations in the 1930s.[23] In addition, he argued that the integration of the Jews of Worms into their surroundings was based on their own recognition of their "distance" from the German people. This was a major tenet in the Zionist critique of modern emancipated Jewry. The idea of distance (*Distanz*) signified what was perceived as an unbalanced relationship between Germans and Jews in the emancipation era. To Loewenstein, distance was at the core of a very old Jewish legacy that enabled the Jewish people to survive even in periods of integration.[24] This balanced path of integration, he argued, faded during the nineteenth century and was replaced by a drive for radical assimilation.

Loewenstein recounted the Worms legacy, as did liberal spokespeople, as a positive model for integration of the Jews in their surroundings. However, unlike the liberal spokespeople, Loewenstein did not associate this with nineteenth-century emancipation; rather, he emphasized the difference between the two periods. The disagreement between Hirschberg and Loewenstein was not in their assessment of the legacy of Worms but was instead in their judgment of nineteenth-century German Jewry. Had it been radically assimilated, more so than the medieval Jewry in Worms, or had it been integrated in a respectable and self-preserving manner?

A much more direct and radical criticism of the way in which the Worms anniversary was marked by Jewish liberal spokespeople was presented by the Zionist publicist and educator Moritz Spitzer (b. 1900). The nine hundredth anniversary of the establishment of the Worms synagogue was marked respectfully, Spitzer asserted, but should it have even been marked as a Jewish festival in the first place? The speeches at the central ceremony, like the articles in the liberal Jewish press, that highlighted the continuity of the Jewish history of Worms and primarily its integration into the surroundings missed the true meaning of the anniversary. The real reason to mark the anniversary, Spitzer wrote, was because it expressed both the strong spirit of Jewish survival in the exile and the power of its sacrifice within the pressures of the outside environment. Therefore, Spitzer links the memory of the Worms synagogue to the martyrdom of the great Jewish sage Rabbi Akiva ben Yosef and his disciples who were killed by the Romans following the Bar Kokhba Revolt in Judea in the second century. For Spitzer, Worms also represented Ashkenazi medieval Jewry's deep devotion to Judaism in the Rhineland, which peaked at the time of their martyrdom:

> These martyrs and their sanctification of God's name are commemorated in synagogues all over the world, at least in Ashkenazi ones, in the memorial services of Tish'ah b'Av and in the time before and during the Yamim Noraim [Days of Awe] and in poetry [*selichot* and *kinnoth*], which are based on eyewitness depictions of these events. Only they reflect the spirit of "true Worms," the spirit that has not disappeared yet in the broad

Jewish world for which this synagogue, that survived, is a real monument.[25]

Whereas Loewenstein's critique of the liberal memory of Worms was quite mild, Spitzer proposed a totally different meaning to the anniversary. For him, the spirit of true Worms had nothing to do with the integration of the Jews into their surroundings. It was all about the Jewish power of survival in a hostile environment and therefore should be associated with the memories of Jewish martyrdom. Naturally, the inspiration that German Jews in the 1930s could draw from this spirit of true Worms was entirely different from what Hirschberg or even Loewenstein interpreted from the event. Both Loewenstein and Spitzer immigrated to Palestine in 1939.

The Pantheon of Heroes in German Jewish Public Memory

In addition to the commemoration of anniversaries and their attitudes toward places of memory, German Jewish publicists in the 1930s turned to Jewish and non-Jewish historical figures and reinterpreted their accomplishments against the needs of the present. In this manner they preserved a German Jewish tradition that had originated in the late eighteenth century.[26]

Historical figures from the pantheon of heroes of German Jewry were widely discussed in the Jewish press around the anniversaries of their births and deaths. Sometimes they were also invoked in ideological disputes between adversarial political Jewish sectors. But German Jewish public discourse did not limit itself to heroes; antiheroes and other controversial figures were discussed as well. As a result of the great variety of figures included in the pantheon, the discussion here will focus only on a few of them and primarily on Mendelssohn.[27]

In September 1929 German Jews celebrated the two hundredth anniversary of the birth of Mendelssohn. The German Jewish press—mainly the journals associated with the central liberal camp—devoted special issues to the anniversary, portraying Mendelssohn as the founding father of modern German Jewry. Mendelssohn's memory was also connected to a series of ceremonies and exhibitions. In 1929 he was depicted, sometimes dogmatically and sometimes in a more critical way, as an admirable philosopher and the forerunner of the emancipation.[28]

However, even then other voices on the margins of the Jewish discourse, mainly within the national Jewish milieu, could be identified. One of the critics claimed that Mendelssohn had failed to advance a bona fide integration of the Jews into German society.[29] In the Zionist journal *Jüdische*

Rundschau, the Berlin educator Israel Auerbach (b. 1878) referred to the gap between the original Mendelssohn and his image in 150 years of history.[30] Auerbach claimed that Mendelssohn had been a major opponent of the mass abandonment of Judaism in the emancipation period and had actually provided Jewry with the spiritual resources that it needed for its self-emancipation and survival in the new age. However, Auerbach continued, many of Mendelssohn's self-identified disciples went much too far toward full Germanization, which amounted to spiritual suicide.

A few years later during the first months of the Nazi regime, Mendelssohn's image became more and more prominent in the German Jewish press and was widely used as a metaphor for the various writers' perceptions and visions, especially among liberal writers. They were confused by the collapse of the emancipation and needed to reinterpret the past in light of the new reality.

In August 1933 Heinz Kellermann (b. 1910), who was active in the youth section of the CV, implored his readers to acknowledge that the "external emancipation" of German Jews had been abolished but that they should nevertheless continue their identification with German culture and the fatherland. He referred to this as "internal emancipation."[31] As a member of the minority of Jews who in the first months of 1933 still believed that Jews could take part in the new German national revolution, Kellermann insisted on the indispensability of preserving the internal emancipation, which he associated with Mendelssohn's heritage. Only people such as Mendelssohn, Kellermann claimed, would be able rebuild the foundations of the synthesis between Germans and Jews.

Kellermann drew an analogy between the current crisis of German Jewry and Mendelssohn's period. However, most CV senior speakers did not accept Kellermann's position. Like most German Jews, they began to recognize that the emancipation period, which had begun in Mendelssohn's time, had not come back to its starting point but instead had reached a dead end.[32]

A different Jewish liberal attempt to grant actual meaning to Mendelssohn's heritage was expressed by Rabbi Ignaz Maybaum (b. 1897).[33] Maybaum asserted that the model that Mendelssohn had developed to achieve the integration of the Jews in the modern world while preserving Jewish tradition was still relevant 150 years later. Writing more than a year after Kellermann, Maybaum did not stress the connection of the Jews to "Germanness" but instead focused on the more general ideal of humanistic education and *Bildung.* For Maybaum, Mendelssohn represented the right balance between the humanistic German cultural heritage and the Jewish tradition, a balance that should not be upset by either side. Thus, Maybaum rejected those who left the Jewish tradition in the post-Mendelssohn era and turned it into no more than a *Bildungsjudentum* (Judaism of *Bildung*), a superficial modern substitute to the original rich Jewish tradition. He also opposed the tendency in the mid-1930s tendency to take children out of school in order to prepare them for physical work in Palestine.[34] In an era in which the political chances of renewing emancipation seemed close to impossible, Maybaum invoked Mendelssohn's memory as a symbol that might prevent the deterioration of the young generation into what he saw as a segregated primitive cult. In 1939 Maybaum left Germany for England, where he would become a leading religious philosopher in the British Reform movement.

An entirely different representation of Mendelssohn was included, as we saw in the previous chapter, in Joachim Prinz's harsh critique of emancipated Jewry. Prinz mentioned not only Mendelssohn's political vision but also his relatives who had stayed behind in the ghetto as well as his offspring who had mostly converted to Christianity.[35] The representation of Mendelssohn was discussed by Prinz's liberal reviewers and critics. Thus, in a contrasting historical narrative to that of Prinz, Weil depicted Mendelssohn as the utmost icon of Jewish ascent and success in the era of emancipation, a great man who was attached to the variety of cultural treasures of his time.[36]

It is interesting to note that not only liberals but also most Zionist commentators did not accept Prinz's image of Mendelssohn. Such an attitude is exemplified in the introduction to an article about Mendelssohn's relationship to the German philosopher Gotthold Ephraim Lessing by the editors of *Jüdische Rundschau.* "It is important for us," the editors of the journal wrote, "to become acquainted with the period when the foundations that shaped the path of German Jewry until recent years had been set."[37] Mendelssohn's friendship with Lessing, they claimed, can serve as a positive model for the formation of Jewish-Christian relationships, since each one of them was deeply rooted in his own tradition and since Mendelssohn never considered abandoning Judaism. Similar to the way that Kurt Loewenstein viewed the legacy of Worms, *Jüdische Rundschau's* editors tried to utilize the myth of the Mendelssohn-Lessing friendship in order to support the Zionist view that Jewish-Gentile relations can be productive and stable only when founded on a clear awareness of a certain distance and on the maintenance of Jewish dignity. Still, in spite of the differences between them and the liberal commentators, it seems that the Zionist editors shared a positive view of Mendelssohn as the founding father of modern Judaism and preferred to focus their critique of the modern path of German Jewry on other, mostly later, historical figures.

This line of historical interpretation—the positive evaluation of Mendelssohn as a loyal Jew and the critique of his children and disciples—also appeared in some of the Orthodox interpretations of that time. Rabbi Joseph Carlebach (b. 1883), one of the well-known leaders of communal Orthodoxy (*Gemeindeorthodoxie*) who served as a rabbi in Altona and Hamburg, clearly articulated this. In a programmatic essay about the path and legacy of modern German Jewish Orthodoxy, Carlebach asserted that Mendelssohn was the first to shape the boundaries of the Jewish assimilation process and to establish the principle that Jews will not deviate from their religious laws for the sake of political rights.[38] Mendelssohn, he further claimed, wanted to free the Jewish masses of their estrangement from European culture and to lead them to "internal emancipation" and cultural regeneration before the coming of the "external emancipation."[39] Carlebach's critique of Mendelssohn focused only on the way he tried to transfer his heritage to the next generation. According to Carlebach, Mendelssohn's naive expectation that others would follow him in the smooth integration of the two worlds led him to prematurely initiate his modernization plans and to hastily pass the torch to other less reliable Jews, who later did not maintain his legacy.[40]

In January 1936 German Jews marked the 150th anniversary of Mendelssohn's death. This anniversary occurred a few months after the enactment of the Nuremberg Laws, which deprived Jews of German citizenship and prohibited marriage between Jews and other Germans. The 1936 anniversary of Mendelssohn's occurred only seven years after the 200th anniversary of his birth but under entirely different historical circumstances and gave Jewish publicists a new opportunity to reshape his image. Some of the participants in the discussion acknowledged the gap between their current perspectives on Mendelssohn and the one that German Jews had voiced during the previous anniversary.[41]

The participants in the 1929 anniversary, claimed Fritz Bamberger (b. 1902) in 1936, had been fully justified in celebrating Mendelssohn's achievements, which still seemed valid at that time. However, after the Nuremberg Laws had brought the course of emancipation to an end, there was an opportunity to understand Mendelssohn in a different way.[42] Bamberger, a lecturer at the Berlin liberal Hochschule für die Wissenschaft des Judentums, rejected the image of Mendelssohn as the founding father of emancipation, instead presenting him as an apolitical figure. From the perspective of January 1936, Bamberger opposed the image bestowed upon Mendelssohn during the 150 years of emancipation, what he described as a shallow and distorted image that ignored the real uniqueness of the philosopher who had lived between two worlds. Bamberger proposed that the situation in 1936 offered an opportunity to expose the other sides of Mendelssohn, those that had been neglected before but had gained new relevance after the enactment of the Nuremberg Laws. Bamberger thus presented Mendelssohn as the "Founding Father of Modern Hebrew" and stressed that his motives for his Bible translation project originated not from emancipation aspirations but rather from inner Jewish values.[43]

The way that Bamberger, a central figure in the Jewish liberal education system in Berlin, presented Mendelssohn can be viewed as an internalization of the new situation of German Jewry and an attempt to cope with it by new means. An apolitical Mendelssohn with more doubts and questions about the German Jewish synthesis could be a useful icon for those Jews who needed to accept the loss of the nineteenth-century political achievements. Therefore, Bamberger strove to dissociate Mendelssohn from the vanishing achievements of the nineteenth century and to describe his legacy as independent of non-Jewish sources. Only then could German Jews who lived in 1936—according to Bamberger "out of the emacipatory legal status"—adopt this legacy, which actually originated before emancipation.[44]

Devoted to Mendelssohn's anniversary, the central article in the *Israelitisches Familienblatt* added new dimensions to his image.[45] Mendelssohn's image, claimed the anonymous author, had gone through an unjustified process of Germanization, Hellenization, and liberalization by the generations that followed him. During the nineteenth century his figure became an idol, a misleading light (*Irrlicht*), and a mere cliché of the emancipation; his adherents totally ignored the darker and the more ambiguous sides of his biography. The events of 1933 had ruined this figure, and now the time had come to rediscover Mendelssohn as a Jew.

In a more popular mode than that of Bamberger, the *Israelitisches Familienblatt* author associated Mendelssohn first and foremost with traditional Jewish roots, extensive religious education, and a warm Jewish heart. Mendelssohn's initiatives and ambitions were rooted, according to the writer, in thousands of years of Jewish fate. This was the fate that had made him so great but that had also brought him face to face with tragic dilemmas that his followers in the nineteenth century chose to ignore. Thus, the obstacles that European society had placed in the way of Mendelssohn's integration as well as the inherent contradiction between his ambition to free the Jews from ghetto life and his wish to preserve the uniqueness of the Jewish fate had tragic significance that could only be fully understood in the 1930s.

Historical interpretations such as these reflected a major shift in the state of mind of the German Jewish mainstream and its dissociation from the narrative of progress. This was clearly expressed in the fact that Mendelssohn, the most prominent icon of Jewish modernity, was described in the post-1933 era as using terms such as "tragedy" and "fate," which were associated, as we saw in the previous chapter, with the growing sense of historical pessimism and with the archaic-mythic historical discourse.

In fact, these interpretations were not essentially different from Zionist ones, which suggested their own version of the real Mendelssohn as opposed to his nineteenth-century representations.[46] In the mid-1930s there was a growing consensus on how to present Mendelssohn in the German Jewish public arena. There was considerable consistency in the emphasis on his deep Jewish roots and on his significance independent of the integration into the surrounding society.[47] Almost all spokespeople of German Jewry tried to associate Mendelssohn's image with the current line that they supported, and almost none of them turned directly against his memory, as Prinz had done a few years earlier.

The historical evaluation of individuals in the post-Mendelssohn generation was based mostly on comparisons between them and Mendelssohn. In the 1930s the main challenge in this regard involved coming to terms with what had gone wrong in the earlier period and why. Liberal writers who dealt with these questions did not wish to disqualify the entire nineteenth-century heritage and were therefore driven to develop a more nuanced position vis-à-vis this period.

According to some, the gap between Mendelssohn's generation and the succeeding one paralleled the crisis of German Jewry in the 1930s. Mendelssohn's era, argued Selma Stern-Täubler not long after the Nuremberg Laws were passed, was characterized by the abandonment of old prejudices and the preference for reason.[48] This atmosphere had created a comfortable setting for German Jewish synthesis. Romanticism had a different agenda, however. Having emerged at the end of the eighteenth century, Romanticism was dominant in the post-Mendelssohn generation. Romanticism strove to create an organic community based on nation and race and refused to recognize any connection between German and Jewish entities. Alluding to the 1930s, Stern-Täubler asserted that in the ideal Christian German state (*christlich-germanische Staat*), which was the vision of Romanticism, there was no place at all for Jews as Jews.[49]

Stern-Täubler was not alone in implying that the problems of the post-Mendelssohn generation were similar to those of the 1930s. The Berlin writer and critic Arthur Eloesser (b. 1870), cofounder of the Jüdischer Kulturbund (Jewish Cultural Federation), linked the crisis of the late eighteenth century to the transition from the enlightened absolutism of Friedrich II to the more conservative regime of his son, Friedrich Wilhelm II.[50] According to Eloesser, the new regime replaced the rule of reason with a reactionary regime and transformed Berlin from Athens to Sparta. This was another clear allusion to the transition from the Weimar Republic to Nazi Germany.[51]

The most discussed figure among Mendelssohn's so-called disciples was, without doubt, the Berlin Jewish writer, banker, and communal leader David Friedländer. Several writers drew a distinction between the Mendelssohnian emancipation path, which they regarded as constructive and balanced, and Friedländer's route, particularly his 1799 proposal that the Jews should join the Protestant Church, which they described as dangerous and destructive. Exemplifying these sentiments was a popular article, composed in 1936, that equated Friedländer's proposal with the "liquidation of Judaism" (*Entjudung*). This, according to the writer, was typical of the post-Mendelssohn generation and in fact of the entire period until the Nazis' rise to power in 1933.[52] In a more academic presentation, the historian Ismar Freund, a rabbi and a lecturer at the Hochschule für die Wissenschaft des Judentums, described Friedländer's proposal as an example of the readiness to surrender Judaism for the sake of civil equality, an obvious betrayal of Mendelssohn's concept of emancipation.[53] Alongside these negative assessments, however, there were liberal writers, mostly in 1934 around the one hundredth anniversary of Friedländer's death, who highlighted certain positive aspects of his activities and rejected any sweeping disqualification of his memory.[54]

An especially interesting historical discussion was conducted in the German Jewish public sphere in 1936 around the eightieth anniversary of the death of the poet Heinrich Heine, who converted to Christianity at the age of twenty-eight. In spite of his conversion, most of the publicists who wrote about Heine included him in German Jewish history and tradition. The Berlin author and dramatist Leo Hirsch (b. 1903) stated that "Heine the Jew" is no less significant to Judaism than the famous medieval Jewish Spanish poet Rabbi Yehuda Halevi. Hirsch even attributed to Heine a prophetic power because Heine had said that Christians would never disregard the Judaism of Jews even after their conversion, a remark that proved to be a tangible reality in the wake of the Nuremberg Laws.[55]

In his 1936 book *Vom Ghetto nach Europa,* Eloesser undertook a much more comprehensive discussion of Heine's image. Eloesser, who turned to Zionism in his later years, defined himself as "an old man but a young Zionist."[56] However, it seems that his choice of Heine as the central figure in a book about the nineteenth-century German Jewish experience indicates that Eloesser preferred a wider German Jewish perspective to a narrow Zionist one. Throughout Heine's biography, Eloesser used terms such as "fate" and "tragedy." He concluded that the poet's very tragic circumstances were a clear manifestation of the essential problems facing the Jews in nineteenth-century Germany. Heine's fate, Eloesser claimed, was "in its inner conditions the one fate of all German Jews."[57]

In his discussion of Heine's Jewish identity as well as that of Ludwig Börne, the other well-known German Jewish convert and writer from the Romantic period, Eloesser suggested an interesting parallel between their understanding of their German identity while being political refugees in Paris and his views on their Jewish identity. Thus, he referred to Börne's remarks that it was a "misfortune" (*Unglück*) and a "hard task" (*schwere Aufgabe*) to be German, adding that their being Jewish was a bigger misfortune, a harder task, and even a tragedy for both Heine and Börne.[58] Eloesser therefore emphasized the Jewish perspective of Heine's and Börne's suffering and in this way made them more meaningful for his generation.

Throughout his extended discussion of Heine, Eloesser hardly referred to the poet's conversion and avoided judging it as a final act of dissociation from his Jewish origin. Instead, he accentuated Heine's contribution to European culture, describing him as a person whose Jewish legacy was in his blood and explaining his conversion as an act reflective of the times and even expected by his own family.[59] In the wake of the Nuremberg Laws, when the concept of the Jewish fate seemed to force itself even on those German Jews who chose to convert, Eloesser explained Heine's conversion as a result of the poet's fear of an "old German" (*Altdeutscher*) who will not recognize Heine's newly gained Germanness and will stab his "non-German heart," blaming him for disregard of his homeland.[60]

Through such descriptions, Eloesser transformed Heine from a Jew who had betrayed his heritage into a major representative of Jewish suffering with whom the German Jews of the 1930s could identify. This also seems to be why Eloesser describes Heine again and again as a lost son who returned to his heritage in his last days.[61] Furthermore, Eloesser's emphasis on Heine's Jewish identity did not come at the expense of his German one. It seems that here too Eloesser directed his writing to his expected readership. Heine is characterized throughout the book as bonded to Germany with all his heart. His dualism, his being both a German and a Jew, is the only way to understand his tragic life story.[62]

Eloesser's Heine does not propose any sort of solution to the misery of the German Jews in the 1930s, but the way that Eloesser shaped Heine he may have contributed to their efforts to retain a positive memory and ascribe meaning to the emancipation period. It had been a time of cultural achievements for which they could still be proud, but it had also produced tragic figures who predicted its decline.[63] From this perspective the gap between the nineteenth century and the 1930s seemed to be more bridgeable, and the previous century's legacy could still be a source of strength and comfort for German Jews in the 1930s.

In addition to Friedländer and Heine, several other Jewish figures from the post-Mendelssohn generation were widely discussed in the 1930s. These figures included the salon women, primarily Rahel Varnhagen (the 100th anniversary of her death was marked in early 1933); Gabriel Riesser, the politician, lawyer, and prominent spokespeople for Jewish emancipation (the 130th anniversary of his birth was marked a few months after the Nuremberg Laws were enacted); and Leopold Zunz, one of the founding fathers of the science of Judaism (the 50th anniversary of his death was marked in 1936).[64]

Although the central figures in the German Jewish pantheon were, as we have seen, German Jews, Jewish writers included certain non-Jewish Germans. It is noteworthy that while the assessment of Jewish figures was primarily integrated into the debates among the various Jewish orientations (liberal, Zionist, and Orthodox), the evaluation of non-Jewish Germans was mainly part of the Jewish writers' struggle against anti-Semitic historical interpretations. Evidence of this trend can be found in the last years of the Weimar Republic, predominantly surrounding the one hundredth anniversaries of the death of the Prussian statesman Karl Freiherr von Stein (1931) and of the poet and humanist Johann Wolfgang von Goethe (1932). In both cases Jewish writers, mostly from the liberal sector, depicted these famous figures as liberals and strong supporters of Jewish emancipation and opposed any representation of them as antiliberal conservatives and even anti-Semitic.[65]

In April 1935 under very different political circumstances, the one hundredth anniversary of the death of Wilhelm von Humboldt was marked. Reacting to an unfavorable assessment of Humboldt in the Nazi press, Jewish publicists related primarily to his position on Jewish emancipation. Fritz Friedländer, who represented the liberal Jewish narrative in this context, depicted Humboldt's interactions with various Jewish groups in Berlin, including a few of Mendelssohn's disciples and certain salon women, as a formative experience that demonstrated the great potential of the German Jewish encounter.[66] Humboldt's essay concerning Jewish emancipation, which was published in 1809, was distinguished by Friedländer as one of the major sources of the 1812 Prussian Emancipation Edict. Friedländer also recognized the failure of Humboldt's vision—the suspension of the 1812 edict as a result of Prussia's retreat to a Romantic conservatism that was hostile to the Jews—in a description that could be read as hinting at the experiences of German Jews in the 1930s.[67]

Whereas Friedländer articulated a wholeheartedly positive assessment of Humboldt, Ludwig Feuchtwanger (b. 1885), a lawyer and a publisher from Munich, provided a Zionist perspective soliciting a more balanced and critical evaluation of his positions and rejecting any glorification of Humboldt. The beginning of the emancipation era was, in fact, an age of freedom and humanism, Feuchtwanger asserted, but in retrospect there were also elements of "groundless impressions" (*Wesenlose Scheine*).[68] From his Zionist perspective, and with reference to the failure of Humboldt's political vision during the period of reaction in early nineteenth-century Prussia, Feuchtwanger presented him as far too optimistic and unrealistic, as in fact having accepted part of the conservative critique.

In addition to the attention given to German Jewish and non-Jewish figures, Jewish spokespeople, primarily from 1935, began writing and reflecting on the legacy of non-German Jews of earlier generations. Two major examples of this growing phenomenon were Rabbi Moses ben Maimon (also known as Maimonides) and Don Isaac Abravanel, the most prominent representatives of the Sephardic Jewish legacy. Maimonides and Abravanel had been central figures in the historical imagination of German Jewish spokespeople since the Enlightenment period, and their memory played an important role in the emergence of the so-called myth of Sephardic supremacy that German Jews had developed in the nineteenth century.[69] Anniversaries in 1935 and in 1937, respectively, of their births gave German Jewish spokespeople an opportunity to reassess their legacy vis-à-vis the current crisis.

In late March 1935 the eight hundredth anniversary of the birth of Maimonides was celebrated in Spain in a public ceremony in Córdoba (where he was born) and in a series of events all over the Jewish world, including Berlin.[70] Some of those who wrote about Maimonides' legacy focused on the agony of the German Jews. In 1935 the liberal educator Fritz Bamberger published a research paper on the philosophy of Maimonides. Bamberger asserted that Jewish history had known eras of open-mindedness and less open-mindedness, but the legacy of Maimonides cemented the bond between Jewish and non-Jewish cultures, establishing the bond as a crucial element of the mission of the Jewish culture. Facing the misery of German Jews, which had motivated some to dissociate from the general culture, Bamberger relied on Maimonides to encourage his readers to commit to what still promised to be a fruitful encounter with non-Jewish culture, even in times of crisis.[71]

Devoting a festive volume to the anniversary, the editors of the Zionist

Jüdische Rundschau presented Maimonides' legacy as part of the humanist culture, which at that time was under threat. The eight hundredth anniversary of the birth of Maimonides, they wrote, occurred "exactly at this time, when a major assault that seeks to bring to an end spiritual developments of centuries is being conducted in front of our eyes. . . . In Germany there is an awakening of a new living sentiment, which turns against the deeds of many centuries. . . . Vast cultural eras are reopening in front of us, [and] our ancestors are becoming our contemporaries." Unable to articulate their view explicitly on this new spirit in Germany, the Zionist editors expressed it implicitly through their depiction of Maimonides, whom they referred to as an "emigrant."[72]

In addition to the special volumes circulated by Jewish journals, Maimonides' anniversary was also marked by the publication of several books on his religious legacy. One writer, the Lithuanian-born Orthodox educator and publicist Selig Schachnowitz (b. 1874), drew upon Maimonides to validate positions on a number of contemporary issues, such as Jewish settlement in Palestine, Hebrew language, and Jewish education.[73]

As conditions worsened, in 1937 German Jews marked the five hundredth anniversary of the birth of the Spanish Jewish statesman, philosopher, and Bible commentator Don Isaac Abravanel. The relevance of Abravanel's memory, deeply linked to both the greatness of medieval Iberian Jewry and to its tragic demise and expulsion, was quite apparent in 1937.[74] Abravanel was commemorated in this year in a variety of ceremonies as well as in a memorial exhibition organized by the Berlin Jewish community.[75] "Isaac Abravanel had experienced more than any other person," wrote Elbogen in February 1937, "the instability of the Jewish fate." Reviewing Abravanel's dramatic life story, "a life that was full of misery and hard tests," Elbogen emphasized Abravanel's political and economic activities, his humanistic devotion to science and thought, and his achievements in the religious sphere. Eventually Elbogen returned to the term "fate": "Don Isaac Abravanel, in his rise and fall, is a symbol for Jewish fate; in his faith and his hope he is a model for Jewish religiousness."[76]

For the young Zionist rabbi Max Nussbaum of Berlin (b. 1910), Abravanel's life story demonstrated what Nussbaum called "the law of centers"—the cyclical pattern of history of the decline and eventual disappearance of a major Jewish center—that paved the way for the rise of a new center. Thus, Nussbaum aptly described the eve of the 1492 expulsion of the Jews from Spain in a way that resembled the situation of the German Jews on the eve of the Nazi era: "Each year has brought new difficulties. The Jews of Castile and

Aragon had to feel that their future in Spain was unsafe, but they decided not to emigrate and closed their eyes to the reality. The explanation for this is that they loved Spain more than anything. . . . They were convinced that no other country could take the place of Spain."[77]

Nussbaum also discussed Abravanel's various activities as well as his philosophy, but it is clear that Nussbaum was most interested in Abravanel's biography because it helped Nussbaum demonstrate his view of the cyclical pattern of Jewish history, a pattern that had clear implications for the future of German Jews. Nussbaum left Germany in 1939 for the United States, where he served as a reform rabbi in Hollywood.

Other German Jewish sectors also depicted Abravanel's figure. While liberals praised the duality of his worldly economic and political activity balanced with his authentic religious and spiritual legacy, the Orthodox commentator Selig Schachnowitz viewed Abravanel's worldly success as a temporary and marginal element of his heritage, compared to his religious philosophy and biblical interpretation. Another description of Abravanel was included in a volume of biographies published by the Reichsbund jüdischer Frontsoldaten (National League of Jewish Frontline Soldiers). Generally the league presented Abravanel as a hero who defended his fellow Jews in an age of expulsion and emphasized his Jewish pride by including a story about an encounter with the Spanish royal couple.[78]

The discussions about Maimonides and Abravanel were only two prominent examples of the German Jewish press and public's growing interest in the biographies of premodern Jews. The *Central Verein Zeitung* published a long series of biographies in a section called "Jewish Figures in Their Epochs" during 1935–36. Major historians and publicists, including Elbogen, Friedländer, Feuchtwanger, Isaak Heinemann, and Max Wiener, contributed articles about a variety of historical Jewish figures, from the biblical Moses and David to Jewish leaders in the early modern period.[79] Another series titled "Personalities in Jewish History," which mostly spotlighted Talmudic scholars, was published in the Jewish communal journal of Berlin and, later, of Frankfurt. Most of these biographical articles were written by the young Polish-born rabbi Abraham Heschel (b. 1907), who later became an important Jewish theologian and philosopher in America.[80] It is noteworthy that liberal spokespeople used the ancient Jewish sages more than did the Zionists, who were more focused on the development of the Jewish national home in Palestine.

Emigration and Diaspora in Historical Perspective

A major topic on the agenda of German Jews from the beginning of the Nazi period and, even more so, in the second half of the 1930s was the question of Jewish emigration. At first it was mainly Zionists who called on the Jews to leave Germany, while most liberals continued to identify Germany as their motherland. However, the growing agony that had already led tens of thousands of Jews to leave Germany and the somber future of German Jewry made emigration the central subject of discussion for all the Jewish parties.[81] Internal Jewish debates about this topic resembled how certain historical issues were approached, that is, trying to create a usable past.

In his September 1934 plea urging Jewish historians to be more responsive to the needs of the Jewish public and to engage realistic problems rather than abstract questions, Fritz Friedländer mentioned emigration as a key present-day issue. Emigration, he stated, had been a major phenomenon throughout Jewish history, but its new crucial implication required fresh historical reflection. Friedländer also mentioned the concept of Diaspora and the problem of Jewish-Gentile relationships as another fundamental topic that had to be illuminated for the sake of the community.[82]

German Jews understood their current situation by comparing it to the relatively recent emigration of Jews from certain German states in the nineteenth century. The young Polish-born historian and sociologist Bernhard Weinryb (b. 1905), writing in the spring of 1934, insisted that the motives for this emigration, though not identical to those leading to the current emigration from Germany, were quite similar. In both cases there was a decline in the legal status and economic situation of the Jews due to government policies, including the 1813 Bavarian Jewish law, Prussian Jewish policy in the post-Napoleonic period, the failure of the 1848 revolution, and, most recently, the laws passed under the Nazi regime. Weinryb added that in both the nineteenth and twentieth centuries emigration was linked to a change in the Jewish occupational structure (*Berufsumschichtung*) and also included internal migration (mostly from the country to the city) and immigration abroad and overseas (mostly to the United States).[83]

Preference for Palestine as the favored destination for German Jewish emigrants during the first three years of the Nazi regime was a result of the rise in Zionist influence and the 1933 transfer agreement, known as the Haavara Agreement, between the Nazi regime and the Jewish agency to Palestine. As a result, various Jewish liberal spokespeople were motivated to defend their legacy, partly through a growing interest in the concept of Diaspora.[84] The CV monthly magazine *Der Morgen* opened its June 1934 volume with a comprehensive discussion of this concept. The harsh shock felt in Germany, the very country where the integration of the Jews seemed to be most successful, stated editor Eva Reichmann-Jungmann (b. 1897), evoked fundamental questions that were of concern to the entire Jewish world: "If German Jewry could be thrown away by the forces of history, one may get the feeling that this generally concerns the Diaspora as a Jewish option."[85]

This issue, Reichmann-Jungmann continued, also raises questions regarding Jewish fate during generations of dispersion and regarding the concept of the Diaspora as a mission in Jewish history: "The Diaspora, first and foremost the German one, is in danger. It is not only threatened materially, but also in the sense of denial of its value as a Jewish mission."[86] Reichmann-Jungmann emigrated in 1939 to England and was very active there in the milieu of the former CV activists.

The next two articles in the magazine attempted to legitimize and rehabilitate the Diaspora in Jewish history in contrast to the Zionist vision. Rabbi Ignaz Maybaum described the Diaspora element in Jewish life as religiously valuable and employed the term "exile" in this context: "The exile is sociological space for Jewish chosenness. Exile is not a mere geographic term that means 'abroad' (outside of Palestine). Exile means powerless existence. In this context the Jews in contemporary Palestine are also in a similar situation like ours. *The exile is our fate.*"[87]

In a more intricate historical discussion, Grigori Landau defined the Diaspora as part of a cyclical process in which dark times always follow more enlightened ages. The Jewish uniqueness of the Diaspora, he asserted, relates to political powerlessness. This fact, which has a universal meaning that concerns the fragility of human existence, was forgotten and repressed in the nineteenth century because of the rise of the idea of progress:

> During the last century we (not only the Jews but all modern humanity) have forgotten the fundamental truth of human life, the eternal ups and downs and the instability of the soil on which we walk in our earthly life. . . . The formative power of a few decades made us accustomed to stability and relative quiet. . . . We became used to the exceptional and temporary affluence, to the unprecedented rise in the standard of living and to the stabilization of human society—to the overall progress of the recent era. This brief and exceptional era seemed to us to be the norm and we started to assess history at large accordingly. . . . The Jews, too, evaluated the Diaspora according to the norms of a few decades in the nineteenth century.[88]

The truth is, Landau added, that the Diaspora is far from the ideal; it is a difficult and dangerous path that genuinely represents the fragility of human life. While in the Diaspora the Jews had been confronted by many hardships, but without them the Jews would have declined and disappeared, as many other peoples did. Landau attributed most of the Jewish creativity to the Diaspora and attacked the Zionist worldview, claiming that even in the biblical period the formative ideas of Judaism originated outside the Land of Israel. Citing the exile of Egypt and the exile of Babylon, he viewed the Land of Israel as the only place for the realization of the formative ideas of Judaism.[89]

A few months later liberal spokespeople, on the subject of the Diaspora, went several steps further in a discussion conducted in the youth supplement of the *Central Verein Zeitung*. For example, the young rabbi Franz Rosenthal (b. 1911) criticized the Zionists, stating that in spite of what he called the pseudomessianic movements, including Karaites, Kabbalists, Hasidim, and also Zionists, and in spite of the ideas raised by figures such as the medieval Spanish Jewish poet and philosopher Rabbi Judah Halevi, Rabbi Moses ben Nahman (Nahmanides), the sixteenth-century Portuguese Kabbalist Solomon Molcho, and also Theodor Herzl, Jewish life continued and would continue in the Diaspora due to "the law of Jewish existence." Rosenthal dated this historical principle to the destruction of the Second Temple and affiliated it with the legacy of the first-century Rabban Yochanan ben Zakai, who successfully converted the Jewish Temple ritual into spiritual worship. As a result, the Jewish bond with the Land of Israel became less territorial and more spiritual. Thus, the Jews could become more attached to their new homelands.[90] Rosenthal immigrated to the United States in 1939.

The growing fear that the emigration of the Jews from Germany would eventually bring an end to German Jewry motivated certain Jewish writers, mostly liberals, to stress the uniqueness of the German Jewish legacy in the Jewish Diaspora and to sometimes ruminate on the endurance of this legacy outside of Germany. Rabbi Ignaz Maybaum singled out German Jewry as the only rooted representation of "Western Judaism" (*Westjudentum*), the Jewish entity that combines Jewish tradition and world culture and expresses Jewish values in a way that is meaningful to other nations.[91] This Western Jewish legacy, he asserted, originated in the Greco-Roman era in both Alexandria and Babylon. East European Jews do not represent this legacy because they are too focused on their particular Jewish existence. French and British Jews could not embody this legacy, as they had become too distant from authentic Jewish experience. For Maybaum, German Jewry epitomized the Western Jewish legacy and bore responsibility both for the manifestation of such a consciousness in the United States and for the emergence of modern Judaism in the Land of Israel.

Ten months later in late 1934 Maybaum returned to this topic, speculating on the continued existence of this Jewish legacy, which he then called *Bildungsjudentum,* if the Jews were not able to remain in Germany:

> The history of German Jewry is a Jewish history. This is why the question whether German Jewry will continue to exist has [general] Jewish implications. It means: Will the new Jewish era, which German Jewry succeeded to accomplish after the vanishing of the Jewish Middle Ages, be lost? Such a loss is possible; we have seen this with Spanish Jewry. The era of prosperity of Spanish Jewry brought spiritual development, which could have marched the Jews to the new time. . . . [T]hen came 1492. The historical struggle for achieving a new Jewish era was lost, [and] only a medieval Jewry was left until much later[;] starting only with Moses Mendelssohn, German Jewry has taken upon itself the struggle for a new Jewish era. We are still in the midst of this struggle. Can we collect its fruit or will we, like Spanish Jewry, not reach anything beyond some grand beginnings?[92]

Maybaum viewed the potential loss of the German Jewish legacy as parallel to the catastrophe of 1492 but did not yet raise the idea of its survival by emigration.

The importance of emigration in the German Jewish discourse arose after the Nuremberg Laws officially brought the emancipation to a close.[93] A few weeks after the laws were enacted, Fritz Friedländer expressed the view that emigration is the only way to secure the future of the nineteenth-century legacy: "This century of assimilation, which has now come to its end, has not been, as certain people state today, in vain, since our youth, which is today pushed to leave Germany because of its agony, is carrying the fruit of these times to new homelands."[94]

This quote reflects the beginning of a change in the position of non-Zionist spokespeople vis-à-vis the issue of emigration and, along with it, the Jewish past. In early 1936 Hirschberg claimed that the Jews had kept the pure Jewish spirit all through the generations by living among the nations as a minority lacking any political power. The fate of such a minority had forced it, and may still force it in the future, to wander among the nations, but this should not be viewed in a negative sense: "The image of Ahasuerus [the Christian medieval mythological figure of the 'wandering Jew'], who is compelled to wander as a curse and a symbol for the Jews, is not the desired model of our community, it was rather coined by others. Whoever is destined to wander, fulfills the mysterious blessing, on which Judaism is founded, and carries with him the mission of his community to be a blessing."[95] Three years later, in 1939, Hirschberg left Germany for England and in 1940 settled in Brazil.

In his 1936 book, Hungarian-born Orthodox rabbi and spokesman Adolf Altmann (b. 1879), who served the Trier community, articulated a fundamentally similar position regarding the place of emigration in Jewish history. He asserted that the basic law of Jewish existence is the law of "movement and rest." This is embodied in two well-known verses from the book of Numbers: "And it came to pass, when the ark set forward" (Numbers 10:35), "And when it rested" (Numbers 10:36). Throughout thousands of years of history, Jewish existence was thus characterized by a tension between the poles of movement and rest, a tension that shaped the achievements as well as the failures of the Jewish people.[96] Altmann emphasized the blessing and fruitfulness in the process of movement and wandering, a process that liberated the Jews from the dangers of remaining at a standstill and of falling victim to assimilation. Altmann did not endorse any of the positions that emerged during the liberal-Zionist debate regarding the meaning of Diaspora vis-à-vis the Land of Israel in Jewish history; rather, he stressed the need for a synthesis of the two directions.[97]

It is interesting to note that the memory of Abravanel, which, as we have seen, was extensively discussed by German Jewish spokespeople in 1937, was also adapted to a usable past in the context of emigration. "As Isaac Abravanel has lost his homeland," wrote one publicist in the Berlin communal journal, "he was bound to lead the emigration[;] . . . his life and memory were therefore bound to the emigration of Jews from one country to other regions." The article linked the "wandering staff" (*Wanderstab*) held by Abravanel to the contemporary experience of German Jews and to the tasks set before their leadership. The search was for new destinations of settlement for European Jews around the world as well as for the formation of coordinated action for the support of immigration.[98]

A 1937 article by the historian and businessman Hanns Reissner (b. 1902) contains an additional historical perspective on emigration. While emigration was difficult during this period, emigrating was more difficult in the nineteenth century, something that seemed to have been forgotten. The emigrants then were totally cut off from their original community, even when they only moved from Bavaria to Prussia.[99] In regard to the immigration history of his own family, Reissner described their economic achievements as well as their complicated attempts to preserve the cultural heritage of their homeland. He also presented their assimilation and the abandonment of Judaism by some of them as an unavoidable price of immigration. By presenting this family story, he tried to encourage contemporary German Jews who were struggling with similar problems.[100]

The German Jewish liberal leadership's increasing recognition of the inevitability of emigration in the second half of the 1930s had transformed the discussion about the Diaspora. Liberal writers now dealt with the Diaspora in their work not in order to legitimate the continuation of Jewish life in Germany but instead to express their position regarding the historical meaning of the emigration and the preferred destinations. A clear expression of this position was articulated by the lawyer Ernst Herzfeld (b. 1875), the president of the CV from 1936. Herzfeld acknowledged emigration as an essential solution for the German Jews, but he did not accept the idea that Palestine should have a unique status in the debate: "It is not right that only in Palestine Jews will be able to escape from superficiality, lack of creativity, assimilation and eventually also excommunication. If this had been even partially true then, after seventy generations of life in the Diaspora, there would have been no Jews and no Judaism."[101]

Herzfeld's argument for a fair evaluation of destinations echoed his plea for a balanced assessment of the emancipation era in German Jewish history. He called for an acknowledgment of the errors along with an appreciation of the achievements of the 150-year emancipation period that ended with the Nazi rise to power. A few months later Herzfeld produced a systematic analysis of the terms "assimilation," "dissimilation," and "emigration," which he integrated into a cyclical view of Jewish history.[102]

Zionist writers criticized Herzfeld's perspective on the Diaspora as well as his plea not to hold the 150 years of assimilation responsible for the contemporary need for emigration. By 1936, as it had become clear that Palestine would not be able to accommodate mass Jewish immigration, the Zionists could no longer rule out Jewish immigration to other countries. Their disagreement with Herzfeld was therefore primarily about his interpretation of the past and his evaluation of the term "Diaspora." "We, the Zionists," one of them argued, "oppose the transformation of German citizens of the Mosaic faith, or their children, into Brazilians and South Africans of the Mosaic faith, since we understand that what has failed in Germany will eventually fail in Brazil or South Africa as well." Unlike Herzfeld, the writer added, Zionism did not accord with any positive value in the Diaspora. The persistence of the Diaspora could be justified only insofar as it retained a Jewish national consciousness.[103]

The rapid deterioration in the situation of German Jews in 1938 had a clear effect on how the Jewish spokespeople referenced emigration in Jewish history. Nobody wishes to emigrate, to leave his homeland and his parents' graves, wrote Manfred Swarsensky in an article for Passover in 1938, but the Jews today are facing a Divine decree of *"Lech Lecha"* ("go forth"), which commands them to find a new space to preserve and develop their Judaism.[104] Ignaz Maybaum, who in 1934 expressed his concern about the future of Judaism in Germany, framed overseas immigration four years later as a Jewish liberal religious mission:

> The promotion of the immigration overseas must be understood as a mission, a mission that should be seen as Jewish and holy in the same way that Zionists experience their activity in favor of the immigration to Palestine as a holy Jewish vocation. . . . The fate of Judaism depends on the question of how many Jews we will able to bring to North and South America, to Australia and South Africa. . . . The fate of Judaism depends on the turning of these new Jewish centers into halls of Torah. This is the mission of contemporary Jewry.[105]

Jewish history was entering a post-Zionist era, Maybaum added, an era in which the major challenge would be the formation of "global Diaspora Judaism" that would carry the Western Jewish legacy, including the pluralistic modern German Jewish heritage, to the new homelands.[106]

Others who discussed emigration in 1938 referred to the establishment of the Beth Midrash (House of Learning) in Yavneh by Rabban Yochanan ben Zakai as the beginning of the change in Judaism to a scholarly culture based on centers that could be transferred from place to place (Babylon, Spain, Germany). Germany was the pioneer in advancing the scientific approach to the study of Judaism in the nineteenth century, one writer asserted, but it should be recognized that historical circumstances would no longer permit this activity to continue in Germany. Therefore, new centers of Jewish research should be established in other countries, primarily in Palestine and in the United States.[107]

Every end is also a beginning, stated the historian and CV activist Ernst Fraenkel (b. 1891) in October 1938. He demonstrated this principle by recounting Yochanan ben Zakai's new initiative after the fall of ancient Jerusalem and by referring to the quarter of a million Jews who strengthened

American Jewry after leaving Germany in the nineteenth century. Fraenkel's historical examination of the emigration was summed up with the comforting reference to the cyclical character of Jewish history: "Simon Dubnow, the great historian, has spoken once in his memoirs about the fact that all the historical lives are turning around in a circle. . . . In these days of calamity and destruction, more than ever, we can and we should recognize that Jewish history is demanding . . . a belief in times of building. . . . The necessity of the farewell can be a bitter agony, but the divine movement can always . . . turn the agony into joy."[108] These sentences were published a few weeks before the *Kristallnacht*.[109] From this point onward, the relatively free German Jewish press, which had served as the framework for the discourse discussed in this chapter, was utterly silenced.

Conclusion

Various German Jewish spokespeople—political activists, publicists, rabbis, educators, and professional historians—frequently used the past when addressing their readers in the first years of the Nazi regime. As we have seen in this chapter, this helped them encourage their readers to believe in a better future and to gain inspiration from major past events and historical figures. Spokespeople for German Jewry also turned to the past to justify certain actions that they believed were necessary in response to Nazi threats and, especially in the late 1930s, to legitimize emigration as a well-established pattern in Jewish history. In addition to these common aims, there were two major differences in the ways that spokespeople of the various Jewish groups—primarily liberals and Zionists—made use of the past.

Liberal Jewish spokespeople, who embodied the legacy of Jewish integration in Germany, emphasized patterns of continuity. The undeniable end of the emancipation era as well as the growing recognition of the general decline of modern liberal values motivated these spokespeople to turn to historical symbols from the remote past. Thus, in addition to their use of Mendelssohn, who was reshaped into a form that fit the new position of German Jews, they revived symbols such as the medieval synagogue of Worms and figures such as Maimonides and Abravanel. The discussions about emigration and Diaspora in Jewish history were also founded on the continuity of the German Jewish legacy.

In response to an argument based on continuity, various Zionist spokespeople criticized the liberals and offered their own interpretation of some of these symbols and figures. One Zionist writer asserted that the true spirit of Worms did not represent a Jewish tradition of integration into the surroundings but instead represented a legacy of martyrdom. Another Zionist writer associated Abravanel's memory with the shortsightedness of Spanish Jews in the late Middle Ages and connected this to the impending catastrophe of German Jews in the twentieth century. Such ideas, however, did not represent the full spectrum of Zionist writers, who increasingly used less polemical arguments when writing about the past.

The turn of German Jews to the past reflected a gradual process of the narrowing—though not the disappearance—of the gaps in the positions of the various sectors of German Jewry vis-à-vis the steady deterioration of conditions in the 1930s. As time passed, liberal spokespeople desisted from implying that the emancipation in Germany was to be restored as part of a cyclical historical movement. They now recalled images from the past in order to emphasize the deep-rootedness of the German Jewish legacy as well as to engage in a more general discussion about the Diaspora. The positions of Zionist and Orthodox spokespeople, on the other hand, softened in comparison to the harsh polemics of Prinz and Schwab (discussed in the chapter 1). Their assault on what they saw as the assimilating positions of the mainstream Jewish liberals became rather pointless as the approaching calamity raised doubts regarding any possible solution for the future of German Jews. Amid this harsh reality, the creation of a usable past focused increasingly on an attempt to comfort German Jews in their agony, to encourage them to believe in a better future, and eventually to ease the experience of being uprooted from their homeland and forced to emigrate.

PART 2

FRANCE
1932–40

3

FACING THE CRISIS AT HOME AND ABROAD

In the period between World War I and World War II, French Jewry was divided into two main groups: native French Jews and the east European immigrants. Each of these groups, neither of which was monolithic within itself, maintained its own organizational frameworks and political culture. Their spokespeople reported and interpreted the daily developments in different newspapers and periodicals and even in different languages (French and Yiddish). These distinctions were also articulated in the historical narratives and symbols that spokespeople of the two groups drew from the past. This was the dynamic that unfolded in response to the difficult challenges that Jewish emancipation faced in Germany, all over Europe, and even in France itself during the 1930s.

In 1919 there were approximately 150,000 Jews living in France. By 1939 the number climbed to around 300,000.[1] This rapid growth, which was primarily the result of increased immigration, not only reflects the demographic transformation of French Jewry during this period but also had a great impact on the community's political and public agenda. Since the French Revolution and, even more so, from the mid-nineteenth century, the native Jewish population had been undergoing an integration process within the state, society, the economy, and culture. Led by the Central Consistory of the Jews of France, which had been founded during the Napoleonic era, local French Jews had developed a clear sense of patriotism that enabled them to cope with the challenge of the Dreyfus Affair and was strengthened during World War I.[2] The French Jewish ideology of assimilation, which became fully crystallized in the late nineteenth century, presented the Jews as an indispensable part of the French nation and based itself on the legacy of the great Revolution and the Napoleonic regime.[3]

While the local Jews were becoming more and more integrated, the immigrant Jews—mostly concentrated in Paris—tended to preserve their linguistic and ethnic characteristics and to develop their own political subculture.[4] The immigrants' political tendencies could be compared to those of the Jewish east European immigrants in England and in the United States. For east European Jews who tended toward political activism and especially for those who identified with left-wing movements (Bundists, Communists, and others), France and primarily Paris symbolized the universal values of the Revolution. This symbolic value was one of the reasons that they preferred France as their immigration destination. England seemed to be more conservative, and the United States was viewed as too materialistic.[5] As we shall see in this chapter, those who wrote for the immigrant press and shaped public opinion had their own interpretation (or even interpretations) of French history, values, and heritage. In their journals there could also be found articles by Yiddish publicists and intellectuals from other countries (mostly Poland and the United States), and therefore they reflected the trends in the thoughts and moods of the wider Yiddish literary readership. These trends did not always match the conceptualizations or interests of the local French Jews.

The Jewish community of France, and especially of Paris in the 1930s, was therefore unique in comparison to other European Jewish communities insofar as it consisted of two communities with approximately equal standing. Although almost equal in size, they were very different in their language, origin, and political culture and therefore in their approach to questions of Jewish identity and in their reaction to the Nazi threat.[6]

For these reasons, French Jewry of the 1930s offers an interesting case study. Through it we can examine the reception, interpretation, and political mobilization of national, Jewish, and universal historical narratives and symbols in response to the Fascist and Nazi onslaught on the achievements and values of the emancipation era.

The various ways in which Jews in France—both locals and immigrants—came to terms with the developments of the 1930s and attempted to mobilize historical memory can be fully interpreted only in consideration with the French political and social setting during this period and the use of historical symbols in the general French political arena. The world economic crisis that began to be felt in France in the early 1930s, the rise of the Nazis to power in Germany in 1933, the internal French political split that became much sharper after 1934, and the escalation in the French public discourse about the refugee problem all threatened the status of the Jews in France and evoked a variety of responses.

France in the 1930s: Social and Political Crisis and Conflicting Images of the Past

During the 1930s, France experienced a series of events and processes that deepened the political and social divisions and created an atmosphere of crisis. These processes, which were partially a belated outcome of World War I, exposed French society as being especially vulnerable within the Western world. Eugen Weber opens his comprehensive study of 1930s' France by presenting this decade as the decade "before the war" (*l'avant-guerre*) in contrast to the 1920s, which was the decade "after the war." This does not mean that World War II or the swift French defeat were predetermined outcomes of the 1930s, but it does reflect the French loss of self-assurance and the pessimistic atmosphere during this decade and also serves as a justification for presenting the 1930s as a period unto itself.[7]

The formative experience of French society in the 1930s was the memory of the horrors of World War I. Preventing the outbreak of another war was therefore a matter of supreme importance, perhaps more so for France than for any other European nation.[8] The number of French soldiers who had fallen in the war—more than 10 percent of the country's active young men—was higher than for any other European country. What made France more unique and deepened the pessimistic mood in French society was the acceleration of the country's demographic decline following the war, a process that reached its peak in the 1930s.[9]

The anxiety over the possibility of another war also pertained to the French view of German society as young, dynamic, and aggressive in contrast to the defense-oriented French society of which the Maginot Line became a major cultural symbol.[10] These images became more threatening during the 1930s after the rise of the Nazis to power in Germany. The memory of the war and its terrible consequences were interpreted by many as having led to the ultimate lessons of "no more war" and "never again." The day of the declaration of the cease-fire (November 11, 1918) thus became a very important date in the French calendar, one of the central places of memory of French society in the interwar period.[11]

In addition to the demographic crisis and the anxiety over another war, the French experienced a deep economic crisis in the 1930s. Following the successful rehabilitation of the French economy in the 1920s, at which time it returned to its prewar level of production by the end of the decade, France was affected relatively late by the world economic crisis. But France was also late in recovering from the crisis. The French economic decline started only in 1931 or even in 1932 but was far from coming to an end in the mid-1930s, when England, Germany, and other countries seem to have begun to pull themselves out of the recession.[12]

The economic crisis also led to a series of social confrontations. The most severe concerned the question of foreigners and refugees. After France encouraged immigration during the 1920s in the period of economic growth, the number of foreigners in France grew from 1.5 million in 1921 to 3 million in 1931. These included east European Jewish immigrants. However, during the recession the French felt that they did not need any more immigrants. This mood led to the growth of hatred of foreigners in general and to anti-Semitism in particular.[13] In the later years of the 1930s this trend intensified in reaction to the pressures of refugees seeking asylum from the Central European Fascist regimes and, later on, after the republican defeat in the Spanish Civil War.

The economic crisis and the social confrontations of the 1930s in France also led to the polarization of the political system. The weakening of the republican establishment, whose reputation was severely damaged by a series of corruption scandals in the early 1930s, destabilized the regime, sharpened the political tensions, and brought on significant political violence. Furthermore, the decline and fall of democratic regimes in other European countries—particularly the rise of the Nazis to power in Germany—evoked substantial concern for the Fascist danger also in France.

On February 6, 1934, France experienced the most violent night in its political history since the days of the Paris Commune in 1871. Right-wing demonstrators gathered in the Place de la Concorde to protest the newly formed government of the radical leader Édouard Daladier and also protest against the democratic regime of the Third Republic. The violent eruptions that night, when fifteen French citizens and one policeman were killed and more than fourteen hundred people were wounded, resulted the following day in Daladier's resignation. The French Left understood these events as an attempt at a Fascist putsch. From the perspective of the French Right, however, February 6 represented its rooted unwillingness to accept the legitimacy of the Third Republic. This was a direct continuation of a series of events that France had experienced since the republic's establishment in 1871, among them the Dreyfus Affair. The protest also reflected a deeper reservation of certain elements within French society toward the heritage of 1789.[14] The Left's initial reaction to these events was a mass demonstration on February 9 and a call for a general strike on February 12. These events resulted in the deaths of more citizens but were interpreted as a national mobilization for the values of the French Revolution against the Fascist danger.[15] February 6, 1934, can be said to be the beginning of a French civil war, an overall struggle between the supporters of the legacy of 1789 and their opponents. This struggle lasted until the fall of the Third Republic in 1940 or even until the fall of the Vichy regime in 1944.[16]

In spite of the reality of the Fascist threat, after a few months it became evident that the Fascist element was still too weak to bring down the republic. Furthermore, the republic's supporters—initially the Socialists and the Communists and then also part of the center-left radicals—turned gradually to a strategy of political unity in order to cope with the threat, trying to learn the lesson from the fall of the German republic. The French Front populaire (Popular Front), which was formed as a coalition of these parties, saw itself as the authentic representative of the 1789 principles and therefore as being obliged to save France from a Fascist overthrow. The Popular Front first appeared as a public power in a mass demonstration that was held in Paris on July 14, 1935, and was officially established in January 1936. Later the Popular Front rose to power in the elections, after which the Socialist Leon Blum was nominated as prime minister (June 1936). The Popular Front celebrated its victory, symbolically, in a mass demonstration that was held on Bastille Day on July 14, 1936. The ideas of unity and the legacy of July 14 were presented by the Popular Front as the answer to the internal Fascist challenge of February 6, 1934, as well as to the growing external threat of Nazi Germany.[17] Granting mythical meaning to the symbols of the republic and the Revolution was therefore a major source of power and inspiration, and the Popular Front used this method to enlist mass support.

However, the Popular Front's rise to power did not bring the confrontation between the Left and the Right, or between the legacy of July 14 and the challenge of February 6, to a clear end. The Spanish Civil War, which erupted only three days after the demonstration of July 14, 1936, and the Spanish Republic's request for help from the French forced Blum to choose between military intervention and neutrality. Blum's decision not to intervene is seen by many as the first signal of his eventual fall. Symbolically this decision can be interpreted as preferring the lesson of November 11—that is, "no more war" or even "never again"—to that of the July 14 legacy and the unconditional commitment to fight Fascism with all possible means.[18]

France's past and its historical symbols—the most important of which was the historical interpretation of the French Revolution and its heritage—thus became in the 1930s burning issues among intellectuals and in the general French public. Deepening political divisions also sharpened the histori-cal disputes, and such issues became key methods for mobilizing the masses to political aims. French politicians and public figures tended to choose their cultural heroes according to their current political views: conservative republicans took hold of the 1789 symbols as representing progress, radi-cals tended to present figures such as Georges Jacques Danton and the Gi-rondists as the real representatives of the revolutionary spirit, and the clearly left-wing speakers presented Maximilien Robespierre, Louis-Anton-Léon de Saint-Just, and other Jacobins as their heroes.[19] The spokespeople of the conservative Right, on the other hand, tended to describe the ancien régime in a more positive way and related the problems of France to the damages resulting from the revolutionary spirit. Extremist right-wing representatives went further and related the ideas of 1789 to the influence of foreign sources (mostly Jewish and German Protestants) that had turned France away from its authentic Catholic royalist heritage.[20]

Facing the Rise of Nazism: The Local French Jewish Perspective

After the Nazi rise to power, French Jewish publicists began to cope with the meaning of this new and threatening development. As in other countries, including Germany itself, French Jewish spokespeople initially expressed their hope that the Nazi regime would not survive for long and that Hitler's government would soon fall like its predecessors.[21] However, as the weeks and months went by and the lasting power of Nazism as well as its destruc-tive impact on the German Jews became clear, French Jewish writers felt a growing need to explain what was happening in Germany not only in the immediate political context but also from a wider historical perspec-tive.[22] The developments in Germany were so threatening that they moti-vated Jewish spokespeople in France to react even before the signs of the political destabilization in their country appeared. Not surprisingly, many writers referred to the question of precedents: does Hitler represent a totally new danger to the Jews, or is the Nazi power perhaps only a new version of experiences with which Jews have already coped in the near or distant past? French Jewish spokespeople were also concerned with the problem of German Jewish refugees trying to enter France and asked themselves how French Jews should cope with this phenomenon. Furthermore, facing po-litical developments elsewhere in Europe—and from early 1934 in France itself—they were bothered by a more general question: was Nazism a unique German phenomenon, or did its rise to power perhaps herald a general turn-ing point in European history and possibly even in France?

The first explanation offered by French Jewish spokespeople described Nazism as a movement rooted in the Middle Ages. Its ideology of hatred of the Jews was a new form of the hatred that had appeared in the Dark Ages and at the time of the Inquisition. Hitler's gang, wrote one commentator in the *Archives Israélites* in February 1932, wants to return to the policy of the medieval kings who tried to extort money from the Jews in every possible way. Nazism was viewed as simply a newer version less cruel perhaps than the first one, that is, in terms of the behavior of the Inquisition leaders.[23]

After the Nazi rise to power, French Jewish writers drew a parallel between the misery of the twentieth-century German Jewish refugees and the suffering of those expelled from Spain. The Nuremberg Laws were presented by some as being akin to the Inquisition's racial-purity principle, while the decline of Spain after the expulsion of its Jews foretold, in their view, Germany's future without its Jews.[24] Others, among them writers for the Parisian *L'Univers Israélite,* the most widely distributed community weekly of the local French Jewish establishment, went even further back in history. "The Hitlerian oppression," stated one of the writers of *L'Univers Israélite* in April 1935, "is nothing but another episode, one of the darkest and the most recent, in the long-term martyrdom of Israel," which started, according to this writer, with the false accusation of the Jews for the death of Jesus.[25] A year later *La Tribune juive,* the conservative journal of the Jews of eastern France, theorized that the policy toward the Jews had always been a decisive criterion by which to measure the general situation of a civilization. Thus, Jews were typically oppressed in ages when law and justice were generally in decline and enjoyed freedom and equality at times when law and justice were respected. Eventually, declared *La Tribune juive* optimistically, history has proven that Judaism always overcame its opponents due to its morality, and this would also be the outcome of the present crisis.[26]

Finding among the French Jewish writers of the period a systematic cyclical presentation of Jewish history, as had been developed by certain 1930s' German Jewish writers, is difficult. Nevertheless, it is still possible that the citation of historical precedents to Nazi racism served as a comforting and calming interpretation of contemporary events. Moreover, this interpretation took the position that the tragedy of German Jewry was by no means unprecedented in Jewish history and therefore also implied hope and the belief that the Jews would eventually recover from this crisis. Critical evaluations of the emancipation period, especially with regard to its optimistic historical views, also figured prominently in the French Jewish discourse. Certain writers even used concepts such as Jewish fate and sometimes returned to traditional symbols of preemancipation Jewish memory.

An interesting example of this phenomenon can be found in an article that was published in July 1934 by Hippolyte Prague, the editor of the *Archives Israélites,* to mark Tisha B'Av, the memorial day of the destruction of the Jewish Temple in Jerusalem.[27] The emotions and the pain surrounding the disasters that took place on Tisha B'Av, Prague asserted, could not be maintained for centuries without the occurrence of new disasters, whose impact kept reopening the old wounds each time they were beginning to heal. In the modern era after the bestowal of civil and political rights and the old Jewish misery began to be forgotten, the annual observance of Tisha B'Av began to seem irrelevant. There were even those who suggested turning it into a new Jewish holiday in honor of the great fatherland (i.e., France), which had emancipated its Jews. The current events, claimed Prague, proved that efforts to cancel Tisha B'Av as a day of mourning and remembrance were too hasty. In light of developments in Germany and perhaps also influenced by the internal threat facing France after February 1934, Prague stressed the duty of the Jews to preserve the memory of their defeats and of their martyrs, which turned out again to be very meaningful in the 1930s. At this stage, however, Prague's position did not necessarily seem to be a pessimistic historical evaluation but instead was an attempt to relate the new reality in historical and cultural terms.

Alongside the emphasis on the historical precedents to the Nazi anti-Semitism, certain writers tended to connect it more specifically to German anti-Semitism. This position, whose spokespeople sometimes even related radical anti-Semitism to the fundamental characters of the history of the German nation at large, had an unmistakable impact on the Jews in France: if the events in Germany are the outcome of the unique German character, Jews should not feel threatened by similar developments in France. Certain writers even presented French history and heritage as essentially opposing those of Germany and as therefore being immune to Fascism and anti-Semitism.[28]

In July 1933 Rabbi Mathieu Wolff published in *L'Univers Israélite* an article marking Tisha B'Av. He referred to the various historical catastrophes that are bound up with this day in the Jewish tradition: the destruction of the First and Second Temples and the expulsion from Spain.[29] Relating to medieval anti-Semitism, Wolff emphasized events that related to Germany at that time, such as the massacres in the era of the Black Death, and claimed that the Germans had even then tended toward a unique anti-Jewish animus. Jews, he explained, already embodied the spirit of freedom that was diametrically opposed to the gregarious character of the German people. Tisha B'Av, Wolff added, had tangible meaning for German Jews of the twentieth century, whereas it reminded French Jews of their obligation to be generous to the refugees from the other side of the Rhine. This meaning also emphasized the enormous gap between the French worldview—representing the noble aspects and universal values of the Western world—and the worldview of Hitlerian Germany.

A somewhat different attitude was expressed in an article published a few months later by Robert Loewel on French and German anti-Semitism.[30] Anti-Semitism, Loewel claimed, was imported to France from Germany. Hostility in Germany toward the Jews was therefore chronic like a plague, whereas such hostility in France was never chronic. In spite of this historical interpretation, Loewel also noted a similarity between the rise of French anti-Semitism in the late nineteenth century—a process that started after the failure of the 1889 Boulanger conservative right-wing coup d'état and peaked during the Dreyfus Affair—and the rise of Nazi power in post–World War I Germany. In both cases, he claimed, anti-Semitism emerged in countries that had to cope with severe military defeats (France in 1870 and Germany in 1918) and the moral crises that followed those defeats. In both countries the anti-Semites used pseudoscientific slogans. If we read between the lines, we can sense the fear that France in the 1930s would not necessarily be protected from the influence of German anti-Semitism.

The tendency of some of the French Jewish spokespeople to view their country's heritage as immune from events such as those taking place in Germany was made clear in a review article devoted to Joachim Prinz's *Wir Juden*. This review was published in *L'Univers Israélite* during the very days of the February 1934 events in Paris. Prinz had addressed the broader Jewish world, criticizing the French Revolution and its impact on the Jews. He even foresaw that the "iron fist" of the Jewish fate would also reach the Jews in the Western countries—France, England, and the United States—and would put an end to their pride.[31] Prinz's reviewer, however, portrayed him as a critic of Jewish assimilation as it was manifested specifically in Germany. In contrast to what Prinz himself stated, the reviewer claimed in Prinz's name that unlike Germany, where anti-Semitism was persistent, there had been other countries, among them France, England, and even Italy, where the Jews had participated in the life of the country.[32] Clearly, this French Jewish spokesman felt more comfortable relating the problem of anti-Semitism to Germany and to east European countries, thus removing France from the discussion.

For Frédéric Sternthal, another writer in *L'Univers Israélite*, the 125th anniversary in 1937 of the Prussian Emancipation Edict of 1812 was an opportunity to present the frailty of the emancipation in Germany from its very beginning. Unlike revolutionary France, which granted its Jews full emancipation after a short time and by free choice, "the Prussian king declared on March 12, 1812, emancipation for the Jews in the largest German state unwillingly, only because of political pressures."[33] This heralded the future historical course in the German states, which granted political rights to the Jews only reluctantly and always tried to diminish them. More generally, Sternthal claimed, unlike in France and other countries such as England, Italy, and the United States, progress came to Germany and Austria only under the pressure of external events (such as the Napoleonic wars, the 1848 revolution, the 1866 and 1870 wars, and finally World War I) and was always followed by reactionary anti-Semitic movements. Sternthal also minimized the duration of full Jewish emancipation in Germany to a decade and a half, starting only in 1918 when the German Jews were granted full access to state services. Seen from this point of view, the upheaval of 1933 did not break a sequence of 150 years of progress but instead involved a much shorter period of time. This break therefore could not be seen as an indication of future developments in countries with a much more rooted tradition of emancipation, first and foremost France.

Emancipation and Assimilation: Their Reexamination in the French Jewish Discourse

In addition to the political and historical interpretations of the turning point in Germany, local Jewish spokespeople in France tended to more general evaluations of the process of Jewish emancipation and assimilation in Europe. Of course, the events in Germany were the immediate background for such discussions, but they were also inspired by the deterioration in the status of the Jews in eastern Europe (mostly in Poland), the internal political tension in France, and the escalating refugee crisis. Furthermore, these discussions continued ideological polemics that had been present in the French Jewish public arena even before the 1930s.

In 1928 the French Zionist intellectual Baruch Hagani, a disciple of Zionist leader Max Nordau, published *L'Emancipation des juifs*. Hagani's historical interpretation clearly did not represent the views of the central French Jewish camp. Still, his attitude can be used as a point of departure for a discussion about critical—though not necessarily representative—interpretations of the emancipation period that were raised in the French Jewish press.

Hagani challenged the conventional Jewish interpretation of the emancipation period in France and Germany. In the first part of his book, he described at length Moses Mendelssohn, "the first emancipated Jew," as the representative of Jewish solidarity; he was devoted to the struggle for his brothers' rights without giving up his Jewish commitment.[34] The decline of German Jewry in the nineteenth century, claimed Hagani, like other Zionist publicists from the other side of the Rhine, was largely an outcome of the positions and actions of several of Mendelssohn's disciples as well as other German Jews: David Friedländer, the "salon women," and other German Jews from their generation who chose to resolve the tension between tradition and modernity and fulfill their integration aspirations by giving up their Jewish commitments.[35]

Hagani's critique of the emancipation was not directed only toward the German Jews. Indeed, in the second part of his book he emphasized the uniqueness of the emancipation that was granted to the Jews of France during the Revolution as a genuine expression of the French people's will, unlike the German emancipation.[36] However, he claimed, one must remember the indifferent and sometimes even hostile attitude of most of eighteenth-century French philosophers toward the Jews and, even more, the price that the French Jews were required to pay for their civil rights.[37] Hagani's ambivalence toward the impact of the French Revolution on the Jews is reflected in his choice to emphasize the late eighteenth-century Alsatian Jewish attempt to preserve the Jewish traditional corporative rights and their ethnic distinctiveness. His cultural hero in this period is Berr Isaac Berr, the head of the Alsatian Jewish delegation to the French National Assembly. Hagani described Berr as striving not only toward emancipation but also for an intellectual regeneration of the Jews as well as the preservation of their communal privileges.[38]

If Hagani's interpretation of the emancipation that the revolutionary National Assembly granted to the Jews was ambiguous, his view of Napoleon's Jewish policy as well as of the behavior of the French Jewish leadership of that time was clearly negative.[39] Napoleon's motives in settling the status of the Jews are presented by Hagani as anti-Semitic. The whole episode was a "comedy," and the reaction of the French Jewish leadership to the emperor's actions was an irresponsible surrender: "The members of the Notables assembly and the grand Sanhedrin threw the dead body of Judaism before Napoleon, but unlike the priests of the other religions they were not able to preserve its soul."[40]

This point is the peak of Hagani's critique of the emancipation heritage. He sees an honest interpretation of these formative developments as the key to understanding the rapid decline of Western Jewry in his own time.

More than five years after Hagani's book was published but in a very different historical setting, Maurice Liber (b. 1884), a prominent Paris rabbi, a historian, senior member of the Central Consistory, and the author of a well-known biography of Rashi (Rabbi Shlomo Yitzhaki), chose to criticize Hagani's thesis. Liber did this in a lecture that he gave in January 1934 under the title "Did the Emancipation Fail?" Hagani, wrote the *L'Univers Israélite* reporter who summed up Liber's lecture, claimed that there was a major historical mistake in the process of emancipation. It is possible, therefore, to understand Hagani's thesis as an acceptance of what was taking place at the time in Germany. Liber, acting as a historian "with a warm heart but cold mind," felt obliged to cope with this challenge and answer a basic question: did the Jewish leaders in revolutionary France make a crucial mistake when they strove for full equal rights for the Jews?[41]

The French Revolution, Liber asserted, launched the integration of the Jews first in France and then in other nations after they had been ostracized from society and civilization from the time when Christianity became the state religion in fourth-century Rome. After France granted citizenship to the French Jews, the Revolution gradually brought justice to the Jews in Germany and Central Europe and, after the 1919 peace agreements, also in eastern Europe. Liber presented the Revolution as a clear product of Western culture, represented by France, and this was his interpretation of the spreading of its values eastward and the threat that these values were facing in the present: "Modern civilization marched from the west to the east and the great problems that are rising today evoke the question if the east will now drag the west to barbarism."[42]

As a Jew who was proud of the emancipation heritage, Liber also associated it with a positive impact on the development of the Jewish religion. In the ghetto there was no Jewish pride, he claimed, and the religious spirit could not develop within its borders. The emancipation therefore not only granted rights to the Jews but also led to a Jewish renewal and put the Jewish religion on an equal standing with the other religions. Even Zionism, he added, could not have been possible without the emancipation. Thus, the idea of the return to the ghetto should be utterly rejected, as should the concern that Judaism would not be able to survive under Western conditions of freedom.

In spite of all this, Liber's position was not totally free of criticism regarding the emancipation era. He focused his critique on what he called "the passive emancipation," that is, that Judaism is merely a religion and that belonging to it is a purely individual act.[43] The hasty implementation of this concept led to the decline of Judaism and to the loosening of the inner Jewish association. Liber therefore called for a renewal of the collective element in the Jewish existence. Unlike national Jewish critics, however, he did not see any contradiction between this call and his belief in the heritage of the emancipation. In fact, he believed that this renewal had already started within the existing French Jewish community: French Jews had understood the dangers of the "passive emancipation" already in 1860 and had consequently established the Alliance Israélite Universelle, and through this organization they had worked for general Jewish solidarity. Another shortcoming of the emancipation era that Liber pointed out and called for repair of was exaggerated optimism. Some of the adherents of the emancipation, he claimed, had been uncritical in their belief that the Revolution was the total solution to the Jewish question, whereas in fact the realization of progress and the fulfillment of the Revolution's values were a slow, gradual, and multigenerational process.[44]

A more critical reassessment of the concepts of emancipation and assimilation appeared in that period in the Alsatian *La Tribune juive,* a more traditional and somewhat more nationalist Jewish journal than the Parisian *L'Univers Israélite.* In two articles published in *La Tribune juive* in late 1932 and early 1933, an anonymous writer presented a more or less balanced picture of the emancipation and assimilation period, with all its achievements and shortcomings.[45] The emancipation opened the ghetto gates for the Jews and enabled them to take part in general society but, on the other hand, shook the foundations of Judaism by transforming it into a mere religion, thus paving the way for the weakening of the Jewish nationalist instinct. Indeed, the Jewish collective survived this era, but its will to live was deeply hurt because of the assimilationist formula.

"The Luxemburg Page" ("La page de Luxemburg"), which was included in *La Tribune juive* as a German supplement, offered very interesting discussions on this topic. In a lecture delivered in late 1933 to a Jewish youth group in Luxemburg, Eugen Schoemann suggested a systematic elaboration of the concepts "ghetto" and "assimilation."[46] The ghetto Jews, Schoemann asserted, were the creators and preservers of the Jewish tradition that had been so seriously weakened during the emancipation era. The Jews paid for their emancipation by means of the depletion of the inner traditional Jewish values; nevertheless, in the course of the nineteenth century this would still not bring about their full integration into their surroundings. Unlike what seemed to be close to Hagani's position, Schoemann saw a historical mistake not in the process of assimilation but instead only in the way it was actualized, mostly in the confusion between the fields of culture (*Kultur*) and civilization. The Jews had to do their best, he claimed, in order to integrate into

European civilization, but they should not have relinquished their culture for a foreign culture that they were not really capable of joining. In an original metaphor, Schoemann described Judaism as a cog integrated within the larger mechanism of history: its outer part must be adapted and integrated into the broader course of the other larger cogs, but its diameter—a metaphor for its inner and essential qualities—cannot and should not be changed in this process of adaptation. The failure to act in this way, he implied, is the reason for the decline of German Jewry and might also prove ominous for other emancipated communities.

A different approach appeared a few months later in an article published by Marcel Greilsammer in the Jewish national journal *Chalom*. Greilsammer tried to present a pluralistic model regarding the relationship between the Zionist model of Jewish identity and the assimilationist model.[47] Most of the Zionists, Greilsammer argued, believe that assimilation is totally bankrupt; they see the assimilated (*assimilé*) Jews as a slack, degenerate, and unworthy element within the people of Israel. This position, he argued further, is simplistic and one-dimensional. Its representatives forget that in various countries, especially in France, political emancipation was a process over several generations and that the Jews became a vital element within the synthesis on which their homeland was founded. Greilsammer granted positive value to assimilation not solely on the basis of French Jewish history. He supported his thesis with other examples from Jewish history, showing that also in other eras Jews assimilated within other cultures. The tendency of nationalist Jews to strive to put an end to the oppression of the Jews in other countries by declaring war on assimilation in all cases might therefore, according to Greilsammer, be harmful and actually damage the homeland of their assimilated brethren in France.

This, however, was only one aspect of Greilsammer's position. On the other hand, he claimed, the assimilated Jews, for whom Judaism was merely a religion, tended to ignore the situation of their brethren in countries in which political assimilation is not a realistic option and Zionism represented the only alternative for the future. Greilsammer asserted that the position of those Jews, who strove to sacrifice totally their Jewish distinctiveness in order to become like others, must be particularly refined in an age when ghetto life was again being imposed on Jews in certain countries, a direct hint regarding the events in Germany. The crossroads at which Jews were positioned in the mid-1930s therefore suggested two different Jewish solutions—two options—each with its own historical foundation and political justification. Still, it was vital that those holding each of these options recognize the vitality as well as the value of the other solution in its political and historical context.

At times, French Jewish writers expressed a degree of criticism toward the emancipation process and primarily toward assimilation, but almost none focused criticism on French Jewish history. Instead they tended to criticize and sometimes even condemn the course of German Jewish assimilation, relating in some cases to the more general European historical process. This fact implies how rooted the connection to the French homeland and its symbols was, even among the local Jewish nationalist milieus in France. We will now see how the spokespeople of the various Jewish groups in France in the 1930s described French history and heritage as well as French Jewish history.

The French Past in View of Jewish Memory

Since the beginning of the nineteenth century, the memory of the French Revolution had become a leading idea in French history, a legacy that was never static but instead was subject to an ongoing hermeneutic.[48] For the Jews the ideal of equality and integration in France became the foundation for the Revolution's legacy, but its meaning as such was shaped and reshaped in various ways over the generations. During the nineteenth century French Jewish collective memory tended more and more to repress the fears and anxieties that the Jews in France had experienced during the revolutionary era for the sake of its glorification, an optimistic concept according to which history safely moves forward.[49] This tendency became fully established in the early 1880s with the institutionalization of July 14 as the French national holiday and the official memorial day for the Revolution, a date that also became a major symbol for French Jews.

The centenary anniversary in 1889 of the French Revolution had been an ideal opportunity for the French Jews to express their bond and gratitude as well as their loyalty to the young Third French Republic, which presented itself as the legitimate successor to the Revolution.[50] The status of the Revolution as well as the July 14 holiday continued to develop as key factors in the French Jewish politics of memory after the end of the Dreyfus Affair and, later, during and after World War I. In the 1930s French Jews clearly grasped the Revolution as the central event in modern Jewish history and continued to see the crucial bond between it and their present patriotism.[51] This strong bond to the Revolution's legacy was by no means alien to the east European immigrants living in France. Coming from east European Jewish culture, which already in the nineteenth century had a very positive assessment of the French Revolution, some of the immigrants were attracted to France because they viewed it as the land of freedom and justice. They saw themselves attached to the values of July 14 and especially regarded Paris as a Pan-European symbol for the values of emancipation.[52]

The legacy of the Revolution and the memory of July 14 became issues of public debate in France in the 1930s because of both the rise of Fascist regimes in other European countries and the inner political instability in France itself after the events of February 1934. Still, local French Jewish spokespeople tended to omit the fact that the values of July 14 had became contested within French society. Instead they continued to relate mostly to the festive and ceremonial aspects of the French national holiday, presenting the values of 1789 as a matter of national French consensus.[53] Thus, they continued the strategy that they had employed since World War I by presenting their integration in France as part of the national sacred union (*l'union sacrée*) of the French nation without mentioning any inner disputes. This strategy, which to a great extent also called on the memory of World War I and the myth of Verdun, motivated the representatives of the French Jewish establishment to take part in interfaith memorial services for the fallen soldiers during the 1920s and even in the 1930s, when their acceptance as Jews within the World War I veterans' unions began to be problematic.[54] Furthermore, representatives of the French radical right-wing organizations, among them the Croix-de-Feu (Cross of Fire), who were clearly identified with the political struggle against the Third Republic continued to be invited by the Central Consistory to memorial services for the Jewish soldiers.[55]

Anti-Semitism, asserted Paris rabbi Jacob Kaplan (b. 1895) at one of these ceremonies, is fundamentally an anti-French ideology, and therefore the Jews must encourage a wide French consensus to oppose it, in the spirit of *l'union sacrée*.[56] It is noteworthy that Kaplan, who delivered this speech in the presence of the representatives of the Croix-de-Feu, avoided connecting the French values to the legacy of July 14. The very fact that at this time the 1789 legacy had become disputed in the internal French political struggle was not in accordance with the worldview and political strategy of the Central Consistory representatives, and therefore they tended to conceal it.[57]

In addition to the Revolution's legacy and World War I, spokespeople for the French Jewish public also dealt with other historical issues that concerned French Jewry and tried to use them to support their agenda. A central aim of many of these writers was to show that the Jewish presence in France had a long and deep-rooted history. In March 1934 *L'Univers Israélite* published a series of articles written by S. Posener, the pseudonym of Solomon Vladimirovich Pozner (b. 1876). Posener's articles, which dealt with the immigration of German and Polish Jews to France during the Napoleonic era, strove to dispel the impression that modern french Jewry was composed predominantly by foreign Jews from the East had gone to France ever since it granted emancipation to the Jews in 1791. On the basis of a review of historical documents, Posener concluded that Jewish immigration to France was marginal, which confirmed that French Jews were deep-rooted inhabitants of their homeland.[58]

A more systematic attempt to present French Jewish history was made in a book on French Jewish history written by Léon Berman, chief rabbi of Lille. Berman, who was formerly Maurice Liber's disciple, opened his account by describing the great diversity of French Jewry, composed of a variety of groups with different cultural traditions. In fact, Berman claimed, until the Revolution there was no single French Jewish history but rather several, each of which had developed separately.[59] Berman emphasized the long period of continuity of Jewish settlement in France and presented the 1394 expulsion decree as a severe injustice to a community that had lived in France and had contributed to its wealth and development for fourteen hundred years.[60] In contrast to the fourteen centuries described by Berman, the next four centuries, between 1394 and 1791, seem to have been no more than a temporary hiatus. This period eventually came to an end with the emancipation, which returned justice and restored the natural order. Published in 1937 in the midst of growing confrontations in the French political system and public opinion regarding the entry of Jewish immigrants and refugees to France, Berman's book created a French Jewish narrative that was accessible to the Jewish immigrants. He especially emphasized the mobilization of thirteen thousand Jews without French citizenship to the French army in World War I and their willingness to risk their lives for the country that had granted them asylum from the oppressive anti-Semitic regimes in their former homelands.[61]

Another approach to French Jewish history and an attempt to use it for a different purpose can be found in an article published in *La Terre Retrouvée,* the French journal of the Keren Kayemeth LeIsrael (Jewish National Fund) in October 1932.[62] French Jewry, claimed the writer Robert Lévy-Dreyfus, had played a key role in the medieval Jewish world. Above all this was due to the Talmudic commentary of Rashi (Rabbi Shlomo Yitzhaki), who was presented by Lévy-Dreyfus as the cultural hero of medieval French Jewry, and Rashi's successors, the Tosafists. Hundreds of years later after French Jews had been so severely hurt by the harsh fate and grave injustice that they had to endure, Rashi's descendants took it upon themselves to challenge leading French Jewry in the revolutionary era. In both cases, claimed Lévy-Dreyfus, French Jewry had played a key role for the benefit of the entire Jewish people: because hundreds of years in the Jewish ghettos were imprinted on the experiences of French Jewish life in Rashi's time; in modern times the French emancipation played a key role in the liberation of the Jewish people after eighteen hundred years of enslavement.

However, at that point Lévy-Dreyfus abandoned the idea of French Jewish patriotism for the sake of the Zionist point of view. The desire for emancipation and the enthusiasm surrounding assimilation, he claimed, had pushed French Jews to sacrifice the national and historical foundations of their Judaism and had driven them away from the grand Jewish family. Indeed, during the Damascus Affair and later with the activities of the Alliance Israélite Universelle, French Jewry again represented Jewish solidarity and had an impact on the entire Jewish world.[63] However, the indifference of most French Jews to Zionism posed the question as to whether contemporary French Jews were really the true successors to their communal tradition. Jewish history in France was therefore employed by Lévy-Dreyfus to criticize and challenge the 1930s' French Jewish political culture as he saw it.

An additional perspective regarding the encounter between French and Jewish history, which clearly related to the problems of European Jewry in the 1930s, was the image of France as an asylum for refugees. As we shall see, this topic was more central in the Jewish immigrant Yiddish press but can also be found in the local French Jewish press. Hippolyte Prague, the editor of *Archives Israélites,* touched upon this issue in March 1933 as the first Jewish refugees from Nazi Germany entered France.[64] Jewish history repeats itself, claimed Prague, and the Jews are again becoming nomads, victims of an oppression policy that uproots them from their present-day homeland, Germany. Paris, he continued, had become a refuge for Jewish asylum seekers since the end of the nineteenth century. Thus, refugees from the pogroms in Russia found their place in the French capital. This was also true later on for the Jews fleeing from anti-Semitic oppression in Romania as well as in other east European countries. Prague asserted that now Jewish refugees from Germany would follow them. In a clear attempt to make the French history usable, Prague depicted France as the historical asylum for Jewish refugees, the natural refuge for the victims of anti-Semitism in the modern era and therefore also for German Jews. An additional French Jewish attempt to follow this line can be found in a 1936 article in *L'Univers Israélite.*[65]

The French Jewish Immigrant Yiddish Press and Nazi Anti-Semitism

Similar to local French Jewish spokespeople, certain spokespeople from the Yiddish press also emphasized the uniqueness of German anti-Semitism and its contradiction to the French spirit. Being immigrants and sometimes even refugees, their interpretations sometimes originated from their personal experiences as Jews in Germany and France. A. S. Lirik (the pseudonym of Aaron Levi Riklis), who was born in Poland in 1885, lived in Germany from 1920 until the Nazi rise to power in 1933, when he moved to France. In a January 1936 article in *Pariser Haynt,* the most prominent journal of the immigrants in Paris, Lirik related to the 150th anniversary of Mendelssohn's death by emphasizing the shortcomings of the emancipation in Germany, in contrast to France. "The romantic brotherhood between philosophers and artists from both peoples, Germans and Jews, had very little to do with real life and the people themselves," he asserted. Whereas in France the ideas and the humanistic heritage of the Revolution were in the people's blood, such values were never rooted in the German nation, and thus the friendship between German and Jewish intellectuals did not really influence the wider society. It is therefore not by chance that 150 years after Mendelssohn those who did not believe in the idea of Jewish integration in Germany were proven correct: "It began with the brotherhood between Mendelssohn and Lessing and it is over now with Hitler and Goebbels."[66]

On the other hand, in the Parisian Yiddish press there exist more pessimistic evaluations concerning the history and the deep roots of anti-Semitism that transcended the borders of Germany. Thus, certain spokespeople in the Yiddish press claimed that the turning point in Germany was part of a wider deterioration in the status of the Jews and would also have an impact in the West. In a March 1934 article A. Ginzburg claimed that Hitlerism had brought to an end the Jewish assimilationist thinking that distinguished between the religious identity of the Jews and their national allegiance to the nations in which they lived. Furthermore, he added, "Hitler is not the only one, but only the most severe and brutal expression of the anti-Semitism that exists not only in Germany, but can be encountered in almost all the European countries and to a certain extent also in America. Hitler is only expressing in his typical German brutality what many others feel[;] . . . he is only the most noticeable among them."[67] According to this view, Nazi anti-Semitism was not a unique German phenomenon but only a clear expression of an overall failure of emancipation and assimilation at large.

Almost two years later following the enactment of the Nuremberg Laws in Germany, Ginzburg went a step further and described anti-Semitism as a deterministic historical phenomenon, virtually a heritage that non-Jews had been carrying with them since the Greco-Roman period. Writing in December 1935, Ginzburg claimed that already in the ancient world the hatred of the Jews focused on their unique religious way of life. Later on in the Middle Ages it turned into a deeper religious hatred and finally, following the secularization process in modern times, assumed the new form of racism now in Germany and elsewhere. Aside from the deterministic pessimism that surfaces in this article, there is also a comforting aspect: the Jews are expected to continue to live despite this hatred, as they always had done in the past; the hatred will not disappear but is also not a threat to their very existence.[68]

It is especially interesting that A. S. Lirik, who stressed the uniqueness of German anti-Semitism and drew a clear distinction between the German spirit and the French heritage, tended in other articles to present the collapse of the emancipation in Germany as part of a wider historical turning point. The new German push of the Jews back into the ghetto a century and a half after their release from this restriction on their movement, Lirik claimed after the Nuremberg Laws, might well have an impact on the status of the Jews all over Europe and might put their future everywhere in existential danger.[69] A few months later Lirik presented even more clearly the turning point in the fate of the German Jews as the collapse of a general paradigm in Jewish history:

> From the classical example of German Jews, with their gigantic rise and decline, we can all learn that we must change our internal and external position to the whole world. . . . [I]t is impossible to continue in the same way; The time of the zigzag games, of dancing at all the weddings, is now over, because the world does not want it anymore and also we started to understand the disrespect in it, the fact that such a life may lead a people to lose its dignity. . . . Managing dual life as Jews and as non-Jews is not possible anymore, whether we like it or not, and it will be better for us if we will turn back to ourselves out of our own will than to let Hitlerism impose it on us.[70]

The clear inconsistency between this interpretation, which presents the entire emancipation and assimilation course as a failure, and the position that Lirik expressed in his article about Mendelssohn, in which Lirik referred to a specific German crisis, demonstrates a basic difficulty on the part of the Jewish immigrants' spokespeople in France at that time.[71] Thus, these spokespeople, mostly the ones writing for the national Jewish *Pariser Haynt,* were influenced by their surroundings and tended to believe in the positive universal impact of the French Jewish emancipation path. On the other hand, they were more sensitive than the French Jewish press to the deterioration in the status of the Jews not only in Germany but also all over Europe.

As we saw in the discussion regarding local French writers, the harsh events in Germany motivated immigrant publicists to not only discuss the nature of anti-Semitism but also reexamine the whole course of Jewish integration into modern European society. Interestingly, Yiddish writing spokespeople were reacting to historical narratives expressed by German Jewish refugees to France, demonstrating the transnational dimension of the Jewish public discourse of the 1930s. The German Jews, claimed Y. Gotlib in an article published in July 1934 in the *Pariser Haynt,* were still trying to prove to the Germans that the Jews were like any other people, as exemplified by Lessing's play *Nathan the Wise.*[72] Gotlib described several encounters with German Jewish refugees in a Parisian café. They repeatedly discuss the history of Jewish equal rights, relate to the golden age of the Jews in medieval Spain before their expulsion, and try to draw strength and hope also from the modern Anglo-Jewish experience and the French Revolution. Their hope that equal rights are not merely words written on paper and will sooner or later be abolished. This motivates their optimistic faith that the turning wheel of history will eventually bring them to a more comfortable point.[73]

Gotlib himself rejected the cyclical concept of Jewish history in the name of progress, the same idea that was widely used by the supporters of the liberal emancipation until the crisis of the 1930s: "Deep in our consciousness we hold the faith that we have come to this world to see new things every day, to experience and to take part in the progress." The idea that there is nothing new under the sun and, consequently, the expectation that equal rights for the Jews will be revived therefore seemed groundless to Gotlib. Thus, he concluded his article with the following irony: "It could have been interesting to view philosophically at the ever turning wheel [of history]. It could have been also amusing to turn around in such a carousel on which fate seated us . . . if it was not so dizzying for the head and so heavy for the heart."[74]

French Revolutionary Legacy and French Jewish Historical Memory: The Immigrants' Perspective

Unlike local French Jewish communal spokespeople, who tended to ignore the fact that the legacy of the French Revolution and the memory of July 14 became contested within French society, immigrants' spokespeople were not inclined to obscure the internal French dispute. Instead they clearly turned to this legacy in order to support their political agenda.

This strategy was very clearly set forth in the articles of Mark Jarblum (b. 1887), a key figure in the federation of the immigrants' organizations and a devoted Socialist who also served as a political analyst for the *Pariser Haynt.* Jarblum was born in Warsaw and moved to Paris in 1907. In his view, the fate of French democracy following the events of February 6, 1934, was now unequivocally intertwined with the future of democracy all over Europe because the struggle was not only with the external enemies of the Revolution's legacy (i.e., Nazi Germany) but was also an internal French struggle. A victory of the right-wing forces and the Action Française, he added, would result in the eradication of the fundamental human and civil rights and of the values of the great Revolution of 1789, would harm the peace, and would bring chaos to all of Europe.[75]

Jarblum's turn to the legacy of 1789 was more systematically expressed in an article that he published a year and a half later on July 14, 1935, the day on which the Popular Front held its mass anti-Fascist demonstration in Paris.[76] The article pointed out that it was almost 150 years since Parisian masses broke into the Bastille and that it now seemed, after July 14 became merely a formal and not-so-interesting holiday for the French people, that the legacy of 1789 was suddenly being revived and evoked everybody's interest.[77] Jarblum related to the meaning of the choice of July 14 as the memorial day for the Revolution by the leaders of the Third Republic and argued that the events of this day symbolized the resistance to tyranny more than any other event during the revolutionary period. The Revolution essentially stood in contrast to any kind of oppressive regime, including, of course, Fascism and Hitlerism.

In this article Jarblum sharpened his interpretation of the revolutionary legacy, claiming that it was based chiefly on the internal French struggle between the powers of the Revolution and the powers of oppression. The powers of oppression and reaction, he asserted, had followed the same strategy since the resistance of the French aristocracy and clergy to the elimination of their traditional privileges in the late eighteenth century, and this was continued by those French elements that were hostile in 1935 to the values of July 14: "In no other European country did the struggle between the two camps take on such serious forms as in France. Not only the future of the French Republic but also the entire European future is dependent now on the outcome of this confrontation in France."[78] Jarblum concluded by stating his firm belief in the decisive victory of the July 14 anti-Fascist legacy in France and eventually on the entire continent.

It was a historical coincidence that on the very day of July 14, 1935, when the Popular Front held its mass demonstration and the Croix-de-Feu held its counterdemonstration, another event took place in Paris: the funeral of Alfred Dreyfus.[79] In sharp contradiction to the political events of that day, the funeral was a very low-profile event. In the following days the Parisian Yiddish press devoted various articles to Dreyfus the person as well as to the Dreyfus Affair.

The link between the historical affair and the internal French conflict that had peaked on the very day of the funeral was clearly expressed by Yitzhak Chomsky. Born in Warsaw in 1903, Chomsky was a physician who had immigrated to Paris in the mid-1920s and had become one of the main publicists in the *Pariser Haynt*. He was very critical of the fact that the funeral was held almost as a private event. The family had been silent, and the Central Consistory made no announcement: "This seemed suitable to our grand French Jews. A person passed away discreetly. Nobody thought that in fact they are not entitled to remain so discreet especially in this case of a Jewish name that aroused so many empathic feelings and tears in the Jewish world."[80] However, continued Chomsky, the hand of fate had Dreyfus's funeral take place on a uniquely symbolic day. The same person who in 1899 and mostly in 1900 had "the country . . . divided because of him into two camps, Dreyfusards and anti-Dreyfusards, liberals and dark forces," was buried on the same day that masses demonstrated in Paris in support of the republic. Indeed, masses of Jews should have stood in front of Dreyfus's open grave—our ghetto Jews, claimed Chomsky—because his misery was deeply part of the Jewish fate. As a result of the low profile that the French Jewish leadership imposed, the Jews missed the opportunity to turn the funeral into a very meaningful Jewish historical symbol and to link it to the current struggle of the French Republic for its values.

In addition to the revolutionary legacy and the Dreyfus Affair, Yiddish publicists in Paris discussed other aspects of French Jewish history, aiming to make that history usable for their goals. Neither the Yiddish writers nor their readers could relate to French Jewish history directly as their own, since their cultural and historical roots stemmed from eastern Europe. Still, they used that history in order to link themselves to the fundamental symbols of the French Jewish past or to examine them critically. Thus, for example, a series of more than seventy articles concerning French Jewish history published in the *Pariser Haynt* during 1935–36 was devoted to the first of these two aims and proposed to Yiddish readers a widely popular version of that history.[81]

In another series of articles published in the spring of 1937 and dealing with the Jews of Alsace-Lorraine, Joseph Hollander (b. 1896) expressed a more critical view. This position was especially clear in the third article of the series that focused on the history of the Jews in Alsace-Lorraine. In it Hollander judged them with regard to how they treated the Jewish immigrants and refugees in France in the 1930s. The Jews of Alsace-Lorraine acted, according to Hollander, as a poor person who made a fortune and aspires to integrate among the wealthy. By so doing he alienates his former brethren, as they remind him of his miserable origins and might endanger his upward mobility.[82] Until the French Revolution, the Jews of Alsace-Lorraine had shared the same culture and language as their coreligionists in Germany and Poland; they had suffered from the same anti-Semitism and had persistently shown the same commitment to their religion. Only 150 years ago, Hollander added, the Sephardi Jews from southern France had looked at the Ashkenazi Jews of Alsace-Lorraine arrogantly and had emphasized the differences between them. These Sephardim were integrated into European culture and tended to assimilation. What happened later? The Jews of Alsace-Lorraine failed to cope with the challenge of emancipation and paid for it with the price of assimilation. They forgot too quickly all the misery they had experienced and treated the east European Jews the same way that the Sephardim had treated their forebears. According to Hollander, then, assimilated Jews need a scapegoat, and they tend to look for it among those Jews who preserve more of the Jewish tradition. At that time it was the east European Jew.

But the discussion did not end at this point. Hollander also suggested comparing the way that French Jews treated the Polish Jewish immigrants to the way that Polish Jews were treated by German Jewry. According to Hollander, at a time when the German Jews were experiencing such distress, which was pushing so many of them out of their homeland, they found out that east European Jews who had not been influenced so intensively by the assimilation treated them kindly and with Jewish solidarity with regard to their troubles. French Jews, Hollander concluded, should therefore learn the lesson from the German Jewish tragedy, overcome the disintegrative impact of assimilation, and develop a kinder, more hospitable attitude toward their east European brethren.

Hollander's article offers an interesting example of a critical discussion by an immigrant spokesperson on the matter of assimilation. Another attempt by an immigrant intellectual to come to terms with Jewish integration in France appeared in an article titled "La Marseillaise and Hatikvah" by the Yiddish writer and publicist Nissen Frank, who was born in Lithuania in

1889. As much as the Jews would counter the "swallowing assimilation" that threatened to ruin their national identity, Frank claimed, they would still be influenced by their surroundings and the outer world.[83] Thus, the Yiddish speakers in Paris were influenced by the French language, and their Yiddish absorbed new phrases in exactly the same way that Yiddish had developed over the generations in various cultural and linguistic environments. As long as it was not "swallowing assimilation," Frank continued, there was nothing adverse in the influence of the neighboring populations, and it can also be mutual: French living near Jews might be influenced by their Yiddish. Although Zionist in his worldview (he had lived for some time in Palestine before moving to France), Frank had come to view the integration of the Jews in France as a natural process. Thus, Jews from Paris often play the Marseillaise (the French national anthem) and then the Hatikvah (the Jewish national anthem), and they see no problem with this combination. Similar to certain German Jewish spokespeople who were discussed in chapter 1 and to some of the French Jewish publicists, Frank offered his own distinction between the good and the bad versions of Jewish assimilation.

The Jewish Communist Voice

In contrast to spokespeople for the immigrants' federation who published their articles mostly in the *Pariser Haynt* and represented the center or moderate Left political views, Jewish Communist spokespeople developed their own more radical interpretation of French history and French Jewish history. Their representation of the past was closely connected to the fact that the French Communist Party joined the Popular Front and became obligated to the national anti-Fascist unity. This position, which the French Communists adopted in the mid-1930s, motivated them to develop a more active relationship to the French national myths and to form their own version of the Revolution story. They therefore place greater emphasis on the legacy of 1792 (the republican stage of the Revolution, which was more radical than in 1789) as well as of 1848 and 1871 (the Paris Commune uprising).[84] This process also influenced the Yiddish-speaking Jewish Communists who were formerly alienated from the French political culture. From July 1935, French Communists pressed their Jewish comrades to coordinate their activities with other political groups (in the spirit of the ideas of the Popular Front) as well as to take part in the events of Bastille Day.[85] In the ensuing years various Jewish Communist spokespeople tried to integrate the national mythology, Marxist theory, and Jewish pride in their journal *Naye Presse*, thus creating their own version of French and French Jewish history.

On July 14, 1937, the *Naye Presse* devoted a few pages to mark the date, which now stood for two anniversaries: Bastille Day and the second anniversary of the Parisian mass demonstration that had brought about the establishment of the Popular Front. A few weeks earlier in June 1937, Leon Blum's government fell as a result of internal disagreements between its partners. *Naye Presse*'s commentator A. Raiski, the pseudonym of the young Communist activist Adam Raigadski who was born in Poland in 1914 and immigrated to France in 1932, tended even more than Jarblum and Chomsky, the spokespeople of the Jewish immigrants federation, to sharpen the contemporary meaning of the 1789 legacy and to present it as a highly disputed element in the 1930s. In Raiski's view, July 14, the historical symbol of the assault on absolutism, was institutionalized as a French national holiday but had lost its real meaning.[86] According to Raiski, subsequent French regimes had tried to make the people forget the true meaning of the Revolution and had distorted its history; it was only lately (i.e., on July 14, 1935) that this day once again became a day of freedom in its original sense. Fascism is our century's Bastille, asserted Raiski, and as in 1789, so also in 1935 only a coalition of the working class with the petit bourgeoisie (i.e., Communists, Socialists, and radicals, the political components of the Popular Front) would be able to defeat it. Raiski emphasized, however, that the conflict was far from being won, and he condemned the Popular Front government's decision (which was accepted, in his opinion, because of the pressure of bourgeois reactionary powers) to adopt a neutral position concerning the Spanish Civil War.

Toward the end of his article Raiski employed historical symbols in order to mobilize his Jewish readers to join the struggle. Jews, he claimed, had taken part in the 1789 revolutionary events in Paris in spite of their small number. They had also been involved in 1848 and 1871 in revolutionary actions and were still obliged to act with solidarity and cooperation with the French people in its struggle for freedom.[87] In writing such historical accounts, the Jewish Communist publicists strove to uplift the Jewish sense of pride and to make the Jewish left-wing immigrant workers, who were basically alienated from the French Jewish politics of memory, feel more connected to the revolutionary elements of French history.

The differences between the historical representations in the French press and the Yiddish press had to do with the different settings, both of the readership and of the publications themselves. *L'Univers Israélite* and other French Jewish newspapers were published once a week or even less and functioned for their readers as a supplementary source of information. Thus, they did not really cover French national news and international news but instead dealt mostly with matters of Jewish interest, primarily French Jewish interest. The *Pariser Haynt* and its younger Communist rival *Naye Presse* were, on the other hand, daily newspapers that strove to give their readers general news coverage and interpretation of the events in France and the entire world. This was one of the reasons that the events in Germany and eastern Europe had a much more central place in the Yiddish press than in the French Jewish press. The Yiddish readers also naturally tended to follow the news from their countries of origin. They were generally more ethnically Jewish and therefore more sensitive to the overall changes in the situation of the Jews in Europe.

Still, it is important to emphasize that most of the immigrants' spokespeople—national Jewish, Socialists, and Communists alike—shared the French Jewish belief in the heritage of the Revolution. Thus, in spite of their clear awareness of the deep political and cultural splits in French society, they did not tend to readily give up the image of France as the source of universal values and the pioneer of the anti-Fascist struggle. As a result, in the Parisian Yiddish journals there are critical reports and interpretations of the situation of the Jews in Europe and sometimes even general critiques of the entire historical process of emancipation and assimilation. On the other hand, the same journals—and sometimes even the same writers—could still express their deep belief in the heritage of the Revolution and in the ability of contemporary France to withstand the Fascist threat.

The French Jewish Pantheon of Heroes

In contrast to the centrality of historical heroes in the German Jewish memory culture, the French Jewish cultural memory was based more on formative historical events, first and foremost the Revolution. Still, the cultural memory of French Jewry also included the representation of key figures from their history and their adaptation to contemporary needs and challenges. This discourse was naturally dominated by local French Jewish writers who dealt with their own heritage, but as we shall see certain immigrant publicists took an active part in the discourse and enriched the range of critical perspectives.

The most prominent non-Jewish figure in the French Jewish pantheon of heroes was the liberal priest Abbé Henri Grégoire, whose image was fundamentally associated with the French Jewish struggle for emancipation during the revolutionary era. Already in 1881 when the fiftieth anniversary of Grégoire's death was marked, French Jewish spokespeople dealt extensively with his image as the representative of emancipation and of the universal and republican values of the Revolution. These were the values that the young Third Republic strove to adopt against the monarchist and clerical dangers.[88] The one hundredth anniversary of Grégoire's death, which was marked on May 28, 1931, gave the supporters of the republic, including the Jews, another opportunity to commemorate him, now as an anti-Fascist icon. In addition to commemorative ceremonies held in Jewish communities, several Jews—among them the lawyer Paul Grunebaum-Ballin—were involved in the establishment of the Société des Amis de l'abbé Grégoire (Society of Friends of Abbé Grégoire).[89]

In addition to providing historical accounts of Grégoire's efforts to promote the emancipation of the Jews and to liberate Negro slaves as well, some of the articles related to more contemporary aspects of his legacy. One writer in L'Univers Israélite claimed that marking Grégoire's centenary was the appropriate Jewish reaction to the Hilterian propaganda against Jewish immigration, which had also spread to France.[90] Grégoire's legacy was presented as a guarantee—in contrast to the developments in Germany, where the Nazi Party was experiencing remarkable growth—that there was no chance for an anti-Semitic revival in France.

A different view of Grégoire's legacy was expressed in an editorial by Alfred Berl in the journal Paix et Droit. Berl described Grégoire's leading position in the struggle for the emancipation of French Jewry and against those who tended to Judeophobia.[91] Grégoire's tolerant attitude, the writer claimed, was rooted in the Christian doctrine of love and grace. Grégoire was thus portrayed as the representative of the true Christianity, in contrast to the fanatic anti-Semitic priests, still active in the 1930s, who were ostensibly speaking in the name of Christianity. Berl's position on this issue, including his use of Christianity, was quite unique among French Jewish journalists and publicists who tended to present the emancipation as having been founded on the secular principles of the Revolution.

Berl also related to the influence of the Enlightenment on Grégoire and mentioned the tolerant vision of Mendelssohn and Lessing but emphasized that Grégoire's sources of inspiration were mostly French. Berl referred to the French authors of the eighteenth-century Encyclopédie, especially Jean-Jacques Rousseau and Voltaire (Berl simply ignored Voltaire's anti-Jewish views), but reserved a special place for Montesquieu. Montesquieu's Spirit of the Laws (L'Esprit des lois), according to Berl, was the most significant influence upon Grégoire. The retreat from the Revolution's universal values during the Napoleonic era, including the assault on the emancipation of French Jewry at the hands of the 1808 Infamous Decree, are depicted by Berl as a temporary eclipse. He did not believe that this changed the basic direction of overall progress. Berl's firm faith in the idea of progress might have applied as well to his interpretation of the new wave of anti-Semitism in Europe in the early 1930s.

Among French Jewish spokespeople there was a wide consensus concerning the positive image of Grégoire, which was similar to their interpretation of the Revolution's impact on the Jews. However, certain Zionist writers challenged these positive evaluations and proposed a more critical view of Grégoire and, indirectly, of the entire emancipation process in France. Thus, French Jewish poet and Zionist activist Andre Spiré (b. 1868) had claimed in 1928 that Grégoire's long-term vision was the eradication of Jewish national identity in France in exchange for the bestowal of civic equality to the Jews. Spiré was also very critical of the Jews of that period who accepted this formula. About two years later during the events of Grégoire's centennial anniversary, another Zionist publicist argued that Grégoire's motives were basically missionary. This publicist incorporated a mixture of hostility and contempt toward the minorities he wanted to assimilate, among them the Jews, together with Christian love and mercy. Still, these few provocative assertions did not evoke any real disagreement within the French Jewish public.[92]

Facing the deteriorating situation of the Jews in Germany and in other countries as well as the escalation of the problems experienced by refugees trying to enter France, Grégoire's memory continued to be used by French Jews, especially around the annual commemoration ceremony held by the Société des Amis de l'abbé Grégoire. In an article published to mark the 1937 Memorial Day, one writer asserted that it was crucial to remember Grégoire's legacy, especially at a time when the political rights of so many Jews were being denied in the name of racism, when public schools and universities were closing their doors to Jews, and when the statue of Mendelssohn was removed to the sound of the cheering public.[93]

Another reference to Grégoire's legacy and a more pessimistic evaluation of its impact appeared in Nissen Frank's article in the *Pariser Haynt* a few weeks after the formation of the Popular Front government.[94] Grégoire, argued Frank, was one of the major French figures who had struggled for the general principle of equal rights as well as for its implementation for the Jews. Still, the outcome of this struggle had not yet been determined. If Grégoire were to rise from his grave and see how things were, he would not have wanted to live in such a world. Nevertheless, he would have been comforted by the fact that France still remained loyal to its principles. By dealing this way with Grégoire, Frank was led to a more general discussion concerning the question of progress. He actually underwent a conversion from the idea of historical progress to a more pessimistic historical worldview, at least concerning the Jews:

> With regard to the Jews, nothing is final. The world can cheerfully recognize today their right to equality and take this back tomorrow. Here there is no beginning and no end. This is how things are because Jews have always been forsaken and therefore taking something from them is not robbery but a lawful act. . . . The Jewish equality of rights has been recognized already a thousand times. . . . Still it can be denied to them with a stroke of the pen. . . .
>
> The lives of all the [other] peoples are being conducted according to the logical continuity of history. They have a beginning, a middle point and an end. A victory is a victory and it is impossible to go back to the point of departure. There are boundaries, rules and rights. It is impossible to deny them today what they received yesterday. This is why the Jews always live in fear. They can never feel safe with their rights.[95]

Frank claimed on the one hand that France was still preserving Grégoire's legacy, and in this context it was clear that Frank shared the outlook of the mainstream local Jewish spokespeople. On the other hand, his more general view implied that things could change in France and that the values of the great priest could then be rejected in favor of the new anti-Semitic trends. Even the great Revolution could not alter the basic course of Jewish history—as Frank grasped it—and free the Jews from the tragic cyclical course of exile, which might harm their position in the future, even in France.

The other historical figure who was extensively mentioned by Jewish spokespeople as an icon for the values of emancipation was Adolph Crémieux, founder of the Alliance Israélite Universelle, president of the Central Consistory, and minister of justice of France. The attempt to link Crémieux and Grégoire was made clear in an article written in 1931 by Rabbi Maurice Liber. Liber described the encounter between the two in 1819, when the aged priest had to cope with the pressures of the Restoration regime, which had not forgiven him for his support of the Revolution, and the young Jewish lawyer, who was a member of a group that was accused of singing the Marseillaise and who had tried to fight the "white terror."[96] Describing Crémieux's journey to meet Grégoire, Liber claimed that the young Jewish attorney, a son of the first generation of Jews who were able to benefit from the achievements of the emancipation, was a living fulfillment of Grégoire's vision.

Throughout Crémieux's career up until the 1870 decree named for him (the Décret Crémieux), by which as minister of justice he extended political rights and French citizenship to the Algerian Jews, Crémieux was inspired by Grégoire and wanted to continue his work. The story of the friendship between the two, which was popular mostly within the circle of the Alliance Israélite Universelle, is an interesting expression of the French Jewish attempt to establish a homemaking myth.[97] It can also be seen as an endeavor by French Jews to invent their own version of the German Jewish myth about the Mendelssohn-Lessing friendship. As we saw in chapter 2 this myth had reached its peak only two years before, in 1929, when German Jews had marked the double bicentential anniversary of the births of both Mendelssohn and Lessing.[98]

During 1933–34 a two-volume biography about Crémieux, written by S. Posener, was published in Paris.[99] Born in Minsk in 1876, Posener immigrated with his family to Paris before World War I. Raised in a Russian and French cultural milieu, he became a major spokesman of French Jewry in the 1930s in the field of historical representation (he had no real connections with the newer Yiddish-speaking immigrants' milieu). The discourse that developed around Posener's book reveals how Crémieux became a consensus figure among the French Jewish public in the 1930s and was invoked against the threats and challenges that French Jews faced at that time.

It is impossible today to mark Crémieux's memory, insisted one of Posener's reviewers in *L'Univers Israélite* in December 1933, without mentioning the events of the previous few months.[100] According to the reviewer, we can only imagine how Crémieux, who had led so many struggles for the rights of the Jews in and outside of France and had tried throughout his life to initiate plans to improve their situation, would have reacted had he lived in the 1930s, when German Jews were being exiled from their homeland. Another reviewer mentioned Crémieux in more general terms as an icon representing the protest of the civilized world against racism and the oppression of minorities.[101] Crémieux's protest against the oppression of Christian minorities in the Middle East in 1860 was presented as a precedent for how the world ought to unite in condemning the Hitlerian barbarism and supporting its victims. *La Tribune juive* also presented Crémieux as a model of French patriotism and emphasized his reaction to the German occupation of Alsace-Lorraine in 1871, which was a formative experience for all the Jews of the region.[102] Another attempt to render Crémieux's image relevant was undertaken in the autumn of 1936, when anti-Semitic propaganda was mounted against Leon Blum after his nomination as prime minister. One Jewish journal even presented Crémieux as Blum's forerunner, a French Jewish politician struggling generally for the values of 1789 and specifically to defend the rights of the Jews.[103]

An additional use of Crémieux's image—this time for a more internal Jewish aim—was made in early 1935 in another review article of Posener's book. Although Posener may not have intended to argue that loyalty to Judaism can be completely in line with French citizenship, claimed the *Le Journal Juif* reviewer, Crémieux's life story certainly led to this conclusion.[104] The publication of this biography might therefore be valuable precisely when radical nationalistic tendencies were beginning to have an impact on the Jews. These resulted from a misguided interpretation of Zionist principles, a misunderstanding of the universal values of Judaism, and an attempt to imitate several European national movements. The legacy of Crémieux, who affirmed the possibility of integrating Jewish culture and the cultures of the nations among whom Jews lived, is therefore very relevant and significant in an era in which the belief in such a possibility was being undermined.

In addition to Crémieux, though certainly connected to him, French Jewish spokespeople also viewed the Alliance Israélite Universelle, which marked the anniversary of its establishment every June, as an institutional historical hero. In an article published in June 1934, Maurice Leven, the son of one of the organization's founders, described the Alliance Israélite Universelle as the representative of the values of 1789 and 1848.[105] The history of the organization was presented by Leven as a series of activities devoted to defending oppressed Jews all over the world: in Morocco and the surrounding region in the second half of the nineteenth century and, after World War I, in Hungary, Romania, and Poland. Following this account, the question as to the meaning of the Alliance Israélite Universelle's activities was naturally raised in light of the situation of oppressed Jews in Nazi Germany. Leven, who saw the eruption of Nazi anti-Semitism as no more than a reversion to medieval anti-Judaism, claimed that it did not hurt the foundation of the Alliance Israélite Universelle's French values and thus should not arouse any questions concerning the validity of those values.

A critical review of the way in which the Alliance Israélite Universelle was portrayed by the French Jewish establishment appeared a year later in the *Pariser Haynt* in an article by the writer and journalist Aharon Alperin.[106] Alperin, who was born in Lodz in 1901 and immigrated to France in 1928, described the establishment of the organization as a proud Jewish reaction to the series of anti-Jewish offenses following the Damascus Affair and as an expression of Jewish solidarity. He presented the Alliance Israélite Univer-selle not as a French Jewish association but instead as an international Jewish organization established to enlist Jewish support from all over the world, acting everywhere to defend Jews and protect their rights and even preparing for the possibility that it would have to face a future catastrophe, a clear hint to the events in the 1930s.

This depiction of Alliance Israélite Universelle leaders as creating some kind of "world Jewish congress" imbued the image of the organization with contemporary Jewish nationalist political values, which were close to Al-perin's own national values, but at the same time totally ignored the organi-zation's educational activities.[107] The current leaders of the Alliance Israélite Universelle, Alperin claimed, had deviated from the original focus of the organization, such as when they had opposed during the Versailles peace conference the recognition of the Jews in eastern Europe as national minori-ties and had declared that they should be treated as members of religious communities only. Alperin's article is therefore an interesting attempt to use the seventy-fifth anniversary of the establishment of the Alliance Israélite Universelle to prompt its leaders to endorse the national Jewish political tra-dition. He thus portrayed the organization in a fundamentally different way from how it was presented by most of its leaders and members in the 1930s.

Another historical hero whom French Jews adopted in those years was Léon Gambetta. His one hundredth birthday was marked in the spring of 1938 a short while after the *Anschluss* of Austria.[108] Under such historical circumstances, Gambetta became an important symbol for support of a he-roic foundation myth of the Third Republic. He was also associated with the 1789 legacy and with a French tradition of patriotic resistance to the threat-ening militarism of Germany. This tendency was particularly pronounced among several writers in the *Pariser Haynt*. They presented Gambetta as a hero who had acted in 1870 to motivate a confused French society shocked by German military success (a parallel to the French public mood in the spring of 1938) to continue the heroic struggle in defense of the father-land.[109]

Gambetta was presented as the most heroic figure in the pantheon of the Third Republic, the man who had fought for the republican values of freedom under the Second Empire, had led the resistance against the Prus-sians in 1870, and had continued the struggle even after Paris was occu-pied; he actually escaped from the city in a balloon. The French victory came only much later, claimed one of the *Pariser Haynt* writers, but 1918 finally brought the symbolic victory of Gambetta's values over the German aggression, and those values were still valid in the 1930s. Another aspect of

Gambetta's memory, which was raised by French Jewish spokespeople during his spring 1938 anniversary, was his friendship with Crémieux, a friendship myth that can be interpreted as another attempt to endorse the values of the emancipation.[110]

Whereas Gambetta was presented by the *Pariser Haynt* writers as the moral founding father of the republic, *Naye Presse* Jewish Communist writers offered the 1871 Paris Commune as an alternative myth. In 1935 *Naye Presse* related to the memory of the commune, its struggle and fall, as evidence of the necessity of a united anti-Fascist French front. This came in reaction to the threat that erupted in February 1934.[111] More than two years later, the editors of *Naye Presse* devoted a few articles to mark the sixty-sixth anniversary of the struggle of the Paris Commune and related directly to its current implications. Y. Lerman (probably the pseudonym of the Jewish Communist activist Lolke Groynovski, who immigrated to France from Poland in 1929) presented the commune as a model of French Jewish cooperation, a historical precedent for the current collaboration between the Jewish workers and the French working class.[112]

The uprising of the commune in 1871 and its control over part of Paris in the same year, claimed Y. Spera, another Jewish Communist publicist, represented the struggle between the powers of enlightenment and human fraternity against the powers of darkness and barbarism, which were concentrated at that time in Versailles. For Spera, Paris of the commune represented the real French character, whereas Versailles was a distorted image of the French people, full of anti-French "poison."[113] In a tone that seemed to reflect the 1937 struggle of the Jewish immigrants in France to be recognized as part of the French Popular Front, Spera emphasized the contribution of volunteers from various other nations, including Poles, to the activity of the commune, which embodied the belief in equality as a universal principle. The same ethos, he claimed, also led the French Communists to struggle against the French Fascists who had tried to overthrow the republic in 1934 and now aspired to join Hitler. The Popular Front—the united resistance to the Fascists—was therefore the direct continuation of the struggle of the French people against the spirit of Koblenz (the center of aristocratic resistance of the French Revolution) and Versailles (where the opponents of the Paris Commune were concentrated in 1871).

A few months later and a few days after the *Anschluss* of Austria, Spera referred again to the story of the Paris Commune.[114] Against the background of the helplessness felt by many in France in those days, Spera compared the French aristocracy of 1871, which preferred surrender to Otto von Bismarck in order to prevent social reforms in France, to the social French elites of 1938, who had adopted a defeatist position vis-à-vis the Nazis and ignored the struggle taking place beyond the Pyrenees, that is, the Spanish Civil War. After presenting these historical parallels, Spera called on his readers to draw inspiration from the commune for the struggle against Fascism.

Conclusion

During the years under discussion here, the Jews in France, locals and immigrants alike, did not experience any sort of trauma compared to that of the German Jews during those years. Thus, the French Jews did not have the same need to profoundly reexamine their worldview or reshape their historical consciousness. However, the great historical change that was taking place in Germany also had an impact on France. Jewish public opinion in France followed the events in Germany and elsewhere in Europe, and its spokespeople tried to interpret the implications. In addition, the growing internal tensions in French society and politics (even to the extent that certain historians viewed it as a civil war), the escalation of the anti-Semitic atmosphere, and mainly the struggle surrounding the continuation of Jewish immigration to France also influenced the motivation to make use of and sometimes reexamine French and French Jewish history.

Facing these threats to the future of democracy in Europe and to the status of the Jews, local French Jews continued to associate themselves with the values and images of the emancipation and, in most cases, displayed no real tendency to thoroughly reexamine their historical consciousness. France and French Jewish history functioned for them as a reassurance and a source of hope, and they were not willing to reexamine it too critically in light of the events beyond the border. The developments in Germany were therefore understood to be either a product of a temporary turnabout in the inevitable progress of history or, alternatively, a result of the uniqueness of German character and history, which were considered to be fundamentally different from French character and history. French history, stated the local Jewish spokespeople time and again, each in her or his own way, was the best guarantee that France would never follow the example of Nazi Germany. Looking within and relating to French history and cultural symbols, writers from the central camp among the local French Jews consistently presented a picture of inner-French *l'union sacrée,* ignoring or repressing the fact that the fundamental values of the Revolution were deeply disputed within French society itself. French Jewish spokespeople could sometimes relate to the fact that historical assessments of the emancipation were too optimistic with re-spect to the rapidity of Jewish integration but almost never rejected them entirely, certainly not in connection to French Jewish history.

The French Jewish homemaking myth, in the center of which were the legacies of the Revolution and of July 14, also became very rooted within the immigrants' milieu. The spokespeople for the immigrants, however, coped in their journals much more directly with the internal French struggle of those years. Among their articles are essentialist views that present German history as leading to anti-Semitism, as opposed to French history that leads to emancipation. Other writers in the Yiddish press in France suggested that the social and political confrontation in French society in the 1930s ought to be viewed as a continuation of 150 years of internal conflict between supporters of the Revolution and its enemies. This tendency to sharpen the consciousness vis-à-vis the political polarization as well as to attempt to gain support by invoking historical symbols was especially prominent among the Jewish Communists.

The tendency of local Jewish spokespeople to present a harmonic picture was also clear in the representation of French Jewry as a deep-rooted popula-tion in France as well as in undervaluing the historical significance of Jewish immigration to France. This sometimes came at the expense of blurring the break in French Jewish history in the centuries that had followed the 1394 expulsion. Spokespeople for the east European immigrants, on the other hand, tended to emphasize the historical image of France as an immigrant-absorbing state and society and also described the local Jewish community to some degree as a former outside entity that had been absorbed into France.

In addition to the discussion concerning the civil status of the Jews in various countries and to the reassessment of the success and failure of the emancipation in Germany, France, and other places, the French Jewish pub-lic in the 1930s also coped with the question of assimilation. As we have seen in the case of Germany, many Jewish writers in France, native-born and immigrant alike, distinguished between two types of assimilation: good ver-sus bad, or constructive versus destructive. However, the definitions of the boundaries between these different forms of assimilation as well as the attri-bution of certain historical figures or processes in Jewish history in France to one type of assimilation or another could be of considerable dispute among the various writers, each according to his worldview.

4

FROM THE *ANSCHLUSS* TO THE ANNIVERSARY
OF THE REVOLUTION

The *Anschluss* of Austria by the Nazi regime in March 1938 was a crucial turning point that not only was felt in the international arena and contributed to the escalation toward war but also affected the internal politics of France. On March 10, 1938, on the eve of the German invasion of Austria, French prime minister Camille Chautemps submitted his resignation, which was interpreted as an attempt to escape responsibility for the looming crisis. Three days later when Adolf Hitler's army was already in Vienna, Leon Blum's second government was established in Paris; however, this time it survived for only twenty-six days. With its fall, the political existence of the Popular Front for all intents and purposes came to an end, dashing hopes that by combining forces the French leftist and center factions would be able to stop the Fascist threat.

These political upheavals in the spring of 1938 and the growing anxiety concerning another war increased the polarization of French public opinion between the supporters of appeasement and those who demanded a harder line against Germany. Édouard Daladier, who was nominated as prime minister in April 1938, and his foreign minister, Georges-Étienne Bonnet, favored a policy of appeasement, which peaked when France signed the Munich Pact in September 1938. Many French, among them quite a number of Jews, saw this policy as a humiliating surrender that would only deepen the crisis, but many others viewed it as a way to be freed of anxiety over impending war.[1]

The appeasement policy of Daladier's government was accompanied by a sharp turn to the right and a more authoritarian character for the French regime. More immediately important for our discussion, 1938 witnessed a significant escalation in anti-Semitism and xenophobia in France.[2] Jewish refugees from Central and eastern Europe who tried to enter France in considerable numbers were viewed by many within the local population as militant Communists aspiring to drag France into a war against Germany. The refugees were therefore seen as posing an existential threat to French national security. The anti-Jewish incitement peaked after the assassination of the German diplomat Ernst vom Rath by the young Polish Jew Herschel Grynszpan in Paris in November 1938. This action was understood by many as an attempt to damage the French conciliatory foreign policy. Tellingly, the *Kristallnacht* pogrom, which erupted in Germany after vom Rath's death, evoked only minor protests in France.[3]

This escalation in the anti-Jewish atmosphere in France and the growing threat to the Jews in Europe on the whole account for a growing pessimism and even a fatalistic mood among France's Jews.[4] Generally, the leading views and strategies regarding the interpretation and the usage of the past that had emerged among Jewish spokespeople in France in the pre-1938 setting remained prominent after the spring of 1938. But in light of the changing circumstances and the political intensification of the Jewish discourse, especially in the few months before the war, they assumed new meanings. A major development in this context was the return-to-the-ghetto polemic, a Yiddish transnational debate that was uniquely connected to the escalating atmosphere of the late 1930s. In France the most natural venue for this debate was the immigrant Yiddish press, which also touched on problems that concerned local French Jews. The 150th anniversary of the French Revolution in the spring and summer of 1939 gave the Jewish spokespeople an additional opportunity to develop and express their views concerning the meaning and the implications of the past.

Facing the Crisis: Historical Perspectives and Reassessment in the Yiddish Press

The ominous series of events in 1938 evoked a need for historical reassessment among Jewish writers in France. Such discussions were prominent in the Yiddish press and mainly in the *Pariser Haynt,* which combined historical interpretations with daily news. Joseph Milner (b. 1887), for example, in a March 1938 article chose to relate to the destruction of Viennese Jewry by describing its golden age, when Vienna was a center of Jewish enlightenment and culture. Now, claimed Milner, Vienna had been conquered by medieval powers.[5] The feeling of a historical withdrawal, back to the Dark Ages, was expressed in another article that Milner published two days later marking the ninetieth anniversary of the 1848 Revolution in France.[6] No other year in European history, with the exception of 1789, had evoked so many hopes to end despotism. During 1848 barricades were built in several European cities, including Vienna, as part of the struggle for freedom. The year 1848 was also one of high hopes for the Jews, who aspired to the victory of liberalism and emancipation, and saw the political ascendancy of Adolph Crémieux in France and Gabriel Riesser and other Jewish freedom fighters in Central Europe. Ninety years later, however, in the era of radio and aircrafts, this progress had come to an end.[7]

The tendency to locate the growing European anti-Semitism in historical precedents found expression in August 1938 in an analogy edited by Y. Gotlib. Gotlib drew a parallel between the new racial laws of Fascist Italy and the suppression of Judaism and Christianity in ancient Rome in the first century.[8] The Fascist rulers of the 1930s, claimed Gotlib, continued the cruel pagan policy followed by the Roman emperors who saw themselves as gods and therefore opposed Judaism and Christianity alike.

By emphasizing the fact that the racial legislation was not only anti-Jewish but was also directed against the church, various Jewish writers represented the anti-Fascist struggle as a joint Jewish-Christian cause.[9] As we shall see in chapter 5, this strategy, which was designed to mobilize the church in the battle against Fascism and anti-Semitism, gained greater support among Jewish spokespeople in Hungary, where the church became the central anti-Fascist and anti-Nazi moral power.[10] The emergence of such a strategy in France, where the struggle rested on the secular legacy of the republic, demonstrated the growing need to find new allies in order to break out of their political isolation.

Linking the current anti-Semitic outbursts to the history of Vienna, Italy, and above all Germany could imply that such phenomena would not occur in France.[11] As noted in chapter 3, Jewish spokespeople in France tended in the early 1930s to express an essentialist description of the course of German history and characterized it as bound to tyranny and anti-Semitism, as compared to the French path of Revolution and equality. In 1938, however, such views had to face the escalation of anti-Semitism not only in Germany and other European countries but also in France itself. Now, with the rise of Fascism and as the anti-Jewish policy began to assume a normative character in Europe, the essentialist description was directed less to the German case and more to the French case. Thus, for example, Moris Schwarz wrote in the

Pariser Haynt in late July 1938 a few days after the end of the Evian Conference, which failed to find a solution to the problem of European Jewish refugees: "The Frenchman is a totally different creature from other human beings. He has a special space of freedom, and if this space will be diminished . . . he will be ready to risk his life and his children's life in order to fill it. The French need to be free like fish need water."[12] Whereas in other democratic countries, claimed Schwarz, political parties fight each other, in France they only argue, and all of them accept the principle of freedom. Consequently, France can never become Fascist, even if this might happen in England or the United States. It is nonetheless possible, Schwarz continued, that the French could be influenced by the atmosphere around them, which could lead to a closing of the gates of their country to foreign immigrants and to a deterioration in the condition of immigrants already living in France, a clear reference to the disappointing outcome of the Evian Conference and to the escalation of xenophobia and anti-Semitism in the French public arena. Still, he argued, the French would recover from this and soon return to the ideal of freedom, while the Germans will continue to shout "Heil Hitler."

Facing the escalation of the anti-Jewish campaign in Europe in the autumn of 1938, various writers offered reassuring interpretations of Jewish history. This tendency was most apparent in the *Pariser Haynt*, as its writers were more sensitive to developments in the overall status of the Jews in Europe. An interesting example of the comforting use of historical memory can be found in an article by the author and publicist Wolf Weviorka. Born in Poland to a Hasidic family in 1898, Weviorka immigrated to Paris in 1924 after living in Berlin for a few years. He insisted that in late October 1938, panic and mass psychosis had overtaken the Jewish masses throughout the world. As a result the Jews now had begun to react instinctively out of fear, and this impaired their ability to function and struggle. They are right, he added, in feeling that the forthcoming developments will lead to catastrophe, not only for them but for all of Europe. "The Jewish people, the oldest people among all the European nations, would not have survived so many storms without having developed a sense of smell to predict the next storm." Still, he asserted, this is not enough: "A people with historical memory of thousands years can allow itself to look also . . . to the clear sky after the storm, to the sun that will shine after the darkness. Panic is not fitting for such an ancient people. Such a people should have the kind tranquility and the stoic wisdom that we see in one of its most beautiful pieces of literature, Tevye the Milkman."[13] It is therefore historical memory that can be expected to grant the Jews the broader historical perspective and the spiritual balance they need for the approaching long night so that they can anticipate the new day that would follow and thereby free themselves from panic and act more reasonably.

A month later, just weeks after *Kristallnacht,* several writers from the *Pariser Haynt* attempted to calm their readers by presenting the events in Germany in a wider perspective. The wave of anti-Semitism and disturbances in Germany, claimed one publicist, are not unprecedented, although they are more systematic and cruel than those of the past. Some of the ideas expressed by Hitler and Joseph Goebbels, including the expulsion of the Jews and even murdering them, echoed the anti-Jewish campaigns in early nineteenth-century Germany.[14] Nevertheless, this precedent was proposed in order to comfort the Jews. The early nineteenth-century German anti-Semitic wave was shown to have declined after a few years, suggesting that this could happen again. By contrast, another publicist related to the fate of the expelled Spanish and Portuguese Jews as a precedent for the forced emigration of German Jews. Then it was Holland that represented the spirit of tolerance and welcomed the Jewish refugees.[15] Similarly, the publicist claimed, Jewish refugees are now accepted in various countries in the world, and various attempts to settle them are being made. This is civilization's response to Nazi barbarism, he continued, and as in the past, the spirit of tolerance will eventually win out.

World War I: The Memory and Lessons under Debate

As we saw in chapter 3, the memory of World War I was a formative experience for French society in the 1930s, and the day of the cease-fire (November 11, 1918) was even institutionalized as a memorial and an unmistakable symbol of the pacifist cause. The pacifistic orientation was very clear on the twentieth anniversary of the cease-fire in November 1938, when the masses who feared an international escalation expressed the message of "never again."[16]

During the 1930s, French Jews found it difficult to express their positions concerning French policy toward Nazi Germany. On the one hand, many of them—first and foremost the spokespeople of the immigrants but, in growing numbers, also those of the old French community—felt that another war against Germany was inevitable and that there was no other way to stop the Nazi threat. On the other hand, they did not want to criticize the French appeasement policy, which had gained considerable public support; they feared being viewed as warmongers ready to drag France into an unnecessary conflict on behalf of foreign interests.[17] The way in which French Jewish publicists marked the memory of the war during the 1930s by means of the anniversary of November 11 reveals their efforts to come to terms with these difficulties and portrays the continuity as well as the changing atmosphere in late 1938 as the threat of a new war became much more palpable.

Press reports issued by the French Jewish establishment with respect to the cease-fire memorial day in the early 1930s combined the memory of the fallen soldiers with calls for peace.[18] For the Jews in Alsace-Lorraine, this day also symbolized their return to life under French sovereignty after more than forty years of foreign German occupation. At the November 11, 1933, ceremony in Strasbourg, the liberation of the Alsatian Jews from German rule in 1918 was linked to their moral obligation to help the German Jews living in 1933 under Nazi rule.[19]

Two years later the marking of the cease-fire memorial day came after the Nuremberg Laws were passed in Germany. Whereas local French Jewish spokespeople did not link these two events and continued to relate to November 11 mostly from the perspective of peace, the Warsaw-born physician Yitzhak Chomsky delivered a much more pessimistic message in the pages of the *Pariser Haynt*.[20] In the past, claimed Chomsky, November 11 was marked with the hope and belief that a better world would emerge from the ruins of the old. But these hopes had not been realized, since dictatorships and militarism were again on the rise. For the Jews, he asserted, November 11 had meant belief in progress and a better tomorrow but now, given the new events in Europe, symbolized the ever-turning wheel of their fate: hatred and reactionary attitudes assault them again even after it seemed that liberalism had prevailed. Chomsky left France in 1941 with a group of Jewish children whom he led to Spain and Portugal and eventually, with the help of the American Jewish Joint Distribution Committee, came to the United States.

An article that was published two years later clearly showed how the skepticism concerning the optimistic peace vision of November 11 had also begun to influence the local French Jewish leadership. Raymond-Raoul Lambert (b. 1894), one of the most prominent spokespeople of the Central Consistory, described his feelings as a young French soldier when he heard about the impending end of the war.[21] Then, claimed Lambert, there was a growing hope and belief in unity among members of all nations and religions. Now, only nineteen years later, another war was likely. Lambert cautioned French Jews not to demand that their homeland adopt the politics of rancor, that is, a harsher line toward Germany. But he insisted that a totalitarian regime should not be permitted to impose the laws of the jungle onto international relations and enforce the so-called myth of blood instead of human brotherhood. Lambert's strong opposition to what he saw as the repetition of medieval barbarism indicates a call to France to adopt a more aggressive anti-German foreign policy, although he did not state this explicitly.

A few months later following the *Anschluss,* Lambert referred again to the danger of war. Facing the growing threat, he chose this time to mark the memory of the common mobilization, *l'union sacrée,* of July 1914. This was a very different memory than that of November 11, with its pacifistic implications. Lambert understood the urgency of a French national revival and a more aggressive reaction to the German threat and stressed the role played by the Jews in the French struggle for liberty.[22]

The events of the summer and autumn of 1938 and the escalation in the international arena made the memory of July and August 1914—the last days before the outbreak of World War I and the first days of the conflict—increasingly more present in the consciousness of the Jews in France. Several speakers referred to the summer of 1914 as the beginning of the bloodshed, fearing that history might repeat itself. Not even twenty years had passed since the end of the "great war," wrote Mark Jarblum in late September 1938 on the eve of the Munich Conference.[23] The resemblance to the events of 1914, wrote Nissen Frank a few days later after the Munich agreement had been signed, was clear. Today too, Frank stated, peoples and states conduct themselves according to their collective instincts, which tend to outweigh reason. In 1938 as in 1914, he continued, the Jewish public in France—including the immigrants—want to join the struggle of the French people with even greater enthusiasm.[24] Like Lambert, Frank also expressed ambivalence. On the one hand he supported peace and feared the irrational powers pushing to war; on the other hand he returned to the myth of the patriotic mass mobilization in the summer of 1914, stressing that the immigrant Jews also wanted to take part in it.

A month later, a few days after the assassination of vom Rath and the events of the *Kristallnacht* pogrom in Germany, French Jewish spokespeople marked November 11 out of fear that they would be seen as warmongers.[25] Again it was Lambert who best expressed the ambivalence of the Jews, but he could not point to a way out of it. Twenty years after they had participated in the French heroic struggle, he stated, the Jews are now put to a new test:

> [We are being blamed because] we belong to a spiritual or racial group that was interested in a war in September [the time of the Munich Conference]. The absurdity of this accusation must not stop us from struggling against it. After we wore the same uniform we have the right to defend ourselves from this dangerous

defamation. . . . In the past we were accused of desiring peace; after the [Versailles] treaty we were charged with seeking too quick a reconciliation between the nations. Now . . . the accusation has changed.[26]

Throughout the cease-fire anniversary, Lambert emphasized the Jews' loyalty to France and their willingness to defend the country's freedom in times of both peace and war. He also claimed that because of their loyalty to French humanism, Jews would not be ready to accept the pagan blood ideal (implying militarism). Nevertheless, Lambert refrained from stating unequivocally whether the Jews' devotion to French values now meant a belief in peace or a call to prepare for an inevitable war.

In Search of Comforting Memory: Back to Jewish History in France

The growing isolation and distress that French Jews experienced in 1938 led them to increasingly cling to their historical memory as a source of comfort. A major expression of this tendency was a sourcebook compiled by Rabbi Jacob Kaplan, who had served since 1929 as rabbi of the old Parisian synagogue Notre-Dame-de-Nazareth.[27] The book, which resembled similar projects in other countries, is a clear example of a conscious utilization of a usable past.[28] Kaplan compiled hundreds of short entries describing the attitudes of key figures in French history and culture toward Jews and Judaism. These were organized according to topics such as Jewish contributions to France and French views of anti-Semitism. In his introduction Kaplan clearly referred to the shock at the rise of anti-Semitism in Germany and the attempt to come to terms with it by clinging to the French legacy of opposition to anti-Semitism. Today, he asserted, there was a new attempt to drive the French against the Jews, but the way that French scholars related to the Jews over the generations would, he believed, indicate to his Jewish readers how utterly baseless this attempt was.[29]

Kaplan's analysis of French attitudes toward the Jews began in the Middle Ages, from the French Gallic-Roman age. He argued that in a fundamental sense, anti-Semitism is not rooted in the Christian tradition; it became prominent only in the early Middle Ages as a result of the interreligious rivalry. Even in the late Middle Ages there were still Christian theologians who had a liberal attitude with regard to the Jews.[30] Kaplan presents a picture of continuity of the positive view of the Jews in France even in the centuries when Jews did not live in France. But the main thrust of his discussion—both in the introduction and in the sources that he compiled in the book—related mostly to the period since the French Enlightenment and the Revolution. Many of his sources are from the nineteenth century and relate to the contribution of the Jews to world culture.[31] Kaplan could hardly deny the existence of a contrasting view or the fact that many of the authors of the texts included in his collection related negatively to the Jews in other entries. Nevertheless, he preferred to characterize them in the form of the biblical Balaam, who intended to curse the sons of Israel but eventually blessed them. All in all Kaplan presented anti-Semitism as an anti-French, anti-Christian, and antihumanistic phenomenon that was the starting point for an all-out attack against civilization. Thus, his project ought to be viewed as a major contribution to the emergence of an essentialist portrayal of French history and legacy vis-à-vis the Jews.

The nature of Kaplan's project as a political tool to combat anti-Semitism was discussed in a review article published by Lambert in April 1938 shortly after the shock of the *Anschluss.* Lambert argued that the twentieth century might well be known to future generations as "the century of publication," when propaganda had become a conventional weapon used by governments, and that this weapon ought to be also used for the defense of civilians under attack.[32] Thus, the texts that Kaplan had compiled could help in the struggle against discrimination and exclusion of the Jews. It is interesting that Lambert related to another aspect of Kaplan's book: its potential use as a tool to introduce the French Jewish heritage to the Jewish immigrants in France. The basic message that Lambert drew from Kaplan's book was the belief in progress; that is, the current anti-Semitic wave ought to be viewed as a temporary eclipse that would not darken the French sun of freedom for long. In 1941 Lambert became secretary-general of the Union Général des Israélites de France (General Union of French Jews), the central French Jewish organization in Vichy France. He was arrested, along with his family, by the French authorities in 1943 and was sent first to the Drancy camp near Paris and later deported to Auschwitz, where he was murdered.

An additional documentary project compiled by a historian rabbi was the volume published by Nathan Netter on the history of the Jews of Metz, the most important urban Jewish community in prerevolutionary France.[33] Netter, who had served for decades as chief rabbi of Metz and the surrounding area, described the community as a microcosm of Jewish history in France, much as Jewish spokespeople in Germany related to Worms as a model for German Jewry. Drawing on documents from twenty centuries of Jewish communal history, Netter strove to strengthen the link of the Jews to France in general. This objective is clear in the introduction written by Georges Samuel, president of the local chapter of the Central Consistory, who expressed optimism about the future of the Jews in the area in spite of unfortunate contemporary trends.[34]

Metz is described by Netter as a Jewish spiritual center where figures such as Rabbenu Gershom (the "Light of the Exile"), Rashi, and Rabbenu Tam—all viewed as medieval forerunners of modern Jewish scholarship—had resided.[35] Netter presents early medieval Metz as a stronghold of Christian-Jewish fraternity, a city in which the official church leadership had strongly opposed anti-Jewish provocations. After depicting the Jewish suffering in Metz during the Crusades, Netter turned to the modern era and related extensively to the revolutionary period.[36] Later he brings numerous sources concerning the community in the nineteenth and early twentieth centuries in order to call attention to the loyalty of the Jews in Metz to France during the decades of the German occupation.

Review articles that were published in the Jewish press tended to emphasize the contemporary implications of Netter's work. The history of the Jewish community in Metz, claimed one reviewer, epitomized all of Jewish history in France.[37] Another commentator, Jacques Bielinky, chose to emphasize the deep link of Netter's early historical heroes—Rabbenu Gershom and Rashi—to the French language and culture. Bielinky was born in 1881 in Vitebsk and immigrated to France in 1909. As one of the earlier immigrants, he also drew from Netter's book a lesson concerning the burning question facing French Jewry at that time: the refugees. Thus, Bielinky tells his readers about Netter's description of Louis XIV's visit in Metz and his encounter with a rabbi, a survivor of the Khmelnytsky (Chmielnicki) 1648–49 pogroms who had entered Metz illegally.[38] Had this encounter taken place today, he continued, the refugee rabbi would have been arrested and imprisoned for half a year. But the Sun King (Louis XIV) acted in the spirit of traditional French hospitality and settled the rabbi's status. This royal gesture, concluded Bielinky, was very different from the current republican policy.

The tendency to highlight a French tradition of hospitality toward refugees was also clear in *Naye Presse,* the journal of Communist immigrants. A few days after the *Anschluss,* an anonymous writer described the French Revolution and the subsequent republican era in French history as fundamentally friendly toward immigrants and refugees.[39] A much more comprehensive treatment of this issue can be found in an article published in *Naye Presse* a year later by A. Raiski (Adam Raigadski). Raiski presented France as open to Jewish immigration during almost its entire history and described the era of the expulsion of the Jews as a temporary anomaly, a "black spot" in French history that had been removed by the Revolution.[40] This article is one of the most interesting attempts to minimize the meaning of the four-century expulsion era in order to construct a picture of long-term continuity of Jewish settlement in France.[41] We can identify here certain continuity with the series of articles about Jewish immigration that appeared in *Naye Presse* in 1935, as discussed in chapter 3. Nevertheless, Raiski was more radical in minimizing the significance of the medieval expulsion and in emphasizing the prominence of Jewish immigration throughout French history. His article can therefore be viewed as presenting a long-term essentialist description of the French relation to Jewish immigrants.

This attention given to historical themes in general and the growing interest in the Middle Ages in particular found expression in a series of lectures organized in Paris in early 1939 by the Shema Yisrael society. The memory of the life shared by Jews and non-Jews in early medieval France was depicted by Rabbi Hirschler as a source for respectful relations in the present.[42] The Roman civil status enjoyed by the Jews in Gaul, he claimed, set the pattern for centuries. In contrast to the miserable conditions they experienced in other countries, Jews found in France a homeland for approximately one thousand years, that is, until the fourteenth-century expulsion. In the lecture presented by Rabbi Berman of Lille, the Middle Ages were depicted as the era when rabbinic creativity in France reached its peak and represented a legacy that also enriched their French patriotism.[43] The growing interest in the medieval period and the attempt to use it to support the homemaking myth of the Jews in France seems to be reflected in the unwillingness of several Jewish spokespeople to rely totally on the revolutionary heritage while also expanding the historical foundation of their integrality in France.[44]

Jews continued to look to the legacy of the Revolution as they faced the 1938 escalation. This was expressed in an article published in the *Pariser Haynt* by Bernard Lecache, president of the Ligue internationale contre l'antisémitisme (International League against Anti-Semitism, known as LICA), an interesting organization that bridged the chasm separating local and foreign-born Jews in France.[45] Lecache related to the legacy of July 14 as an inspiration for present struggles. Nowadays, he wrote, we celebrate the fall of the Bastille, "the celebration of equality, freedom and fraternity, but where in the world does freedom equality or fraternity exist for Jews? . . . There have never been so many new Bastilles[,] . . . new inquisitions."[46] Jews are being persecuted almost everywhere, and even in Eretz Israel they are used by the British as a political tool for their interests, Lecache asserted at the very time that the problem of Jewish refugees was under discussion at the Evian Conference. Still, he continued, French Jews must find inspiration in July 14 and join their forces for a united struggle for the values of the Revolution and against anti-Semitism.[47]

A major expression of the revolutionary legacy as used by spokespeople for the immigrants appeared in the twenty-part series of articles in *Pariser Haynt* about the Jews during the French Revolution. In these articles, which were published between April and July 1938 by Wolf Weviorka, the author did not limit himself to a historical overview of the period but also referred to parallels to contemporary problems. It is only natural, he argued in the opening article published a few weeks after the *Anschluss,* that Fascism, which is leading the current crusade against the values of the French Revolution, combines the general antidemocratic struggle and an attempt to abolish Jewish emancipation.[48] In the ensuing articles Weviorka emphasized the major struggles that preceded the emancipation, implying that the struggle itself was part of the revolutionary legacy.[49] He also portrayed the general French public as having embraced emancipation approvingly and sympathetically; he characterized the antiemancipation opposition in the revolutionary era as mostly products of conservative and religious right-wing groups.[50] This description corresponded to the way Jews in France understood their situation in 1938.

Weviorka did not refrain from relating to the dark side of the Revolution. He discussed at length how Jewish religious life was severely hurt during the Reign of Terror and also referred to the attacks against affluent Jews and speculators that at times had turned into general anti-Jewish assaults. All in all, he still chose to conclude his series with a statement that such destructive events were only temporary episodes, whereas the Revolution had brought to the world civil equality for the Jews and universal humanitarian values. This legacy, he added, would eventually defeat the tyranny and barbarism of the twentieth century.[51]

The Return-to-the-Ghetto Polemic and the Reexamination of Emancipation

Alongside the legacy of the Revolution and the role of history, the 1938 events inspired a more critical discourse concerning the ideas of progress and emancipation. In January 1938 amid the Ukrainian and Lithuanian celebrations of the anniversary of the Khmelnytsky Uprising, which had led to the mass pogroms of 1648–49, one writer in the *Pariser Haynt* asked whether contemporary nations were more tolerant than those of the seventeenth century. Despite the major changes that had occurred over the course of three centuries, not the least of which was the French Revolution, he argued, "in our case the rule that humanity is progressing and that the later times will be better than the earlier proved to be invalid."[52] Consequently, Jews still suffered persecution in many places such as Poland, where the memorial day for Bohdan Khmelnytsky (Bogdan Chmielnicki) was celebrated.

The impact of the crisis mood that prevailed in France after the *Anschluss* emerged clearly in an article by Joseph Ben Aron that was published in the Zionist journal *La Terre Retrouvée* in May 1938. The article was written as a fictional dialogue between two Jews: the narrator, who presents himself as a European-educated Jew who turned to Zionism as an adult, and his friend Shmuel, a Zionist who grew up in a traditional environment and was educated in a cheder (a traditional elementary school that teaches the basics of Judaism and the Hebrew language) and a yeshiva (a school for Talmudic study). The experience that led the narrator to turn to his traditional friend was the frustration and anger of the modern Jew to the collapse of Jewish emancipation in Europe: the events in Austria, the beginning of anti-Jewish legislation in Hungary, and so on. Shmuel, whose fictional figure represents the preemancipation Jewish collective memory, is depicted as much less surprised by these developments. The narrator, who represents the modern Jew, sees the possible reactions of the Jews as either ongoing patriotic loyalty to their European homelands or a hopeless struggle against the new tyrannies. Shmuel, on the other hand, contends that the Jews must devote their best efforts to preserving their unique collective culture and life form, and therefore they must return to the ghetto: "The return [to the Middle Ages] is a fact. The totalitarian, national and corporative regimes have a great proximity to the Middle Ages. We did not want it and cannot prevent or abolish it. Still, we must take the best parts from these new Middle Ages that were imposed on us, and this concerns first and foremost the preservation of our moral strength."[53]

An age in which the world that was founded on individualism and humanism and equal rights was now collapsing, stated Shmuel, and the Jews must now return to their own particular existence, which was based in the ghetto, in order to gather strength. In a reversed version of the 1789 statement by Count Stanislas de Clermont-Tonnerre in the French revolutionary National Assembly that "the Jews should be denied everything as a nation, but granted everything as individuals,"[54] Shmuel asserted that following the abolition of their civil equality, the Jews should again become a nation in Europe, just as they had been in the period prior to the French Revolution.

The different historical perceptions of the two participants in the imaginary dialogue also led to different evaluations of the future of the emancipation. Whereas the narrator was not willing to give up the vision of emancipation and believed that the Western countries, including France, would preserve the equal status of the Jews, his more traditional friend Shmuel focused on the calls of conservative French spokespeople to restrict the rights of the Jews. The dispute between the two positions was not resolved in the article. Shmuel linked the moral decline of Judaism to assimilation and therefore called for a return to the traditional ghetto values, whereas the narrator stated that this idea was in opposition to the Zionist vision.

The same topics that were discussed in Ben Aron's imaginary dialogue—the idea of progress, the future of emancipation in the West, and the reassessment of the ghetto heritage—stood at the center of a wide-ranging transnational Jewish public debate that had begun to develop at that time in the Yiddish press. This debate was conducted primarily in the two major centers of the Yiddish literary world of the 1930s: the United States and Poland. The Yiddish press in France, situated between these two centers, was invariably influenced by the debate and responded to it.[55]

In March 1937 during the anti-Semitic campaign to restrict the Jewish students in Polish universities to special seats that were known as ghetto benches, the Polish Zionist leader Yitzhak Grinboym (b. 1879) published an extensive article about the concept of the ghetto.[56] Although a ghetto could be a place in which a group of people or even a nation is imprisoned, he asserted, it could also serve as the bastion for members of a weak and defenseless people living among foreigners. But the ghetto could also be a home, a place to which people always come back to draw inner strength. Grinboym expressed clear opposition to the imposition of the ghetto as a prison, alluding to the situation in Polish universities. On the other hand, however, he argued that Jews ought to recognize the need for the ghetto as a bastion and, even more so, as a spiritual home that should be developed and enriched.

A year later shortly after the *Anschluss* of Austria the concept of the ghetto was discussed again, this time in the United States. The harsh events in Europe, which were viewed by some Jewish intellectuals and publicists as a betrayal of the Jews by the West, motivated Yiddish writer Yaacov Glatshteyn (b. 1896) to announce in April 1938 his withdrawal from the modern world and return to ghetto life and culture: "Good night," he called to the world, "in a proud step, out of my own initiative, I return to the ghetto."[57]

The Yiddish press in France, primarily the *Pariser Haynt,* began to discuss these issues in July 1938, during the time when the Evian Conference had assembled. On July 3 the newspaper published an article by Moshe Fuks in which he clearly expressed the complicated ambivalence of east European immigrant intellectuals toward the apparent bankruptcy of assimilation.[58] Born in 1890 in Galicia, Fuks lived most of the interwar period in Vienna until his arrest by the Germans after the *Anschluss;* he subsequently left for Paris. We "Jewish Jews," Fuks claimed, have observed the assimilation process of west European Jews from the outside. Whereas the assimilating Jews believed that their Judaism carried a fruitful culture to the other nations, Fuks asserted, we chose to oppose the national disintegration and viewed it as an unnecessary sacrifice for the sake of false universal humanism. The bankruptcy of assimilation in Germany furnished proof that the humanistic ideas were not eternal but instead were temporary. The Jews, explained Fuks, had paid for assimilation with a period of stagnancy in their national creativity, and the latest events proved that it was in vain. Nevertheless, he did not end his discussion with this point. He concluded his article by stressing that he did not deny the universal mission of the Jews and even their possible impact on humanity, ideas that continued to be valid for him even after the collapse of assimilation.[59]

Further historical assessments concerning the position of the Jews in the late 1930s vis-à-vis the preemancipation era became more intensive among Yiddish-speaking intellectuals in Paris primarily after the *Kristallnacht* pogrom.[60] In December 1938 the publicist Israel (Jacques) Efroykin (b. 1884 in Lithuania), former president of the immigrants' federation in Paris, organized a public debate among several immigrant Jewish intellectuals concerning the topic of the return to the ghetto.[61] The historian Eliyahu (Elias) Tcherikower, who opened the discussion, introduced the polemic about the return to the ghetto that had developed mostly in the United States since April 1938. The opponents of this idea, he said, argue that the ghetto had never been a privilege for the Jews and that it had always been imposed on them. However, Tcherikower added, this was not true. The Jews themselves had chosen to live in a designated area, separating themselves from their neighbors for many years, and only later was the ghetto imposed on them. According to Tcherikower, the problem of the polemic was that the various spokespeople did not really clarify what they meant by a return to the ghetto. For him, he asserted, this was a call for dissociation from the non-Jewish world and concentrating inward in order to find a new historical path.

Most of the immigrant intellectuals who took part in this debate, including Socialist activist Charles Rapaport (b. 1865) and former Bundist Avraham Menes (b. 1897), expressed their clear support for the idea of progress and described the revisionist movement as a kind of debility in the spirit of the anti-Nazi struggle. A different point of view was articulated by Dr. Singalovski—probably the Russian-born Zionist educator Aaron Singalovski (b. 1889), who after World War I was among the founders of the Organization for Rehabilitation through Training (ORT) in Berlin, an organization devoted to the advancement of Jews through training and education—who expressed greater understanding for the return-to-the-ghetto idea. In the beginning, he said, the ghetto was a privilege for the Jews. Only later on, when it became associated with their forced concentration under harsh conditions, its advantages were forgotten, and modern Jews aspired so much to leave it for the sake of assimilation. But this tendency was founded only on a partial understanding of Jewish history, he added: "There are two tendencies in Jewish history: the first is to get outside into the world and the second is to dissociate from the world. These two contradicting tendencies have appeared throughout Jewish history and were internalized into the people's soul so that a full rift between them might lead to a schism within the people itself."[62] The solution that Singalovski eventually offered was Zionism, but in this context it is more important that, unlike most other speakers, he did not embrace the idea of linear progress. Instead he adopted a cyclical concept of the history of Diaspora Jews, running backward and forward between separation and integration, between ghetto and assimilation.

Another article that was published in the *Pariser Haynt* a few days later expressed the upsetting atmosphere that prevailed in the immigrants' milieu at that time. This was one of the only articles published in France that suggested a revision in the understanding of Jewish history similar to what was being offered by certain German Jewish spokespeople after January 1933. The article openly criticized not only the general ideas of progress and assimilation but also the specific way in which emancipation had been granted to the Jews after the French Revolution. The impact of the speedy escalation in late 1938 can be clearly seen here, because the writer was no other than Wolf Weviorka, who only a few months earlier had published the series of articles about the Jews during the French Revolution. "Let us not play with words," he wrote. "The Jews should have the courage to admit that they signed a bill for the emancipation they got 150 years ago, a bill that (in their national subconsciousness) they had no intention to repay, a bill that they could not have repaid even if they had wanted. . . . The bill that the Jews signed in exchange for the rights that the French Revolution granted them obliged them to disappear as a nation."[63] We the Jews, Weviorka continued, had then supported our friends in the National Assembly who had invited us to join the French nation in exchange for this promise. We had struggled against our enemies who argued that we should not receive rights, because we will never give up our national identity. Now, Weviorka asserted, it turns out that our enemies were right.

This historical lesson is relevant today, Weviorka stated, not only for the emancipated Jews who had already left the ghetto but also for those who were still living within the ghetto walls (i.e., the Yiddish-speaking immigrants as well as the Jews of eastern Europe). We should not repeat the mistake of our forefathers and surrender our national identity for the sake of integration. East European Jews including the most secular among them, such as the Bundists, claimed Weviorka, are still ghetto people (*Ghettniks*); therefore, the return-to-the-ghetto slogan does not relate to them. But, Weviorka concluded, the return to Jewish uniqueness is necessary today, first and foremost in the United States, where the Jews are losing their national identity, and in France as well.

A few days later another publicist, A. Kremer, related to the return-to-the-ghetto polemic and criticized positions such as Weviorka's.[64] The call to return to the ghetto, Kremer wrote, is both optimistic and naive because it assumes that anti-Semites will be satisfied after pushing the Jews back to their neighborhoods and yeshivas and will let them live there. Unlike Weviorka, Kremer asserted that Nazi anti-Semitism is not a rehearsal of medieval hatred but a new much worse and unprecedented phenomenon in Jewish history. The Nazis, he claimed, do not aspire to enclose the Jews in ghettos but instead intend to exterminate them; no return to the ghetto will counter this effort. Whereas the more optimistic Jewish spokespeople (mostly Jewish Communists and Bundists) denied the uniqueness of Jewish suffering and continued to cling to the idea of progress while on the other hand the more conservative and national publicists criticized the course of modern Jewish history and called for a return to traditional values, Kremer opposed both directions. His radical view of Nazi anti-Semitism led to a fatalistic understanding of the Jewish suffering. Neither progress nor the return to Jewish tradition would grant real meaning to Jewish suffering or suggest a solution.

The voices that most emphatically rejected the idea of a return to the ghetto—politically, as giving up the struggle against Fascist forces, and culturally, as a futile return to religion and tradition—belonged to the Jewish left wing: Jewish Communists and Bundists. Those who called for a return to the ghetto, argued the Communist Y. Lerman—probably the pseudonym of the Polish-born Lulke Groynovski (b. 1904), who immigrated to France in 1929—in *Naye Presse* in early 1939—ignored the fact that not only Jews but also Spanish, Chinese, and Czechs were suffering at the hands of Fascist forces.[65] On the other hand, he added, they also ignore the freedom of Jews in the United States, the Soviet Union, France, and other countries. According to Lerman, the idea of a return to the ghetto originated among the defeatist Jewish bourgeoisie. The other Jewish camp, led by the working class and supported by most of the intellectuals, was obligated to the international democratic struggle against Fascism. Its members joined the republicans in the Spanish Civil War, and they took action against anti-Semitism in Poland and also joined other confrontations in France, the United States, and other countries. Similar to Lerman's position, Bundist spokespeople also condemned the return-to-the-ghetto movement as an expression of decline and despair among Jewish bourgeois intellectuals, who had turned to mysticism and superstitions as a result of their political helplessness.[66]

Discussions about the future of emancipation and the return to the ghetto were also concerned with the future of the Jews in the new world. As the feeling that an overall crisis was enveloping, as Nazi Germany grew stronger, and as the pessimistic assessments concerning the Jewish future on the European continent and sometimes even in France itself became more common, the question of the status of the Jews in America began to be discussed more widely.[67] An especially original discussion on this topic can be found in an article published in January 1939 by Y. Gotlib.[68] It is commonly said, and with some justification, claimed Gotlib, that there is no American people and that American culture has not yet been born. Yet in spite of the fact that masses of people from many nations live today in America and strive to preserve their original cultures and languages, Gotlib continued, the result is not the same as in the European Balkans. The Americanization process, he asserted, is more than a mere linguistic assimilation. It is an adaptation to a particular mentality and a certain way of relating to the world for which Americans are willing to fight. At this point Gotlib pointed out an essential difference between America and Europe:

> It is impossible to understand the style and character of the European jungle if one forgets that Europe is no more than a peninsula of Asia. Europe is Asia, Europeans are Asians. They boast that they originate from the Aryans, from the race that was dominant in Asia for thousands of years. When one looks at the Europeans who are in power in public life one can identify the sparkle of the past Asian tyrants. . . . For many Europeans the idea of life is mixed with the idea of control.[69]

The Asian character, Gotlib continued, accounts for the fact that feudalism was so rooted in Europe, and it is also the reason for the Inquisition and for events such as the St. Bartholomew's Day Massacre. It is interesting to note that the Gotlib article did not mention the French Revolution. After relating to several examples from medieval and early modern European tyranny, he claimed that the European dictatorships of the 1930s were just another expression of the political culture that had originated in Asia.

America, on the other hand, represented for Gotlib the utter antithesis of the European worldview. He presented the Americans as former Europeans who had dissociated themselves from the impact of feudalism when they reached the New World: they left the European jungle and did not accept tyranny any longer. Whereas in Europe, according to Gotlib, political leaders continue to behave like the French monarchs or the Habsburg emperors (a description that might have applied not only to the leaders of the Fascist countries in Europe but also to Daladier's leadership in France in early 1939), the American president understood his position as his country's first civil servant. Facing what seemed to be in early 1939 Europe's inevitable decline, Gotlib did not feel any need to distinguish between the democratic and the totalitarian forces in power either on the European continent in general or in France in particular. Instead, he chose to present America as the sole representative of democracy and therefore also as the last bastion of emancipation.

The return-to-the-ghetto debate was intensively dealt with and conceptualized in the new journal *Oyfn Shaydveg* (At the Crossroads); the first volume (one of two) was published in Paris in April 1939. *Oyfn Shaydveg* disseminated articles by Jewish intellectuals from France as well as from the other centers of the international Yiddish literary world.[70] In the opening programmatic article of the first volume, the editors—Israel Efroykin and Eliyahu Tcherikower—expressed their view that the Jewish world is in a deep crisis and is positioned at a crossroads in a period in which there was a growing need to reexamine the national past:

> The world around us is today at the crossroads; it is living in anxiety and going through a major social, political and ideological crisis. The world will turn out to be different after this crisis. But we, the Jews, if we will not find a real refuge, if we will not find a way, a real support, new ideas and inner forces to maintain our existence as a people, then we might be crushed under the wheels of this era. We are living at the time of the painful liquidation of the Emancipation period, with its humanistic and democratic principles. We are becoming a people of refugees, of homeless standing in front of closed doors without any chance for a new home[;] . . . adversity makes a man wise. We must learn from our bitter experiences. First of all we must look back honestly and seriously to our old Jewish burden and get hold of anything which might help us to preserve our fallen Jewish soul and revive our national energy; [look back to our past] not only for mere criticism but in order to find there new methods for the

struggle for the Jewish existence. Looking for such ways—this
is the aim of our journal.[71]

The most important contributor to the first volume of *Oyfn Shaydveg*
was Tcherikower, who in addition to being one of the editors wrote two
major essays: a programmatic article and a critical review of the return-to-
the-ghetto debate in the Yiddish literary world.[72] Born in Ukraine in 1881,
Tcherikower was a student of Simon Dubnov in St. Petersburg. In 1915
Tcherikower moved to New York, and after the outbreak of the February
Revolution of 1917 he returned to Petrograd. Following the Bolshevik Revolution he moved to Kiev, where he participated in the experiment of Jewish
national autonomy in Ukraine. Later on he moved to Berlin and lived there
until moving to Paris in 1933.[73] In 1939 he was interested mainly in the
question of whether the Jewish people would be able to mobilize national
energies for a future revival after the forthcoming catastrophe, which seemed
inevitable. The Jewish soul, he argued, had already proven its ability to survive previous national disasters, such as the destruction of the First Temple
and the Second Temple, the Crusades, the expulsion from Spain, and the
1648–49 Khmelnytsky pogroms. After each of these disasters the Jews had
gone through a process that led to a spiritual revival and sometimes even to
a cultural revolution: Yavneh after the destruction of the Second Temple, the
Ashkenazic medieval literature, the Lurianic Kabbalah after the expulsion
from Spain, and Sabbateanism and Hasidic Judaism after the pogroms in
Ukraine. The eruption of modern anti-Semitism in late nineteenth-century
Europe had also inspired Jewish creativity and brought about the emergence
of the national revival movement in Eretz Israel on the one hand and the free-
doms enjoyed by Jews in America on the other hand. Against the backdrop
of these precedents, Tcherikower raised the question of the Jewish struggle
to meet the challenges posed by the crisis of the late 1930s, which he called
"the swastika crusade."[74] Will the Jewish people, Tcherikower asked, be able
again to cope with the approaching disaster in a creative way and turn the
catastrophes into a source of power?

Tcherikower's position regarding this question was very skeptical. In
spite of all the harsh experiences that Jews had gone through in Europe,
they had still avoided, in his judgment, a true self-examination. Referring
to the various cultural developments among German Jewry, he asserted that
they "could not understand what lies in the depth of the ghetto, even when
the ghetto walls were closing around them." In other countries, he added,
including Hungary, Jews were reacting to the anti-Semitic pressure with self-
denial and even with religious conversion. In countries where the pressure

was less intense—such as France, England, and the United States—Jews were not exhibiting enough solidarity with their suffering brethren. The blame for the feebleness of the Jewish reaction lies, according to Tcherikower, with the historical worldview that had become so popular among Jews: "For many years a blind and endless belief in the iron rule of Emancipation became so rooted. The Emancipation exhausted the basic foundations of Judaism."[75] This belief in emancipation became even stronger after years of suffering by the Jews in Germany, who were not prepared to let it go. The power of this belief was in contradiction to the very spirit of the Jews that should have been the precondition for a real self-examination:

> For several decades we have ceased to nurture the reserves of power that we have inherited from previous generations, their iron discipline, which they created over such a long period of work and efforts, and now we are in a position of [spiritual] bankruptcy. We failed to transfer the old wine into new bottles. We have [instead] enabled assimilation to spread to all areas of our daily life. . . . We were divided into seventy languages and seventy-seven parties. We were enriched by universal values and contributed to the general culture while neglecting our old heritage with its determined spiritual resistance power. And then, when the huge catastrophe appeared to the world, we were caught with a weak backbone and a fragile national will.[76]

After this clarification of his criticism of emancipation and assimilation, Tcherikower expressed his position on the question of the return to the ghetto. It is true, he argued, that this idea might seem naive, romantic, and even reactionary. However, he added, the meaning of the call to return to the ghetto is not to draw the Jews physically back behind the walls. Rather, it is to make them aware of the collapse of emancipation and to restore the deep national powers that they had lost after surrendering to dry rationalism. "We have gambled on the card of emancipation and fraternity," he wrote, "and this card has lost . . . but we should not leave the game now desperately. . . . We need now a new national will. . . . Jews should now become active in their history."[77]

Expressing the mood of some Jewish immigrant intellectuals, Tcherikower's criticism of the emancipation era went hand in hand with his interpretation of the call to return to the ghetto as a manifestation of a deep need to draw strength from historical sources.[78] This pessimistic position was not religiously driven, but it was endemic to Jewish tradition. It was therefore fundamentally different from the position of the left-wing spokespeople whose commitment to the revolutionary legacy as well as their militant anti-traditional approach motivated them to reject any idea of returning to the ghetto. Tcherikower's position was also essentially different from the views of the vast majority of French Jewish spokespeople at that time.

Whereas the Yiddish press in France, which was an integral part of the international Yiddish literary world, was very interested in the whole European and even global implications of the emancipation's decline, the French Jewish press did not take a significant part in the return-to-the-ghetto polemic.[79] The leaders of the Central Consistory related generally to the need to return to Jewish tradition and to reinforce the Jewish spirit, but the French Jewish establishment, whose views were expressed in the journal *L'Univers Israélite*, could not identify with a revisionist interpretation of the emancipation era.

The escalation in Europe, however, had a deeper impact on several French Jewish spokespeople who represented other, more peripheral, milieus. Two clear examples of such positions will be presented here: one was raised by an Alsatian Jewish writer, and the other was raised by a young national Jewish activist in Paris.

In December 1938 the Alsatian journal *La Tribune juive* published an editorial that related to the harsh events in neighboring Germany.[80] The editorial stated that after 150 years, during which we had made an extensive effort to share in European culture, we must admit now that we have failed. The aspiration to create a synthesis between Judaism and Western culture, which will be free of pagan heresy and superstitions, has proved to be an illusion. Furthermore, the editorial claimed, the failure is not only spiritual: our brethren who served as the avant-garde of modern militant Judaism (i.e., the German Jews) are today in a process of destruction.

Lucien Dreyfus (b. 1882), the author of the editorial (written under the initials L. D.), endeavored to explain this development in religious terms. The racism and atheism that had taken over the European soul epitomized the antithesis of the Jewish tradition, he argued, and the sole explanation for their ascendancy is God's plan to reveal His will through history. However, the new historical reality was exposing the depth of the illusion on the part of those Jews who had lost their belief in Jewish uniqueness for the sake of integration among other nations. In Dreyfus's view, the only way to cope with the current predicament was to return to what he called the eighteen hundred-year-old legacy of Jewish martyrdom, which had begun with the rejection of Paul's missionary attempts and had continued under the Inquisition in the Middle Ages. Only such a reaction could grant meaning to the current Jewish suffering.

It is interesting that this conservative revisionist reading of Jewish history related primarily to the disaster of the Jews in neighboring Germany. The decline of emancipation in Germany, claimed Dreyfus, and the failure of attempts to turn the Jews into an integral part of the local population could be linked to previous historical experiences in Jewish history: the Babylonian exile, the Jewish exile in Hellenistic Alexandria and in Rome, and the Jewish experience in medieval Andalusia (in Spain).[81] In each of these cases, many Jews had sacrificed the Jewish ideal for the sake of integration, but the activity of several loyal Jewish families saved the patient and stubborn Jewish soul, which refused to pass away.

In spite of these positions, which were not entirely distinct from those being expressed by Yiddish writers of the time, the Alsatian publicist clearly avoided applying his basic view to the French Jewish experience. Unlike other countries, Dreyfus argued, France had remained loyal to the principles of 1789 and to civic equality, and its Jews should therefore be grateful. Nevertheless, he was also critical of those Jews who believed that patriotism obliged them to fully abandon the Jewish uniqueness for the sake of integration into the French nation. Thus, the argument can be made that *La Tribune juive*'s editor presented two different historical narratives at the same time. In presenting the emancipation of German and Central European Jews, he viewed it as a total collapse and portrayed the entire process as erroneous from the very beginning; it was another historical case among failed Jewish attempts to integrate into foreign nations and cultures. In relation to France, on the other hand, Dreyfus continued to cling to the essentially positive narrative of emancipation while turning his criticism only to the question of the differentiation between a positive integration model and a negative one, which led to full and unrestrained assimilation.[82]

In January 1939 a new Jewish weekly, *Affirmation*—a joint initiative of young local and immigrant Jews—was founded in Paris. *Affirmation*'s declared aim was to develop a new Jewish discourse: to contribute to the crystallization of a new and more united positive Jewish identity in France by turning to common Jewish historical memory.[83] In February and March 1939 *Affirmation* published a few articles by Arnold Mandel (b. 1913), the son of a Galician immigrant family who had grown up in France. Mandel's articles clearly revealed the impact of revisionist historical interpretation on certain Jewish writers in the French language.[84]

The ability of the Jews to revitalize their self-consciousness and to achieve greater unity depends mostly, claimed Mandel in February 1939, on their disillusionment with certain perceptions that had developed under assimilation.[85] They should overcome the tendency to identify Judaism with abstract trends of thought (Kantian, Hegelian, Nietzschian, etc.). They must defend their freedom and uniqueness everywhere without identifying their heritage with any political ideology, not even with progress or democracy. As much as Jews wanted to be treated better by democracies, Mandel added, they should depend on that but must shape their future on the basis of their own unity and inner strength.

Mandel's tendency to dissociate political ideologies from national identities was recognizable as well in his broader historical interpretation of the events of the 1930s. Just as the French Revolution, while having erupted in France, was an event of universal significance, Nazi anti-Semitism, which started in Germany, had expanded to other countries. Mandel decoupled the essentialist link between Nazism and the German character much as he disconnected the revolutionary legacy and the French character. From this people could learn, at least implicitly, according to Mandel that France too was not immune to the impact of Nazism.

Mandel's interpretation of the European turn to Fascism and his historical narrative concerning the rise and fall of Jewish emancipation were expressed more sharply in another article published in March 1939.[86] Mandel argued that the key values for the Jews in the twentieth century were those of Western civilization. Not only did assimilated Jews see it this way, he emphasized, but so did many Zionists and nationalist Jews. They were continuing Theodor Herzl's vision by planning to import emancipation to Palestine, that is, found a Jewish state on liberal values, as in England and the United States.

In contrast to this attitude—which Mandel felt was so rooted among Western Jews, even Zionists—he offered an alternative narrative to the connection between the Jews and Western culture. Looking at it from the perspective of the spring of 1939, Mandel diagnosed the West as a declining culture full of inner contradictions. The integration of the Jews into the West was therefore very shallow. This integration was based on the Jewish imitative acceptance of "Europe's cheap ornaments." The Jews were tempted by Europe's "sweetness," Mandel continued; kind Europeans who were influenced by major historical developments had even granted them emancipation.[87] Now, as the honeymoon of the liberal and humanistic era was over, the West viewed the Jews as responsible for its major historical error even though they had had nothing to do with it.

Mandel was very critical of the historical choice made by European Jews to sacrifice so much in order link their fate with the West. Unlike many other publicists, he did not distinguish between the different forms of assimilation (good and bad) or between the German and the French cases. Instead, he maintained a broader view of the entire Western world in which humanism was on the decline: "Western humanism is bankrupt. All the grand achievements of European civilization cannot serve humanity now against the cruel and arbitrary forces—the masses, the class, the race. Nowadays the real Westerners are the Nazis. Hitler does not speak only for Germany but for all Europe, and in fact no other European is more authentic than Mr. Hitler."[88]

This severe judgment of European culture was one of the sharpest public attempts in the French language to revise the perception of modern Jewish history, not only in Germany but also generally in Europe. Mandel chose not to relate directly to France and the position of its Jews, but it is clear that he saw France as an integral part of the problem. One can identify here a cyclical view of Jewish history and perhaps also of world history. This historical interpretation rejected the belief in the idea of progress and therefore viewed Nazism not as an unexpected and temporary anomaly in the normal course of history but rather as an authentic expression of the modern era and of western culture. Such a position was of course fundamentally different from that of the mainstream French Jewish spokespeople whose obligation to the revolutionary legacy was being reconfirmed at that very time.

The 150th Anniversary of the Revolution and the Outbreak of World War II

In the spring and summer of 1939, France marked the 150th anniversary of the French Revolution. The anniversary events were naturally affected both by the political situation in France and the escalation in the international arena. Following the Nazi invasion of Prague, which was in clear violation of the agreement that Germany had undertaken in Munich, public opinion in France and Britain began to view war as inevitable. During this period the French government, led by Daladier, canceled a substantial part of the social reforms that had been advanced by the Popular Front. The French regime also adopted certain authoritarian characteristics; in fact, several historians refer to this period as "Daladier's dictatorship."[89] During these months there were also certain signs of recovery in the country as the economy began to pull out of the recession and as France began an intensive armament process and diplomatic offensive against Nazi expansion plans. Parallel to the pessimistic mood and the rising anxiety over the approaching war, the French regime tried to arouse a patriotic revival and, for this purpose, also made use of the anniversary of the Revolution.[90]

The marking of the Revolution's anniversary in this way was compatible with the tendency of Jewish spokespeople in France to emphasize the contrast between French and German values. This was clear in an article by Joseph Milner, one of the older immigrants, who had lived in Paris since 1906 and who was engaged in researching ancient Jewish communities in France. Because the Revolution's anniversary, insisted Milner, would be marked in 1939 at a time when the dark forces are trying to obliterate its spirit, people should expect the celebration to contribute to a renewed awakening of France. Milner was optimistic about the stability of the revolutionary legacy: no Koblenz (i.e., the antirevolutionary monarchic-aristocratic alliance of the late eighteenth century) and no Fascism would be able to defeat it.[91]

In February 1939 the French Jewish press began to follow the preparations for the anniversary celebrations, repeatedly emphasizing Jewish support and participation.[92] Even the *Affirmation,* which tended to a more reserved evaluation of the emancipation era, took the position that the 1791 bestowal of citizenship was the watershed of French Jewish history: the Jews had been lifted from the Dark Ages to an enlightened era of participation in universal freedom.[93] In contrast to such positive evaluations, other writers were more skeptical in their assessment of the long-term impact of the Revolution. Thus, in the *Pariser Haynt* the question was raised as to how the Jews should mark the anniversary of the Revolution: as a celebration or as a memorial and mourning day (*yahrtzeit*) for the late emancipation.[94]

In an article published in the *Affirmation* in May 1939, Jacques Bielinky expressed doubts concerning the "naive" idea of progress due to the fact that "Hitlerism" had exposed the fragile status of the Jews in Europe.[95] Bielinky added, however, that it would be better to try to understand the historical facts than to merely lament the Jewish plight. He therefore related to a series of reforms initiated under Louis XVI in prerevolutionary France in order to improve the civil status of the Jews. Bielinky claimed that if the Revolution had not occurred, French Jews might have been granted the same civil rights by the king and perhaps even more. Furthermore, in an explicit reference to the problem of Jewish refugees in France, Bielinky added that Louis XVI had begun to view Jewish immigration more favorably, in contrast to the more restrictive policy of the Third Republic in 1939.

Bielinky's criticism of the idea of progress and of the conventional view of the Revolution as taking the Jews from darkness to daylight had somewhat of a Tocquevillian spirit. Like Alexis de Tocqueville, Bielinky rejected the very idea of the absolute innovation attached to the Revolution, pointing to the rudimentary changes that had already begun in the ancien régime. This led him to a cyclical view of Jewish history, renewed continually by an "*éternal recommencement.*" This view, however, did not yield any real comfort vis-à-vis his understanding of the condition of the Jews in 1939: "150 years after the Revolution millions of Jews are facing the problem of attaining human rights again in harsher and under more painful circumstances than those of the eighteenth century."[96]

Jewish spokespeople in France related to the anniversary of the Revolution with great complexity. On the one hand, in a series of ceremonies that took place in June 1939 Jewish representatives emphasized their commitment to the values of the Revolution while marking its great contribution to the status of the Jews. On the other hand, they compared the gap between these values and achievements to the situation of the Jews in certain European countries where conditions were described as worse than for Jews in prerevolutionary France. Some of the writers also claimed that a tolerant attitude toward immigrants and refugees was an integral part of the Revolution's legacy.[97]

As we have already seen, left-wing immigrant Jews stated more explicitly that the enemies of the Revolution—not only outside of France but also within French society—were opposed to its values and challenged its legacy. In a special volume of the Communist *Naye Presse* published in February 1939, Y. Panin made a Marxist distinction between the prerevolutionary Ashkenazic Jews in Alsace and the wealthier and more privileged Sephardic Jews in Bordeaux, a distinction that hinted at the gap between the twentieth-century native Jewish population and east European immigrant Jews. In late eighteenth-century France, Panin argued, it was the Ashkenazi Jews who had joined the Revolution enthusiastically in order to obtain their freedom.[98] Time and again, he asserted, left-wing Jewish spokespeople, who rejected revisionist interpretations of the Revolution, emphasized their support for a joint French Jewish struggle.

The memory of the Revolution and the war between revolutionary France and its enemies, especially its victory over the antirevolutionary powers at the September 1792 Battle of Valmy, became increasingly relevant as the war with Nazi Germany grew more imminent. The war atmosphere can be felt in a speech delivered by Rabbi Nathan Netter in Metz at a ceremony marking the Revolution's anniversary. Republican France, claimed Netter, is standing today before the tribunal of history; the values of July 14 and Valmy as well as the legacy of the World War I battles of the Marne, the Somme, and Verdun ought to be its source of power in the current confrontation. French Jews, he added, must remember their liberators—Mirabeau (Honoré-Gabriel Riqueti), Emmanuel-Joseph Sieyès, Grégoire, Clermont-Tonnere, and others—and serve France today for the sake of all mankind.[99]

The Battle of Valmy and the mass mobilization of the French in defense of their homeland, which was under attack at the time, was also offered by Yitzhak Chomsky as a legacy of inspiration to French society fighting for its freedom in the past as well as in the future. The confrontation with the Germans, claimed another commentator in the *Pariser Haynt* while relating to the Revolution's anniversary, is above all a struggle for freedom: although they had great philosophers, the Germans had always lacked the ability to live in freedom because they had never conquered their own Bastille.[100]

The second volume of *Oyfn Shaydveg,* which appeared in Paris in August 1939, included an interesting polemic concerning the historical meaning of the Revolution. In an open letter to the journal's editors, the elderly historian Simon Dubnow (b. 1860), who lived in Riga at that time, argued that the recommended revision to the Jewish historical orientation, as it was expressed in the first volume of the journal, was out of place. The Jews, he asserted, are not living now on an ideological crossroads but instead on the eve of a battle, and therefore they should concentrate on the struggle and postpone the critical self-examination. Dubnow also referred in this context to the anniversary of the French Revolution, which he called "The Time of Our Freedom." The Jewish people's future would be decided as part of the struggle for the values of the Revolution, he asserted, and therefore they should join the struggle rather than involve themselves in an unnecessary dispute about the return to the ghetto.[101]

In his response to Dubnow, Tcherikower, Dubnow's ex-student, argued that there is no contradiction between being on the crossroads and being in a struggle. A member of a disillusioned generation, Tcherikower had spent a year in the czarist prison after the 1905 Russian Revolution and was highly disappointed by the 1917 Russian Revolution. He later experienced the Nazi rise to power in Germany and could not identify with Dubnow's rationalistic optimism. Instead, Tcherikower felt the deep need for a historical self-examination. While stating that the great achievements of the Jews in the French Revolution should not be underestimated, he argued that he could not forget the lesson of this era as he had learned it from Dubnow: the price of the emancipation was the abandonment of Jewish collective existence, a historical decision whose impact was an integral part of the current crisis.[102]

The Jewish public discourse on the French Revolution's anniversary came to a close in a celebratory volume of *L'Univers Israélite,* which coincidentally was published on September 1, 1939, the first day of World War II. Members of the French Jewish establishment responded to the skeptical assessments of the Revolution's legacy. One member questioned how they ought to deal with having been propelled back to the Middle Ages after their golden age of emancipation in the nineteenth century.[103] In one of the most interesting articles in the volume, the historian Robert Anchel argued that the Revolution had not only developed in France as a result of the writings of the Enlightenment philosophers but also stemmed from the old French tradition whose roots were in the Gallic-Roman and Merovingian eras. The long historical presence of the Jews in France, he added, paved the way for the decision of the French National Assembly to grant them emancipation. Anchel clearly underestimated the extended period following the expulsion of the Jews from France. He presented it as only a temporary interruption in the much longer continuum of Jewish settlement in France and in a French tradition of hospitality to Jews that had prefigured modern emancipation. On the other hand, despite his Tocquevillian tendency, he still emphasized the innovativeness of the Revolution and the courage of the French for having granted the Jews citizenship while having abandoned the deeply rooted idea that only Catholics could be "real" French.[104] This article reveals the complex consciousness of some of the French Jewish spokespeople. On the one hand, their bond to France rested squarely on the revolutionary legacy, but, on the other hand, they worried about the decline of the legacy and therefore tried to find other ways to embrace French history. Anchel's argument that the position of the Jews in prerevolutionary France had not been so hopeless clearly did not match the opinions of other writers who, in the same volume, stressed the misery of the Jews in pre-1789 France in order to glorify the Revolution.[105]

The most systematic reaction to the skeptical view of the emancipation legacy—and indirectly also to those who called for the return to the ghetto—was formulated by the Paris rabbi and historian Maurice Liber. On the one hand, Liber clung to the Revolution's legacy and expressed his gratitude to several major French figures who had taken part in the beneficence exhibited toward the Jews. On the other hand, he related to the collapse of the emancipation ideas in Germany and other countries:

> We lived under a great illusion when we thought that enlightenment, reason and justice would easily disperse the dark forces that originate in passions and interests and the prejudices that stem from lack of tolerance. The powers of the past had proved to be stronger than the victory of liberty in the public life of the masses who were not mature enough [for the progress] and were easily entrapped by the unrestrained propaganda. This is the reason that parties and governments abroad that wished to destroy freedom turned first against us, the Jews. We have a bond

with freedom. We cannot live without it. We are the witnesses
of freedom in history.[106]

Liber's criticism of the inflated optimism on the part of emancipated Jewry
was not fundamentally different from that of certain Yiddish writers, such
as Sh. Niger, but the fact that a chief spokesperson of the local population
of Jews expressed himself in this way demonstrated the change in the atmosphere all the more emphatically. Liber clearly admitted that the optimistic
perception of history had not materialized, but he still rejected the idea of
the return to the ghetto and presented the future status of the Jews as a major
topic in the general struggle for freedom. Judaism, he asserted, is not a religion of the ghetto and could not have survived in the modern world with the
communal framework of the old regime. Not only had the Jews benefited
from emancipation, but Judaism had benefited as well; if not for emancipation, Judaism would have degenerated amid the old oppressive state. In the
new world the Jews became the witnesses of liberty.

Toward the end of his article, Liber drew a direct link between the Revolution's anniversary and the forthcoming war. He presented the anniversary
as the festival of the Jews in those countries—France as well as England and
the United States—that had decided to integrate them: "the Western solution to the Jewish question." This Western path addressed not only the status
of the Jews but also the approaching international conflict: "Is it by chance
that today, 150 years after the Revolution, the three Western democracies
oppose the dictatorships, the tyrannies that suppress their minorities, the
enemies of liberty and equality?"[107]

The war against Germany motivated Jewish writers in those journals that
continued to be published in the first months of the fighting to emphasize
even more the deep contrast between the French revolutionary legacy and
German barbarism. Immigrant writers linked this to French generosity toward immigrants and refugees as well as to the patriotism of immigrant Jewish volunteers in the French army both in the present and the past.[108]

Another historical symbol that the French Jewish press employed during
the first months of the war was Émile Zola; the one hundredth anniversary
of his birth was marked in April 1940.[109] One of the writers in *L'Univers
Israélite* linked Zola's legacy to the current French patriotic struggle and presented it as a basis for a Christian-Jewish alliance against the power that
wanted to ruin France. The Yiddish press described Zola as a man of truth
and peace who had displayed empathy toward the agony of the Jewish immigrants. Zola's struggle was linked more generally to the image of France as
representing truth and justice in the war against Germany.[110]

On May 27, 1940, when the German army was already deep into French soil and total defeat was at hand, Wolf Weviorka published an article titled "I Believe in France." This article was one of the last public opportunities by a Jewish spokesperson in France to come to terms with the question of progress in history before all the Jewish journals in France were shut down. Weviorka argued that the European nations, headed by France, were responsible for the development of modern culture and civilization and "are threatened now by the dark and evil Middle Ages that we thought had already passed away."[111] Weviorka described the war as a total event, a struggle not over territories or economic interests but instead between worldviews; a conflict between the human and the devil, between day and night; and a struggle against the darkness of the Middle Ages, which aspires to erase a whole chapter of one thousand years of progress from European history.

Weviorka wrote at a time when France was fighting for its life, and he thus avoided skepticism and expressed his firm belief in the victory of progress. From his Jewish point of view, he called for the mobilization of ancient sources for the sake of the belief in France and for a better European future: "Such a belief means a belief in the world, a belief that there is meaning and purpose to history. Such a belief is not weaker than religion; it may even be stronger. We Jews know this belief. It protected us for thousands of years, it enabled us to raise our eyes and look beyond the Middle Ages—the real Middle Ages and not only their twentieth-century shadow, which will, as we hope, totally disappear—to the end of the day. We know the power of this belief."[112] Weviorka survived part of the Nazi occupation in southern France but was eventually captured by the Nazis and was murdered in Auschwitz.

Conclusion

The deterioration in the condition of European Jewry from the time of the *Anschluss* of Austria, coupled with internal developments in France in the late 1930s, had a profound impact on the agenda of Jewish public spokespeople in France. These developments motivated them to reexamine their historical worldview and their belief in the idea of progress. A common interpretive line that characterized most French Jewish establishment publicists and also some immigrant Yiddish writers emphasized the uniqueness of France vis-à-vis Fascist countries and France's loyalty to the revolutionary legacy. As we saw in chapter 3, after 1933 French Jewish writers tended to present an essentialist negative description of the course of German history as having paved the way to Nazi anti-Semitism, whereas the spread of Fascism and anti-Semitism in Europe in the late 1930s shifted the emphasis to positive essentialist representations of the French legacy vis-à-vis the expanding Fascist threat in Europe. Such voices became even more common in 1939, when the 150th anniversary of the Revolution was marked. Another nuance of this attitude presented France together with Great Britain and the United States as representatives of Western progress and emancipation against the medieval barbarian anti-Semitism that had overtaken Germany and its Central and east European allies.

Aside from these positions, the worsening situation brought an increase in revisionist Jewish historical interpretations. This was a phenomenon that was part of the larger 1938–39 transnational debate that took place in the Yiddish literary world, from Warsaw to New York. Certain publicists expressed total hopelessness concerning the ideas of progress and emancipation and yearned for a return to the ghetto. Others, whose criticism of these ideas was more cautious, presented a different historical view, raised questions about the validity of the idea of progress, and even favored a cyclical view of Jewish history. Such immigrant Yiddish voices were joined by certain spokespeople from the periphery of the French Jewish press, older immigrants, and local Jewish writers with conservative or nationalist Jewish tendencies.

A major memory to which the Jews in France referred in this context was World War I. There was an interesting gradual transformation from messages such as "no more war" and "never again," which had been associated with the memorial day of November 11, to a more militant use of World War I memory with an emphasis on heroic myths such as *l'union sacrée.* This new tendency became especially dominant beginning in the spring of 1939. As a war with Germany seemed inevitable, the Anglo-French appeasement policy proved to be a failure, and therefore the fear that Jewish spokespeople would be seen as warmongers had declined. In 1939 the 150th anniversary of the Revolution also helped to link the memory of the united patriotic mobilization of World War I with the older memory. Thus, the 1792 Battle of Valmy, where the French revolutionary army had stopped the monarchic-aristocratic Koblenz alliance, was presented as the predecessor of the French struggle against the Berlin-Rome axis.

Another reaction to the escalation that had begun in the spring of 1938 was articulated chiefly by local Jews but also by immigrants, who attempted to deepen their connection to the Jewish distant past in France. The source-books that were compiled by Rabbi Jacob Kaplan and Rabbi Nathan Netter were only the most prominent examples of many endeavors to accentuate the image of centuries of Jewish historical continuity in France, concealing the era of the expulsion and sometimes even ignoring it. Whereas local Jewish spokespeople strove to foster the impression of historical continuity, immigrant spokespeople wanted to establish the sense of a solid French tradition of tolerance toward immigrants and refugees, with clear implications for the current refugee crisis.

Toward the late 1930s, several Jewish publicists presented a Tocquevillian interpretation of prerevolutionary Jewish history in France, implying that by granting emancipation the Revolution had only continued a well-rooted French tradition of tolerance to the Jews. The tendency to engage in this historical interpretation can be explained by a desire to invest Jewish emancipation with French national authenticity and thus free it from a total dependence on the revolutionary legacy. This was also the background of the attempts by certain spokespeople, almost all of them local Jews, to link the French resistance to anti-Semitism and Fascism to France's Catholic Christian heritage, a historical foundation with deeper roots than the secular revolutionary ethos.

All in all, the memory and myth of the French Revolution and the emancipation continued to serve as the major form of historical identification for the Jews in France even in the late 1930s, and there were no real attempts to challenge it fundamentally or to argue that the entire historical path of modern French Jewry had been a mistake, as it appeared in the post-1933 German Jewish discourse. Of course, the firm belief in unconditional progress with regard to the future status of the Jews in Europe and, more specifically, in France was undermined. Certain writers became very critical toward what they now saw as the exaggerated and even naive optimism that had characterized French Jewry during the golden age of emancipation that had since elapsed. Nevertheless, the vast majority of Jews in France, native-born and immigrants alike, would eventually fight the Germans in the name of French patriotism and universal revolutionary values.

PART 3

HUNGARY
1933—44

5

FACING THE DECLINE OF EMANCIPATION
Hungarian Jews in the 1930s

In the second half of the nineteenth century, primarily from 1867 when Hungary granted its Jews full emancipation, a major Jewish movement emerged that was profoundly committed to the ethos of integration and emancipation. First and foremost within this camp were the Neolog (liberal) communities, headed by the community of Pest. Gradually the Neolog movement was joined by the more Western, modern sector of Hungarian Jewish Orthodoxy. Despite deep religious differences with the Neolog movement, the more modern Orthodox still fundamentally shared their political worldview. Politically, emancipated Jewry therefore comprised two major sectors in pre–World War I Hungary, although its political culture did not have the vast majority support that the liberal emancipation political culture enjoyed in German and French Jewry.

Aside from the modern integrating communities, there were also extreme Orthodox communities—mostly Hasidic—that were located primarily in northeastern Hungary. These groups continued to dissociate themselves from modernization, declining to adopt Hungarian language, culture, or political identification.[1]

The central political aim of modern Jews in Hungary, Neolog as well as modern Orthodox, in the last decades before World War I was to consolidate their emancipation and to become integrated within the Hungarian state as equal citizens. Since they saw themselves as belonging to the Hungarian political culture, they also shared in the predominant public discourse that centered on images and memories from the national history. Politicians and public spokespeople discussed not only events from the relatively recent past such as the Hungarian Revolution of 1848–49—the struggle for liberation (*szabadságharc*) against the Habsburgs—but also much earlier memories. These included the Hungarian defeat by the Turks at the Battle of Mohács in 1526 and even the legacy of the first king of Hungary, Saint Stephen (Szent István), whose kingdom was recognized by the pope in 1000 CE.[2]

Nathaniel Katzburg, who has described the main trends of Hungarian Jewish historiography, asserted that this was a major tool used in Hungarian Jewry's struggle for emancipation and integration. According to Katzburg, the prominent Jewish historians who were active during the dual Austro-Hungarian monarchy era (1867–1914), headed by Sámuel Kohn (b. 1841), focused on the antiquity of Jewish settlement in Hungary, Jewish Hungarian patriotism, and the Jews' contribution to the country. Those historians also tried to create the impression that anti-Semitism was fundamentally far removed from the Hungarian nation.[3]

The decline of the emancipation of Hungarian Jewry began after World War I and accelerated dramatically in the 1930s. It was in the 1930s that the growing influence of Nazi Germany as well as the internal threat of a Fascist overthrow severely undermined the political stability in Hungary and brought about an increase in anti-Semitic pressure. The intensification of the debates about the Jewish question in these years motivated Hungarian Jewish spokespeople to relate to both Hungarian national history and the history of Hungary's Jews. Images of the past were employed extensively in the public and political struggle against the abolition of Jewish political rights and in order to consider the significance of the predicament in which Jews found themselves. The efforts of Jewish spokespeople to use such images and develop a usable past during the 1930s concentrated primarily on the promulgation of the first two Jewish laws in 1938 and 1939.[4]

Hungary and Its Jews in the Interwar Period

With the defeat of the Central Powers in World War I and owing to the Treaty of Trianon that was forced upon the Hungarians by the victors, the historical Kingdom of Hungary effectively disintegrated. Hungary ceded nearly 60 percent of its population and more than two-thirds of its territory to Romania, Czechoslovakia, Austria, and Yugoslavia and had to acquiesce to the fact that more than three million Hungarians would be under the rule of the country's new neighbors. The drastic reduction of Hungary's territory and population, the country's separation from the wider Central European economy, and the need to cope with an influx of hundreds of thousands of refugees had a devastating effect on Hungary's economic infrastructure. In the year following the conclusion of the war, Hungarians also experienced a series of blood-drenched revolutionary events that peaked during Béla Kun's Communist regime, which sent profound shock waves through the old Hungarian elites. The state was restabilized under the rule of the traditional Christian conservative elite, under the regent Miklós Horthy, only in the early 1920s.[5]

The change in the demographic structure and the political atmosphere in Hungary in the post-Trianon era transformed the situation of the Jews who remained on Hungarian soil. Formerly the Jews held the balance in a multinational liberal state whose rulers needed their support in order to maintain a Magyar majority. This accounts, at least in part, for their having been awarded full emancipation in 1867 and for the elevation of the Jewish religion to parity status with Christianity in 1895. However, following the outcome of World War I and the Treaty of Trianon, the Jews had become the most prominent minority in a nation-state with a clear Catholic majority.[6] Moreover, the shock occasioned by Béla Kun's revolution, led mainly by Jews, radicalized the anti-Semitic atmosphere in Hungary. Under these new circumstances, increasing numbers of Hungarians found insufferable the salient presence of Hungarian Jews in diverse industries and in the liberal professions. Even more significantly, the Hungarian government no longer had any real reason to protect the Jews.[7] Thus, it is no wonder that in 1920 Hungary became the first European state, after czarist Russia, to pass a *numerus clausus* law against Jews in universities. This set in motion a process of de-emancipation.[8] In response to public pressure, the Hungarian government officially retreated from the liberal tradition of the nineteenth century that the new Hungary could no longer embrace. With its curtailed powers and owing to the international circumstances that prevented it from attaining its aspirations of irredentist Magyarization vis-à-vis neighboring countries, Hungary in the post-Trianon era implemented a policy of internal Magyarization. Ultimately this meant de-Judaization.[9]

After the crisis of the early 1920s, the new Hungarian regime was stabilized under the conservative prime minister István Bethlen. The radical anti-Semitism was somewhat restrained, and in response to international pressure, the *numerus clausus* law was even eased.[10] But this relative stability began to be undermined in the early 1930s, especially owing to the global economic crisis that did not bypass Hungary. Bethlen's resignation from the premiership in 1931 and, more significantly, the appointment of Gyula Gömbös to the post in 1932 symbolized the shift. The supremacy of the Christian conservative Right had been upset, while the ascent of extreme right-wing

Fascist elements that were patently pro-Nazi became evident. Gömbös was known as the key figure in this extreme rightist constellation; he had been one of the leaders of the violent anti-Semitic campaign that swept Hungary in 1919 and 1920 after the Communist revolution had been quelled.

Although under the pressure of economic circumstances in the 1930s Gömbös refrained from undermining the Jews' legal status any further, his regime was still deeply influenced by Nazi Germany. Beyond its ideological affinity to Nazism, the Hungarian regime was hopeful that the Germans would help them regain the territories that they had lost in the Treaty of Trianon.

After Gömbös's death in 1936, the Far Right—particularly the Nyilas-keresztes Párt (Arrow Cross Party)—grew stronger. This was a result of a number of factors, including the ascendancy of Nazi Germany.[11] In the late 1930s, Hungarian politics was characterized by a struggle between the conservative right-wing establishment, which had a relatively mild anti-Semitic orientation, and the Arrow Cross Party, whose racial anti-Semitism was modeled after that of National Socialism and posed an existential threat for Hungarian Jews.

The consequences of World War I also brought about a sea change in the internal structure of the Jewish community in Hungary. From a population of 911,000 in prewar Hungary, the number of Jews decreased to approximately 470,000 within the Treaty of Trianon borders in the immediate aftermath of the war. In the next two decades their number was further reduced—mostly because of the low birthrate, emigration, and religious conversions—to around 400,000 in the late 1930s. Hungarian Jewry was now much more urban than the prewar community, as reflected in the fact that more than half the population lived in Budapest. A major part of the Orthodox Jewish population, mostly the radical Hasidic sector, was left outside the borders of Hungary by the Treaty of Trianon. The Neologs were now the majority, whereas the Orthodox minority became mostly a modern urban sector.[12] Paradoxically, the circumstance that led to the erosion of Jewish emancipation in Hungary had created also a situation in which the vast majority of Hungarian Jews now shared the modern political culture of emancipated Jewry.

In interwar Hungary there was also an active Zionist movement that promoted the idea of Jewish nationalism and challenged the concept of full Jewish integration into the Hungarian nation. The power of the Zionists increased following the crisis of emancipation, but the Zionists nonetheless remained quite a tiny minority, much smaller than what had existed in Germany in the pre-Nazi era.[13]

The Hungarian National Historical Perceptions: From Liberal Nationalism to Christian Conservatism

The transformation of Hungarian political culture from the liberalism of the Austro-Hungarian period to the Christian conservatism of post–World War I exerted a profound impact on perceptions of the national history and its representations. Pre–World War I liberal Hungary, where the political elite granted civil rights to all its citizens and strove to assimilate the sizable national minorities who lived within its borders into the Hungarian nation, had developed a historical narrative suitable for these aims. The establishment of national historians, dominated then by Kálmán Thaly, collected and published sources supporting Hungary's dominion over its full historical territory—Saint Stephen's Land (Szent István országa)—and legitimized its rule over non-Hungarian ethnic minorities. The emphasis on Hungary's national sovereignty, which was regained in 1867, also produced the idolization of the Hungarian national struggles against the German Habsburg domination, primarily the Hungarian Revolution of 1848–49, and the national leaders of this period, headed by Lajos Kossuth.[14]

This liberal national orientation culminated with the 1896 millennium celebration of the 896 occupation of the Hungarian homeland by the Magyar tribes, known as the Conquest (*honfoglalás*). By marking this anniversary—and especially the prominence of the ancient pagan leader Árpád—Hungarians expressed what appeared to be the victory of the secular, national, and liberal orientation over the influence of Catholicism.[15] The uniqueness of Hungarian nationhood was located in its Eastern origin, and its history was depicted as an enduring struggle against Western powers (Rome, Germany, and Vienna). King Stephen was represented in this context not as a Catholic saint but instead as a national symbol with whom Calvinists and Jews could also identify.

After World War I this construction of national identity lost its validity for most Hungarians. Instead, the trauma of the disintegration—*összeomlás* (collapse)—of the Hungarian kingdom became the new point of departure for historians and publicists intent on interpreting the course of Hungarian history. The consequences of the Treaty of Trianon were presented as parallels to those of the 1241 Mongol invasion of Hungary and especially to the 1526 Mohács defeat of the Turks, which led to the division of Hungary between the Turks and the Habsburgs.

The foremost attempt to interpret the significance of the new national catastrophe was the book *Three Generations* by the historian Gyula Szekfű. Published in 1920, it soon became a major source of the so-called culture

of defeat in interwar Hungary.[16] Deeply influenced by the German tradition of *Geistesgeschichte* (the history of ideas), the representation of the Hungarian national history in *Three Generations* can be termed archaic-mythic
(see chapter 1 in the present volume). Like the German historians of his
time, Szekfű used concepts such as eternal and frequently referred to collective spirits and moral forces in history.[17] He viewed Hungarian nationhood as part of a Christian European entity with predominantly Catholic
roots. Consequently, Szekfű associated the threats toward Hungary and its
historical national enemies not with the West (i.e., the Habsburg influence
and, more generally, the German influence) but instead with the East (the
Mongols and Turks and apparently the Bolshevist threat of the 1920s).

In the spirit of this position, Szekfű challenged the foundations of the
Hungarian historiography as it was shaped in the pre–World War I period.
Thus, he denied the greatness of Kossuth and criticized the 1848–49 anti-
Habsburg liberation struggle. Hungary's present catastrophe, Szekfű asserted, was not the outcome of World War I. It stemmed from a "declining
era" (*hanyatló kor,* part of the subtitle of his book), the national liberal era
that deteriorated during the dual monarchy into shallow materialism. Influenced by anti-modernists and cultural pessimists in German Central Europe,
Szekfű described the moral, cultural, and economic decline and atrophy of
the Hungarian national class. He claimed that only foreign elements—first
and foremost, the Jews—had benefited from the economic modernization
of Hungary, whereas the historical uniqueness of the "Hungarian soul" had
been severely damaged.[18]

Needless to say, Szekfű's ideas encountered considerable criticism. However, Hungary's situation in the 1920s—the problems that the country faced
as well as its new conservative political culture—enabled these ideas to shape
the image of the Hungarian past. They were also used by the new regime to
launch a national revival. Between 1927 and 1934, Szekfű and the medieval
historian Bálint Hóman, the Hungarian minister of culture in the 1930s,
published a series on Hungarian history (*Magyar történet*) that proposed a
conservative Christian reinterpretation of Hungarian history from the post-
Trianon perspective.[19]

The growing popularity of the conservative interpretation of Hungarian national history and its institutionalization made modern emancipated
Hungarian Jews very uncomfortable, and they naturally held on to the liberal
political culture. Nevertheless, the redefinition of Hungarian nationhood on
a conservative Christian basis had a certain impact on the public discourse
of Hungarian Jews.[20] As in the case of French Jews, Jewish liberalism and
optimism in Hungary were also challenged by the Nazi rise to power in Ger-

many and by the escalation of anti-Semitism. In the late 1930s this process even led to an anti-Semitic government policy and, in fact, to the beginning of the end of emancipation. Yet despite the turn toward illiberal and even anti-Semitic trends within Hungarian historical writing, liberalism, faith in emancipation, and the idea of progress continued to dominate post–World War I Hungarian Jewish historiography.[21]

Facing the Rise of Nazism in Germany

After the Nazi rise to power, Hungarian Jewish publicists began to cope with the meaning of this new and threatening development. Like Jewish spokespeople in France, Hungarian Jews also tried to come to terms with events in Germany. They asked whether those developments were the result of forces unique to Germany and what implications they held for the future of emancipation specifically and for the idea of progress in Jewish history in general. Implicitly, they were struggling with the question of whether similar events might occur in their own homeland.

The initial responses of Neolog liberal spokespeople to the rise of the Nazi regime reflected their difficulty in accepting the new situation. That such things could have happened in the land of Goethe and Schiller is difficult to believe, asserted the old liberal economist and statesman Pál Sándor (b. 1860) in June 1933 in *Egyenlőség* (Equality), the main journal of the Neolog community. It is true that Jews had lived under oppression for thousands of years, he added, but this time the change was taking place in the midst of European culture. The Jewish world was being brought to an unprecedented crisis that was even more severe than the Inquisition.[22]

Ernő Ballagi (b. 1890), a Neolog publicist and member of the editorial board of *Egyenlőség*, attempted to discover the deeper meaning of events in Germany by introducing an imaginary dialogue between two voices. One was an optimistic voice that still believed in the ultimate victory of progress and viewed the events in Germany as no more severe than the pogroms in Russia; the other was a pessimistic voice that portrayed German anti-Semitism as the strongest in many centuries and as having exposed the idea of progress as an empty shell.[23] A year later when the Nazi regime marked its first anniversary, Ballagi inclined toward the more optimistic view: one should not see the rise of the new regime in Germany as the beginning of a new age in Jewish history, since only German Jews had experienced such a tragic downfall. As a liberal, Ballagi also related in detail to the internal disputes between German Jewish liberals and Zionists and clearly disapproved of the Zionist view that called on Jews to acknowledge the failure of emancipation and turn voluntarily to self-dissimilation.[24]

The fact that developments in Germany undermined the Hungarian Jewish belief in the idea of progress was expressed in an article published by Sámuel Löwinger (b. 1894) in the *Magyar Zsidó Szemle,* the yearbook of the Budapest rabbinical seminary. Löwinger, who served as a professor of the Bible in the Budapest Neolog rabbinical seminary, compared the crisis under the Nazis to the oppression of German Jews during the Reformation and the Counter-Reformation. In his view, the present-day calamities were typical of unstable revolutionary periods; Jews had experienced such misfortunes in the past and would continue to endure them in the future. Historical developments might lead them to new places and new conditions, but they would continue to suffer for the fundamental Jewish ideals to which they remained committed: "For the Jews there is no antiquity, Middle Ages or modern era, even not the latest modern times."[25] Löwinger immigrated to Israel in 1950.

It is noteworthy that at this stage Neolog spokespeople avoided linking their interpretation of events in Germany explicitly to the question of the future of emancipation in their own homeland. This was related to their belief that events in Germany would not impact their own situation in Hungary. Similar to French Jewish spokespeople, these Hungarian Jews preferred to see Nazism as a unique German phenomenon and believed that the national culture of their homeland was immune to this kind of anti-Semitism. An anonymous writer could therefore still assert in early 1935 that any attempt to imitate anti-Semitic racism in Hungary would ultimately fail because racial distinctions were foreign to the Hungarian national spirit, which was based on religious values.[26]

Zionist spokespeople, on the other hand, naturally tended to portray the turn of events in Germany as a crucial step in the broader process leading to the decline of emancipation. In an article that was published in the Zionist journal the *Zsidó Szemle,* the prominent Zionist leader Ede Iszák placed events in Germany within the context of the rise of emancipation after the French Revolution. He related to the tragic choice of those Jews who, when freed from the ghettos, chose the path of assimilation and self-denial. We, the Zionists, he added, do not have the illusion that France, England, and the United States will save us. We know that what is happening in Germany can also happen tomorrow in other Western countries.[27] Iszák therefore called upon his readers to accept the Jewish fate, realize that Jews should not count on other nations, and consequently join the Zionist enterprise. On the other hand, he called upon them to continue to act as loyal citizens of their home countries and support social and liberal goals within them. By this he attempted to continue to embrace, at least in part, the political values of emancipated Jewry. And similar to Neolog spokespeople, Iszák also avoided explicitly comparing the tragic developments in Germany to the plight of the emancipation in Hungary.

Aside from dealing with the historical significance of events in Germany, Hungarian Jewish spokespeople continued to adhere to the liberal narrative of Hungarian history and the history of Jewish emancipation in Hungary. Thus, for example, the fiftieth anniversary of the publication of Sámuel Kohn's book on the history of Hungarian Jews was marked by a favorable examination of the Hungarian Jewish historiography based on the values of the emancipation.[28]

The ongoing reconstruction of the Jewish struggle for emancipation in Hungary, as well as the depiction of the positive attitude of central figures from the Hungarian national historical pantheon toward the Jews, were especially prominent in *Egyenlőség*. During 1935–36 the liberal Jewish journal published two series of historical articles titled "Hungarian Jewish Past" ("*Magyar zsidó múlt*") and "Unfamiliar Pages from Jewish History" ("*A zsidó történelem ismeretlen lapjai*").[29] Furthermore, the turn to nineteenth-century Hungarian national historical figures such as Lajos Kossuth and Sándor Petőfi in an attempt to use them against the rising tide of anti-Semitism can be traced in Orthodox and even Zionist journals.[30] Similar to what we saw in France, these Hungarian Jewish spokespeople turned to history in order to illuminate the roots of anti-Semitism and disprove its arguments.[31]

A more systematic attempt to confront the conservative Christian narrative of Hungarian history—primarily the deeply rooted view regarding the problematic character of the integration of the Jews into the Hungarian nation—can be found in a February 1934 article by the Jewish journalist György Kecskeméti (b. 1901). In a comment to Szekfű, who had asserted in *Three Generations* that the Jewish presence in the pre–World War I Hungarian press was a result of a foreign and harmful influence on the Hungarian nation, Kecskeméti claimed that the prominent activity of Jews as journalists in the Hungarian press promoted genuine Hungarian national values. A cultural struggle between a liberal pro-Western and a national conservative line was in fact going on in Hungary at that time, Kecskeméti continued. However, Jews and Christians alike were associated with both camps, and both were fundamentally loyal to the Hungarian national cause.[32] In his attempt to defend the Jews against the dominant narrative in conservative Christian Hungary, Kecskeméti depicted the Jewish presence in Hungary as rooted and authentic. In his view the Jews consciously joined the Hungarian nation in the 1840s, a much earlier date than that cited by Szekfű.

The growing impact of developments in Europe—primarily but not only in Germany—was recognizable two and a half years later in another article that Kecskeméti published in the national Jewish monthly *Múlt és Jövő* (Past and Future). A year after the Nuremberg Laws, he expressed his views on the general condition of the Jews in Central and eastern Europe, although without any explicit reference to the Hungarian situation. He called on his readers to accept the fact that the liberal era had come to end. According to his view, they had to come to terms with the destructive implication of this fact on the future of the Jews. Kecskeméti, whose worldview seemed to have changed following the Nuremberg Laws, even expressed a certain understanding of the decline of nineteenth-century liberalism and the emphasis on the gap between the Jews and their surroundings and called on his Jewish readers to absorb the lesson of what had happened:

> If we leave aside the pseudoscientific [i.e., racist] attitudes, we will find that there is something real in this simple thing: The Jews are an alien body within the peoples that absorbed them. Their ways of thought, their practices and their fields of interest differ from those of Christian society. Liberalism was not correct in its unwillingness to recognize these differences and their significance. Now, it is necessary to abandon this error and to remove the Jews from the society that was willing to absorb them only feebly and halfheartedly.[33]

While Kecskeméti did not express here a disapproval of either liberalism or emancipation, he did accept the fact that these values had weakened. He also emphasized that the decline of liberalism stemmed from a crisis of European civilization, which should be analyzed and corrected.

Kecskeméti's new critical position toward liberalism was far from typical of the Neolog spokespeople, who as we shall see predominantly continued to cling to the traditional liberal narrative. Still, this change foreshadowed a process that other publicists would also go through during the decline of the status of the Jews in Europe generally and in Hungary specifically in the late 1930s.

Facing the First Jewish Law

In late 1937 the Jewish press in Hungary marked the seventieth anniversary of the emancipation of Hungarian Jewry following the compromise settlement with Austria in 1867. Various writers, chiefly in the liberal Neolog camp, which accounted for the majority of post-Trianon Hungarian Jewry, reviewed the process that had led to the enactment of what one had called "the Magna Carta of Hungarian Jewry."[34] As they were well aware of the contemporary struggles to preserve the achievements of emancipation, Jewish writers related to the Emancipation Law of 1867 not merely as the victory of one political camp but as a national decision by the Hungarian people.[35] The seventieth anniversary was also mentioned in speeches made at an assembly of the Budapest *kehillah* (Jewish community) in 1938. There it was more directly linked to the lack of confidence that typified the new era and the imminent threat to emancipation. "Only the grandeur of past history," one speaker declared, "can constitute a basis for our confidence in the future."[36]

The confidence of Hungarian Jews was already declining by 1937 due to local political developments. New Hungarian prime minister Kálmán Darányi stated clearly that Hungary indeed had a Jewish problem. It was necessary in his view to strike a balance between Jews and non-Jews in Hungarian economic life by passing legislation that would restrict the Jewish emancipation. At the same time, the increasing pressure of the extreme Right's grassroots anti-Semitism also contributed to the Jews' rising sense of impending danger. Along with attempts by community leaders to persuade top state officials to refrain from discriminatory legislation and to curb the violent anti-Semitism, Hungarian Jewry's spokespeople attempted to fight the anti-Semitic propaganda by appealing directly to public opinion in their newspapers and journals.

Various Hungarian Jewish periodicals described the struggle over shaping the past as an integral part of the Jews' broader political struggle for their civil status and their future. In early 1937, for example, *Egyenlőség* reported dangerous attempts by the Fascist Arrow Cross Party to revise Hungarian history and impugn the reputation of those who had emancipated the Jews in the nineteenth century. *Egyenlőség* urged Jewish organizations in Hungary to unite so as to defend the legacy of Kossuth, Petőfi, and the other heroes of the 1848 liberation struggle.[37] "It is a luxury," wrote István Virág (b. 1904) in *Libanon*, a more intellectual and scholarly journal, at approximately the same time, to claim today that historiography is a discipline in and of itself: "Nowadays, when false old slogans are being presented in a new form and used as the foundation of a new anti-Semitic wave, which attacks also Hungarian Jewry, it is crucial that the truths of historical science will be presented as a mighty weapon in the struggle to defend ourselves." Jewish history in Hungary, especially the history of the emancipation era, he continued, is particularly important at this time, when Hungarian Jewry is fighting for reemancipation, that is, the full reestablishment of liberal emancipation and a halt to the attempts to curb or repeal it.[38]

The adherence to the emancipation era was clearly expressed in the positions taken in the spring of 1938 during a public debate regarding the proposed law to limit the Jews' participation in Hungary's economic and cultural life. This law later came to be known as the First Jewish Law.[39] In a typical attempt to portray Jewish emancipation as a factor rooted in Hungarian history, one of the writers stressed in March of that year that the rights of Hungarian Jews had not been granted ex nihilo in 1867 and described at length how they had been awarded gradually, starting from the reign of Emperor Joseph II in the late eighteenth century.[40] The depiction of the Jews' status as being rooted in the national Hungarian heritage was also evident in an article marking March 15 (the memorial day for the Hungarian Revolution of 1848–49), which was observed in 1938 in the shadow of the grim news of the *Anschluss* in neighboring Austria and the discussion surrounding the First Jewish Law in Hungary. In view of the events that were reshaping world history, the article argued, the values of liberty, equality, and fraternity continue to beat in the breast of Hungary, which unlike its neighbors has not lurched to the Right.[41]

On the eve of the enactment of the First Jewish Law, the key political figures in Hungary certainly did not identify with these values. Even at that time, however, the adherence to the legacy of March 1848 by the Jewish columnist in the Neolog periodical *Zsidó Élet* was not devoid of a basis in Hungarian political culture. Since 1937, the columnist stated, "the ideas of March" had been the focal point of the activities of an anti-Fascist Hungarian political coalition—the Márciusi Front (March Front)—that opposed the political and military alliance with Nazi Germany and characterized it as an affront to the Hungarian national heritage.[42]

In April 1938 after the lower house of the Hungarian parliament passed the First Jewish Law, Lajos Szabolcsi (b. 1889), the editor of *Egyenlőség*, considered the most important periodical associated with the liberal Neolog stream, published an article titled "We Grieve."[43] The new statute, Szabolcsi asserted, had brought seventy years of emancipation to an end, and the Jews of Hungary should therefore mourn the end of the era of equality. *Egyenlőség* was founded by Szabolcsi's father, Miksa, who was considered a symbol of emancipation.

After discussing some of the practical effects of the new law on the economic future of Hungarian Jewry as well as questions about the future of the younger generation and the possibilities of emigration, Szabolcsi returned to the question of how to evaluate the seventy years of emancipation. In the spirit that was typical of most important personalities in the liberal Neolog camp—although not of all of them, as we shall see—Szabolcsi stated that the Jews had no regrets about what had happened during the period that had now come to an end. Indeed, he added, from now on the Jews would have to turn more inward and become more of a "Jewish fate community" (*zsidó sorsközösség*).[44] This, however, should not in any way be construed as a return to the ghetto, which the Jews had resolutely chosen to leave seventy years earlier.

After the bill was passed into law, Samu Stern (b. 1874), head of the Neolog community in Pest and president of the Neolog Communities of Hungary, published a pamphlet titled *The Jewish Question in Hungary*, which can be considered the official response of the liberal Neolog Jewish leadership to the new law.[45] The pamphlet's importance in our context is due to its systematic presentation of the Neolog conception of Hungarian Jewish history, a conception whose foundations were laid in the work of the late nineteenth-century historian Sámuel Kohn. Stern's historical outlook was based on the premise that Jews were not recently arrived migrants from abroad but instead were longtime residents of the homeland who had lived in Hungary before its conquest by the Magyar tribes in the ninth century. Moreover, Stern depicted the era of the founding of the Árpád dynasty that ruled Hungary until the early fourteenth century as the first golden age of Hungarian Jewry. At that time, he wrote, the Jews had many privileges and had made important contributions to the country. Hatred of Jews, Stern asserted—in much the manner of other Jewish writers at the time—had always been alien to the Hungarian national character: "From abroad, from the West, together with the Crusades, the initial elements of hatred of Jews infiltrated into the country. Anti-Semitism is not a Hungarian creation; to this day it is alien to the soul of the Hungarian people, which was tolerant since the times of the ancient occupation of the homeland. From abroad, from the West, primarily from Germany, the seeds of the hatred of the Jews penetrated here."[46]

Reflecting his reading of the situation in the spring of 1938, Stern portrayed medieval anti-Semitism as a movement of foreign ideas that had been imported to Hungary chiefly from Germany, where the rulers had repressed the Jews.[47] In Stern's view, the decline of the Hungarian national dynasty had deeply damaged the status of Jews in Hungary, but the real nadir for the Jews was the period following Hungary's defeat by the Turks at the Battle of Mohács in 1526, the event that marked the end of independent national Hungary, which was then partitioned between the Turks and the Habsburgs.[48]

In the wake of events following World War I, the defeat at Mohács became very important in the Hungarian national consciousness and memory.

In Szekfű's view of Hungarian history, for example, the era of the Turkish occupation was described as the source of all of Hungary's disasters and of the destruction of its national demographic fabric.[49] In Hungarian public opinion and among prominent users of history, a parallel was often drawn between the Mohács's defeat and the ensuing partition of Hungary and the Treaty of Trianon catastrophe—the breakup of historical Hungary after World War I—as the two darkest points in Hungarian history. The comparison also suggests that just as the country recovered from the first defeat, so would it be able to recover from the second. In his pamphlet, Stern applied these ideas to the Jewish context by drawing a parallel between the anti-Semitic repression in Hungary after Mohács and the outbreak of anti-Semitic hatred and the onset of discriminatory legislation—the *numerus clausus* law—after the Treaty of Trianon. He even asserted that the two disasters might have had an effect on the demographic decline of Hungarian Jewry.[50]

Stern was not alone in maintaining that the current emancipation crisis in Hungary was not unprecedented and that knowing the history of previous crises might enable the Jews to cope with their situation.[51] As we saw in the first part of this book, such historical interpretation was typical also of German Jewish liberal spokespeople (primarily Bruno Weil), who used it in order to come to terms with the emancipation's demise. When it seemed that the historical narrative centering on the idea of progress had lost its validity, liberal European Jews balked at the idea of accepting the opposite historical narrative, which depicted the emancipation era as an age of decline. Instead, they attempted to portray the current crisis as part of a lengthy historical process of ups and downs that characterized the dynamic of the Jews' integration into their surroundings or at least, as we saw with regard to France, to point to historical precedents.

The presentation of a cyclical historical view and the denial of the unique character of the decline of emancipation in the 1930s could nonetheless be articulated in various ways. Stern's cyclical perception of history had a pronounced apologetic tone and lacked any dimension of soul-searching. His pamphlet stressed the Jews' loyalty and contribution to Hungary, expressed no criticism of their behavior, and even portrayed the Dual Monarchy period as a golden age, an almost unblemished era of harmony and tranquility. Stern's tone and above all his apparent unwillingness to consider self-criticism prompted Nathaniel Katzburg to assert that "the old ideology of assimilation was capable neither of reassuring the Jewish community, nor of imbuing it with a new spirit at a time when Emancipation was collapsing."[52] Stern made no effort to offer any new meaning to the current events, and the strong contrast between his historical picture and the one that typified Hungarian society in the post-Trianon era (which viewed the liberal age as the source of all Hungary's woes) seriously hampered his ability to help Hungarian Jewry cope with their calamity. Evidently Stern, who was a businessman and public figure but not an intellectual, found it very hard to confront the demise of liberalism critically. His response was typical of the attitude of many of his supporters who belonged to the Hungarian Jewish Neolog bourgeoisie, which continued to adhere to the traditional formulas of emancipation.

A more critical attempt to explain the misfortune of Hungarian Jewry from a liberal Neolog viewpoint was made by Endre Sós (b. 1905), one of Budapest's outstanding Jewish essayists and journalists.[53] Sós based his assessment of Hungarian Jewry's situation on the broader perspective of Central and east European Jewry. He described the time of his writing (1938) as a "storm zone" (*viharzóna*) and attributed the suffering of the Jews of Germany, Austria, Romania, Hungary, and other countries to the pagan menace that was threatening to take over all of Europe. Realizing that the main counterforce to the growing Fascist-Nazi threat in Hungary was religion and not secular liberalism, Sós stressed the need to revive religion and to incorporate it into the efforts at social reform. This, he claimed, was how social Christianity had been established, in the same way that a social Judaism had to emerge.[54]

Sós depicted the crisis of Hungarian Jewry not only as the outcome of external pressure but also as an internal, primarily cultural, Jewish crisis. In this context, he compared Hungarian Jewry with German Jewry: while German Jewish writers such as Jakob Wassermann chose to present themselves as both Germans and Jews, Hungarian Jewish artists and writers in the age of emancipation tended to hide their Jewishness, a tendency that did much to fuel the Hungarian public's general disdain for the Jews. Sós offered his readers the example of the German Jewish Jüdischer Kulturbund. In the midst of oppression, this German Jewish organization was firmly resolved to maintain Jewish cultural life without enclosing the community in a ghetto. Sós advised Hungarian Jews to build cultural lives of their own before even harder times came upon them by bringing together the finest Hungarian Jewish art and by working to promote it.[55] Sós's call for change was rooted in criticism of the course of Hungarian Jewish history in the emancipation period, a criticism that would become more pointed a year later in response to the Second Jewish Law.

Zionists were much more inclined than liberal Neologs to attribute the crisis of Hungarian Jewry to its own actions and oversights. Zionist journalist and writer József Patai (b. 1882) was the editor of the monthly *Múlt és*

Jövő, which focused mainly on Jewish cultural affairs and maintained a readership beyond the narrow circle of the Zionist movement's members. Writing in a confessional style, he listed the sins of Hungarian Jewry, which, in his opinion, had brought the new law upon the community. He singled out the sin of shortsightedness for having duped them into regarding emancipation and equality as everlasting laws: "We have sinned in listening to false prophets when they declared that there was no more Jewish question, that there was no need for Jewish repentance, that there was no more Jewish hope and Jewish truth. For the sake of assimilation they had to detach themselves completely from any remnant of Jewish culture."[56]

Like the liberal Sós but in a far harsher tone, Patai criticized the Hungarian Jewish artists who had opposed Jewish culture. Among the sins of Hungarian Jewry he also counted the abandonment of Hebrew, the cool response to Theodor Herzl's vision, and even the grim fate of Jews in other countries and conversion, which, Patai asserted, was more rampant in Hungary than anywhere else. Patai proposed a solution that combined the Zionist vision of immigration to Palestine with a call for Jewish cultural autonomy in Hungary. In certain respects, Patai's vision of a Zionist revival was not essentially different from that of the non-Zionist Sós, as they both lauded the endeavors of the German Jewish Jüdischer Kulturbund as a role model for Hungarian Jewry. Patai immigrated to Palestine in 1939 but continued to be actively involved in the monthly *Múlt és Jövő* until 1944.

The similarity between Sós's vision of cultural revival and the Zionists' idea of cultural autonomy is even more apparent in an article by another Zionist, Lajos Fodor (b. 1883), who stressed that the Zionist call for the rebirth of a Jewish national entity (*népiség*) in Hungary should not be construed as opposition to "Hungarian life." Fodor expressed general criticism of the way Jews integrated into modern Western countries. Above all, he questioned the assumption that the Jewish question could be resolved by applying the principles of liberty, equality, and fraternity and by relinquishing the national (*népi*) component of the Jews' identity. Nevertheless, he did not call for uprooting the Jews from Europe but instead demanded the creation of a new basis for Jewish life within the European surroundings. The Jewish revival would lead to a solution of the "internal" Jewish question, Fodor asserted, and would thereby help solve the "external" Jewish question, that is, the Jews' status in Hungarian law.[57]

The Orthodox press, which reacted to the First Jewish Law in a manner similar to Samu Stern, stressed the Jews' patriotism, noted the antiquity of the Jewish presence in Hungary, and depicted the new law as contradictory in spirit to the foundations of the Hungarian constitution and the legacy of the great nineteenth-century Hungarian statesmen.[58] More interesting was a proposal by an anonymous Orthodox writer in early March 1938, following Prime Minister Darányi's pronouncement of the need to find a legislative solution to Hungary's Jewish problem.[59] In view of the new political atmosphere in Hungary and claiming that the era of liberal emancipation was over, the writer proposed redefining the status of Hungarian Jews in the spirit of the arrangements made by King Béla IV in the thirteenth century. The medieval king, argued the writer, had given the Jews privileges and letters of protection in return for their contribution in specific fields to the country's development. The writer portrayed a Hungary with a strong medieval Christian tradition that was much more established than the liberalism of the nineteenth century. It was this original Hungarian tradition, according to the writer, that inspired Casimir the Great when he made similar arrangements for the Jews of Poland. The Orthodox writer claimed that only an arrangement based on this tradition, which would be supported by Hungarian clergy, could ensure social harmony, restore the balance between Jews and Christians as the initiators of the anti-Semitic legislation demanded, and thereby stem the tide of pagan anti-Semitism in Hungary.

The Ninth Centenary of Saint Stephen and the Jews

In the spring and summer of 1938 Hungary celebrated the nine hundredth anniversary of the death of King Stephen, who according to Hungarian tradition had been crowned by the pope in the year 1000. The jubilee marked the culmination of a full year of events that had begun in the summer of 1937 during what the Hungarians called Saint Stephen's Year (Szent István év). Saint Stephen, who had always been a central symbol in Hungarian national consciousness, became a key icon in the reformation of post–World War I conservative Hungary.

In Horthy's Hungary in the early 1920s, August 20 (Saint Stephen's Day on the Catholic calendar) became a national holiday. The regent and the aristocratic elite around him used the founder-king's memory as a highly important instrument in their efforts to create an awareness of historical continuity that would legitimize their government's domestic and foreign policies. Saint Stephen symbolized Hungary's wide historical borders—Saint Stephen's Land—and his memory served as the basis for Hungary's irredentist ambitions. His persona was also the main element in the shift of Hungarian political culture to a more Christian religious direction after the decline of the secular liberalism of the Dual Monarchy era and the defeat of atheist Bolshevism in the quashing of Béla Kun's uprising.[60]

The destabilization of the Christian conservative government in Hungary in the early 1930s and, even more so, the perceptible ascendancy of Ferenc Szálasi's Arrow Cross Party in 1937 gave new meaning to the conservative elite's preoccupation with the legitimist tradition of Saint Stephen. Now, the persona of the founder-king and the legislative tradition attributed to him became a central symbol of traditional authority not only against the Bolshevist menace but also, and mainly, against the rising popularity of the new extreme Right. The latter drew inspiration from Nazi Germany and was depicted by its Catholic opponents as a neopagan threat to the future of Christian Europe.[61] This struggle between the conservative Christian Hungarian establishment and Fascism, as manifested by the Arrow Cross Party, culminated after the appointment of Béla Imrédy, one of the architects of the First Jewish Law, as prime minister of Hungary in May 1938. Imrédy battled the Arrow Cross Party directly and in July 1938 ordered the imprisonment of the party leader, Szálasi, an act that triggered a mass protest by Szálasi's supporters. The nine hundredth anniversary of Saint Stephen's death occurred at a time when the political and public struggle between these two factions of the Hungarian Right was at its peak.

It is important to emphasize that the struggle between the conservative Hungarian Right and the Fascist-Nazi extreme Right, as in the symbolism of Saint Stephen as well, was not solely an internal Hungarian affair. After the *Anschluss,* the Vatican believed that it was facing a far-reaching Nazi anti-Catholic campaign and considered Hungary the next target for a European-wide confrontation between Catholicism and Nazism. By deciding to hold the 1938 International Catholic Congress (Eucharisztikus Kongresszus) in Budapest in honor of the commemorative events for Saint Stephen, the Vatican intended to stress its view of Hungary as a bastion of Catholicism, a Regnum Marianum (Kingdom of Mary), that should be fortified against the dual threat to Christianity of godless Bolshevism and pagan Nazism. The fact that Adolf Hitler did not permit Catholic delegates from Germany and Austria to attend the congress in Budapest, which took place under official Hungarian patronage, only intensified the standoff.

Another aspect of the struggle for shaping the founder-king's image was reflected in the position of the largely Calvinist Protestant establishment, which was very wary of turning the national figure of King Stephen into a Catholic saint and his appropriation by the Vatican. In July 1938 the Calvinists organized a congress of their own in Debrecen (the center of Calvinism in Hungary, also known as the Hungarian Geneva), where they memorialized the first king primarily as a national figure for all of Hungary.[62]

Hungarian Jewish leaders themselves were hardly indifferent to the debates about the memory and legacy of King Stephen. These were an integral part of the political struggle that was so crucially important for them. The way they approached the subject clearly demonstrates their efforts to shape Hungarian history and heritage in light of their needs and worldviews, as the Catholics and Protestants tried to do. In addition, the Hungarian Jewish leaders repeatedly manifested concern, as Jews, about issues that pertained ostensibly only to Christians and Christianity.

The basic attitude of Hungarian Jewry toward the legacy of King Stephen was expressed in the speeches delivered at the assembly of the Budapest *kehillah* in January 1938. One of the speakers stressed the identification of Hungarian Jewry with the rest of the Hungarian nation—particularly with Catholics—and its struggle to fulfill the heritage of justice that the founder-king had set forth, that is, the war on paganism and extremism. The speaker asserted that Catholics, Protestants, and Jews—or, as he put it, worshippers who prayed in Latin, Hungarian, and Hebrew—were united under a patriotic banner that combined allegiance to "faith and homeland" (*hit és haza*), a patriotic monotheistic alliance against the pagan menace.[63] The Orthodox press expressed a similar attitude, portraying the International Catholic Congress as an important front in the monotheistic struggle that united all of Hungary.[64]

Following the International Catholic Congress and the final passing of the First Jewish Law, the Jewish press continued to focus on Saint Stephen and his legacy, perhaps with even greater attentiveness. An article in one of the liberal periodicals in early June 1938 stated that Saint Stephen's policy for Hungary had been based on the principle of settling the country with immigrants and tolerance toward the weak. This policy, the writer added, should remain in effect and should be instilled in the younger generation even after the festivities passed.[65]

Dezső Korein (b. 1870), a prominent Orthodox figure, went so far as to draw a parallel between the Catholic conference and the Jewish festival of Shavuot, which fell at roughly the same time. He argued that only through peace and an interfaith alliance could Hungary attain stability.[66] Bernát Heller (b. 1871), a teacher at the Neolog Rabbinical Seminary of Budapest, noted more directly the painful contrast between what was taken as the legacy of Saint Stephen's Hungarian rule of justice and the First Jewish Law. Heller's article compared the Treaty of Trianon, which Hungarian public opinion unanimously opposed, and the First Jewish Law. The article defined both of them as injustices that conflicted with the legacy of the founder-king. Although the ostensible purpose of these injustices was to provide justice to victims of discrimination (Romanians, Serbs, Slovaks, and Czechs in the case of the Treaty of Trianon and Christian Hungarians in the case of the First Jewish Law), in fact they were seriously—and unjustifiably—harmful to others (the Hungarians in the case of the Treaty of Trianon and the Jews in the case of the First Jewish Law).

In the spirit of the tendency to trace all of Hungary's woes to German influence, Heller alleged that there was a contradiction between the humanistic legacy of Saint Stephen and the more parochial patrimony bequeathed by Charlemagne, the medieval lawgiver of the German tribes. The Hungarian legislation enacted by the first king was formulated in conjunction with the bishops and the subjects, asserted Heller, and thus emerged as a tradition that could not be reconciled with the practices of contemporary dictators, a clear allusion to Hitler and perhaps even to Szálasi's pretensions.[67]

Ernő Munkácsi (b. 1896), the director of the Jewish museum in Budapest and a major spokesman for the liberal Neolog stream, addressed himself frequently to historical issues. Munkácsi subjected Saint Stephen's legacy for Hungarian Jewry to a systematic discussion and interpretation. Before the official memorial day for the founder-king, Munkácsi wrote that Saint Stephen was an important personality not only for Christians but also for the adherents of all accepted religions in Hungary: "The association of Hungarian Jewry with the ideas of Saint Stephen's Land is essentially based on a history of communal life. Members of our faith and blood have resided here as early as the days of the Hungarian king and were already among the supporters of the motherland. . . . If we seek Saint Stephen's political ideas, we have to turn first and foremost to his own laws."[68]

In a description that reflected his view of the situation in Hungary in 1938, Munkácsi contended that Saint Stephen's legislative heritage had developed under pressure from the neighboring German states to the west and dangers from the east. Munkácsi also pointed to similarities between the principles of Saint Stephen's regime and the liberal national principles of nineteenth-century Hungary: "Saint Stephen's kingdom was not based on a racial concept [*faji*] but on the national [*nemzeti*] idea. A common fate [*sorsközösség*], a common culture, love for the motherland, the life in the same state in a real bond and the readiness to sacrifice money and shed blood for it—all these make a group of people into a nation. This is the fundamental idea of the national historic Hungarian constitution: the worldview of the holy crown."[69]

Munkácsi argued that these were the political ideas that had developed in Hungary during the Árpád dynasty (from the eleventh century until the early fourteenth century) and had remained central themes in the fourteenth and fifteenth centuries. They had been put to the test—successfully—when one of the Árpád kings closed the borders to an embittered Christian rabble during the Crusades and another king granted Jews political rights at a time when no other European ruler did so. It was only the Mohács calamity that had had such a devastating effect on the nature of the country and deprived the Jews of the historical rights that they had enjoyed since Saint Stephen's time.[70]

The positions expressed by Munkácsi and other Jewish writers about the legacy of Saint Stephen were rooted largely in the liberal integration ideology of the second half of the nineteenth century.[71] However, they were not totally divorced from attitudes found in certain Christian circles in Hungary in the late 1930s. Jewish writers were aware of the use made by Christians—particularly Catholics—of the first king specifically and of Hungarian history generally against Fascism.

In the absence of any real secular, liberal power center on which they could rely—the type of center that had existed in the late nineteenth century—Jewish writers tended to probe the Catholic Church's positions again and again. Two weeks after his article on the legacy of King Stephen appeared, Munkácsi made note of comments by the pope against racism and mentioned the universal interpretation that the pope had lent to the concept of Catholic as race laws in Italy were being debated.[72] The Orthodox Dezső Korein also tried to base his arguments on the antiracist voices emanating from the Vatican and even to anchor them in what he described as the traditional opposition of the medieval popes to anti-Semitism.[73]

Recourse to the Hungarian historical legacy as a tool against Nazi influence was characteristic not only of the clerical establishment but also of other Hungarian groups. At the time, Hungarian rulers and elites tended to favor an alliance with Nazi Germany in the belief that only through such an alliance could Hungary regain the territories that it had lost in the Treaty of Trianon. However, Hungarian intellectuals, who were increasingly averse to the Nazi propaganda and considered its penetration in Hungary a menace to the country's Christian middle class, endeavored to evoke the Hungarian past—especially the Christian national age of the Middle Ages—in order to mount a spiritual national defense (*szellemi honvédelem*) against this propaganda. One of the most prominent activists in this field was the historian Gyula Szekfű.

As noted above, about two decades earlier Szekfű had depicted Hungary as part of a German Christian civilization and expressed unambiguous anti-Semitic views. From the mid-1930s on, however, he displayed disapproval of

Nazism, mainly of its biological-racist ideas. At this time Szekfű, along with other Hungarian intellectuals tended to stress the uniqueness of the Hungarian national tradition in contrast to the past and present German world. In his growing opposition to racism, Szekfű stated that the Hungarian nation had acquired its collective character through the adoption of common cultural traditions by diverse ethnic groups that coexisted through tolerance. The medieval Hungarian kings, he added, had made it their policy to protect the national minorities who lived under their rule.[74]

There was no essential difference between this approach and the attitudes of Munkácsi, Heller, and other Jewish spokespeople, although they emphasized primarily the Jewish angle. These Jewish publicists could therefore find justification for their view that the anti-Jewish laws were a deviation from the mainstream Hungarian national legacy. Some of them also expressed similar positions regarding the international circumstances pertaining to Hungary in the late 1930s. The portrayal of Hungary as a country that had been pinioned between the cruel Turkish power and the foreign German influence in the sixteenth and seventeenth centuries—a view that was typical of the opposition circle that gathered around Szekfű during those years—was therefore also articulated by a Jewish writer who termed Hungarians and Jews "partners in distress" vis-à-vis these forces.[75]

Reexamining Emancipation and Assimilation in View of the Second Jewish Law

The plight of Hungarian Jewry took a severe turn for the worse in the spring of 1939, when the Second Jewish Law was passed. While the First Jewish Law was meant to ensure "greater balance" in Hungarian social and economic life, the new statute imposed much tougher restrictions on the Jews and marked a perceptible escalation at the rhetorical level as well. Furthermore, the new statute defined the term "Jew" in racist terms, stating that even people who had been converted to Christianity after August 1919 (when Béla Kun's Communist regime was overthrown) would be considered Jewish.[76]

On January 1, 1939, the authorities shut down the main organs of Hungarian Jewry—foremost among them the long-standing liberal Neolog *Egyenlőség* and the Orthodox *Zsidó Újság*. However, both of the new journals that were founded then—the *Magyar Zsidók Lapja* (Journal of Hungarian Jews) on the Neolog side and the *Orthodox Zsidó Újság* (Orthodox Jewish Newspaper)—turned out to be rather unrestricted forums of expression for Hungarian Jews. These publications highlighted the Jews' struggle for their rights and provided a platform for the coping and soul-searching efforts of leading Jews in response to the grim developments.[77] It is noteworthy that the reactions of Neolog and modern Orthodox spokespeople at this stage were not fundamentally different. Publicists from both groups associated themselves with similar political values even when their modes of expression were at times quite dissimilar.

In April 1939 shortly before the upper house of the Hungarian parliament ratified the Second Jewish Law, a contributor to the new Orthodox newspaper made an unusual comparison. He argued that the grim events in Germany and Austria—which he construed a reversion to the Crusader attacks that had swept through the towns of the Rhineland in 1096—and the bill that Hungary was about to legislate were reminiscent of difficult Jewish memories during the period of the counting of the Omer (between Passover and Shavuot). According to another article in the same issue of the newspaper, the contents and, no less important, the phrasing of the law pointed to the end of an era in the history of Hungarian Jewry. Both writers, however, continued to cling to what they considered the Hungarian tradition and the true Hungarian spirit, and in an act of parting of sorts they expressed their gratitude to all the Hungarian politicians, past and present, who had promoted Jewish rights.[78]

Bidding farewell to a bygone era while concurrently adhering to the Hungarian Jewish historical heritage as a source of consolation and hope were also expressed in graphic and emotive language in May 1939 in an article in the new Neolog journal. Under these circumstances, the encounter with the text of the 1867 Emancipation Law during a visit to the Jewish Historical Museum evoked in the writer's mind glum reflections regarding the upheavals of the Jewish fate. Later, however, he also expressed thoughts of hope and comfort:

> How eras pass and the spirit of the ages changes, I thought to myself. How the Jewish fate is decided. How the happy days come to an end so rapidly, and long eras, deeply shadowed, follow the short periods of light. I heaved a big sigh. Suddenly a stranger looked at me as though he was reading my thoughts. He told me: "Don't sigh. The seventy-one years and five days that stand between these two laws will have to be examined from a historical perspective. . . . There is no better place than the Jewish museum to try to understand the upheavals of fate. Look—he continued to speak, now with an pedagogical and confident voice—every document here, since the age of the

Árpád dynasty, describes how ages of our agony were always, ultimately, followed by bright days."[79]

An article by Ernő Munkácsi exemplifies the challenge of reexamining Hungarian Jewish history in light of the turnabout embodied in the Second Jewish Law. In his response to the First Jewish Law, Munkácsi had claimed that one might view the statute as only an "outward offense" of the Jewish interest in the general welfare; it did not necessarily contradict the principle of equality. The Second Jewish Law, however, he said, marked a historic turnaround and returned Hungarian Jewry to the pre-1867 period, to the era preceding the reforms of Josef II in the late eighteenth century.[80]

While Munkácsi admitted that the emancipation, which had been won after centuries of struggle, belonged to the past, he urged Hungarian Jews—in a manner similar to that of liberal Jewish spokespeople in Germany a few years earlier—to continue to struggle for a new emancipation. It is also necessary, he said, to reject the Hungarian legislature's assertion that a Jew is unassimilable (*asszimilálatlan*) as long as he adheres to his ancient faith. In order to assess the new historical situation of Hungarian Jewry and its struggle for survival, the two key concepts of the preceding era—emancipation and assimilation—therefore needed to be reelucidated.

Munkácsi explained his own views on these issues in two additional articles. He dismissed the racist anthropological definition of the term "nation," which indeed implied that Jews were not assimilable. Instead, he described assimilation as a process by which groups of diverse origins and religious backgrounds integrate into the Hungarian nation and culture and become partners in Hungarian fate.[81] He defended his belief that a Jew could assimilate (*asszimilált*) sufficiently—that is, well enough that the new Hungarian law would allow him to retain his rights—even without converting to Christianity. True Christianity, the kind that is inspired by religious conviction, could be a path to assimilation, he admitted, but it was not the only path. Furthermore, those who thought that they had found their own solution to the Jewish question by having themselves baptized for opportunistic reasons had actually chosen a path desired neither by the state nor by the church, who were, after all, the main players at the focal point of the Jewish question.[82]

One reflection of the public debate surrounding the reassessment of the emancipation in Hungary was the appearance of the term "new emancipation." This term, which had already been used in some liberal Neolog responses to the First Jewish Law, suggested that a new formula for the integration of Hungarian Jewry might be possible. Even then, one of the Zionists objected. A new emancipation, asserted Lipót Sás in 1938, cannot be achieved if the Hungarian people do not accept it, and they will not accept it as long as the Jews continue to deny their origins.[83] Only love of the soil of Palestine and immigration by young Jews to that country might make the Hungarian people emotionally receptive to those Jews who choose to remain in Hungary. Developments in Hungary, Sás continued, proved that the idea of emancipation as a practical barter arrangement involving the forfeiture of cultural values was ill-fated from the start. He concluded that conditioning emancipation on assimilation was the cause of its failure.

From the Orthodox perspective, an interesting struggle over these concepts appeared in an article published by Dezső Korein several weeks after *Kristallnacht*. German Jewry, he asserted, was in the throes of "unhealthy assimilation" (*beteges asszimiláció*) and "hyperassimilation"; many Jews in Germany had embraced German culture slavishly until the entire edifice collapsed around them like a house of cards. What concerns us, he added, is not the past per se but the lesson that Hungarian and all of the world's Jewry could learn from the appalling tragedy of German Jewry. Korein then steered his readers toward the conclusion—which was fundamentally similar to that of Neolog spokespeople—not to abandon the road to assimilation totally but instead to moderate its course. Korein urged Jews to oppose "religious assimilation," which he blamed for the calamity of German Jewry, but he presented "national assimilation," including the cultural integration of Hungarian Jews and their loyalty to Hungary, in a positive manner.[84]

This tension between a fundamental aversion to the idea of assimilation—that is, the renunciation of the Jewish faith—on the one hand and principled acceptance of assimilation as an expression of integration on the other hand was expressed in an article by another Orthodox writer, Jenő Groszberg (b. 1894), in March 1939. Groszberg praised the Jews of the Middle Ages for adhering to the true faith and resisting assimilation but tried to refute the Hungarian anti-Semites' argument that Jewish assimilation constituted a deviation from Hungarian history.[85]

The Orthodox found it easier to subject the processes of emancipation and assimilation to critical analysis, since in most instances they placed the blame for past mistakes at the door of the liberal Neolog majority. The liberal Neologs tended to portray the reversal in the condition of Hungarian Jewry as an injustice inflicted on loyal Hungarian Jews or as the result of an unstoppable global process. However, when the crisis intensified in 1939 and particularly after the shock of the Second Jewish Law, certain liberal Neolog writers themselves gradually began to treat the history of the emancipation era more critically. This certainly narrowed the gap between them and the Orthodox spokespeople.

Several months after the Second Jewish Law was passed, Endre Sós, a writer of liberal Neolog origin, wrote a hard-hitting article on assimilation among Hungarian Jews. As discussed above, in 1938 Sós had spoken forcefully about the pressing need to develop an autonomous Jewish cultural life in Hungary. Now he published an anthology of stories by Hungarian Jewish writers that he had edited. In his preface, written in 1939, he addressed the difficult subject of conversion to Christianity. In contrast to Munkácsi, Sós claimed that conversion and the idea of assimilation on which it was based were not a minority aberration but instead reflected a widespread phenomenon typical of an era he called "the decades of false understanding of assimilation."[86] In his attempt to present his own position on the matter, Sós asserted:

> We, too, are motivated by and follow a natural and realistic process of assimilation[;] . . . we too acknowledge that only he who feels Hungarian and joins the Hungarian nation totally, for the good and for the bad, could enjoy his rights and live a full life in Hungary. However, the Hungarian sentiment, at its most virtuous, and the intensive Hungarian communal life are not dependent on any religious framework, group of origin or national-ethnic [népi] association. . . . The natural and realistic assimilation must not strive to contradict religious values, to dismantle racial bonds or to dissolve national forces. On the contrary! Countries and nations [nemzetek] that aspire to realistic assimilation, strive, out of their own interest, to adequately preserve all the religious energies, the racial diversity and the national passions and, if needed, to recruit them for the right aims.[87]

Sós chose his words deliberately. From now on his comments, like those of several other liberal Neolog writers, would express the understanding that the Jewish experience is not only a religious one and that its national-ethnic dimension should not be denied, even when it is integrated in the Hungarian nation.

The tragedy of modern Hungarian Jewry, according to Sós, was that Jews, unlike members of other groups, were being forced to deny their religious, ethnic, and national background in order to take part in the culture of their country of birth. "We Jews of Hungary," Sós responded to remarks by one Jewish parliamentary representative as the bill was being debated, "were good Hungarians and bad Jews."[88] The Jewish public, Sós said, had divorced itself from its Jewish roots and had lost its Jewish spine. As can be inferred from his words, herein lay at least some of the reasons for the calamity that now had to be endured.

In spite of the fact that Sós's position was fundamentally different from that of the official Neolog leadership as well as from that of many Orthodox spokespeople who continued to see the Jews as followers of the Mosaic faith only, Sós did not become a Zionist. He continued to believe in the integration of the Jews into the Hungarian nation. However, the ideological gap between him and those Zionists who developed a more Diasporic Jewish nationalism became narrowed considerably.

Remarks made in late 1939 by Rabbi Yehiel Michael (Mihály) Hacohen Guttmann (b. 1872), a teacher at the Neolog Rabbinical Seminary of Budapest, provide another critical perspective on the age of emancipation. Writing in the Hebrew section of the seminary yearbook, Rabbi Guttmann described the period as "a time when the gates of Emancipation closed on the Jews of Central Europe and on some of those in the northeastern corner [of the continent]." He explained in retrospect the nature of "that enlightened age, which took the Jewish world by storm at the time and now is quite suddenly sentenced to death due to hatred of Judaism."[89] The first generation to experience emancipation, Guttmann claimed, was so delighted with the turnabout in its destiny that it fully believed in the stability and moral strength of the age and felt that it rested on firm foundations: "After all, all the Jews have trusted the Emancipation because of its sublime moral content; they all saw the demolition of the ghetto's walls as a kind of historical restoration, since they did not receive at that time new rights, only the rights of which they were deprived in the Middle Ages."[90] This, in Guttmann's view, was the Jews' first mistake. Their second mistake, he continued, was their excessive eagerness to exercise their rights immediately and absolutely, a passion that prompted many of them to renounce basic Jewish principles and turn Judaism into "merchandise with a price tag."[91] Similar to the presentation offered by Joachim Prinz of Germany, Guttmann noted the unexpected abruptness of the Jews' departure from the ghetto and their lack of maturity in seeking a balanced integration in the modern era.

Guttmann went on to claim that those who had taken this path—particularly the extremists who had converted to Christianity—were the ones who had in fact prompted the anti-Semites to invent the racist creed. Ironically, this doctrine was turning them and their descendants into full-fledged

Jews now that the honeymoon of emancipation was over. The third mistake, which Guttmann characterized as the greatest mistake that the Jews had made during the emancipation era, was the *Kulturkampf* between enlightened and ultra-Orthodox Jews, two opposing extremes. Modern Jews were fragmented along party lines and could not achieve unity. Guttmann did not refer specifically to Hungarian Jewry, but there exists in his words an appeal to this community—certainly the best-known community in the Jewish world for its internal religious polarization—to join forces in this new grim situation.[92]

The erosion in the civil status of Hungarian Jewry therefore led Guttmann to present emancipation as a historical path that was bound to fail, almost inevitably, from the beginning. But this was only a minority voice in the Hungarian Jewish discourse of that time. Other spokespeople—both Neolog and Orthodox—continued to believe in the principles of emancipation and assimilation and therefore tended to present their decline as a consequence of wrong and unbalanced implementation. It was not emancipation as such that had failed. The problem, in their estimation, was that emancipation was associated with the wrong kind of assimilation and was thus unable to engender a genuine balance between Jewish and Hungarian identity. They believed that if this balance was more effectively realized in the future, the foundation for integrating the Jews within the Hungarian nation would be restored.

Conclusion

Out of concern for shaping the image of the past, those who spoke for Hungarian Jewry in the late 1930s endeavored to legitimize emancipation vis-à-vis the threats with which they had to cope. They therefore portrayed the emancipatory legislation as rooted in the Hungarian national tradition and anchored in the political thought and action of the forebears of the Hungarian nation since the time of Saint Stephen. These spokespeople also repeatedly stressed Hungarian Jewry's loyalty to their country and the roots they had set down there since time immemorial. By contrast, the spokespeople depicted the dangers confronting Hungarian Jews since the Crusades as having derived from foreign sources, particularly Germany. In this vein, they portrayed the processes of decline and crisis in the status of Jews in Hungary as but one aspect of the crisis that had beset Hungarian national life since the post–World War I catastrophe, successive reflections, as it were, of the dreadful crisis that Hungarians and Jews had experienced after the defeat at Mohács some four centuries earlier. This representation of the Jewish past in

Hungary and in particular the attitude to the unique Hungarian legacy, as opposed to that of Germany, were not expressed in a vacuum. Rather, they were consistent, at least in part, with ideas that were current among anti-Nazi Hungarian opposition circles at the time.

In the Hungarian Jewish discourse on the past, as in the modern Hungarian political culture in general, a major place was devoted to the Middle Ages.[93] Of course, Jewish spokespeople had also dealt with nineteenth-century history and national heroes. Still, in comparison to France, where the Jewish usable past was focused primarily on the events and implications of the French Revolution, and to Germany, whose Jewish spokespeople had concentrated on the Enlightenment and emancipation, Hungarian Jewish writers tended more toward discussing the Middle Ages. Furthermore, unlike most Jewish writers in Germany and France, many Hungarian Jewish spokespeople emphasized their homeland's Christian legacy rather than its liberal tradition as the main barrier to the penetration of anti-Semitism—particularly racial anti-Semitism as developed under Nazism—within their homeland.

These forms of discourse on the past reflected the political power shift in Hungary since the early 1920s: the marginalization of the Left and the liberals and the fact that only the conservative Catholic Right, whose sources of inspiration were in the Middle Ages, could offer substantial resistance to the threat of Nazi Fascism.

The shaping of historical awareness also served the community's internal needs, which had become increasingly important as the isolation of Hungarian Jewry intensified. Invariably the decline in their confidence in the emancipation and in the idea of progress in general motivated them to look to the past for support and consolation. When they realized that the present carried ominous overtones for the future, they looked to the past for signs of the cyclical character of their situation, perhaps in order to draw hope that the wheel of fortune would spin in a more propitious direction.[94] Some also stressed the special importance of teaching Jewish history to young people as a part of molding their Jewish identity and preparing them to cope with the harsh circumstances of the life that lay ahead.[95]

Sociologist Viktor Karády claimed that the various strategies of identity formation pursued by Hungarian Jewry in the late 1930s—that is, to remain attached to Hungary, to dissimilate (as the Zionists urged), and to rely on a universal ideology—were all postassimilatory.[96] He argued that although these approaches were based in one way or another on the conceptual and cultural heritage of the age of assimilation, it was necessary at the same time to reevaluate that heritage. In the same way, in this chapter we have shown how Hungarian Jewish spokespeople, primarily liberal Neologs, who were forced to acknowledge little by little that the age of liberal emancipation had ended tried to reaffirm the concepts of emancipation and assimilation by reexamining them for possible new facets.

Some of those who reassessed history did so with the recognition that Hungarian Jewry, or perhaps modern European Jewry in general, bore partial responsibility for the disaster that had befallen them. Those who adopted this approach availed themselves of the past—primarily the emancipation period—to note mistakes that had been made and to call for lessons to be learned. The Zionists, for whom criticism of the emancipation era was a hallmark of their worldview, were the most naturally inclined to do this. The Orthodox too, who stood outside the mainstream of interwar Hungarian Jewry, found it relatively easy to fault secularization and estrangement from tradition and therefore urged Hungarian Jews to return to religious observance.

This tendency, however, did not characterize only spokespeople of these two sectors. As we have seen in this chapter, certain liberal Neolog writers, such as Sós and Guttmann, that the sectors to which they belonged had traditionally viewed the emancipation era as a golden age, tended now to examine it more critically. As we shall see in the next chapter, this tendency continued and even strengthened during the deterioration in the situation of Hungarian Jews in the early 1940s.

6

IN THE SHADOW OF THE HOLOCAUST

In the short term, the outbreak of World War II had little influence on the life and status of Hungarian Jews. This was because the country—despite its diplomatic treaty with Germany—was not really involved in the war. In the last months of 1939 and the first months of 1940, Hungarian Jews were thus coping primarily with the repercussions of the Second Jewish law, which had a severe impact on their economic strength. The course of anti-Jewish legislation was renewed in the summer of 1941 under Prime Minister Bárdossy. The Third Jewish Law, which banned marriage between Jews and non-Jews, was a clear expression of the regime's rejection of the very idea of Jewish assimilation into the Hungarian nation.

Parallel to this development, Hungarian Jewry was transformed as a result of the return of territories that had been lost in World War I to Hungarian rule. Due to its treaty with Nazi Germany, Hungary had already annexed southern Slovakia in November 1938 and Carpathian Ruthenia in March 1939. These annexations augmented the Jewish population by 146,000 and changed the character of the Jewish community as a whole. The transformation was exacerbated when northern Transylvania, consisting of around 164,000 Jews, was returned to Hungary in August 1940. And the process was completed with the April 1941 annexation of territories from Yugoslavia, with an additional 14,000 Jews.[1] Hungarian Jewry, which numbered around 401,000 people in early 1938, had thus grown to 725,000 by the spring of 1941.

The Jews in the annexed territories were generally more traditional than their coreligionists living within the 1938 borders, and they also lived in more crowded Jewish communities. Many of them still spoke Hungarian and were attached to the Hungarian culture, but the two decades of their political separation from Hungary had found expression in a new national Jewish political culture, which influenced their views on Hungarian nationalism and Jewish memory culture alike.[2]

An important turning point that also had an impact on the fate of Hungarian Jews was Hungary's entry into the war on the side of the Axis powers following the Nazi invasion of the Soviet Union. In August 1941 Hungary became directly involved in the Final Solution when some eighteen thousand Jews with foreign citizenship were expelled from its territory to Galicia. There most of them were murdered by the Germans with the assistance of Hungarian soldiers.[3]

The recruitment of thousands of Jewish men into the Hungarian labor service under harsh conditions was another ominous sign for the future of Hungarian Jewry. Furthermore, the foundations of Jewish emancipation in Hungary were greatly weakened by the abolition of the 1895 Law of Reception that had regulated the status of the Jewish religion in Hungary as equal to that of the Christian churches. This enactment brought to an end most of the state support to Jewish communities by the summer of 1942 and also banned Christians from converting to Judaism.[4]

In spite of these developments that resulted in the growing social isolation and economic decline of Hungarian Jews, they remained in a fundamentally much better situation than their brethren in the neighboring countries. The Arrow Cross Party—the Hungarian force that seemed to epitomize the existential threat to their future—was weakened in the early 1940s, and Hungary's ruling conservative elite did not give in to the Nazi pressures concerning the Jewish question in Hungary. Even after the legal offensive on their position, both major Jewish communities—the Neolog and the Orthodox—continued to function. They were still able to publish their journals and also conducted quite extensive social welfare activities.

The government of Miklós Kállay, which took over in March 1942, had tried to moderate Hungary's pro-German orientation. As a result, the Christian conservative character of Hungarian state anti-Semitism became more prominent, and the gap between it and Nazi racial anti-Semitism widened. This changed with the March 1944 Nazi occupation.[5]

In contrast to the German Jewish and French Jewish cases, Hungarian Jewish conceptualizations and representations of the past, from the outbreak of the war in the autumn of 1939 until the Nazi conquest of Hungary in the spring of 1944, permit us to examine the Jewish historical discourse based on the emancipation narrative during the Holocaust years. It is difficult to determine what the leaders of Hungarian Jewry in the early 1940s knew about the tragic fate of other Jews in Nazi-occupied territories, but it is clear that they could not have been entirely disconnected from these events. Jewish refugees from the neighboring countries naturally contributed to the rising awareness of the atrocities taking place beyond the border.[6]

All in all, in spite of the fact that Hungarian Jews were isolated in Nazi occupied Europe during the harshest years of the mass murder of their brethren, it seems that the vast majority of Jews in Hungary as well as their public spokespeople believed that the catastrophic fate of the Jews in the neighboring countries would elude them. It also appears that the very fact that such atrocities remained beyond the border (until early 1944) strengthened their faith that their fate would be different, a faith that was supported by their historical memory. The Hungarian Jewish public agenda, as it was expressed in a variety of communal periodicals and publications, was generally concentrated within the borders of their homeland; most Hungarian Jews truly believed that Hungary would preserve its sovereignty. Their press therefore did not relate much at all to the tragic developments beyond the border.

The external and internal censorship to which the Jewish press in Hungary was subjected must also be considered. The freedom of expression of the writers in the Jewish press and literature was more limited than during the prewar years, yet it seems that they were still relatively free, primarily with regard to internal Jewish matters.[7] On the other hand, in response to the progressive isolation of Jews in Hungary, which involved being cut off almost entirely from Hungary's public life and the nearly exclusive concentration of Jewish spokespeople on internal Jewish matters, the Jewish press related much less to Hungarian politics and foreign policy. From a typological perspective, there are four forms of Hungarian Jewish historical narrative in this period. Thus, we can speak about the common narrative of the Neolog establishment's spokespeople, about an additional group of intellectuals from a Neolog background that developed a more critical liberal narrative, and about the historical interpretations that were expressed by Hungarian Orthodox spokespeople and by Zionist and Jewish nationalist writers. Such a typological perspective may help point to various parallels between certain usable-past strategies employed by Hungarian Jews in the early 1940s, in comparison to those of German Jewish and French Jewish spokespeople.

Hungarian Nationalism and Jewish Patriotism:
The Neolog Perspective

In February 1940 the Neolog journal *Magyar Zsidók Lapja* marked the centennial anniversary of the legislation that had led to Jewish emancipation in Hungary. The law that was enacted by the Hungarian Diet in 1840 was described as the point of departure for the process that continued with the bestowal of equality to the Jews in 1849 during the Hungarian Revolution of 1848–49 and was finally completed with the Law of Emancipation (1867) and the Law of Reception (1895).[8] Ernő Ballagi, one of the prominent Neolog spokespeople, published a more systematic overview of the historical background of this anniversary in the annual published by the Hungarian Jewish literary society. Ballagi described the path to Hungarian Jewish emancipation from the late eighteenth century until 1867 as the result of the noble worldview and initiatives of prominent Hungarian statesmen and thinkers. Their support for Jewish integration contrasted with the conservative Austrian policy. Hungarian Jews, from their perspective, had also chosen the Hungarian nation: "from the beginning, the Jews viewed Hungarianness as a safe anchor for their rights vis-à-vis the Viennese court."[9]

Ballagi's article revealed how Neolog writers continued after the Second Jewish Law and also during the war in Europe to embrace the national liberal narrative of emancipation that linked the liberation of the Jews with the realization of Hungarian national sovereignty. In a similar fashion, March 15 was marked by special articles and speeches that combined Hungarian national pride with an emphasis on the patriotism of the Jews from the Hungarian Revolution of 1848–49 until World War I. Even in 1944 a few days before the German occupation, Neolog spokespeople continued to associate March 15 with Hungarian national independence and freedom and joined those who used this historical symbol to oppose cooperation with Nazi Germany.[10]

The efforts by Jewish spokespeople to balance their support for the Hungarian national cause on the one hand and their sensitivity to the status of the Jews on the other hand was expressed in their attitude toward the Treaty of Trianon (1920), which had forced Hungary to surrender an extensive part of its historic fatherland. In June 1940 the Jewish journal *Képes Családi Lapok* (Illustrated Family Journal) published an article to mark the twentieth anniversary of the treaty. Whereas the Hungarian defeat at the hands of the Turks at the Battle of Mohács (1526) was the result of internal struggles that had weakened Hungary, asserted an anonymous writer, the Treaty of Trianon was the outcome of a military defeat by foreign powers. In response to accusations that the Jews were responsible for the disintegration of Hungary at the end of World War I and for the Treaty of Trianon, the writer offered his own explanation as to what had led to the *numerus clausus* law and to other forms of discrimination against Jews. As a Hungarian national and as a Jew, he argued that Hungary's national humiliation was also the source of the humiliation of the Jews: "We should not forget that there is a source that nourishes the elimination of our rights and [our] humiliation: Trianon."[11] The degradation of the Jews was therefore only a reflection of the fundamental humiliation of Hungarian nationalism that resulted from the Treaty of Trianon, which led to the distortion of Hungarian nationalism.

Another writer asserted a few months later in the *Képes Családi Lapok* that the legacy of Saint Stephen delineated not only the territorial borders of the fatherland but also its fundamental values. The Treaty of Trianon had therefore damaged not only the territorial integrity of Hungary but also the idea that the Hungarian nation was based on the integration of the various peoples of which it was comprised, including the Jews. Whereas the anti-Semites presented the exclusion of the Jews as the key to Hungary's national rehabilitation, this Jewish writer expressed the opposite position and presented this very exclusion as a manifestation of the decline of the original Hungarian national character.[12]

The adherence of the Neolog spokespeople to the Hungarian national past was also expressed by their use of national heroes and their association with the Jewish question. István Széchenyi, the most prominent Hungarian statesman of the Reform age (the second quarter of the nineteenth century), had generally supported the integration of minorities. Yet he had expressed his reservation about the naturalization of the Jews in Hungary because of their relatively large number. In the early 1840s Széchenyi compared the Jews who were integrated into Western countries to a bottle of ink poured into a lake. But in Hungary, he insisted, this will be like pouring ink into a pot of soup: the soup will be spoiled.[13] In spite of this famous statement, often cited by Hungarian anti-Semites, an editorial published in the *Magyar Zsidók Lapja* in August 1941 presented Széchenyi as pro-Jewish. This attempt to associate the great Hungarian reformer with the values of the Jewish emancipation was supported by other statements by Széchenyi in addition to his personal respect for certain Jewish individuals.[14]

Another Hungarian national hero to whom Jewish spokespeople often related was Lajos Kossuth, the leader of the Hungarian Revolution of 1848–49. Kossuth's ambivalence concerning Jewish emancipation—on the one hand his support in principle but on the other hand his assertive requirement that the Jews relinquish any sign of religious and cultural distinctiveness that might separate them from the Hungarian nation—could be interpreted in different ways. Adherents of the Fascist Arrow Cross Party depicted him as an anti-Semite, whereas Jewish spokespeople strove to refute this claim.[15] On March 16, 1944, a few days before the conquest of Hungary by the Nazis, an editorial in the *Magyar Zsidók Lapja* referred to Kossuth on the fiftieth anniversary of his death as the figure "whose name represents forever the ideals of national independence, the nation's freedom, general and proportionate sharing of taxation and equality before the law. Kossuth is a person who became an idea; there are only a few like him in world history."[16]

The nineteenth-century Hungarian statesman who was most identified with the emancipation was József Eötvös. In the summer of 1940 the Jewish press marked the one hundredth anniversary of his essay on Jewish emancipation. It is true, Ballagi asserted, that some of Eötvös's ideas had become outdated, but his deep love for the excluded Jews of his time was not out of date. A hundred years ago, Ballagi added, it was clear that those who struggled against the emancipation were primarily materialistic and narrow-minded, whereas the wider interest of the nation's development was linked to the integration of the Jews. This was a clear indication of Ballagi's view of the situation in 1940.[17] In February 1941 the editors of the *Magyar Zsidók Lapja* commemorated the seventieth anniversary of Eötvös's passing by describing him as "our closest friend in Hungary of the previous century." They also published a segment from his 1840 essay, "the nicest words ever written for us and for our freedom."[18]

In March 1942 the legacy of Eötvös and of the generation of the 1840s was subjected to a more critical examination. It is a common error, asserted writers of the *Magyar Zsidók Lapja,* to equate the Reform era with the rise of liberalism and the attainment of Jewish emancipation without a struggle. Eötvös and his allies had to combat a very powerful opposition to their cause, and the fact that they won this struggle was largely an outcome of long-term economic processes. Furthermore, the ascendancy of liberalism during the Hungarian Revolution of 1848–49 was overturned in the subsequent period of the Austrian tyranny, only to be renewed two decades later. It seems that in the harsh reality of 1942, such a description of the past struggles served the liberal Neolog worldview better than a simplistic linear narrative of the progress of emancipation. Like certain German Jewish liberal commentators in the 1930s, Hungarian Jewish spokespeople sensed that the image of the emancipation era as a dynamic struggle with ups and downs could be useful in granting meaning to the present situation and in raising hopes for a better future. The article concluded with a hint to the 1942 situation of Hungarian Jews: "The world of emancipation declined. Our present [is] struggle, our future [is] vague without security, until it will improve and the light of the past will appear again, the same light that came in the 19th century . . . to the fate community [*sorsközösség*] of Hungarian Jewry."[19]

The claim that the history of Hungarian Jewry followed a cyclical pattern rested on evidence culled from earlier periods as well. So argued historian Emma Lederer (b. 1897) in a 1940 article on Jewish involvement in the economic life of Hungary and other countries. Periods of economic growth and development were typically succeeded by periods when increased competition provoked anti-Jewish hostility, sometimes leading even to expulsion. The rule of Hungarian king Mátyás Hunyadi (1458–90), portrayed as the culmination of political power and cultural prosperity when Hungary adopted the values of the Renaissance and of humanism, was an era of tolerance toward the Jews. Lederer likened this period to the image of the nineteenth-century liberal golden age of modern Hungarian Jews. Anti-Jewish hatred had begun to emerge in Hungary, but it was much more restrained than in German Central Europe. Following the decline of the Hungarian state and its diminished sovereignty and territorial integrity, both golden eras came to an end in a similar manner. Clearly, for Lederer the external catastrophes of the Battle of Mohács and the Treaty of Trianon—and not internal developments within the Hungarian nation—had aggravated the anti-Jewish tension.[20]

With the decline of the nineteenth-century emancipation of Hungarian Jews, the community's national self-consciousness came to depend on a historical narrative of continuous Jewish settlement and integration in Hungary dating back to the Middle Ages. The Magyarization of the Jews, it was argued in a 1941 editorial in the *Magyar Zsidók Lapja*, did not begin in the liberal era, which was now being called "the fiction" by its opponents. Their Magyarization developed over centuries, beginning with the tolerant Christian reception that they were granted by the Hungarian founder-king Saint Stephen. Neither the emancipation nor the literary, cultural, and spiritual output of nineteenth-century Hungarian Jews could have come into existence without the centuries of these previous developments. The Jews' identity and attachment as Hungarians were not dependent on the civil status that they had received in the nineteenth century or on the ideologies of the present century: "There is no 'ism' [*izmus*] and no tendency that is able to cut off the Jews from Hungarian sentiment and Hungarian history. They are tied by many generations and by an unbroken chain to the Hungarian people and its struggles. It is not possible to disconnect from the past. . . . This [Hungarian Jewish] togetherness is not somebody's plan[;] . . . the passing waves of the moment cannot undermine it."[21]

This strategy was not unique to liberal Hungarian Jews. As we saw in the previous chapters, German Jewish liberal spokespeople and, to a lesser extent, the French Jewish liberal spokespeople also turned to the premodern era, primarily to the Middle Ages. Facing the threat of the abrogation of emancipation and the annulment of the achievements of the nineteenth century, these spokespeople sought an alternative and deeper foundation for the Jews' attachment to their homeland. The formation of such a historical memory, they hoped, would protect the Jews against those forces that were resistant to the liberal principles of the nineteenth century and were threatening to overturn them. This tendency seems to have been more common in Hungary than in Germany, which did not have a monolithic national foundation story from the Middle Ages similar to that of the Hungarian kingdom in the eleventh century, or in France, where the legacy of the Revolution overshadowed previous memories. It is interesting to note that the turn of the Jews to the Middle Ages was meant to legitimize their struggle against anti-Semitism but, at the same time, reflected a certain acceptance of the Hungarian conservative political culture that related with skepticism to the developments of the nineteenth century.[22]

An additional strategy that was used by Neolog writers in their attempt to defend the ethos of emancipation was to contrast the distinctive features of Jewish emancipation in Hungary vis-à-vis other European countries. In a general article that was published in 1941 in the annual *Magyar Zsidó Szemle*, Ballagi outlined the fundamental characteristics of the emancipation in Hungary, describing the latter as a unique Hungarian story. The question of Jewish rights in Hungary was first raised in the Hungarian Diet during 1790–91 almost immediately after Jewish rights were discussed in the French National Assembly. Still, he asserted, the discussion in the Diet was based on the Hungarian national perspective and on the recognition of the Jews as genuine sons of the Hungarian homeland; "these were not slogans drawn from outside sources."[23] Nevertheless, Ballagi did not idealize the decisions of the Hungarian Diet. His aim was to sever or, at the very least, loosen the connection between the acceptance of the Jews into Hungarian civil society and the wider story of the European Enlightenment. As he clearly stated, "The best evidence that the improvement in the status of the Jews [in Hungary] was not dependent on the ideas of the [Enlightenment] era was that in the following era of reaction there was no change in their status."[24] Similarly, the subsequent advancement in the civil status of the Jews, primarily from the 1840s, was presented by Ballagi as independent of the European movement in support of human rights. Rather, it was the idea of the Hungarian nation (*nemzet*) that promoted, step by step and not without struggle, the acceptance of the Jews as equal members of the nation.

The historical interpretation that accounted for the integration of the Jews in nineteenth-century Hungary was, in Ballagi's view, directly relevant to the situation facing Hungarian Jews in the early 1940s. The denial of a connection between the general European course of Enlightenment and emancipation on the one hand and the Hungarian case on the other hand, like the depiction of Jewish integration in Hungary as a genuine national development, could reasonably sustain the hope that the decline and fall of emancipation in Europe would not adversely affect the status of the Jews in Hungary. This attempt to present Jewish integration in Hungary in the context of the development of the Hungarian nation, instead of the more abstract context of human rights, was also more suitable to the dominant Hungarian political culture of the early 1940s.

To conclude that Ballagi renounced the universal ideals and foundations of the emancipation would be incorrect. His ongoing commitment to these values was subsequently expressed in an article that he published to mark the 150th anniversary of European Jewish emancipation, which had originated in France.[25] Ballagi's views can therefore serve as an accurate representation of the mainstream Neolog position. On the one hand, he continued to believe in the values of emancipated Jewry, refraining from linking the decline of emancipation to any fundamental errors that the Jews might have committed and also emphasizing the uniqueness of Jewish integration into Hungary. On the other hand, since Ballagi could not deny the historical crisis of emancipation in Europe, including in Hungary itself, he chose to present it as part of the Jewish fate, a term that he used more and more as he realized how severe the situation of European Jews had become.

Another method invoked by Neolog spokespeople to produce a usable past was the editing and publishing of a variety of historical and literary sources from the emancipation period. This was similar to what Rabbi Jacob Kaplan and Rabbi Nathan Netter had done in France in the late 1930s. Ballagi was prominent in this context as well. In 1940 he edited a sourcebook dealing with one hundred years of Hungarian Jewish struggle for emancipation (from 1840 to 1940) and published it under the series title *Új Zsidó Könyvtár* (New Jewish Library). The publication of this sourcebook, he stated in the introduction, demonstrates the importance of the struggle that continues even under the present circumstances.[26] In the same year Jewish intellectuals also published a literary anthology devoted to the one hundredth anniversary since the publication of Jewish literature in the Hungarian language. This project was presented by the editors as reflecting the ideal era in the Hungarian Jewish encounter. Three years later Jenő Zsoldos (b. 1896), one of the editors who served as the principal of the Jewish high school for girls in Pest, published another anthology in which he presented the views of Hungarian authors vis-à-vis Jews and Judaism, emphasizing the adjustment that the Jews had made to Hungary and its culture.[27]

In writing about the emancipation period, Neolog spokespeople had to contend with the very different way that anti-Semitic spokespeople presented the nineteenth century. Their efforts to save the historical dignity of the emancipation period, despite its political decline in the twentieth century, were quite similar to those of liberal German Jewish spokespeople, such as Fritz Friedländer, in the 1930s. "Our opponents," claimed a Neolog writer in the spring of 1943 in the *Magyar Zsidók Lapja,* "even try to use the nineteenth century against us and to present it as the century of anti-Semitism, but the truth is that it should be remembered as the century of Hungarian reform." Anti-Semitism was far from being dominant at the peak of Hungarian liberalism, and even the attempt to link national figures such as Széchenyi and Kossuth to anti-Jewish ideas was doomed to fail. It is true, the Neolog writer added, that the national-liberal political culture began to decline with the rise of anti-Semitism after World War I, but the present situation, he insisted, should not undermine the foundations of the past: "We do not want to fall victim to the erroneous view that past life truly reflects the present situation. This world declined, its ideals faded away in many aspects, but it is perhaps natural that as much as the wheel of fortune is greater, as much as the present demands more struggles, so the past is giving us more comfort."[28]

Neolog spokespeople therefore continued to cling to the fundamental ideas of the emancipation period, even when it became clear that its political values were crashing around them. The situation facing Hungarian Jews in the early 1940s drove some of them to point to the historical uniqueness of the Hungarian Jewish path of emancipation in order to strengthen their hope that the fate of Hungarian Jews would be different from that of the Jews in other European countries. In their efforts to find meaning in their situation, some of them also pointed to the cyclical course of Jewish history. Most of them—with a few exceptions, which will be dealt with in the following section—did not offer any fundamental criticism concerning the historical course followed by Hungarian Jewry during the emancipation. They also did not acknowledge any connection between the actions of the Jews in this past era and the present decline in their status.

Integration and Its Boundaries: The Critical Neolog Narrative

Whereas the mainstream Neolog narrative criticized neither Hungarian liberalism nor the Hungarian Jewish actions in the period of emancipation and explained the decline of emancipation almost only as a result of foreign influence, certain Neolog publicists and spokespeople suggested more critical interpretations. They avoided an idealistic description of modern Hungarian Jewry and related to the problems and difficulties in both the past and the present. The more moderate criticism focused on the internal strength of the Jewish community. These spokespeople pointed to divisions among Jews during the emancipation and to the lack of a healthy balance between Judaism and Hungarianness. Others related to misplaced efforts and actions undertaken by Hungarian Jews in the emancipation period as at least partial explanations for the current crisis. These writers, however, still remained loyal to the fundamental Neolog vision. They turned to neither Orthodoxy nor Zionism but instead strove to continue on the historical course of Jewish integration into Hungarian society, albeit on the basis of a different formula than that followed by the preceding generation of Hungarian Jewry.

In October 1939 the Országos Magyar Zsidó Segítő Akció (National Hungarian Jewish Aid Association), or OMZSA, was established in Budapest. The OMZSA was a Neolog-Orthodox-Zionist coalition that aimed to consolidate the Hungarian Jewish self-aid actions. Jewish public activists saw the establishment of the OMZSA as an opportunity for both self-renewal and a growing inner solidarity among Hungarian Jews. In this context Ernő Munkácsi, a Neolog publicist, raised a critical historical interpretation in the OMZSA's yearbook. Since the nineteenth century, Munkácsi wrote in September 1940, Hungarian Jewish history included a long list of missed opportunities. Affected by various forces, the misfortune of Hungarian Jewry stemmed from the dispersal of its powers. The tranquility and comfortable life afforded by the emancipation had undermined internal Jewish unity and had prevented, almost entirely, broad Jewish cooperation.[29]

In the ensuing years during the period when the distress of Hungarian Jewry deepened, Munkácsi continued to publish articles containing caustic historical criticism. In an article published on the occasion of Tisha B'Av in the Jewish year 5702 (1942), he painfully asked, "Is there Hungarian Jewry at all?" He went on to state that "The Jews are torn and divided. . . . The price for the sin of the abandonment of their ancestral tradition is being paid now."[30] The social misery of Hungarian Jewry and its internal rifts were presented as a failure of the emancipation. In this spirit Munkácsi called on Hungarian Jews to return to their historical roots and to find there the foundations for their common fate. He also pointed to the decline and fall of the magnificent medieval Spanish (Sephardi) Jewry as a warning sign for the future of Hungarian Jewry.

Munkácsi's writings in the early 1940s combined a commitment in principle to the course of Jewish integration into the Hungarian nation with a critical examination of their modern history. He turned his readers' attention to the historical legacy of Hungarian Jewry primarily in the medieval era, implying that the similarity between this period and the current crisis could be a source of comfort.[31] In the introduction to his collection of essays titled *Küzdelmes évek* (The Years of Struggle) and published in 1943, he developed his historical view further. Unwilling to disqualify the fundamental course of emancipation, he believed that without strengthening Jewish communal solidarity and historical self-consciousness, Hungarian Jews would face destruction.[32]

A different critical interpretation of the position of Hungarian Jews was expressed in an article published in the 5703 (1943) OMZSA yearbook under the title "Three Hungarian Jewish Generations." This was a paraphrase of the renowned and influential book *Three Generations* by the Hungarian historian Gyula Szekfű.[33] Most members of the first generation of the emancipation, claimed the lawyer and writer Hugó Csergő (b. 1877), had preserved their Jewish cultural legacy while also adopting Hungarian culture and identity. The second generation, which matured at around the turn of the twentieth century, integrated faith (*hit*) and motherland (*haza*) but also produced many cases of full assimilation. Jewish sentiment had turned pale, communal education had declined, and large segments of the Jewish intelligentsia had become alienated from the Jewish tradition. In the third generation, which had come to age in the period of the disintegration (*összeomlás*) of Hungary following World War I and during the decline in the Jewish status, Csergő stated, there was a reverse tendency toward Jewish revival. The danger for the current generation, he continued, was the possible alienation from Hungarian identity amid the growing anti-Semitic pressure. His interpretation hinted at the influence of Zionist ideas. The historical memory preserved by the three generations since the emancipation therefore led Csergő to call for a renaissance of the integration between fatherland and faith, denouncing de-Judaization and de-Hungarization alike: "The lessons of two generations, their memory and their experiences, should serve and show the way to the third generation. . . . We live in a tragic era, in trying times. Only those with powerful spirits will be able to pass this test and withstand the tragedy; only they will be able to prevent the situation in which the strengthening of their Jewishness will bring about the weakening of their Hungarianness."[34]

Csergő's depiction of the threat of the decline of both the Jewish and Hungarian identities as two facets of the same problem was exceptional. Most critical perspectives focused on the decline of Jewish identity and represented the crisis of Hungarian Jewry as part of the broader historical course undertaken by emancipated European Jewry. Jewish intellectuals, asserted rabbi and educator Sámuel Kandel (b. 1884) in 1942, had worked since the mid-eighteenth century to attain civil equality and viewed the advancement of assimilation as necessary for achieving this goal. Their identification with these universal values motivated them to integrate into the nations in which they were living and to adopt their languages and cultures. However, this was not enough. The Jewish elite was not aware that in certain countries such as Hungary, the full "melting in" (*összeolvadás*) of the Jews could not be completed without touching on the religious aspect of Jewish life. Therefore, assimilation had ended in baptism in certain cases and in at least the attenuation of Jewish religious identity in many more cases. Abandoning the religious ceremonies of Rosh Hashanah (Jewish New Year) and Yom Kippur (Day of Atonement) also amounted to separation from the national (*népi*) element of Judaism and brought about the alienation of many modern Hungarian Jews from their coreligionists. However, this process changed its course after World War I as the anti-Semitic pressure led to cruel and unprecedented dissimilation and to a growing exclusion of assimilated Jews from the surrounding society and culture: "This Jewish group is now asking questions and searching for a new path, a Jewish path that is still possible for it, because it does not have any other path. This is the path where it must find its strength . . . to return to the community[,] . . . a path that will teach us again to draw strength from within our current suffering."[35]

Kandel appealed for a return to the Jewish sources, although he did not believe that it was possible to turn the wheel of history backward. Similar to several German Jewish commentators whom we discussed in chapter 1, he realized that in spite of their deep agony, modern Jews could not erase at once the impact of modernity and the results of assimilation. He therefore called on his readers to strive for religious renewal and restore their living bond with the roots of Jewish people to the greatest extent possible.[36]

The similarity—and difference—between the worldview and historical interpretations of the critical Neolog spokespeople and the Zionists, about whom we will deal later in this chapter, was clearly expressed in the writing of the Neolog publicist Endre Sós. Sós identified with the fundamental values of the Neolog political culture and believed that the Jews were an integral part of the Hungarian nation. In 1940 he published a book on Jewish history in six Hungarian towns, emphasizing the contribution and deep involvement of the Jews in the history of these towns. Like the common Neolog position, he also presented anti-Semitism in Hungary as originating from foreign influence.[37] However, as we saw in chapter 5, Sós was already exceptional among the Neolog spokespeople in 1938, when he interpreted the crisis of Hungarian Jews in a wide historical context and called for an internal renewal of Hungarian Jewry. His complicated critical position was articulated in a lecture that he presented in 1941 in front of the members of the Magyar Cionista Szövetség (Hungarian Zionist Bond).[38]

Sós claimed that many Hungarian Jews, first and foremost a significant part of those who belonged to the Neolog trend, live an unbalanced spiritual life and had not come to terms with their Judaism. For them, being Jewish was nothing but a misery that they were born to by chance and could not shake off. Sós admitted to his audience that among the Zionists there were more Jews who were aware of the meaning of the present crisis and viewed the renewal of a connection to Judaism as the fundamental foundation upon which they constructed their world. Still, he identified himself as non-Zionist and consequently had to offer his own explanation for the crisis of Hungarian Jewry and for the decline of emancipation at large.

Sós went on to state that emancipation, which certain Zionists had come to underestimate, was fundamentally a positive historical development. Even the Zionists, he added, must recognize their debt to the political culture that originated in the nineteenth century. This era also laid the foundation for the rise of modern Zionist leadership, which consisted of many physicians and engineers (i.e., educated and modern persons). Still, this historical path was also bound up with an error:

> The error was that European Emancipation, more accurately, the Emancipation in eastern and Central Europe, liberated only the individual Jew but not Judaism. The American emancipation process made it possible, because in the New World the liberated Jew never strove to be liberated from his Jewish character. The European Emancipation was founded on an erroneous interpretation of the term "assimilation" and expected the Jews to alienate themselves, at least in part, from their Jewishness.[39]

Unlike most of the Neolog spokespeople, Sós did not associate the crisis of emancipation and assimilation only with other countries, primarily to Germany, but also cited the Hungarian case as a clear example of this failure. The generation of the fathers, he asserted, could still build bridges between traditional Jewish culture and the new world in an attempt to shape a balanced

Hungarian Jewish identity. The generation of the sons, or at least the major part, had deviated from this balance for the sake of "hyperassimilation" and had given up its religion as well as its national Jewish heritage. As did certain German Jewish liberal spokespeople in the 1930s, Sós distinguished between the positive aspects of assimilation—a natural and respected integration accompanied by a preservation of the basis of Judaism—and its negative qualities, namely the exaggerated and sometimes even distorted expressions of the "overassimilated" (*túlasszimilálódott*) Jewish life. This discussion about assimilation helped him to clarify this point to his Zionist listeners: "Ninety percent of Hungarian Jews will be lying if they do not admit their attachment to the Hungarian nation . . . but it is an error that these Jews, who are one hundred percent Hungarian in their spirit and nationality, should suppress their Jewish self-awareness and their historical consciousness[;] . . . the right, honest and respected position of assimilation is vital."[40]

Parallel to such statements, Sós expressed perhaps more than any other Neolog spokesperson his willingness for a dialogue with the Zionists and his tolerance for their political and historical views. Palestine, he asserted, could become the spiritual center for world Jewry as Rome is for the Catholics, and this should not undermine the Hungarian Jewish common fate. Sós implied that the common denominator uniting his liberal non-Zionist views and Zionism was much more broadly based than the disagreements. This was an exceptional position at the time but foreshadowed post-Holocaust Jewish political culture: "The Hungarian Zionist Bond entitled [Sós's lecture] as 'Assimilation or Zionism?' We should drop the question mark and the word 'or.' Assimilation and Zionism! Both are crucial. In our motherland, Zionism means that Jews here are more Jewish. In Palestine, the wandering Jews can declare themselves as a nation [*nemzet*]. . . . If this will be the case, Hungarian Jewry will weather the storm."[41]

A major figure in the discourse was the literary historian, writer, and poet Aladár Komlós (b. 1892), who served as a prominent teacher and educator in the Jewish high school in Budapest. Komlós attempted to combine Hungarian identity and deep Jewish awareness in a critical manner. In 1921 he published his programmatic essay "Jews at the Crossroad." He related to the difficulties that assimilating Hungarian Jews had encountered when hiding their identity and suppressing their origin. He therefore called on his readers to create a more stable balance between the Hungarian and Jewish components in their identity.[42] In the 1920s and 1930s Komlós was active in various literary and cultural efforts that attempted to promote his vision.

Komlós's interest in Hungarian Jewish literature was founded on the view that the Jews were part of the Hungarian nation. In 1940 he defended this view against anti-Semitic statements—some of them inspired by the Nazis—on Jewish involvement in Hungary during the assimilation period.[43] Responding to writers who blamed the Jews for introducing cosmopolitan elements into the original Hungarian culture, Komlós disputed the depiction of modern Hungarian culture as a monolithic phenomenon and claimed that the Jewish influence had actually contributed to its improvement and prosperity in the early twentieth century. Nevertheless, he did not idealize the Hungarian Jewish cultural integration and did not conceal its shortcomings. The Jewish cultural elite, he wrote, tried to become assimilated into a very thin elite of intellectuals whose cultural and political orientation was fundamentally different from those of most Hungarians. This, he argued, explained why the assimilation process could not succeed in the long run and ultimately collapsed during the profound transformation that Hungary experienced after World War I.[44] Yet Komlós refused to see this development as final. He still believed in the value and fruitfulness of Jewish integration in Hungary if it was founded on the right balance: "It was an integration in which both sides acted like cog-wheels. Now one of the wheels is dismantled. It should be replaced and then the car will be able to proceed again better than before."[45]

It was primarily as the editor of the Hungarian Jewish yearbook *Ararát*, which was founded in 1939 and published until 1944 by the Jewish girls' orphanage in Pest, that Komlós's perception of the past and his political-cultural vision found expression. As *Ararát*'s editor, he advanced his critical view of the emancipation era, which involved a substantive discussion of the relation between past and present. Ultimately he aspired for a Jewish cultural renaissance in Hungary.[46] *Ararát* was edited with a clear awareness of the circumstances that endangered the future of Hungarian Jewry, a situation that Komlós depicted in 1940 as "a second flood that is threatening us." He asserted that the yearbook aimed not only to support the Jewish orphanage financially but also to help its Jewish readers—many of whom were spiritual orphans—to recognize and accept Jewish fate and the need for Jewish unity.[47] Komlós strove to develop the yearbook as a pluralistic publication that would represent all Hungarian Jewish factions. *Ararát* therefore published various public debates, with the participation of a variety of Jewish spokespeople from different parties, on topics such as the Hungarian Jewish path (1941) or what makes a person Jewish (1944).[48]

Throughout the war years Komlós tried more than once to clarify his historical-cultural position, which rested on his views regarding Hungarian Jewish literature. The source of the illness of Hungary's Jews—and at least implicitly also of Jews in other countries in Europe—could be traced, according to Komlós, not to their acceptance of the nineteenth-century process of emancipation and assimilation but instead to a later point in history. Whereas the writers of the first generation of the emancipation knew how to strike a balance between their ancient Jewish tradition and their new Hungarian identity, the younger ones—those who came of age at the turn of the twentieth century—felt that the very idea of the Jewish people was provincial. They also thought that there was no sense in dealing with it since the Jewish question was already resolved. Komlós described this state of mind in a 1942 article: "Jewish traditions and modern culture seemed to be mutually exclusive; if somebody chose one of them he gave up the other. The traditional Jew did not strive at all for the values of modern culture. The poet who lived within modern culture did not care anymore about Judaism. As assimilation proceeded, the social group that continued to be associated with Jewish tradition became increasingly narrow."[49]

A year later in an article titled "Judaism, Hungarianness, Europe" (1943), Komlós came to terms with this problem in a more systematic way.[50] Like the liberal German Jewish writers a decade before, Komlós presented assimilation as an inevitable historical process that was fundamentally healthy. He claimed that it was natural that 150 years earlier, as the very narrow traditional Jewish world began to open, European Jewry was attracted to Europe like a planet orbiting around the sun. Using sharp language—which can be interpreted as a reaction to the intensifying Zionist assaults against the legacy of the assimilation era—Komlós disputed the position that related the decline of emancipation to assimilation and offered an alternative historical explanation:

> We do not want to accept an incorrect argument that the mistakes of the assimilation have brought us to the current situation, have torn us apart from Europe and led to the rebuilding of the ghetto's wall around us. On the contrary! The Jewish ghetto culture was not only shallow; it was also more dangerous to life! A people living behind closed walls will necessarily grown faint. . . . If we do not want European culture to flood us destructively, we should not build a floodgate to block it but rather a channel to it.[51]

Here Komlós confronted the ultraconservative rabbinical attitude and presented it as being responsible for the unbalanced burst of assimilation. He asserted that only a moderate and reasonable step-by-step integration of the Jews into their surroundings—what he called "the continuous assimilation" (*folytonos asszimiláció*)—could counter the risk of radical assimilation. Komlós also condemned the other extreme pole of Hungarian Jewry: radical left-wing Jews.[52] Among them were the writers for the journal *Huszadik Század* (Twentieth Century), who dared to criticize the Hungarian motherland too severely.[53] Whereas the first-generation assimilated Jews were still aware of their Jewishness and found a way to integrate into Hungarian society tactfully and respectful of boundaries, members of the radical Left, not conscious of their Jewish identity, caused the decline of Hungarian Jewish relations by blurring the differences between them. On the basis of this historical analysis, Komlós called on his readers to readopt a Jewish consciousness and to restructure their relationship with their Hungarianness (*magyarság*), which would require maintaining a certain distance. He also appealed to them to surrender the overly central role that they had played in Hungarian national life. Only in this way, he stated, would the Jews be able to preserve both their European and Hungarian identities and restructure their relationship with their fellow Hungarian Christians.

As the clear representative of the position that has been presented here as critical Neolog, Komlós strove to balance his harsh criticism of radical assimilation, which sometimes resembled Zionist criticism, and his belief in the possibility of Jewish integration in Hungary in the future. In 1939 and more so in 1941, he emphasized time and again that his call for a revision of radical assimilation and for deeper Jewish self-consciousness should not be interpreted as a call to dissociate from the Hungarian and European culture and return to the ghetto.[54] Despite his awareness of the ongoing deterioration of the status of Hungarian Jews, Komlós continued to believe in the possibility of their future integration as well as the crucial contribution that they could bring to the Hungarian nation and to all mankind. However, such a contribution could materialize, he believed, only if the Jews would first embrace their Jewish sources.

The Orthodox Narrative

Demographic changes in the structure of Hungarian Jewry resulted from the return of territories containing an extensive Orthodox population, including to a great extent the more conservative and sometimes even antimodern Eastern Orthodoxy. Despite these changes, the central Orthodox community in Hungary was still administered from Budapest. This fact was significant because Western Orthodoxy, which had developed in Hungary's urban centers (primarily in Budapest) since the late nineteenth century, had undergone a process of Hungarian acculturation and was much more integrated than the Eastern, mostly Hasidic, Orthodoxy.[55] The historical discourse that is presented here thus reflects the variety of positions that emerged among the spokespeople of the modern Orthodox establishment in its journal *Orthodox Zsidó Újság*.[56]

As they shared the fundamental liberal political ideas responsible for the integration of the Jews in modern Hungary, some of the Orthodox spokespeople continued to express a positive evaluation of the emancipation period even in the early 1940s. The *Orthodox Zsidó Újság*, for example, published articles about the Jewish contribution to Hungarian society and economy and described the positive attitude of Hungarian national heroes to the Jews.[57] Such articles, which were founded on a positive view of the emancipation and Hungarian nationalism, were combined in various ways with the unique Orthodox agenda. Thus, for example, Dezső Korein was pleased by the return of northern Transylvania to Hungarian sovereignty both because he favored the Hungarian national irredentist cause and because he believed that it would help Hungarian Jewish Orthodoxy as a result of the character of the Jewish population in this area.[58] Another favorable expression of the association of Orthodox spokespeople with the emancipation was the marking of the seventieth anniversary of the approval by the Hungarian National Assembly in 1870 of the separate Orthodox organization. This step was depicted as a realization of the principle of freedom of belief and as an integral part of the emancipation's legacy of liberty.[59]

The misery that Hungarian Jews experienced from the early 1940s led to a significant transformation in the way that the Orthodox communal establishment acted. This produced a greater understanding of the need to cooperate with the Neolog community in welfare activities and in other fields.[60] This tendency also influenced the discourse on the past. The long years of struggle between Neolog and Orthodox were history, stated Dezső Korein, one of the most prominent Orthodox publicists, in an article that documented the struggle for domination by one of the communities. Today, he added, Hungarian Jews have a wider view of the reality, and the representatives of the different camps understand that they must unite in times of crisis.[61]

The enactment process of the Third Jewish Law, which forbade in 1941 marriage between Jews and non-Jews in Hungary, posed an interesting challenge to the spokespeople of Hungarian Orthodoxy. On the one hand, this law clearly contradicted the principles of emancipation. On the other hand, it banned marriages that the Orthodox had strongly opposed and condemned. In an editorial published in the *Orthodox Zsidó Újság* a few days after the Jewish holiday of Shavuot, the writer addressed the question of distinguishing between the Jewish law that forbade mixed marriages and the new anti-Semitic law to ban these marriages.

The support for mixed marriages during the emancipation, the article stated, originated from the initiative of non-Jewish powers—most prominent among them Napoleon—that attempted to force mixed marriage upon the Jews. Furthermore, said the Orthodox spokesman, the extensive rise in mixed marriages during the nineteenth century now presented a severe demographic threat to the future of the Jews in various European countries, among them Germany and Hungary. The rise in mixed marriages had also caused tragic situations in many families and had produced numerous anti-Semitic leaders who were the offspring of mixed families. Even though the Orthodox writer clearly realized that the new law would be a major offense to what was left of Jewish emancipation, he could not oppose it directly: "Mixed marriages damaged Judaism and now it turns out [that] the European society rejects them, too. . . . If we still see today a necessity to prevent mixed marriages, we should not avoid [banning them] even for one moment, even though it somehow damages the social equality [of the Jews]. We should understand that this does not originate from hatred . . . but from the defense of one's race."[62] Instead of presenting a clear position vis-à-vis the new regulation, the writer chose to demonstrate his belief in the ancient Jewish law. He even expressed his hope that the new legal prohibition would motivate many Jews to devote themselves now to Jewish family and faith.

Chapter 5 discussed Hungarian Jewish Orthodox writers who, after the November 1938 pogrom, explained the catastrophe of German Jews as a result of their choice of the path of assimilation. The deterioration of the situation of the Jews in Hungary, and moreover in the neighboring countries, further motivated Orthodox spokespeople to blame the Jewish liberal historical path as the source of the present crisis. The Orthodox way was consequently presented as the positive alternative for the future.

In the spring of 1940 a few weeks before the surrender of France to the German army, Korein published an article to mark the 150th anniversary of the first emancipation edict granted to the Jews in France. The central question that he addressed was the objection of the Orthodox French Jews to the emancipation. These Jews, he asserted, were not fanatics or anticultural. Their position regarding the emancipation only reflected their commitment to defend their faith from the almost unbounded freedom that they were about to enjoy without really knowing how to deal with its ramifications. Indeed, he claimed, the upper classes in France and later among German Jewry did not pass the test of emancipation. The new liberty had eventually brought them to abandon their faith and sometimes even to be baptized, as

Moses Mendelssohn's family members and disciples had. The alternative path that he set forth, that of the believing Jews, was not based on the rejection of the emancipation but rather on its gradual acceptance as the foundation for civil equality. Moreover, they were even ready to identify with the national patriotic point of view of the peoples among whom they were living and thus prove their willingness to sacrifice for their new homelands. However, Korein asserted, the Orthodox, unlike the other Jews, resisted any kind of assimilation in the religious sphere. For them the appropriate integration was determined by their refusal to relinquish unnecessarily crucial elements of their religious legacy, a position that Korein formulated in the present tense: "The Emancipation is crucial for us from the perspective of our civil rights, but we are obliged to care for and preserve our [internal] framework[;] . . . we should not offer a higher price than other groups for our patriotism."[63]

A more direct criticism of the liberal Jewish orientation was expressed by the Orthodox spokesman Salamon Stern in a 1941 debate among representatives of the various Hungarian Jewish factions. Stern related to two opposite views of Judaism: the Orthodox view, which was based on the preservation of religious law, and the liberal view, which presented the humanistic, monotheistic, universal spirit as the foundation of Judaism.[64] The choice that many Jews had made to follow the path of assimilation was supported, he stated, by the vision that regarded assimilation as a realization of the Jewish universal mission. Today, he claimed, it is absolutely clear that assimilation and religious reform have only diluted Judaism and have not contributed to its survival at all. From the current perspective, Stern added, we can see how this position denied the very essence of Judaism itself and led it to internal destruction. Stern also rejected the Zionist option and stated that any attempt to establish Jewish life on a foundation that is neither religious nor ritualistic cannot last; the only ways to preserve Judaism amid the turmoil of history are a religious revitalization and loyalty to the Jewish law.

The nineteenth-century Neolog leaders had followed the fashionable liberal views and had created the illusion that the emancipation that was granted to the Jews in 1867 would put an end to anti-Semitism, asserted another Orthodox commentator in 1941.[65] Facing the harsh circumstances, many Neologs now understood that their efforts at dismantling the religious tradition and ancient laws was not advantageous; they even admitted that the Orthodox were right in their cause.

The deterioration of the status of the Jews motivated Orthodox interpreters to discuss the historical significance of the crisis in light of Jewish cultural memory. In the spring of 1942 with the beginning of the days of the counting of the Omer (Sefirat Ha'Omer), which in Jewish tradition is a mourning period, the *Orthodox Zsidó Újság* published an article about this topic. The article summarized the eras of persecution and mourning in Jewish history from the enslavement in Egypt through the Babylonian exile and the destruction of the Second Temple by the Romans up to the Crusades and the Khmelnytsky massacres (1648–49). Based on this broad historical perspective, the writer pointed to certain positive consequences of these harsh events: "We are like this legendary king who is laughing in one eye and crying in the other. The memories of the past are granting Israel reasons for this [laughing] and for this [crying]. . . . The ongoing oppression in our history, which brought great anguish to many individuals, was not only negative from the communal perspective. This can be seen in all the eras of exile." Based on this argument, the writer described how persecution had always led to religious revival: "Israel can never be destroyed for an entire era as the oppressing tyrants want."[66]

From the Orthodox point of view, the cyclical view of Jewish history did not imply an expectation for a recovery of the civil status of the Jews and the restoration of a liberal regime that would tolerate them. Instead, the Orthodox point of view saw the inferior position of the Jews as a point of departure for a religious and spiritual revival. The writer of the article thus explained that the destruction of the Temple by Rome led to the writing of the Mishnah and the Talmud, the medieval oppression helped the Jews to preserve their Torah in the ghettos, and the Khmelnytsky massacres set the stage for the rise of Hasidism. In his attempt to give his readers an optimistic message despite all, the writer stated that "The external fate leads us many times from misery to salvation."[67]

Although this view denied the historical uniqueness of European Jews in the early 1940s and drew parallels between it and previous periods of crisis and catastrophe in Jewish history, the Orthodox journal expressed more than a year later—on the eve of Rosh Hashanah 5744 (the Jewish New Year)—a very different position. The continuation of the war in Europe and probably the availability of more information concerning the fate of the Jews in Poland and eastern Europe led the journal writers to express a new and much more pessimistic assessment of the situation: "In the age of totality the crisis is also total. In Jewish history we have had so far only partial crisis eras that had an impact on certain Jewish groups or on this or that community. There was also a part of the community left as the foundation of recovery. . . . Up to now each crisis had a direction for a solution: emigration. Today, the option of emigration does not exist anymore."[68] This anonymous writer emphasized the difference between the peaceful and stable world of the nineteenth century, which was the age of liberalism and individualism, and the twentieth century, which was characterized permanently by tension due to the rise of the antiliberal ethos. He warned his readers to shun groundless optimism regarding the future but also to avoid dark hopelessness, which brought him to an inevitable conclusion: only God could help the Jews in this unprecedented crisis in Jewish history.

The deepening pessimism was also expressed in the escalation of criticism on the part of Orthodox spokespeople regarding the course of modern Jewish history. Salamon Stern, who in 1941 pointed to the Orthodox path as the right Jewish choice, two years later called on his readers to recognize that both the Neolog and Orthodox had been mistaken in preferring secular education over Jewish religious teaching.[69]

Korein, who as we have seen expressed in 1940 a clear identification with Hungarian nationalism and in 1941 was careful not to totally denounce assimilation, was much more pessimistic by the autumn of 1943. The politics of assimilation, he stated, was totally bankrupt. The motivation for the Jews to surrender their ancient religious customs was rooted in their expectation that this step would neutralize anti-Semitism. However, this idea proved to be a complete failure particularly in Germany, where anti-Semitism had not spared any Jew even if he had totally renounced his tradition. Furthermore, Korein denounced modern life in general as materialistic and ostentatious, which he viewed as responsible for the disintegration of social solidarity. He therefore blamed the previous generations for not having anticipated the consequences of their choices. A few months before the German invasion of Hungary, Korein denied the very possibility of creating any lasting balance among assimilation, modern life, and the preservation of Jewish distinctiveness. Instead, he called on his readers to recognize the total bankruptcy of assimilation and to banish all alien ideologies from Jewish life.[70]

Such ideas seem similar to the radical positions espoused by Rabbi Simon Schwab, the most extreme Orthodox spokesperson among German Jewry in the 1930s. Still, it is important to emphasize that unlike Schwab, who attacked the course of German Jewry's assimilation from the very beginning, Korein avoided even in late 1943 explicitly dissociating himself from the Hungarian Jewish path to modernity. His disapproval of modernity and assimilation reflected an attempt to draw communal values and social solidarity as well as a deeper historical perspective of the Jewish plight from the premodern era.[71] Moreover, the denunciation of assimilation by Hungarian Orthodox spokespeople such as Korein and Stern was mostly directed toward the French and Germany Jewries and almost never at Hungarian Jewry as a whole. It seems therefore that even they continued to cling, at least in part, to the faith that characterized almost all Jewish commentators in

Hungary from the beginning of the Nazi era: that in their homeland things would unfold differently.

The Crisis of Assimilation and the National Revival: Zionist Interpretations

The political discourse and the historical interpretations that we have followed so far in this chapter appear to be a continuation and sometimes an intensification of the discourse of the late 1930s. Indeed, the lack of significant differences is difficult to understand. Even if Hungarian Jewry could not comprehend the full scope of the catastrophe enveloping its neighboring Jewish communities in the early 1940s and in spite of the fact that their press was not completely free, the expectation is that the calamity of European Jewry would have had a greater impact on them. This limited effect seems to have originated first and foremost within the modern Hungarian Jewish political culture, which had tended to concentrate on its own problems for at least two generations. From this perspective, the rumors about the events in the German-occupied zones as well as the expulsion of eighteen thousand so-called alien Jews from Hungary to their murder in Galicia in 1941 did not lead to a significant transformation. Even the tragic fate of the Jewish recruits in the Hungarian labor service did not have a profound impact on the Hungarian Jewish discourse, perhaps because this took place in peripheral areas in times of war.

This self-centered consciousness was convenient for those who still believed, one way or another, in the future of Jewish life in Hungary and helped them avoid dealing with the Pan-Jewish consequences of the European Jewish catastrophe in terms of their own future. However, the Zionist spokespeople looked at the situation differently. Essentially, Zionist ideology in general tended to a broader perspective. As early as the 1930s Hungarian Zionist commentators related to the overall Jewish significance of the events in Nazi Germany and sometimes also implied that there would be consequences for Hungarian Jews. This tendency became more common in the early 1940s.

In an article published in *Ararát* in 1940, György Kecskeméti coped with these questions. In chapter 5 we saw how Kecskeméti spoke about the end of the liberal era directly after the Nuremberg Laws took effect. Now he stated that the war in Europe was going to determine the complexion of world Jewry for the coming generations. German, Austrian, and Czech Jewries had already been destroyed, and now Polish Jewry was undergoing the same process, he argued. According to Kecskeméti, the catastrophe had begun to develop after World War I with the eradication of the monarchies, which had damaged the idea of a free liberal state and had raised the power of nationalism everywhere. Under these circumstances it turned out that the nineteenth-century path of assimilation had been a mistake, a conclusion that also should be applied to the Hungarian case. The course of the integration of the Jews into the Hungarian society, economy, and nation, which began in the nineteenth century, seems to have failed. Kecskeméti's conclusion from this discussion is clear: the Jews should go through a transformation, turn themselves from a religious group into a nation, and prepare to immigrate to Palestine, despite all the difficulties.[72]

In the first year of the war Zionist spokespeople dealt with the historical meaning of the events from the perspective of the chain of suffering throughout Jewish history. It is true that the Crusades are considered to be a murderous era, claimed the Zionist publicist Lajos Fodor in May 1940, but in fact there had never been so many Jewish victims as in the twentieth century. Moreover, he added, it is more difficult for twentieth-century Jews to cope with this victimization because of the weakening of Jewish self-consciousness during the emancipation period: "Perhaps the twentieth-century barbarism hit us because of our internal life, a retribution for our destruction."[73]

The abandonment of the tradition, Fodor asserted, was much more radical in the case of the Jews, as compared to other peoples. Whereas Germans, Slovaks, and Romanians, for example, had created a modern collective identity that combined faith, nation, and culture, only the modern Jews had decided to eliminate their communitarian ethos and national awareness. Fodor concluded that the only way to cope with the present crisis and avoid an even greater one was for the Jewish national consciousness to be rejuvenated.

A more systematic presentation of the Zionist criticism regarding the emancipation appeared in a series of articles published in 1941 by József Junger in the Zionist monthly *Múlt és Jövő*. Until the mid-nineteenth century, he argued, the Jews were rooted in their nationality (*népiség*) even while being in touch with their surroundings. This situation fundamentally changed in the mid-nineteenth century as the Jews began to turn to total assimilation. Junger linked this turning point to the overall liberal mood in Europe during this time, including positivistic thought, the rise of natural sciences, the materialistic worldview, and the radical individualism that regarded the nation as no more than a collection of individuals. The Jews, Junger argued, were hurt by this Western influence more than any other group, and it led some of them to strong self-hatred.[74]

From this historical analysis Junger turned after a few months to a sociological generational analysis of Hungarian Jews and their historical perceptions. Members of the older generation in the Hungarian Jewish community, whose worldview was shaped before World War I, continued to see the emancipation as the real solution to the Jewish problem. From their perspective, he asserted, the whole process of the enactment of the anti-Jewish laws was a mere historical error, a fleeting episode. However, it was more than just the influence of the worldview of their formative years that led them to this position. Their social standing within the bourgeoisie, which was less offended by the new enactment, also helped them to preserve the historical views that had originated at the turn of the century, even when they became totally unrealistic. On the other hand, the members of the younger generation, who had matured during the post–World War I period and had personally experienced the exclusion of the Jews from Hungary's universities and economic life, already realized at that time that the emancipation had become no more than an illusion. As a result of this awakening, these young Jews strove—and continued to strive—to openly express their national Jewish affiliation.[75]

The Jewish national awareness to which Junger related focused not on Palestine but rather on the redefinition of the position of the Jews within the Hungarian nation. The assimilating Jews, Junger argued in September 1941, should reshape their life in Hungary as a national minority within the Hungarian ethnic majority. Such a step should not be seen as a departure from the nation in which Jews had lived for centuries but instead should be seen as a return to the normal situation in which two groups live together as members of different nationalities (*nép*) within the same nation (*nemzet*).[76] Junger attempted to interpret Hungarian Jewish history as it had been shaped from the Middle Ages until the Reform period (1825–48) as a healthy balance between two nationalities within the same nation. Pointing to the source of the failure that had upset this balance, Junger was clearly inspired by the views of the Hungarian historian Szekfű in his book *Three Generations:* "The great break came in the compromise era [1867–1914]. Pure Hungarian ideas were suppressed then from Hungarian politics and the [newly] dominant alien Western national ideas required not only the nation's unity but also the people's uniformity. This led to assimilation."[77]

These ideas from the second half of the nineteenth century had caused a blurring of the boundaries between the two peoples. This led in turn to pressure on the Jews to renounce the collective elements of their identity and eventually to embrace the idea of total assimilation in order to achieve full emancipation. Accordingly, the rehabilitation of the national Jewish awareness in Hungary and the restructuring of Hungarian Jewish relations would not lead to a break in the historical continuity but instead would lead to the restoration of the centuries-old historical balance. This would also enable the Jews to achieve a new emancipation that was more significant and stable.

Junger was aware of the great practical difficulty in realizing his vision.[78] The central obstacle in the way of national Jewish politics (*zsidó népi politika*), he claimed, was the lack of willingness on the part of the high-ranking bourgeois official Hungarian Jewish leadership to relinquish its idealistic but totally mistaken idea of emancipation and assimilation. Martin Buber's insistence that the process of Jewish assimilation in Europe was no less than a process of atomization—the disintegration of the traditional communal solidarity—was perhaps the most apt description of the situation in Hungary more than in any other country, Junger added. In relating to Buber's ideas, Junger associated his interpretation of the decline of Hungarian Jewry with the wider Jewish context. Junger's vision of national Jewish politics was in fact very similar to ideas that had been raised by German Zionists before 1933.[79] His call for a new emancipation also resembled an argument that had been raised by German Jewish spokespeople before and primarily after 1933, as we saw in chapter 1.

The historical perspective and the political-cultural vision proposed by Junger were not fundamentally different from those that were raised by Komlós, whom we have presented here as a critical Neolog spokesman. Unlike Junger, Komlós was not a Zionist, yet in this context it seems that the gap between the critical liberal attitude of Komlós and the Diasporic Zionism of Junger was quite minimal. Both regarded modern Jewish assimilation in Hungary as a violation of the historical balance between Judaism and Hungarianness and tried to outline the path for the renewal of Jewish consciousness and communal solidarity in order to restore this balance.

Their positions differed slightly with respect to the beginning of the crisis. Komlós related it to the second generation of emancipation, that is, to the turn of the twentieth century, and presented the first generation of emancipation in Hungary as a golden age for the integration of Hungarian Jewry. Junger, on the other hand, pointed to the compromise era as the time when Jews first abandoned the previously balanced Hungarian Jewish tradition. It is interesting to note that Junger related explicitly to Komlós and described him as a positive exception within the Neolog camp. Junger also mentioned a small group of Jewish intellectuals who were active in Transylvania under the leadership of Ernő Marton (b. 1896). They were trying to become the Jewish spiritual avant-garde who would lead the cultural transformation.[80]

The most systematic and comprehensive discussion by a Hungarian Zionist spokesperson regarding the crisis of Hungarian and other European Jews in the early 1940s can be found in the publications of Marton, who was active in Kolozsvár (Cluj) in Transylvania. Marton represented a different type of national Jewish politics than what had developed in Hungary in the interwar period. Following the separation of Transylvania from Hungary and its annexation to Romania, he established the Hungarian Jewish weekly (from 1920 it became a daily) *Új Kelet* (New East), which became the main Zionist journal in the area during the interwar period. A central figure in the Romanian Zionist movement, Marton also served in the 1930s as the representative of Transylvanian Jews in the Romanian parliament. During that period he was also well known in Zionist circles outside Romania. His comprehensive articles on the situation of the Jewish people and its problems were translated and published in various countries.[81]

Marton continued his public and publicist activity after the annexation of northern Transylvania by Hungary in 1940. From 1941 he presented his worldview to the wider Hungarian Jewish public in a series of publications. In writing about Jewish history in Europe and specifically in Hungary, Marton was significantly freer from the narrow Hungarian perspective than were most Zionists in Hungary. Thanks to his tendency to consider contemporary events from a broader Jewish perspective, Marton developed a usable past that was more comprehensive than that of other Hungarian Zionists spokespeople.

In the book *A magyar zsidóság családfája* (The Origin of Hungarian Jewry), which was published in Kolozsvár in 1941, Marton challenged the fundamental assumptions of the homemaking myth that Hungarian Jews had developed during the emancipation. The crisis facing Hungarian Jewry, he argued in his introduction, was spiritual as well as physical. Among other things, it stemmed from the failure on the part of Hungarian Jews to realize what was taking place around them. One way to cope with this crisis, he added, was to develop a more critical understanding of the past as a foundation for a clearer consciousness in the present. Hungarian Jews, however, seemed incapable of this: "There are only a few groups in the entire world whose self-consciousness is in such a bad state as ours, Hungarian Jews. We know so little about ourselves, and what we do know is, mostly, wretched and distorted."[82]

Marton briefly reviewed Hungarian Jewish historiography, concluding that it was highly fragmented. In fact, he argued, it had failed to develop for several decades. His explanation for this miserable situation revealed his assessment of the general situation of Hungarian Jews:

> Why did Jewish historians become silent? Why did Jewish historical research in Hungary decline so dramatically from the

beginning of the twentieth century? Aside from many other signs, this is another manifestation of the decadent process that can be recognized in the internal life of Hungarian Jewry since the turn of the century. An additional expression of this decline, which began with assimilation, can be recognized in the biological and spiritual life of Hungarian Jews in the last 30–35 years. . . . During the first decades of this century, Hungarian Jewry did not feel a real bond to its past. . . . This was an expression of the fact that this period was for it a period of national death.[83]

Marton's harsh criticism of Jewish historiography in Hungary was inspired by general developments outside Hungary, especially the emergence of a new national Jewish school of thought that dissociated itself from the nineteenth-century historiography that had developed under the impact of Jewish assimilation. In the spirit of Simon Dubnow, whom Marton presented as the most prominent spokesperson of this new school, Marton portrayed the Hungarian Jewish historiography as an initiative that aimed to shatter the entire Jewish national consciousness of common fate in order to pave the way for the integration of Jews in Hungary.[84] The new political reality, he stated, made this historical view irrelevant and demanded a new historiography that would present more realistic images of the past vis-à-vis the situation that Jews were now facing:

> Nowadays, when we sit on the ruins of Emancipation, the task of Jewish history will be to depict, scientifically and objectively, the balance of the Emancipation era, what we achieved and what we lost in this rich and interesting chapter of our history, where we went wrong, what we missed and what lesson we can learn from this clear, rich but also irresponsible era. [We should learn all this] for the sake of the life of our people, which is entering now a more difficult era, with much heavier responsibility.[85]

In his discussion of the origin of Hungarian Jews, Marton sharply disproved the myth that they were the offspring of the Khazars and that they had taken part in the Conquest in the late ninth century. Hungarian Jewry, Marton argued, originated with the massive waves of Jewish immigration as an integral part of the Central European medieval Jewry. Later after the liberation of Hungary from the Turks, modern Hungarian Jewry was re-created by various waves of immigration of Ashkenazi Jews from Central Europe (Germany, Austria, and Moravia) and primarily eastern Europe (Poland).[86]

Here Marton challenged the tradition relating the unique origin and the fate of the Hungarian Jews, presenting them instead as an integral part of the "community of fate" (*sorsközösség*) of Central and east European Jewry. This had tangible consequences for the current situation of Hungarian Jews, as his words implied: "It is therefore impossible to speak about a unique Hungarian Jewish fate with its own distinct mission, its own course and its own dynamic in contrast to the other Jews. . . . It will be a great mistake if we cling to the illusion that due to the ostensible Hungarian uniqueness the historical events will not reach us. . . . We must always examine our fate in view of the universal Jewish life."[87]

Another key assumption of the modern Hungarian Jewish historiography that Marton clearly refuted was the idea that the Hungarian nation had always been exceptionally friendly and hospitable to the Jews. This myth, he claimed, was created by modern Jewish historians who were Hungarian patriots and who felt committed to "fix" the Hungarian past by removing any anti-Semitic traces. A new Jewish historiography would be able to depict the past without revamping it, to point to the anti-Semitic elements in the Hungarian past and try to explain them. In this spirit Marton pointed to a series of anti-Jewish riots in Hungarian history and argued that the expulsions in the late Middle Ages had produced a great demographic decline among Hungarian Jews even before the Battle of Mohács and the Turkish occupation of most of its territories.[88] This thesis diminished the accepted image of the relatively undisturbed continuity of Jewish life under Hungarian rule, which was interrupted only by the foreign Turkish occupation. This position also had bearing on the present, as it challenged the claim that the condition of Hungarian Jews in the early 1940s was relatively better than in neighboring countries due to the historically more tolerant attitude of the Hungarians.

Marton, who called for a broader examination of the situation of the Jewish people, contended with this challenge in two other publications dating from 1941: "The Future of the Jewish People" ("A zsidó nép jövője") and "The Worldwide Situation of the Jewish People in 1941" ("A zsidó nép világhelyzete 1941-ben"). Inspired by Dubnow's historical thought, Marton attempted to delineate in these essays the forms of regularity that characterized Jewish life in the Diaspora. The law of the exile in Jewish life (*gáluti lét törvényszerűsége*), he stated, shapes Jewish history in a cyclical course that periodically gets cut off by catastrophes. These catastrophes cause the end to the decline of a historical Jewish center, as the situation in 1941 clearly heralds the decline and ruin of the Jewish center in Europe. A broad look at Jewish history from the exile by ancient Egypt and Rome through the Crusades, the Black Death, the expulsion from Spain, and the Khmelnytsky massacres shows, however, that in spite of these catastrophes, it is not possible to destroy the Jewish people, as the decline of one Jewish center is always followed by the rise of a new one.[89]

A further historical characteristic to which Marton referred in his discussion of dangers to the future of the Jewish people was the threat of assimilation. In this context he related to the naturalization of the Jews in revolutionary France and later in Prussia and Hungary. He argued that these rights had been granted to them in exchange for their renunciation of their collective ethos, Jewish communal life:

> Western Jewry manifested its readiness to intermingle with the peoples of the countries in which the Jews were living and those people were ready, in exchange, to accept the Jews. The spirit of the epoch was supposed to enable such a deal; both sides were sincere in their intentions and actually wanted this great experiment to succeed and the thousands-years-old Jewish problem to be finally solved. But this attempt still did not succeed, even though some 150 years had passed since the [ideas of the] French Revolution had begun to spread through the world with an enthusiastic zeal. Not only did it not succeed; on the contrary, it brought exactly the opposite result.[90]

The failure of assimilation clearly shows, Marton argued, that declarations and even sincere intentions were not enough. Thus, the historical regularity that he outlined determines that assimilation of a minority within the majority society can be successful only if it is an unconscious process. Western Jews, however, have acted in exactly the opposite way (he did not differentiate here among German, French, and Hungarian Jews). They have manifested their patriotism noisily and attempted to adopt their new motherland's language and culture consciously and openly. Furthermore, an assimilation process might be successful only if it unfolds slowly; it should endure for several generations and can by no means be accelerated. This was another mistake of west European Jews: they were hasty to pick the fruits of assimilation before they were ripe. The Jewish assimilation in Europe had therefore developed in a compulsive and unnatural manner, which had eventually evoked an opposite reaction by the European peoples and an exclusion of the Jews to forced dissimilation.[91]

Seeking to give his readers a broad picture of the situation of the Jewish people, Marton expansively related as well to the problems of the Jewish communities in the United States and the Soviet Union. His conclusion in both essays was that only the establishment of a sovereign Jewish settlement in one country could put an end to the cyclical regularity of exile in Jewish life.[92] However, even during the darkest days of the Holocaust, he did not express the idea of the elimination of the Diaspora, and his Zionist path still joined together the Jewish settlement in Palestine and the rehabilitation of Diaspora Jewish life in the framework of a new emancipation:

> The new Emancipation, if it would seek to avoid the errors of the first one, should be deeply rooted in the principle of human fraternity. If there is a hope that majority and minority would be able to live peacefully side by side—and this is our belief—it would be materialized only on the foundation of mutual sincerity and openness. *The Jews would be able to live among the peoples only as a people.* . . . A new Emancipation can be possible only if there will be [in addition] *a political Jewish community,* in which Jews will live a fully independent national life. . . . The setting up and the development of the Jewish state will grant the new Emancipation in the Diaspora a new genuine foundation.[93]

It is noteworthy that Marton chose to use the term "new Emancipation," which had also been used by a variety of Jewish publicists in Germany during the first years of the Nazi period. The use of such a term proves that Marton was resistant to the idea of a return to the ghetto and, like Komlós and other critical Neolog writers, was seeking a new and better formula for Jewish integration in Hungary.

Marton was the most prominent but not the only Zionist spokesperson who, in the midst of the Holocaust, offered Hungarian Jews a new and comprehensive Jewish historical perspective. This was influenced by the historiographic tradition of Dubnow as a substitute to the nineteenth-century Hungarian Jewish historiography.[94] These positions did not evoke any extensive or self-critical public debate in the Hungarian Jewish public, since the vast majority of its spokespeople continued to cling to the narrative of Hungarian Jewish integration. The fact that there were relatively few comments that these Zionist voices evoked demonstrated the deep roots of the integration narrative in the self-awareness of the spokespeople of Budapest Jewry, even amid the Holocaust.[95]

Conclusion

The paths of Jewish public debate in Hungary in the years reviewed in this chapter represent an interesting and unique case study of how an integrated European Jewish community coped with the meaning of the events that occurred in Europe during the Holocaust years. Insofar as the catastrophic events of the Holocaust took place (until the spring of 1944) beyond their country's borders, most spokespeople for Hungarian Jewry continued to cling to the homemaking myth that had linked them to their homeland since the emancipation. In their search for meaning and comfort, they turned and returned to this myth.

As we have seen, the formation of modern Hungarian Jewry and its efforts to be incorporated within the Hungarian state and nation were naturally bound up with the development of a distinctive Hungarian Jewish self-consciousness and, at the same time, a weakening of the wider Jewish collective. The circumstances of Hungarian Jewish life in the early 1940s granted concrete meaning to this distinctive self-consciousness, which had been shaped in the decades of the emancipation. This image of the Hungarian Jewry was the community used by Neolog spokespeople as their reference group as they endeavored to interpret their present position vis-à-vis their history. They believed that Hungarian Jews constituted a unique Jewish community in terms of its historical experience over the centuries. This entrenched view was supported by the more general perception of Hungarian nationalism as unique in relation to other European national traditions, primarily in Germany. The Neolog spokespeople could not of course ignore the decline of the civil status of the Jews in Hungary and their economic and social exclusion. Still, the forms of their usable past enabled them to paint for their readers a picture of a unique Hungarian Jewish fate in the present and reinforced their belief that they were not going to share the disastrous fate of their brethren in Nazi-occupied Europe.

Modern Orthodox spokespeople, who fundamentally shared the same political assumptions, also continued to resort to Hungarian national symbols and heroes from the emancipation era. But they also interpreted the decline of the emancipation in Germany, France, and sometimes even in Hungary itself as clear evidence of the bankruptcy of the modern liberal Jewish path. By 1944 Orthodox spokespeople, particularly Korein, tended more than the Neologs to recognize the failure of emancipation. Nevertheless, they would not deny the uniqueness of the Hungarian case.

This chapter, in addition to having analyzed the positions espoused by the Jewish establishment, has also presented a more critical Hungarian Jewish discourse, which emerged very prominently in the early 1940s. Certain Neolog spokespeople and in an even sharper manner Jewish nationalist spokespeople also pointed to the connection between present events and the past deeds, mistakes, and failures of Hungarian Jews during the emancipation. In some instances they even challenged the basic assumptions of Hungarian Jewish historiography and memory culture. Some Neolog spokespeople depicted the historical course of emancipation in Hungary as imbalanced and argued that it severely weakened the Jewish community and had made the Jews more vulnerable. This was quite similar to the idea advanced by certain liberal German Jews in the 1930s. Publicists such as Sós and Komlós also presented the weakening of Hungarian emancipation as part of a more extensive Jewish crisis but, at the same time, continued to believe in the future possibility of a healthier and more balanced cultural and communal synthesis between Hungarianness and Judaism. Zionist spokespeople, first and foremost Marton, challenged even more directly the idea of a unique Hungarian Jewish path. They presented the historical errors of modern Hungarian Jewry—primarily its readiness to assimilate—as integral to the failure of Western Jewry. Still, even the Zionist vision that was articulated by Marton in those years envisioned a future Hungarian Jewish community that would learn from its past errors and develop under the more respectable, suitable, and stable terms of a new emancipation.

CONCLUSION

The decline of liberalism, the rise of Fascism and Nazism, and most of all the growing anti-Semitic threat drove European Jewish leaders and public activists to develop an intensive and complicated historical discourse. In many respects this passionate preoccupation with the past served to preserve ideas and tendencies that had characterized Jewish public thought throughout the emancipation era. In other aspects, however, it reflected various reactions to the new crisis.

In each of the three case studies presented in these pages, Jewish spokespeople from various communities and political camps related to the local homemaking myth that had been formed by their communal political and rabbinical establishments during the emancipation era. This myth combined a universal belief in progress, a liberal interpretation of the history of their particular nation (Germany, France, or Hungary, as the case may be), and the perception that the local Jewish population was an integral part of the nation. Many of them, primarily but not only from the liberal integrationist camp, attempted—at least in the first stages of their grappling with the changes in the 1930s—to preserve certain parts of this myth or at least to adapt them to the new reality. These spokespeople portrayed the history of the emancipation in their respective countries as a golden age for the Jews. Others who also continued to believe in the validity of the fundamental values of emancipation nevertheless pointed to certain historical errors and shortcomings of this period. Looking back to the late eighteenth century and the nineteenth century, they criticized the way that the state and society had regarded the Jews as well as the choices made by the Jews themselves.

Only relatively few voices, primarily from the Orthodox or Zionist camps, categorically denied the positive evaluation of the emancipation and viewed its decline as an inevitable outcome of the course it had followed from the very beginning.[1]

The validity of the comparative perspective and the fact that in spite of many differences there was still a common denominator in the three case studies are apparent in the reactions of the various Jewish political camps in Germany, France, and Hungary. In each of these three Jewries there was in the interwar period a central liberal camp whose spokespeople represented the communal establishment and continued to cling to the legacy of the emancipation. Although historical circumstances in each instance were quite different, there were also significant parallels. Spokespeople for the integrationist liberal camps in all three countries turned to certain similar strategies when determining how to represent the past.

Associated predominantly with the Centralverein deutscher Staatsbürger jüdischen Glaubens (Central Union of the German Citizens of the Jewish Faith [CV]), spokespeople for the integrationist camp in Germany turned in the last years of the Weimar Republic to the German liberal legacy in an attempt to use its symbols in their struggle against the rise of Nazism. Since a direct political struggle became impossible following the Nazi rise to power, they had to confront the collapse of emancipation in Germany and come to terms with it. In Germany, the nature and the intensity of this process made denying the collapse of emancipation or relating it to foreign (non-German) influence inconceivable for the Jews. As was seen in chapter 1, they had to acknowledge not only that the Weimar Republic had fallen but that this was the end of an era that had lasted 120 or even 150 years. Still, spokespeople for this camp continued, even in the first years of the Nazi regime, to embrace emancipation perceptions, symbols, and images even as they tried to adjust them to the gloomy situation.

Under the new circumstances, which precluded any possibility of explicit public condemnation of the regime, German Jewish liberal spokespeople— including historians, publicists, and public activists—tended more than ever to turn to the past and developed a discourse that expressed veiled criticism. One of the most prominent spokespeople of this camp, the Berlin educator and CV activist Fritz Friedländer, expressed his view in the following argument: Just as Napoleon's defeat at Waterloo should not make us forget his great victory at Austerlitz, it would be wrong to minimize the historical era of Jewish emancipation, despite its present decline. Friedländer therefore continued to cling to the legacy of the German Enlightenment even after the Nuremberg Laws were enacted, going so far as to contest the positions of the Nazi historian Wilhelm Grau. Similarly, other liberal spokespeople tried to preserve the dignity of the emancipation period that was no longer and to find comfort in its memory, even if they were compelled to agree that its political impact had become diminished at present. Sometimes they turned as well to a more distant past, particularly to the medieval era, seeking there the deep roots of the Jewish presence in Germany. These roots, they believed, might well survive even after the decline of the era that had begun with the Enlightenment and the French Revolution. The nine hundredth anniversary of the establishment of the ancient synagogue in Worms, which was celebrated in 1934 (discussed in chapter 2), is a clear example of this tendency.

In the 1930s French Jews enjoyed much better conditions than their German Jewish coreligionists. Still, the French Jews had to cope with the historical and political significance of the decline of liberalism in Europe, the rise of Nazism in Germany, and the escalating political polarization in France. The legacy of the French Revolution, which was at the core of the central myth of emancipation in France, continued to be used by the spokespeople of the Central Consistory throughout the 1930s. To this was added the myth of internal sacred union (*l'union sacrée*) during World War I. It is noteworthy that they tended—primarily around the marking of July 14—to ignore the fact that the fundamental values of the Revolution were deeply disputed within French society between the Right and the Left. The positive image of the Revolution as a national French consensus enabled integrationist French Jews (as seen in chapter 3) to depict the emancipation of the Jews as a product of such a consensus. By nurturing the image of France as the home of the Revolution, they were also able to link the sources of the modern anti-Semitic movement to Germany and to portray it as fundamentally foreign to the French spirit.

Spokespeople of the immigrants' federation, which represented the central camp among the large east European Yiddish-speaking immigrants' community in France, were not integrationist liberals like the CV members in Germany or the Central Consistory in France. However, in their declarations, especially in the national Jewish daily *Pariser Haynt*, the impact of the Franco-Jewish culture of memory is evident. Sensitive to developments in the wider Jewish world, these spokespeople related to the struggle concerning the status of the Jews as a general European problem but also as having a key role in the unique French legacy. Thus, the spokespeople of the federation as well as those of the left-wing Jewish parties (the Jewish Communists and the Bund) that were active among the immigrants related fervently to the meaning of July 14. Unlike the Central Consistory's spokespeople, east European publicists also invoked the concrete political meaning of the

Revolution in the internal French debate. As tensions between Germany and France rose in the spring and summer of 1939, local and immigrant Jewish spokespeople did not fail to mark the memory of the Revolution while also commemorating the victory of the revolutionary army in the Battle of Valmy over the Austro-Prussian coalition.

In the 1930s Hungarian Jews were forced to cope with the hostile political climate and legislation that affected them so adversely. In the early 1940s their legal status and social condition continued to deteriorate, but unlike German and French Jews of the early 1940s, they were not exposed to the Nazi extermination policy. Until the German occupation of March 1944 they could continue to conduct an active communal life, to publish books and periodicals, and to articulate various positions regarding images of the past. Under these circumstances the integrationist Jews—predominantly the leaders and spokespeople of the Neolog community—continued to cling to ideal images of Hungarian nationalism. They dealt with Hungary's liberal legacy and commemorated Hungarian national heroes from the nineteenth century. It is noteworthy that whereas French Jewish and, to a lesser extent, German Jewish writers shaped the local Jewish homemaking myths chiefly around the legacy of emancipation and assimilation of the late eighteenth century and the nineteenth century, the Hungarian Jewish spokespeople turned much more extensively to the medieval era. This tendency, which partly originated from the dominant conservative mood of the Hungarian political culture at large, was expressed, for example, in the deep involvement of Jewish leaders in the summer of 1938 in the nine hundredth anniversary of Saint Stephen's death.

The idea of the uniqueness of Hungarian nationalism in Europe and specifically its tolerance toward the Jews was a central component in the historical awareness of the integrationist Jews of Hungary. Accordingly, some depicted anti-Semitism as fundamentally at odds with Hungarian nationalism, as an outcome of German influence that Hungarian nationalism was able to resist when it was strong enough even as far back as the era of the Crusades. Like French Jews but under very different historical circumstances, the past images of liberal Hungarian Jews portrayed the victory of Nazi anti-Semitism as a foreign phenomenon that stood as a fundamental contradiction to the national-political culture of their homeland. As shown in chapter 6, this image endured even in the early 1940s in spite of the political and military treaty between the Hungarian regime and Nazi Germany and despite the deterioration in the status of the Jews.

Integrationist Jewish bodies in Germany, France, and Hungary therefore embraced similar strategies in their representations of the past in order to cope with the difficulties of the present. They made extensive use of anniversaries and of a variety of figures from the national-liberal pantheon of heroes. These methods aimed to legitimate the Jewish acceptance in their homelands and to describe their acceptance as a well-established historical fact. Historical figures such as Wilhelm von Humboldt in Germany, Abbé Henri Grégoire in France and József Eötvös in Hungary were often mentioned by Jewish liberals. This was the case too with national festivals such as July 14 in France and March 15 in Hungary. Jewish historians, rabbis, and public leaders published a variety of historical accounts and source materials that were meant to identify the past images that verified Jewish integration while also aiming to calm their Jewish readers as they contended with the daily harsh reality. In this respect a common perspective united the book written by Berlin historian Ismar Elbogen on German Jewish history (1935), the comprehensive sourcebook *Témoignages sur Israël* (Testimonies about Israel) compiled by Paris rabbi Jacob Kaplan (1938), and the sources that were published by the Budapest Neolog publicist Ernő Ballagi to mark the centennial anniversary of the legislation that had led to Jewish emancipation in Hungary (1940).[2]

Another important area of parallel concern can be discerned in the respective positions regarding the idea of progress. The conviction that history proceeds forward, rationally, toward a better future has been one of the fundamental principles of liberal culture since the age of Enlightenment. In France this view was bound inherently to the Revolution's legacy and became one of the essential principles of republican political culture. Various iterations of the idea of progress, which combined the universal rational elements with national ideologies, were integrated in the liberal streams of the German and Hungarian political cultures.[3] Over the course of the nineteenth century the idea of progress became a central component in the public thought and political culture of emancipated Jewry, which was bound by an abiding optimism in the future of the Jews in Europe.

The decline of liberalism in Europe, which had begun even before World War I and accelerated in the interwar era, was no less than an assault on the idea of progress. One of the principles of the culture of defeat, which characterized Germany and Hungary in the wake of World War I and also had an impact in France, was the prevalence of the pessimistic public mood. As a result, the optimistic linear historical narrative was replaced by the depiction of history as a process of decline or at least as an unending cyclical movement. Inevitably this atmosphere also impacted the shaping of the Jewish culture of memory.

Liberal Jews correctly viewed the waning of the idea of progress as part of the threat against the future of the emancipation. Some chose to ignore or repress that threat. However, the deterioration in the situation of the Jews in the 1930s as well as the arguments that were raised by Orthodox and Zionist spokespeople motivated liberals to reflect carefully on these topics. Bruno Weil, for example, a senior member of the CV leadership, depicted medieval and modern German Jewish history as a wavy path that signified the process by which the optimism inherent in the linear view was discredited. Samu Stern, the president of the Neolog Communities of Hungary, expressed a similar description of Hungarian Jewish history. However, finding a comparable view of French Jewish history clearly expressed by a senior member of the Central Consistory is more difficult. The spokespeople for integrationist Jews seem to have felt compelled to replace the optimistic linear historical view with a cyclical outline of Jewish history in their homeland only when the circumstances left them no other options. In his lectures delivered in late 1933, Weil went in this direction and expressed this position clearly in the book that he published in 1934, after the revocation of Jewish emancipation in Germany was an undeniable fact. Stern assumed this position in 1938 in reaction to the First Jewish Law in Hungary, at the beginning of the end of seventy years of Jewish emancipation in Hungary. Both Weil and Stern preferred the cyclical representation of their respective community's history in order to ease the disillusionment over what seemed then as the defeat of progress in Jewish history. They attempted to present precedents for the current crisis and to evoke hopes for the rehabilitation of the position of the Jews in the long run. In France, in spite of threats both from home and abroad, Jewish emancipation endured until the end of the 1930s. Spokespeople for the liberal establishment continued to cling to the historical narrative of French emancipated Jewry, although this narrative was based on an unreserved faith in the ethos of the Revolution and consequently also in the idea of progress.

Aside from these tendencies, other liberal Jewish spokespeople developed a more critical approach toward the history of emancipated Jewry in their own countries. They remained loyal to the fundamental principles of emancipation, did not turn to Zionism, and continued to believe in the possibility of re-creating an integrated Jewish community. However, unlike most of the spokespeople for the liberal camp, they chose to accentuate the shortcomings and errors in Jewish behavior during the emancipation. The Jews who were granted emancipation, these spokespeople asserted, went too far in adopting the cultural norms of the surrounding society while leaving their heritage behind. Thus, already in 1933 there existed in the *Central Verein Zeitung* a call to Jewish youths to liberate themselves from "the rubble of the old assimilatory Jewish shadow-life" and to shape a firmer Jewish awareness for the postemancipation era.[4] Another spokesperson for the CV, who also belonged to the younger generation, called on his readers to develop a more collective form of emancipation based on the tradition that "all Israel are responsible for one another."[5] Some liberal Jewish spokespeople who wrote in the 1930s about Moses Mendelssohn were very critical of his disciples, who in the view of these spokespeople deviated from his original legacy of finding the right balance between Germanness and Judaism.

The lowering of the status of Hungarian Jewry in the late 1930s and early 1940s as well as the growing awareness of the collapse of emancipation in Germany and in other European countries motivated certain Neolog spokespeople to develop more critical positions about the Jewish past. Endre Sós, for one, accused Hungarian Jews of a distorted understanding of assimilation that led many of them to deny their own culture. Sós also linked this flawed historical path to the fundamentally problematic character of Jewish emancipation, which had freed the Jews as individuals but not as a collective.[6] But despite certain similarities between these positions and the Zionist critique of emancipated Jewry, Sós and other Neolog spokespeople were not Zionists. Even in the early 1940s they continued to believe that the integration of the Jews in Hungary was still possible and even desirable if was carried out in a balanced way.

Critical approaches toward the emancipation were naturally more exceptional among spokespeople for the French Jewish integrationist establishment. The reality of the 1930s still enabled them to link the problems of the Jews primarily to German anti-Semitism and perhaps also to the shortsightedness of the German Jews. These French Jewish spokespeople therefore continued to believe in the historical course that had led French Jews to a well-established and more secure emancipation. But in some cases their message was more complicated. In a 1934 article, Rabbi Maurice Liber, the chief rabbi of Paris and a senior member of the Central Consistory, condemned what he termed "passive emancipation," a nineteenth-century Jewish approach that could have led to the decline of Judaism. A few years later on the eve of World War II, Liber remained attached to the legacy of the French Revolution, but he also asserted that the emancipated Jews had lived under a powerful illusion that enlightenment and progress would solve their problems without a struggle.[7]

Aside from the liberals, there were two other major political camps in the European Jewish public sphere: the Zionists and the Orthodox. Naturally more skeptical than the liberals about the ideals of progress and emancipation, both the Zionists and the Orthodox had a more convenient starting point for explaining the decline of emancipation. Spokespeople from both camps criticized the historical error of the liberal Jewish camp that had led to the policy of Jewish integration. Still, many spokespeople of both camps continued to adhere to their own version of the homemaking myth, which bound the Jews to their European homelands. Only relatively few spokespeople—although sometimes prominent ones—expressed more sweeping reservations of the emancipation and portrayed it as an erroneous path, an inevitable historical failure or even as a religious or national sin.

An analysis of the positions taken by Zionist spokespeople in Germany demonstrates this very well. As we saw in chapter 1, German Zionist publicists called on their readers even before the Nazi rise to power to acknowledge the decline of liberal political values in both German and Jewish politics. Nevertheless, they were far from dissociating themselves totally from the German Jewish liberal heritage. This can be demonstrated by the case of Gustav Krojanker, who expressed in 1932 very radical positions that were not accepted by most German Zionists but still continued to recognize the historical force of this liberal heritage. About a year later Hugo Rosenthal asserted that German Jews should have rejected the very idea of assimilation as a condition for emancipation and should have insisted on the acceptance of their ethnic uniqueness as part of their integration. Nevertheless, Rosenthal also called on his readers to recognize the importance of the historical legacy of a century of emancipation. The position of Joachim Prinz, who in his 1934 book *Wir Juden* rehabilitated ghetto life and depicted the image of emancipated Jewry in purely negative terms, was therefore exceptional among German Zionist spokespeople. Whereas Prinz directed his assault on the figure of Mendelssohn, most other Zionist spokespeople expressed a positive evaluation of the eighteenth-century philosopher as the founding father of modern German Jewry. Since they approved of the decision to leave the ghetto, they generally focused their historical critique on the unbalanced path that Jews had taken in Germany during the emancipation but not against the idea of integration itself.

In France, Zionist and national liberal spokespeople represented a small minority within the local Jewish community but constituted a much larger segment among the east European immigrants. In general, Zionist spokespeople in France perceived the rise of Fascism, Nazism, and anti-Semitism as a threat to European Jewry at large, but on the other hand most continued to identify with the legacy of the French Revolution and Jewish emancipation in their own country. One of the *Pariser Haynt* commentators, for example, portrayed the Nuremberg Laws as a European effort to push the Jews back into the ghetto, which he viewed as a result of the loss of Jewish dignity during the period of emancipation. Almost at the same time, however, the same writer stressed the critical distinction between the German anti-Semitic tradition and the revolutionary legacy of France.[8]

The need to choose between a memory culture that is still influenced by the ideas of integration and progress and the total negation of the emancipation legacy as a hopeless illusion from the very beginning was expressed metaphorically in the spring of 1938 in the French Zionist journal *La Terre Retrouvée*. In an imaginary dialogue between two Zionists (discussed in chapter 4), Joseph Ben Aron gave expression to the confusion and the complicated situation of French Zionists in the late 1930s.[9] Still, even when pessimistic expressions voiced by national Jewish spokespeople in France peaked during the return-to-the-ghetto debate, in most cases they did not reach a total negation of the idea of progress and of the legacy of emancipation; instead, they advanced a more critical interpretation of their meaning. The position of Arnold Mandel, who completely rejected the idea of progress and challenged the very decision of emancipation Jews to bind their fate with the West, was very marginal even on the eve of World War II.

As in France, Hungarian Zionist spokespeople also presented the rise of Fascism and anti-Semitism as an overall European, or even global, Jewish problem that required careful historical reflection. On the other hand, they also avoided, at least in the beginning, linking the decline of liberalism and the dismantling of Jewish emancipation in Germany to the situation in their own homeland. The historical narrative of Hungarian Zionists in the 1930s, expressed most clearly by József Patai, editor of the monthly *Múlt és Jövő*, criticized modern Hungarian Jews for the abandonment of the Jewish national spirit for the sake of unrestrained assimilation. This narrative also related to the shortsightedness of their faith in the inevitable victory of progress. However, in spite of their appeal to Hungarian Jews to return to their roots, Patai and other Zionist spokespeople did not call on the Jews to dissociate themselves entirely from Hungary. Later on as the situation deteriorated in the early 1940s, more radical views were voiced in the Zionist discourse. The Transylvanian Zionist Ernő Marton, the most prominent among these spokespeople, portrayed in depth what he saw as the historical cycle that led to the inevitable failure of emancipation and assimilation in Europe. Marton presented modern Hungarian Jewish historical consciousness and historiography, which were aimed at depicting Hungarian Jewry as a community of fate with a distinctive historical path, as illusory, and he strove to weaken their fundamental principles. Still, in the early 1940s even Marton related to the possibility that even after the establishment of a sovereign Jewish settlement some of the European Jews—in Hungary as well as in other countries—would continue to live in their homelands as a national minority under a new emancipation. That scenario, he assumed, would be more realistic and stable than the old liberal one.

In two of the three communities dealt with in these pages, there was an established Orthodox sector. In Germany and Hungary, nineteenth-century confrontations between the religious streams had resulted in an official schism.[10] The Orthodox communities had their own journals that appealed to the public opinion of their respective communities. In France there was also a traditional communal life as well as traditional publicists, some of whom are discussed in this book, but the particular political dynamics of the communal system during the emancipation did not lead to the emergence of an established Orthodox sector.

Spokespeople for German Orthodoxy, principally those who expressed their positions in the weekly *Der Israelit,* linked the decline of the liberal era to the sweeping abandonment of Jewish tradition during the emancipation, predominantly by the liberal Jews. Most Orthodox commentators, however, avoided a complete rejection of the idea of emancipation. Some of them even pointed to the historical path of their own stream as the golden path: the proper balance between integration into German society and continued observance of the Jewish tradition. Samson Rafael Hirsch was the natural historical hero of these writers, although most of them also had a positive evaluation of Mendelssohn as well. Contrary to this position, the young rabbi Simon Schwab presented the ghetto as the historical norm of Jewish life in general. He rejected the idea of progress and portrayed the period of emancipation as a temporary pause in the tribulations of exile. Schwab discredited all versions of assimilation, including what he presented as the partial assimilation of modern Orthodoxy. He sharply attacked Mendelssohn and asserted that Hirsch's "Torah im Derech Erez" legacy was no more than a transitory solution that had lost its validity. But Schwab was exceptional. Other Orthodox spokespeople who reacted to Schwab's positions continued to embrace the idea of progress. Instead of disqualifying the nineteenth century entirely, they preferred to draw distinctions between the negative and positive elements of Jewish modernity.

Spokespeople for modern Orthodoxy in Hungary, unlike the Eastern ultra-Orthodoxy, were integrated into the Hungarian state and culture and shared most of the principles of the political ethos of the liberal Neologs, in spite of their differences on religious matters. In the late 1930s they also identified with the past images that the Neolog spokespeople presented and likewise turned to Hungarian national historical symbols such as Saint Stephen. Parallel to this, they also differentiated between the negative implications of assimilation, which they associated with diminishing religious observance, and a more balanced version of assimilation. This primarily meant association with Hungarian nationalism. Conditions in the early 1940s deepened the tendency to portray the historical path of liberal Jewry and the process of assimilation in Europe as the source of the disaster facing the Jews and to present the Orthodox path as the only alternative for improvement and renewal. Still, as time passed these writers—among whom the most prominent was Dezső Korein—became more pessimistic to the extent that they sometimes presented all streams of modern Jewish politics and even modern life in general in an entirely negative manner.

Generally, whereas various German Jewish spokespeople appeared to experience and conceptualize the collapse of the emancipation as a challenge to the meaning of Jewish modernity at large, Jewish spokespeople in France and Hungary tended to interpret events in Germany as well as in their own countries as a temporary setback in the inevitable course of modernity. German Jewish writers tended to distinguish between different forms of German nationalism, pointing to instances of toleration in its history as a counterpoint to Nazi barbarism. Under the impact of the disillusions that they experienced in the first years of the Nazi regime, the most that their spokespeople could do was to claim that the enlightened German proemancipation tradition, as it was expressed by Humboldt and others, was a legitimate German legacy in spite of the fact that it became obsolete in post-1933 Germany. By contrast, the vast majority of French and Hungarian Jewish spokespeople portrayed the political heritage in their homelands in monolithically positive terms and chose not to confront its darker side. Accordingly, Jewish spokespeople in France, natives and immigrants alike, presented the revolutionary legacy clearly as the French legacy, asserting that any deviation from its principles, including its commitment to full Jewish emancipation, was the result of foreign, mostly German, influence. Hungarian Jewish spokespeople depicted their country's national legacy as open and tolerant to the Jews from the Middle Ages to the liberal era, a sharp contradiction to the German national legacy from the age of the Crusades to the Nazi era.

In each of the three communities the meaning of the concept of assimilation was discussed extensively. Most liberals, Zionist and Orthodox alike, attempted to draw a distinction between good, fruitful, or positive assimilation and bad, negative, or destructive assimilation. Many portrayed the decline of the assimilation era as having resulted from the absence of clear boundaries between the integration of the Jews in the local culture and the preservation of their collective uniqueness. Only very few of the historical interpretations that have been discussed in this book (a few in Germany and fewer in France and Hungary) actually denounced the entire course of emancipation and assimilation in modern Jewish history.

A major difference between Jewish public discourse in Germany and Hungary on the one hand and in France on the other hand stemmed from the two-tiered structure of the French Jewish community. The German and Hungarian Jewish historical discourses can be characterized as two distinct enclaves in the Jewish world. Due to their relative cultural and linguistic homogeneity (in spite of their religious and political diversity), German and Hungarian Jews concentrated mainly on their own problems and dealt with Jewish history from their own particular perspectives. The public discourse of the Jews in France, primarily the one that was conducted in the Yiddish press, related much more to the global perspective of the Jewish experience and was clearly part of a transnational discourse. This found clear expression in the return-to-the-ghetto polemic.

Spokespeople representing the various Jewish streams who were active in the countries where Jews were emancipated utilized images and representations of the past both to legitimize their political and religious positions as well as to increase the feeling of safety or, at least, of comfort among their readers. When the political situation permitted it—in Germany before 1933 and in France and Hungary throughout the 1930s—these spokespeople turned to history as part of their struggle against the rise of Fascism and anti-Semitism. The usable past was also an important element in a variety of communal activities. In Germany, historical precedents were used to legitimize emigration and to offer encouragement to emigrants. Jewish spokespeople in France turned to the past to support their position on the absorption of Jewish immigrants and refugees. In Hungary, it was recourse to the Jewish past that made a united social-welfare effort possible.

A further point of comparison concerns the background of the various individuals who took part in shaping and restructuring the expressions of Jewish communal memory. In this regard, the most prominent element in the Jewish public arenas in Germany, France (natives but not the immigrant population), and Hungary was the central role of rabbis, mostly liberal but also Orthodox graduates of the modern rabbinical seminaries in Berlin, Breslau, Paris and Budapest. These rabbinical seminaries, a product of nineteenth-century emancipated Jewry, dealt intensively with the study and research of Jewish history in their homelands.[11] Senior and relatively older rabbis—such as Max Eschelbacher, Caesar Seligmann, Max Dienermann, and Moses Auerbach in Germany; Maurice Liber, Jacob Kaplan, Léon Berman, and Nathan Netter in France; and Sámuel Löwinger, Bernát Heller, Yehiel Michael Guttmann, and Sámuel Kandel in Hungary—therefore represented mostly mainstream positions in the public debate about Jewish history and the rise of Fascism.

Another noteworthy phenomenon was the involvement of young rabbis, publicists, and intellectuals, some only twenty-five or thirty years old, in the public discourse on Jewish memory. This was most prominent in Germany, where three rabbis—the Zionist Joachim Prinz, the liberal Manfred Swarsensky, and the Orthodox Simon Schwab—expressed exceptional and at times even radical opinions. Their young age might explain the occasional audaciousness or naïveté that is found in their articles. It is noteworthy that the three rabbis immigrated to the United States from Nazi Germany and continued their public and rabbinical careers. The phenomenon of young writers who expressed critical and radical opinions was less prominent in France and in Hungary, perhaps because the cultural shock there was less severe. However, such writers did exist in those countries: Arnold Mandel, whose opinions (discussed in chapter 4) was quite radical in the French Jewish context, and to a much lesser extent Endre Sós in Hungary.

All in all, it can be said, following the analysis of the sociologist Viktor Karády about Hungary, that the vast majority of the positions that have been expressed in this book are postassimilatory.[12] Liberal, Zionist, and Orthodox Jews in Germany and Hungary and to a lesser degree in France viewed their past through the conceptual lens and cultural heritage of the age of assimilation but, at the same time, needed to consider a reevaluation of that heritage.

The conclusions reached in this book emphasize the unique profile of pre-Holocaust western and Central European Jewry, with its wide spectrum of Jewish movements. Comparing our conclusions with the findings of recent scholarship dealing with the struggle of Polish Jewry to overcome the crisis they faced during this same period, it is clear that the Polish Jewish experience was distinct from that of the three communities discussed in this book. Most Polish Jews did not experience emancipation before World War I, and the process of their integration into Polish national culture was still in a more primitive stage. Polish Jewry's political framework, which was much larger than the three Jewish communities discussed here, was also fundamentally different. The liberal integrationist camp, which constituted the mainstream of German, French, and, to a lesser extent, Hungarian Jewries, was quite a small minority among Polish Jews. On the other hand, in Poland there were much larger political camps that espoused Zionism, Jewish nationalism, and Jewish ethnic Socialism. Moreover, Orthodoxy was much more segregated than in Central Europe. The comparison with the Jewish communal structure in Poland therefore underscores the similarities shared by the Jews of Germany, France, and Hungary.

Nevertheless, recent scholarship that has dealt with Polish Jewish public discourse in the interwar period and especially during the 1930s describes tendencies that were fundamentally similar to those that have been portrayed in this book. Polish Jewish historians and public figures also turned in the 1930s to representations of the past, asserting that this was part of their struggle against the rising anti-Semitism. They tended to present a positive historical picture of the relationship between Poles and Jews, and they described true Polish nationalism as having been tolerant toward the Jews while relating the anti-Semitic episodes in Polish history to the impact of foreign influence, primarily German. Key figures in modern Polish nationalism were depicted in the Jewish press as representatives of the Polish and Jewish shared fate and sometimes even brotherhood.[13] Even in the early 1940s when Poland was under Nazi occupation and Jews were concentrated in Ghettos, many Jews continued to maintain the positive image of the real Poland and believed in the strength of the historical bond that united them with the Poles. This image that collapsed only with the extermination of the Jews in 1942.[14] We might therefore learn from this comparison that the fundamental characteristics of the Jewish memory culture, as set forth in this book, could develop as well—if only partially—even in Poland. Future scholarship will no doubt examine this from a wider transnational perspective.

Employing the comparative method, this book has demonstrated the strength of the homemaking myths that were central to the self-consciousness of European Jews during the emancipation era. In spite of the dramatic political developments that resulted in the collapse of emancipation in Germany, in its decline and eventual abolition in Hungary, and in a threat to its future even in France, most Jewish spokespeople in these communities continued to adhere to some version of the historical narrative that bound them to their European homeland. Indeed, as we have seen there were those who interpreted the new crisis as a call to return to the ghetto and portrayed the entire emancipation period as a historical mistake or even a sin. However, they were small in number. The vast majority of Jewish commentators, including liberals, Zionists, and Orthodox, could criticize the bygone era and describe its shortcomings yet avoided a total rejection of its essential values and symbols. In the vast majority of political streams and nuances, Jewish public thought in the aggregate continued to have faith in the future integration of the Jews into their surroundings, although this faith relied on a variety of formulas. All in all, in spite of the fact that the new circumstances pushed Jewish spokespeople to develop a more sober view of history, they did not abandon their fundamental faith in the idea of progress.

NOTES

Introduction

1. Alfred Hirschberg, "Der Centralverein deutscher Staatsbürger jüdischen Glaubens," in *Wille und Weg des deutschen Judentums,* 15 (Berlin, 1935).

2. For an overview on modern French Jewish history, see, for example, Paula E. Hyman, *The Jews of Modern France* (Berkeley, 1998); Pierre Birnbaum, ed., *Histoire politique des Juifs de France* (Paris, 1990); and Frances Malino and Bernard Wasserstein, eds., *The Jews in Modern France* (Hanover, NH, 1985).

3. For an overview on modern German Jewish history, see, for example, Michael Meyer, ed., *German-Jewish History in Modern Times* (New York, 1996–98), and Shulamit Volkov, *Die Juden in Deutschland, 1780–1918* (München, 1994). On the complex dynamics of the emancipation process of German Jews, see Reinhard Rürup, "The Tortuous and Thorny Path to Legal Equality: 'Jew Laws' and Emancipatory Legislation in Germany from the Late Eighteenth Century," *Leo Baeck Institute Year Book* 31 (1986): 3–33.

4. For an extensive discussion on the history of the Jewish question in Hungary, see János Gyurgyák, *A zsidókérdés Magyarországon* (Budapest, 2001). For an overview on the Jewish emancipation in Hungary from a comparative perspective, see Guy Miron, "Between 'Center' and 'East'—The Special Way of Jewish Emancipation in Hungary," *Jewish Studies at the CEU* 4 (2004–5): 111–38.

5. Jacob Katz, ed., *Toward Modernity: The European Jewish Model* (New Brunswick, NJ, 1987); Jonathan Frankel and Steven J. Zipperstein, eds., *Assimilation and Community: The Jews in Nineteenth-Century Europe* (Cambridge, UK, 1992); Pierre Birnbaum and Ira Katznelson, eds., *Paths of Emancipation: Jews, States, and Citizenship* (Princeton, NJ, 1995); and Michael Brenner, Vicki Caron, and Uri R. Kaufmann, eds., *Jewish Emancipation Reconsidered: The French and German Models* (Tübingen, 2003).

6. Reinhart Koselleck, "The Limits of Emancipation: A Conceptual-Historical Sketch," in Koselleck, *The Practice of Conceptual History, Timing History, Spacing Concepts,* 248–64 (Stanford, CA, 2002); quotation from p. 262.

7. Jacob Katz, *Out of the Ghetto: The Social Background of Jewish Emancipation, 1770–1870* (Cambridge, MA, 1973).

8. Brenner, Caron, and Kaufmann, eds., *Jewish Emancipation Reconsidered.*

9. In a letter to the Hungarian Jewish historian Joseph Bergel, who claimed that this declaration motivated him to deal with the Hungarian Jewish history himself,

see Joseph Bergel, *Geschichte der Ungarischen Juden* (Kaposvár, 1879), 34, cited in Nathaniel Katzburg, "Jewish Historiography in Hungary" [in Hebrew], *Sinai* 40, no. 2 (1957): 123.

10. Salo Baron, "The Revolution of 1848 and Jewish Scholarship," Part 2, *Proceedings of the American Academy of Jewish Research* 20 (1951): 84. My thanks to Professor Howard Lupovitch for drawing my attention to this article.

11. For a more detailed discussion on this problem, see Miron, "Between 'Center' and 'East.'"

12. For an overview of the life of the Jews in these countries in the interwar period, see Ezra Mendelsohn, *The Jews of East Central Europe between the World Wars* (Bloomington, IN, 1987), which also includes a chapter on Hungarian Jewry.

13. Hobsbawm's position was presented in Eric J. Hobsbawm and Terence Ranger, eds., *The Invention of Tradition* (Cambridge, UK, 1983). For Anderson's position, see Benedict Anderson, *Imagined Communities: Reflections on the Origin and Spread of Nationalism* (London, 1993). See also in this context Ernest Gellner, *Nations and Nationalism* (Ithaca, NY, 1983).

14. Anthony D. Smith, *The Nation in History: Historiographical Debates about Ethnicity and Nationalism* (Hanover, NH, 2000).

15. The scholarly discussion on national forms of memory and commemoration has been very extensive over the last two decades. See, for example, John R. Gillis, ed., *Commemorations: The Politics of National Identity* (Princeton, NJ, 1994), and Dan Ben-Amos and Liliane Weissberg, eds., *Cultural Memory and the Construction of Identity* (Detroit, 1999). For a few examples regarding the three countries discussed in this book, see Etienne Francois and Hagen Schulze, eds., *Deutsche Erinnerungsorte* (München, 2001); Stefan Berger, *The Search for Normality: National Identity and Historical Consciousness in Germany since 1800* (Providence, RI, 1997); Bernd Faulenbach, *Ideologie des deutschen Weges: Die deutsche Geschichte in der Historiographie zwischen Kaiserreich und Nationalsozialismus* (München, 1980); Rudy Koshar, *From Monuments to Traces: Artifacts of German Memory, 1870–1990* (Berkeley, 2000); Pierre Nora, ed., *Les Lieux de mémoire* (Paris, 1997); Robert Gildea, *The Past in French History* (New Haven, CT, 1994); Matt K. Matsuda, *The Memory of the Modern* (New York, 1996); Alice Freifeld, *Nationalism and the Crowd in Liberal Hungary, 1848–1914* (Washington, DC, 2000); and Árpád von Klimó, *Nation, Konfession, Geschichte: Zur nationalen Geschichtskultur Ungarns im europäischen Kontext (1860–1948)* (München, 2003).

16. Orm Øverland, *Immigrant Minds, American Identities: Making the United States Home, 1870–1930* (Urbana, IL, 2000), 7–8, 175. It is important to note that terms such as "usable past" and "homemaking myth" are not being used here pejoratively. These terms, which are part of a much wider vocabulary that was developed under the impact of the so-called cultural turn in history, do not intend whatsoever to doubt the truth value of these memories. They are intended instead to emphasize the importance of past representations as such and to point on their crucial function for the society. About the cultural turn in history, see, for example, Victoria E. Bonnell and Lynn Hunt, eds., *Beyond the Cultural Turn: New Directions in the Study*

of Society and Culture (Berkeley, 1999), and Elizabeth A. Clark, *History, Theory, Text: Historians and the Linguistic Turn* (Cambridge, MA, 2004).

17. On the importance of the historical discourse and the interpretation of the past as a major tool for orientation in the present, see Jörn Rüsen, *History: Narration, Interpretation, Orientation* (New York, 2004).

18. On the concept of cultural memory, which characterizes the long-term memory form of a society and is transformed in a multigenerational process, see Jan Assmann, *Das kulturelle Gedächtnis* (München, 1992). Assmann termed the historical research of these forms of memory "mnemohistory"; see Jan Assmann, *Moses the Egyptian: The Memory of Egypt in Western Monotheism* (Cambridge, MA, 1997), 8–17. On the Jewish collective memory in the premodern era, see Yosef Hayim Yerushalmi, *Zakhor: Jewish History and Jewish Memory* (Seattle, 1982). According to Yerushalmi, the Enlightenment, modernization, and the rise of modern Jewish historiography brought the disintegration of the collective Jewish memory. Amos Funkenstein asserted, on the other hand, that the activity of modern Jewish historians is an additional component in the development of the Jewish memory; see Amos Funkenstein, "Collective Memory and Historical Consciousness," *History and Memory* 1, no. 1 (1989): 5–26. About the historicist ethos in this context, see David N. Myers, *Resisting History: Historicism and Its Discontents in German Jewish Thought* (Princeton, NJ, 2003).

19. Shmuel Feiner, *Haskalah and History: The Emergence of a Modern Jewish Historical Consciousness* (Oxford, UK, 2002), 9–70.

20. See, for example, Ismar Schorsch, *From Text to Context: The Turn to History in Modern Judaism* (Hanover, NH, 1994); Michael A. Meyer, "The Emergence of Jewish Historiography: Motives and Motifs," in Meyer, *Judaism within Modernity: Essays on Modern Jewish History and Religion*, 44–63 (Detroit, 2001); Shulamit Volkov, "Inventing Tradition: On the Formation of Modern Jewish Culture," *Jewish Studies at the CEU* 3 (2002–3): 211–27; Ernst Schulin, "Doppel-Nationalität? Die Integration der Juden in die deutsche Kulturnation und die neue Konstruktion der jüdischen Geschichte," in *Die Konstruktion der Nation gegen die Juden,* edited by Peter Alter, Claus-Ekkehard Baersch, und Peter Berghoff, 243–59 (München, 1999); Christhard Hoffmann, "Die Verbürgerlichung der jüdischen Vergangenheit: Formen, Inhalte, Kritik," in *Judentum und Historismus: Zur Entstehung der jüdischen Geschichtswissenschaft in Europa,* edited by Ulrich Wyrwa, 149–71 (Frankfurt am Main, 2003); and Simone Lässig, *Jüdische Wege ins Bürgertum: Kulturelles Kapital und sozialer Aufstieg im 19. Jahrhundert* (Göttingen, 2004), 278–89.

21. Nitsa Ben-Ari, *Romance with the Past: The Nineteenth-Century German-Jewish Historical Novel and the Creation of a National Literature* [in Hebrew] (Tel Aviv, 1997); Nils Roemer, *Jewish Scholarship and Culture in Nineteenth-Century Germany: Between History and Faith* (Madison, WI, 2005), 66–78; and Jacques Ehrenfreund, *Mémoire juive et nationalité allemanje: Les juifs berlinois à la belle époque* (Paris, 2000).

22. Nils Roemer, "Between the Provinces and the City: Mapping German-Jewish Memories," *Leo Baeck Institute Year Book* 51 (2006): 61–77. For a systematic discussion in the development of the German Heimat concept and the tension between its local and national meanings see: Alon Confino, *The Nation as a Local*

Metaphor: Württemberg, Imperial Germany, and National Memory, 1871–1918 (Chapel Hill, 1997), 97–215.

23. Jay R. Berkovitz, *Rites and Passages: The Beginnings of Modern Jewish Culture in France, 1650–1860* (Philadelphia, 2004), 219–30; Michael Marrus, *The Politics of Assimilation: A Study of the French Jewish Community at the Time of the Dreyfus Affair* (Oxford, UK, 1971), 86–121; Perrine Simon-Nahum, "Jüdische Historiographie im Frankreich des 19. Jahrhunderts," in *Judentum und Historismus: Zur Entstehung der jüdischen Geschichtswissenschaft in Europa,* edited by Ulrich Wyrwa, 91–116 (Frankfurt am Main, 2003); Jay R. Berkovitz, *The Shaping of Jewish Identity in Nineteenth-century France* (Detroit, 1989); and Philip Nord, *The Republican Moment: Struggles for Democracy in Nineteenth-Century France* (Cambridge, MA, 1995), 64–89.

24. See in this context Jacob Katz, "The Identity of Post Emancipatory Hungarian Jewry," in *A Social and Economic History of Central European Jewry,* edited by by Jehuda Don and Victor Karady, 13–31 (New Brunswick, NJ, 1990). For a detailed historical survey of the religious streams in pre-Holocaust Hungarian Jewry, see Kinga Frojimovics, "Who Were They? Characteristics of the Religious Streams within Hungarian Jewry on the Eve of the Community's Extermination," *Yad Vashem Studies* 35, no. 1 (2007): 143–77.

25. Nathaniel Katzburg, "Jewish Historiography in Hungary" [in Hebrew], *Sinai* 40, nos. 2–3 (1956–57): 113–26, 164–76. Regarding the modern Hungarian rabbis who were also historians, see Kinga Frojimovics, "A 'doktor-rabbik' nagy nemzedéke Magyarországon: A neológ identitás kialakítása a történetíráson keresztül," in *Széfer Jószéf,* edited by József Zsengellér, 221–39 (Budapest, 2002).

26. On these developments in German nationalism in this period, see, for example, George L. Mosse, *The Crisis of German Ideology: Intellectual Origins of the Third Reich* (New York, 1964); Otto Dann, *Nation und Nationalismus in Deutschland, 1770–1990* (München, 1996), 197–210; David Blackbourn, *The Long Nineteenth Century: A History of Germany, 1780–1918* (New York, 1998), 424–40; and Uwe Puschner, *Die völkische Bewegung im wilhelminischen Kaiserreich: Sprache-Rasse-Religion* (Darmstadt, 2001). On the rise of German anti-Semitism, see, for example, Peter Pulzer, *The Rise of Political Anti-Semitism in Germany and Austria* (Cambridge, MA, 1988); Peter Alter, Claus-Ekkehard Baersch, and Peter Berghoff, eds., *Die Konstruktion der Nation gegen die Juden* (München, 1999); Shulamit Volkov, *Germans, Jews, and Antisemites: Trials in Emancipation* (Cambridge, UK, 2006), pt. 2.

27. On the developments of such views in France, see Michel Winock, *Nationalism, Anti-Semitism, and Fascism in France* (Stanford, CA, 1998); see pp. 75–84 for an analysis of the ideas of decadence, which opposed the idea of progress. See also David Carroll, *French Literary Fascism: Nationalism, Anti-Semitism, and the Ideology of Culture* (Princeton, NJ, 1995); Charles Sowerwine, *France since 1870: Culture, Politics and Society* (New York, 2001), 57–73; and Rod Kedward, *La vie en bleu: France and the French since 1900* (London, 2006), 44–48. On the rise of anti-Semitic views in pre–World War I France and their relation to the legacy of 1789, see, for example, Pierre Birnbaum, "The Drumont Paradigm," in *Jewish Destinies: Citizenship, State and Community in Modern France,* edited by Pierre Birnbaum, 101–15 (New York, 2000); and Michel Winock, *La France et le juifs* (Paris, 2004), 83–103.

28. On the political and ideological struggle concerning the character of Hungarian nationalism in this period, see Ignác Romsics, *Hungary in the Twentieth Century* (Budapest, 1999), 53–68; Géza Jeszenszky, "Hungary through World War I and the End of the Dual Monarchy," in *A History of Hungary,* edited by Peter F. Sugar, 267–91 (Bloomington, IN, 1994); Gabor Vermes, *István Tisza: The Liberal Vision and Conservative Statecraft of a Magyar Nationalist* (New York, 1985), 150–78. On the development of Hungarian anti-Semitism in this period in relation to the rise of new conservative streams, see Rolf Fischer, *Entwicklungsstufen des Antisemitismus in Ungarn 1867–1939: Die Zerstörung der magyarisch-jüdischen Symbiose* (München, 1988), 42–123, and Nathaniel Katzburg, *Antisemitism in Hungary, 1867–1944* [in Hebrew] (Jerusalem, 1993), 24–88.

29. This difference in the impact on Jewish politics does not mean that the democracy in Germany was essentially weaker than in France. A recent work on Wilhelmine political culture presents the development of democracy in imperial Germany in a much more positive way. See Margaret Lavinia Anderson, *Practicing Democracy: Elections and Political Culture in Imperial Germany* (Princeton, NJ, 2000).

30. On the political transformation of late nineteenth-century German Jewry, see Ismar Schorsch, *Jewish Reactions to German Anti-Semitism, 1870–1914* (New York, 1972); Jehuda Reinharz, *Fatherland or Promised Land: The Dilemma of the German Jew, 1893–1914* (Ann Arbor, MI, 1975); Sanford Ragins, *Jewish Responses to Anti-Semitism in Germany, 1870–1914: A Study in the History of Ideas* (Cincinnati, 1980); Jacob Borut, *"A New Spirit among Our Brethren in Ashkenaz": German Jewry's Change in Direction at the End of the 19th Century* [in Hebrew] (Jerusalem, 1999); and Avraham Barkai, *"Wehr Dich": Der Centralverein deutscher Staatsbürger jüdischen Glaubens 1893–1938* (München, 2002), 19–54.

31. The Ligue des droits de l'homme (Human Rights League), which was founded after the Dreyfus Affair, was not a separate Jewish organization. About the league, see William D. Irvine, *Between Justice and Politics: The Ligue des droits de l'homme, 1898–1945* (Stanford, CA, 2007).

32. On the reactions of French Jews to the Dreyfus Affair and their self-consciousness during and after, see Hyman, *The Jews of Modern France,* 107–14; Marrus, *The Politics of Assimilation,* 163–281; Stephen Wilson, "The Dreyfus Affair and French Jews," *Wiener Library Bulletin* 26 (1972): 32–40; and Richard I. (Yerachmiel) Cohen, "The Dreyfus Affair and the Jews," in *Antisemitism through the Ages,* edited by Shmuel Almog, 291–310 (Oxford, UK, 1988). For comparative discussions about French and German Jews at the turn of the century, see Christian Wiese, "Modern Antisemitism and Jewish Responses in Germany and France, 1880–1914," in *Jewish Emancipation Reconsidered,* edited by Brenner, Caron, and Kaufmann, 140–47, and Jacques Ehrenfreund, "Citizenship and Acculturation: Some Reflections on German Jews during the Second Empire and French Jews during the Third Republic," ibid., 155–63.

33. On the view of the Jewish Neologs in Hungary regarding the emancipation and the Zionist critique of it, see Gyurgyák, *A zsidókérdés Magyarországon,* 225–54.

34. This process was most prominent in Germany. See Roemer, *Jewish Scholarship and Culture in Nineteenth-Century Germany,* 92–100.

35. For the term "culture of defeat," see Wolfgang Schivelbusch, *The Culture of Defeat: On National Trauma, Mourning, and Recovery* (New York, 2003). Schivelbusch deals with the American South after the Civil War and France after the 1870 defeat to Prussia and Germany after World War I; however, his thesis also fits well for the case of post–World War I Hungary. For more in the context of Hungary, see chapter 5 in the present volume.

36. In relation to Germany, see, for example, Dietmar Schirmer, *Mythos-Heilshoffnung-Modernität, Politisch-kulturelle Deutungscodes in der Weimarer Republik* (Opladen, 1992), and Wolfgang Bialas and Gerard Raulet, eds., *Die Historismusdebatte in der Weimarer Republik* (Frankfurt am Main, 1996). For a more detailed discussion of the German case, see chapter 1 in the present volume. In relation to Hungary, see, for example, Irena Raab Epstein, *Gyula Szekfű: A Study in the Political Basis of Hungarian Historiography* (New York, 1987); von Klimó, *Nation, Konfession, Geschichte,* 185–314; and Paul A. Hanebrink, *In Defense of Christian Hungary: Religion, Nationalism, and Antisemitism, 1890–1944* (Ithaca, NY, 2006). For a more detailed discussion of the Hungarian case, see chapter 5 in the present volume.

37. The Volkist ideology is the radical right-wing version of nationalism that rejects the basic assumptions of liberal nationalism. Volkism sees the nation and the people (*Volk*) as exclusive integrative primordial entities.

38. In 1920 the Hungarian government passed the *numerus clausus* law in order to limit the number of Jewish students in higher education. For the late 1930s and early 1940s Hungarian Jews laws see chapters 5 and 6 in the present volume.

39. On France in the 1930s, see, for example, Eugen Weber, *The Hollow Years: France in the 1930s* (London, 1995); Serge Berstein, *La France des années 30* (Paris, 2001); and Rod Kedward, *La vie en bleu,* 151–230. For a more detailed discussion, see chapter 3 in the present volume. About the Fascist public discourse in France, see Zeev Sternhell, *Neither Right nor Left: Fascist Ideology in France* (Berkeley, 1986), and David Carroll, *French Literary Fascism: Nationalism, Anti-Semitism, and the Ideology of Culture* (Princeton, NJ, 1995).

40. On the importance of the transnational perspective in Jewish historiography today, see Moshe Rosman, "Jewish History across Borders," in *Rethinking European Jewish History,* edited by Jeremy Cohen and Moshe Rosman, 15–29 (Oxford, UK, 2009).

41. For a definition of the term "public thought," see Yosef Gorny, *The State of Israel in Jewish Public Thought: The Quest for Collective Identity* (Houndmills, UK, 1994), 3–4.

42. Henry Wassermann, review of Michael Nagel, ed., *Zwischen Selbstbehauptung und Verfolgung: Deutsch-jüdische Zeitungen und Zeitschriften von der Aufklärung bis zum Nationalsozialismus* (Hildesheim, Germany, 2002), in *Zion* 71, no. 1 (2006): 112–16 [in Hebrew].

43. On the Jewish press in Germany during the first years of the Nazi regime, see Herbert Freeden, *The Jewish Press in the Third Reich* (Providence, 1992), and Katrin Diehl, *Die jüdische Presse im Dritten Reich: Zwischen Selbstbehauptung und Fremdbestimmung* (Tübingen, 1997).

44. On the transformation of the Jewish press in Hungary in these years, see Guy

Miron, "Confronting Evil: How the Jewish Press in Hungary Dealt with Anti-Semitism from the Late 1930s until 1944" [in Hebrew], *Kesher* 33 (May 2003): 100–107.

45. See, for example, the articles in Katz, *Toward Modernity,* and Michael Brenner, Vicki Caron, and Uri R. Kaufmann, eds., *Jewish Emancipation Reconsidered: The French and German Models* (Tübingen, 2003).

46. On the Jerusalem school, see David N. Myers, *Re-Inventing the Jewish Past: European Jewish Intellectuals and the Zionist Return to History* (New York, 1995).

47. For a well-known critical view about this orientation, see Todd M. Endelman, "The Englishness of Jewish Modernity in England," in *Toward Modernity: The European Jewish Model,* edited by Jacob Katz, 225–46 (New Brunswick, NJ, 1987).

48. This challenge was clearly presented by Shulamit Volkov in "Jews among the Nations: A Unique National Narrative or a Chapter in National Historiographies" [in Hebrew], *Zion* 61, no. 1 (1996): 91–112. See also Rosman, "Jewish History across Borders." On the challenge of the comparative Jewish history and the difficulties in coping with it, see Todd M. Endelman, "Introduction: Comparing Jewish Societies," in *Comparing Jewish Societies,* edited by Todd M. Endelman, 1–21 (Ann Arbor, MI, 1997).

Chapter 1

1. The literature on the Weimar Republic is vast and cannot be listed here. See, for example, Eberhard Kolb, *The Weimar Republic* (London, 1988), and Detlev K. Peukert, *The Weimar Republic: The Crisis of Classical Modernity* (London, 1991). Regarding the complexity of the situation of the Jews in the republic (the constitution granted full rights to the Jews, but wide segments of society rejected the Jews), see, for example, Peter Pulzer, *Jews and the German State* (Cambridge, MA, 1992), 271–86. For a basic overview about German Jews during the Weimar Republic, see Donald Niewyk, *The Jews in Weimar Germany* (Baton Rouge, 1980), and Avraham Barkai and Paul Mendes-Flohr, *German-Jewish History in Modern Times,* Vol. 4, *Renewal and Destruction, 1918–1945* (New York, 1998), pt. 1.

2. On the remarkable rise of anti-Semitism in the political discourse of the Weimar Republic, see, for example, Anthony Kauders, *German Politics and the Jews: Duesseldorf and Nuremberg, 1910–1933* (Oxford, UK, 1996). On the rise of violent anti-Semitism, see Dirk Walter, *Antisemitische Kriminalität und Gewalt, Judenfeindschaft in der Weimarer Republik* (Bonn, 1999). Regarding attempts to understand and come to terms with this escalation, see Cornelia Hecht, *Deutsche Juden und Antisemitismus in der Weimarer Republik* (Bonn, 2003).

3. On the history of the CV during the Weimar Republic and the Nazi era, see Avraham Barkai, *"Wehr Dich": Der Centralverein deutscher Staatsbürger jüdischen Glaubens 1893–1938* (München, 2002), chaps. 3–8.

4. On the German Zionist movement during the Weimar Republic and its focus on the development of Palestine, see, for example, Hagit Lavsky, *Before Catastrophe: The Distinctive Path of German Zionism* (Detroit, 1996). About the idea of *Volksgemeinde* and the initiative to fulfill it, see Michael Brenner, *The Renaissance of Jewish Culture in Weimar Germany* (New Haven, CT, 1996), chap. 2.

5. The main scholarly work that deals with this group focuses on the Second Reich; see Mordechai Breuer, *Modernity within Tradition: The Social History of Orthodox Jewry in Imperial Germany* (New York, 1992). Regarding the interwar period, see Yehuda Ben-Avner, *Vom orthodoxen Judentum in Deutschland zwischen zwei Weltkriegen* (Hildesheim, Germany, 1987), and Yaakov Zur, "Orthodox Jewry before the Nazis' Rise to Power," in *History of the Holocaust: Germany*, Vol. 2, edited by Abraham Margaliot and Yehoyakim Cochavi, 841–51 [in Hebrew] (Jerusalem, 1998).

6. About east European Jews in Weimar Germany, see Trude Maurer, *Ostjuden in Deutschland 1918–1933* (Hamburg, 1986).

7. The research literature about Jewish life in Nazi Germany is very extensive. See, for example, Barkai and Mendes-Flohr, *German-Jewish History in Modern Times*, Vol. 4, *Renewal and Destruction*, pt. 2; Saul Friedlander, *Nazi Germany and the Jews* (New York, 1997); Jacob Boas, "German-Jewish Internal Politics under Hitler 1933–1938," *Leo Baeck Institute Year Book* 29 (1984): 3–25; Arnold Paucker, ed., *The Jews in Nazi Germany, 1933–1943* (Tübingen, 1986); Wolfgang Benz, *Die deutschen Juden und der Nationalsozialismus 1933–1939* (Bonn, 1988); Otto Dov Kulka, ed., *Deutsches Judentum unter dem Nationalsozialismus*, Vol. 1 (Tübingen, 1997); Marion A. Kaplan, *Between Dignity and Despair: Jewish Life in Nazi Germany* (New York, 1998); and Abraham Margaliot and Yehoyakim Cochavi, eds., *History of the Holocaust: Germany* [in Hebrew] (Jerusalem, 1998).

8. See, for example, Abraham Margaliot, *Between Rescue and Annihilation: Studies in the History of German Jewry, 1932–1938* [in Hebrew] (Jerusalem, 1990), 183–93, and Barkai, *"Wehr Dich,"* 317–41.

9. Regarding the Zionist activity in Germany in the first years of the Nazi regime and the various solutions that they suggested for the future of German Jews, see Margaliot, *Between Rescue and Annihilation*, 217–71; Daniel Fraenkel, *On the Edge of the Abyss: Zionist Policy and the Plight of the German Jews, 1933–1938* [in Hebrew] (Jerusalem, 1994).

10. Yaakov Zur, "Orthodox Jewry in Germany during the Nazi Regime," in *History of the Holocaust: Germany*, Vol. 2, edited by Margaliot and Cochavi, 852–901.

11. On the Jewish press in Germany in the first years of the Nazi regime, see Herbert Freeden, *The Jewish Press in the Third Reich* (Providence, RI, 1992), and Katrin Diehl, *Die jüdische Presse im Dritten Reich: Zwischen Selbstbehauptung und Fremdbestimmung* (Tübingen, 1997).

12. Bernd Faulenbach, *Ideologie des deutschen Weges: Die deutsche Geschichte in der Historiographie zwischen Kaiserreich und Nationalsozialismus* (München, 1980), 2–4. On the role of historians in the formation of the official nationalism in Germany, see Hedda Grameley, *Propheten des deutschen Nationalismus: Theologen, Historiker und Nationalökonomen 1848–1880* (Frankfurt, 2001), 155–273, and Stefan Berger, *The Search for Normality: National Identity and Historical Consciousness in Germany since 1800* (Providence, RI, 1997), 33.

13. Hans Schleier, *Die bürgerliche deutsche Geschichtsschreibung der Weimarer Republik* (Köln, 1975), 22, 47–48; Georg G. Iggers, *The German Conception of History: The National Tradition of Historical Thought from Herder to the Present* (Middletown, CT, 1983), 229–31; and Berger, *The Search for Normality*, 35–37.

14. Robert Gerwarth, "The Past in Weimar History," *Contemporary European History* 15, no. 1 (2006): 1–22; Dietmar Schirmer, "Politisch-Kulturelle Deutungsmuster: Vorstellungen von der Welt der Politik in der Weimarer Republik," in *Politische Identität und Nationale Gedenktage, Zur politischen Kultur in der Weimarer Republik,* edited by Detlef Lehnert and Klaus Megerle, 31–60 (Opladen, 1989); and Peter Schöttler, ed., *Geschichtsschreibung als Legitimationswissenschaft, 1918–1945* (Frankfurt am Main, 1999).

15. Erich Wittenberg, *Geschichte und Tradition von 1918–1933 im Bismarckbild der deutschen Weimarer Republik* (Lund, Sweden, 1969), 285–301. See also in this context Wolfgang Bialas and Gerard Raulet, eds., *Die Historismusdebatte in der Weimarer Republik* (Frankfurt am Main, 1996).

16. Iggers, *The German Conception of History,* 240–43.

17. Faulenbach, *Ideologie des deutschen Weges,* 26–27; Dietmar Schirmer, *Mythos-Heilshoffnung-Modernität, Politisch-kulturelle Deutungscodes in der Weimarer Republik* (Opladen, 1992); and Wittenberg, *Geschichte und Tradition von 1918–1933,* 279–80. On the rise of heroic and violent notions in German culture and mass psychology during the Weimar Republic, see Petra Maria Schulz, *Ästhetisierung von Gewalt in der Weimarer Republik* (Münster, 2004).

18. Karen Schönwälder, *Historiker und Politik: Geschichtswissenschaft im Nationalsozialismus* (Frankfurt am Main, 1992), 20–65.

19. On the attempts to develop and institutionalize a firm Nazi historical worldview, see Karl Ferdinand Werner, *Das NS-Geschichtsbild und die deutsche Geschichtswissenschaft* (Stuttgart, 1967), and Helmut Heiber, *Walter Frank und sein Reichsinstitut für Geschichte des neuen Deutschlands* (Stuttgart, 1966). On the use of the regime's key figures in history for the sake of their political interests and ideological aims, see Frank-Lothar Kroll, *Utopie als Ideologie: Geschichtsdenken und politisches Handeln im Dritten Reich* (Paderborn, 1998). About the activity of German historians under the Nazi regime, see Winfried Schulze and Otto Gerhard Oexle, eds., *Deutsche Historiker im Nationalsozialismus* (Frankfurt am Main, 1999), and Ingo Haar, *Historiker im Nationalsozialismus: Die deutsche Geschichte und der "Volkstumskampf" im Osten* (Göttingen, 2000).

20. About this renewal, see Christhard Hoffmann, "Jüdische Geschichtswissenschaft in Deutschland: 1918–1938, Konzepte, Schwerpunkte, Ergebnisse," in *Wissenschaft des Judentums: Anfänge der Judaistik in Europa,* edited by Julius Carlebach, 139–40 (Darmstadt, 1992).

21. About *Der Morgen,* see Sarah Fraiman, "The Transformation of Jewish Consciousness in Nazi Germany as Reflected in the German Jewish Journal *Der Morgen,* 1925–1938," *Modern Judaism* 20, no. 1 (2000): 41–59.

22. Josef Kastein, *Eine Geschichte der Juden* (Berlin, 1931); for reviews, see S. Levi, *Der Morgen,* June 1932, 157, and Hugo Hahn, *Central Verein Zeitung,* March 3, 1932. Joachim Prinz, *Jüdische Geschichte* (Berlin, 1931); for reviews, see Eva Reichmann-Jungmann, "Geschichte jüdischen Werdens," *Central Verein Zeitung,* December 26, 1930.

23. The contention that the German Jewish discourse of that time should be seen as part of the wider struggle surrounding the character of Germany can be supported

NOTES TO CHAPTER 1

by the concept of German Jewish coconstitutionality; see Steven E. Aschheim, "German History and German Jewry: Junctions, Boundaries, and interdependencies," in Aschheim, *In Times of Crisis: Essays on European Culture, Germans, and Jews,* 86–92 (Madison, WI, 2001).

24. For a more extensive discussion about this, see Guy Miron, "Between History and a 'Useful Image of the Past': Representations of the Jewish and the German Past in the Liberal-Jewish Historical Discourse in Weimar Germany" [in Hebrew], *Zion* 66, no. 3 (2001): 297–330. For a general overview of the Jewish liberal discourse in the last years of the Weimar Republic, see Kurt Loewenstein, "Die innerjüdische Reaktion auf die Krise der deutschen Demokratie," in *Entscheidungsjahr 1932: Zur Judenfrage in der Endphase der Weimarer Republik,* edited by Werner E. Mosse and Arnold Paucker, 349–403 (Tübingen, 1965).

25. A report about Weil's lecture was published in *Central Verein Zeitung* on March 22, 1929. Regarding the critique of various Jewish spokespeople on the narrowing concept of German nationalism at that time, see Eva G. Reichmann, "Diskussionen über die Judenfrage, 1930–1932," in *Entscheidungsjahr 1932,* 520.

26. About the representation of 1848, see, for example, Hermann Funke, "Nationalismus und Liberalismus," *Central Verein Zeitung,* December 19, 1930. About von Stein, see, for example, Ernst Feder, "Karl Freiherr von Stein, Zum 100. Todestage am 29. Juni 1931, Der Vater der modernen Demokratie," *Central Verein Zeitung,* June 26, 1931, and Eugen Wolbe, "Freiherr von Stein," *Jüdisch-liberale Zeitung,* June 24, 1931.

27. Faulenbach, *Ideologie des deutschen Weges,* 116–17, 142, 159–60, and Schleier, *Die bürgerliche deutsche Geschichtsschreibung der Weimarer Republik,* 186, 195–99. For a more extensive discussion about this, see Miron, "Between History and a 'Useful Image of the Past,'" 319–24.

28. For a liberal reaction, see Moritz Stern, "Brauchen wir eine historische Zeitschrift?," *Central Verein Zeitung,* February 22, 1929. For an Orthodox reaction, see Anon., "Geschichte der Juden in Deutschland," *Der Israelit,* January 5, 1933.

29. Selma Stern, "Die Zeitschrift für die Geschichte der Juden in Deutschland," *Central Verein Zeitung,* May 3, 1929. For a discussion about Stern's publicist writing in the last years of the Weimar Republic, see Marina Sassenberg, *Selma Stern (1890–1981), Das Eigene in der Geschichte* (Tübingen, 2004), 184–88.

30. Fritz Friedländer, "Die Juden im Geschichtsunterricht," *Central Verein Zeitung,* September 2, 1932.

31. See, for example, J. Landau, "Lessing und Mendelssohn," *Central Verein Zeitung,* January 18, 1929; Heinrich Meyer-Benfey, "Gotthold Ephraim Lessing als Verkünder der Toleranz," *Central Verein Zeitung,* January 18, 1929; W. Kinkel, "Zum Lessing-Jubiläum, Warum wir Lessings gedenken müssen," *Jüdisch-liberale Zeitung,* January 18, 1929; Fritz Friedländer, "Der Reformator," *Central Verein Zeitung,* August 30, 1929; and Ludwig Holländer, "Was sagt uns-den Deutschen und den Juden-Moses Mendelssohn?," *Central Verein Zeitung,* August 30, 1929.

32. For a comparative discussion on the three anniversaries, see Christhard Hoffmann, "Constructing Jewish Modernity: Mendelssohn Jubilee Celebrations within German Jewry, 1829–1929," in *Towards Normality? Acculturation and Mod-*

ern German Jewry, edited by Rainer Liedtke and David Rechter, 27–52 (Tübingen, 2003). On this topic, see also Elizabeth Petuchowski, "Zur Lessing-Rezeption in der deutsch-jüdischen Presse: Lessings 200. Geburtstag (22. Januar 1929)," *Lessing Yearbook* 14 (1982): 43–59; Andrea Hopp, "Das Jahr 1929: Erinnerung und Selbstverständnis im deutschen Judentum," *Trumah* 7 (1998): 113–34; and Miron, "Between History and a 'Useful Image of the Past,'" 309–13.

33. On the articulation of this attitude in German Jewish family memoirs, see Miriam Gebhardt, *Das Familiengedächtnis, Erinnerungen im deutsch-jüdischen Bürgertum 1890 bis 1932* (Stuttgart, 1999), 91–96.

34. See, for example, G. Weinberg, "Der Weg zurück?," *Central Verein Zeitung,* February 12, 1932.

35. See, for example, Leo Wolf, "Von den deutschen Juden," *Central Verein Zeitung,* January 1, 1932; Fritz Friedländer, "Der deutsche Raum als jüdisches Schicksal," *Central Verein Zeitung,* March 25, 1932; and Ludwig Rosenthal, "Jüdisches Mittelalter in Frankreich und Deutschland," *Der Morgen,* April 1932, 55–59.

36. Jacques Stern, "Die Gesetze der Weltgeschichte," *Central Verein Zeitung,* July 18, 1930.

37. For another Jewish position relating to balanced historical research as valuable in itself as well as a vital need of the Jewish society in Germany, see Ismar Elbogen, "Jüdische Forschung in Not," *Gemeindeblatt der Jüdischen Gemeinde zu Berlin,* August 1932. On the centrality of the value of independent, secular, and impartial science in the ethos of German Jewish scholars, see Hoffmann, "Jüdische Geschichtswissenschaft in Deutschland," 140–43.

38. Hans Herzfeld, "Nationalismus in Deutschland," *Central Verein Zeitung* November 6, 1931; Heinz Cohn, "Nationalismus in Deutschland," *Central Verein Zeitung,* November 13, 1931; and Rudolf Wertheimer, "Nationalismus und Demokratie," *Central Verein Zeitung,* November 20, 1931.

39. Arno Herzberg, "Die Wandlung im deutschen Bürgertum, Wo steht das deutsche Judentum?," *Central Verein Zeitung,* April 8, 1932. For an additional reference in the Jewish liberal press to the end of the liberal era, see Wilhelm Michel, "Was Heisst: Ende des Liberalismus?," *Der Morgen,* June 1932, 83–86.

40. Fraenkel, *On the Edge of the Abyss,* 35–36. This change in the Zionist position can be seen in the Zionist journal *Jüdische Rundschau,* which concentrated throughout the 1920s on the development of Palestine and then at the beginning of the 1930s turned to dealing more and more with questions that concerned the political situation in Germany; see Hecht, *Deutsche Juden und Antisemitismus in der Weimarer Republik,* 207–8.

41. Kurt Blumenfeld, "Die Zionist. Aufgabe im heutigen Deutschland," *Jüdische Rundschau,* September 16, 1932. See also in this context Fraenkel, *On the Edge of the Abyss,* 39, and Carsten Teichert, *Chasak! Zionismus im nationalsozialistischen Deutschland, 1933–1938* (Köln, 2000), 77–89.

42. "Mittelalter als Vorbild," *Jüdische Rundschau,* July 8, 1932.

43. Gustav Krojanker, *Zum Problem des neuen deutschen Nationalismus* (Berlin, 1932). This essay has already been dicussed in research literature; see, for example, Fraenkel, *On the Edge of the Abyss,* 36–38.

44. Krojanker, *Zum Problem des neuen deutschen Nationalismus,* 13–14.

45. Ibid., 29–30.

46. Ibid., 19–25.

47. For an example of liberal criticism, see Ludwig Holländer, "Zum Problem des neuen deutschen Nationalismus," *Central Verein Zeitung,* May 20, 1932. For the evaluation that most Zionists in Germany rejected Krojanker's position, see Jehuda Reinharz, "The Responses of the *Centralverein* and the Zionist Federation of Germany to Antisemitism in the Weimar Republic," in *History of the Holocaust: Germany,* Vol. 1 [in Hebrew], edited by Margaliot and Cochavi, 59–60.

48. Anon., "'Fremdstämmig?'" *Central Verein Zeitung,* March 16, 1933.

49. On the history of the concept of *Stamm* as a definition of the Jewish collective in Germany and as a key for their integration into the German nation, see Till van Rahden, "Germans of the Jewish *Stamm,* Visions of Community between Nationalism and Particularism, 1850 to 1933," in *German History from the Margins,* edited by Neil Gregor, Nils Roemer and Mark Roseman, 27–48 (Bloomington, IN, 2006).

50. Max Eschelbacher, "Der deutsche Jude und der deutsche Staat," *Der Morgen,* February 1933, 404–9.

51. Ibid., 414.

52. Ibid.

53. Fabius Schach, "Vergangenheit redet zur Gegenwart," *Israelitisches Familienblatt,* March 16, 1933.

54. See, for example, Erich Spinaza, "Der Verband der Vereine für jüdische Geschichte und Literatur in Deutschland," *Israelitisches Familienblatt,* April 6, 1933, and Anon., "Stille Feiertage, Volk und Geschichte," *Jüdische Rundschau,* April 7, 1933.

55. Shavuot is the Jewish holiday that commemorates the anniversary of the day God gave the Torah to the entire Israelite nation assembled at Mount Sinai. The holiday, which marks the conclusion of the Counting of the Omer, is one of the three biblical pilgrimage festivals.

56. C. Seligmann (Gemeinderabbiner), "Ein Glück, Jude zu sein? Zum Schowusfest," *Frankfurter Israelitisches Gemeindeblatt,* June 1933.

57. Alfred Hirschberg, "Sammeln und Richtung nehmen," *Central Verein Zeitung,* July 13, 1933.

58. For this view, see Heinz Kellermann, "Ende der Emanzipation," *Der Morgen* 9 (1933): 176–77.

59. Alfred Hirschberg, "Ein Brief an die Breslauer *Jüdische Zeitung,*" *Central Verein Zeitung,* July 27, 1933.

60. For an earlier discussion of the use by CV authors of concepts such as new emancipation in this period, see Margaliot, *Between Rescue and Annihilation,* 183–93.

61. Robert Wohlheim, "Jüdische Jugend Deutschlands sucht ihren Weg," *Central Verein Zeitung,* August 3, 1933.

62. Heinz Warschauer, "Innere Wandlung," *Central Verein Zeitung,* September 20, 1933. See also Friedrich Brodnitz, "Um eine neue Emanzipation," *Central Verein*

Zeitung, January 25, 1934. Brodnitz also raised the concept of group emancipation, tying it to the previous generations' tradition of "all [those in] Israel are sureties one to the other." On the discussion of CV spokespeople about the concept of group emancipation in 1933, see Barkai, *"Wehr Dich,"* 317–30.

63. The most well-known text in this context is Robert Weltsch, "Tragt ihn mit Stolz, den Gelben Fleck!," *Jüdische Rundschau,* April 4, 1933.

64. "Echte oder scheinbare Wandlung?," *Jüdische Rundschau,* May 9, 1933.

65. Hugo Rosenthal, "Die deutsche Judenheit im neuen Deutschen Reich," Part 1, *Jüdische Rundschau,* May 26, 1933.

66. Hugo Rosenthal, "Die deutsche Judenheit im neuen Deutschen Reich," Part 2, *Jüdische Rundschau,* May 30, 1933.

67. "Echte oder scheinbare Wandlung?," *Jüdische Rundschau,* May 9, 1933.

68. For an additional Zionist critique of the liberal historical discourse primarily about the ideas of a new emancipation, see "Um die neue Emanzipation," *Jüdische Rundschau,* June 16, 1933.

69. Elfride Bergel-Gronemann, "Der Sinn des Geschehens," *Jüdische Rundschau,* August 1, 1933.

70. On the activities of Prinz during the Nazi era, see Joachim Prinz, "A Rabbi under the Hitler Regime," in *Gegenwart im Rückblick,* edited by Herbert A. Strauss and Kurt R. Grossmann, 231–38 (Heidelberg, 1970); see also Jacob Boas, "The Shrinking World of German Jewry: 1933–1938," *Leo Baeck Institute Year Book* 31 (1986): 247, and Joachim Prinz, *Rebellious Rabbi, an Autobiography: The German and Early American Years,* edited by Michael A. Meyer (Bloomington, IN, 2007).

71. Joachim Prinz, *Wir Juden* (Berlin, 1934), 19–21.

72. Ibid., 108–12.

73. Ibid., 31.

74. Ibid., 22.

75. Ibid., 23.

76. Ibid., 55.

77. Ibid., 95.

78. Ibid., 32.

79. For Count Clermont-Tonnerre's speech concerning the eligibility of the Jews for citizenship that was given in the French revolutionary National Assembly on December 23, 1789, see Paul Mendes-Flohr and Jehuda Reinharz, eds., *The Jew in the Modern World* (New York, 1995), 114–15; quotations are from p. 115.

80. Prinz, *Wir Juden,* 36.

81. Ibid., 26; see also p. 122.

82. Ibid., 147, 162.

83. Ibid., 142.

84. For example, see ibid., 117–18.

85. On the tendency of the archaic-mythic discourse to portray the past in a cyclical form and on its frequent use of the concept of fate (*Schicksal*), see Schirmer, "Politisch-Kulturelle Deutungsmuster," 36–40.

86. Prinz, *Wir Juden,* 53–54.

87. Ibid., 126–28, 162–72.

88. Karl-Heinz Flietzer, "Noch einmal: Joachim Prinz 'Wir Juden,'" *Central Verein Zeitung,* November 30, 1933.

89. Kurt Alexander Krefeld, "Noch einmal: Joachim Prinz 'Wir Juden," *Central Verein Zeitung,* November 30, 1933, and Fritz Goldschmidt, "Selbstbesinnung nicht erst jetzt," *Central Verein Zeitung,* April 5, 1934. For another less polemical review article see A. K., "Wir Juden," *Israelitisches Familienblatt,* December 7, 1933.

90. Michael Meyer, "Liberal Judaism in Nazi Germany," in *On Germans and Jews under Nazi Germany: Essays by Three Generations of Historians,* edited by Moshe Zimmermann, 291–93 (Jerusalem, 2006).

91. "Joachim Prinz: Wir Juden, Angezeigt von Rabbiner Dr. Manfred Swarsensky," *Central Verein Zeitung,* November 16, 1933.

92. Similar ideas of Jewish history as a cyclical process of ages of integration and synthesis with the surroundings and then ages of separation and isolation were also raised two months earlier by a major CV spokesman; see Alfred Hirschberg, "An der Schwelle des Jahres . . . ," *Central Verein Zeitung,* September 20, 1933.

93. Bruno Weil, *Der Weg der deutschen Juden* (Berlin, 1934). On Weil's public lectures, see "Wir deutschen Juden im Wandel der Zeiten," *Central Verein Zeitung,* December 7, 1933, and "Dr. Bruno Weil spricht im Central Verein," *Israelitisches Familienblatt,* January 11, 1934.

94. Weil, *Der Weg der deutschen Juden,* 13.

95. Ibid., 19–20.

96. Ibid., 21.

97. Ibid., 30–43. About the uniqueness of the 1933–34 events, see primarily p. 42.

98. Ibid., 169–75.

99. Ibid., 24, 180–81.

100. Bruno Weil, "Rechenschaft und Ausblick," *Central Verein Zeitung,* November 1, 1934, and November 8, 1934.

101. Hans Joachim Schoeps, *Wir deutschen Juden* (Berlin, 1934). On Schoeps's movement, see Carl J. Rheins, "Deutscher Vortrupp, Gefolgschaft deutscher Juden, 1933–1935," *Leo Baeck Institute Year Book* 26 (1981): 207–30.

102. Schoeps, *Wir deutschen Juden,* 11–20, 40–42.

103. Ibid., 21–27, 47.

104. Werner Rosenstock, "Hans Joachim Schoeps: Wir deutschen Juden," *Central Verein Zeitung,* August 2, 1934.

105. Fritz Friedländer, "Gabriel Riesser und seine Zeit," in *Jugendführer-Briefe,* No. 1, *Die Grundlagen der Juden-Emanzipation in Deutschland,* 9–12 (Berlin, 1930), and Fritz Friedländer, *Das Leben Gabriel Riessers* (Berlin, 1926).

106. Fritz Frieländer, "Die Juden im Geschichtsunterricht," *Central Verein Zeitung,* September 2, 1932.

107. About his educational activities, see Fritz Friedländer, "Trials and Tribulations of Jewish Education in Nazi Germany," *Leo Baeck Institute Year Book* 3 (1958): 187–201.

108. Fritz Friedländer, "Der Geschichtsunterricht in der jüdischen Schule," *Central Verein Zeitung,* May 10, 1934.

109. Fritz Friedländer, "Hemmung und Ziel jüdischer Geschichtsforschung," *Central Verein Zeitung,* September 6, 1934.

110. Fritz Friedländer, "Jüdische Assimilation im Zeitalter der Emanzipation," *Central Verein Zeitung,* August 30, 1934.

111. About Ranke's view on history, see Iggers, *The German Conception of History,* 63–89. See also Leonard Krieger, *Ranke: The Meaning of History* (Chicago, 1977).

112. Fritz Friedländer, "Jüdische Assimilation im Zeitalter der Emanzipation," *Central Verein Zeitung,* August 30, 1934. See also a similar argument in Friedländer's assessment of Gabriel Riesser: Fritz Friedländer, "Eine Idee und ihre Zeit, 2. April 1806—Gabriel Riesser—2. April 1936," *Central Verein Zeitung,* April 2, 1936.

113. Wilhelm Grau, *Wilhelm von Humboldt und das Problem des Juden* (Hamburg, 1935); Heiber, *Walter Frank und sein Reichsinstitut für Geschichte des neuen Deutschlands,* 411–12; and Patricia von Papen, *"Scholarly" Antisemitism during the Third Reich: The Reichsinstitut's Research on the "Jewish Question," 1935–1945* (PhD dissertation, Columbia University, 1999), 68–77.

114. Fritz Friedländer, "Ein Charakterbild in der Geschichte, Zu Wilhelm Grau: 'Wilhelm v. Humboldt,'" *Central Verein Zeitung,* November 7, 1935.

115. Fritz Friedländer, "Vom Werden des Geschichtsgefühls, Zu Friedrich Meineckes 'Entstehung des Historismus,'" *Central Verein Zeitung,* December 10, 1936.

116. Dr. (Markus) Elias, "Das Ende einer Illusion," *Der Israelit,* August 4, October 13, and October 27, 1932. The discussion here is based primarily on the first part of the article.

117. Regarding this legacy, see Breuer, *Modernity within Tradition,* chap. 6.

118. See, for example, Anon., "Bausteine zur Neuorientierung," *Der Israelit,* March 30, 1933, and Anon., "Ein neuer Umweg der jüdischen Geschichte," *Der Israelit,* June 22, 1933.

119. Anon., "Ein offenes Wort im Namen der Religion," *Der Israelit,* April 7, 1933.

120. See, for example, Rabbiner Elie Munk, "Der Sinn des Geschehens," *Der Israelit,* August 3, 1933.

121. Rabbiner Moses Auerbach, "Die Lehre der Zeit," *Der Israelit,* June 8, 1933. Regarding the phrase "Derech Erez im Torah," the idea is that in fact the adaptation to the modern world came first and only then came the loyalty to Jewish tradition and Jewish law.

122. Nechunia, "Die Lösung der Stunde," *Der Israelit,* March 23, 1933.

123. Simon Schwab, *Heimkehr ins Judentum* (Frankfurt am Main, 1934). Schwab related to the ancient Jewish scholar Nechunia Ben Hakana a few times in the book; see pp. 104 and 124. For another article published under this pseudonym, see Nechunia, "Die grosse Abrechnung," *Der Israelit,* August 31, 1933.

124. Schwab, *Heimkehr ins Judentum,* 27.

125. Ibid., 19–20.

126. Ibid., 109–11.

127. Ibid., 98. See more about Schwab's position toward Zionism on pp. 21–22 and 36–52.

128. Ibid., 113–22.

129. Ibid., 122.

130. Ibid., 127, 140. For a similar position in this context, see Anon., "Golus-Schicksal, Eine Tisch'o-beaw-Betrachtung," *Der Israelit,* August 1, 1935.

131. Anon., "Wo stehen wir?," *Der Israelit,* January 18, 1934.

132. Anon., "Der Aufruf der Geschichte," *Der Israelit,* July 26, 1934. The constant and unconditional clinging of Orthodox spokespeople to Hirsch's legacy was also expressed in a series of articles: "Das Bildungsideal S. R. Hirschs und die Gegenwart," *Der Israelit,* August 23, August 30, September 6, September 21, and October 11, 1934.

133. M. Elias, "Rückblick und Ausblick," Part 3, *Der Israelit,* January 17, 1935.

134. Ibid.

135. Ibid., emphasis in original.

136. "Neue Tendenzen im jüdischen Schrifttum," 051/OSOBI/52, Yad Vashem Archive, Jerusalem.

Chapter 2

1. Ismar Elbogen, "Jüdische Forschung in Not," *Gemeindeblatt der Jüdischen Gemeinde zu Berlin,* August 1932.

2. About Elbogen and his activities, see Erwin Rosenthal, "Ismar Elbogen and the New Jewish Learning," *Leo Baeck Institute Year Book* 8 (1963): 3–28, and Michael A. Meyer, *"Without Wissenschaft There Is No Judaism": The Life and Thought of the Jewish Historian Ismar Elbogen,* Braun Lectures in the History of the Jews in Prussia (Ramat Gan, Israel, 2004).

3. The series title was "Geschichte der Juden in Deutschland" and included the following articles: Adolf Kober, "Die Juden in Deutschland zur Römerzeit," *Central Verein Zeitung,* May 17, 1934; Adolf Kober, "Die Juden in Deutschland bis ins Hochmittelalter," *Central Verein Zeitung,* June 14, 1934; Ismar Elbogen, "Jüdisches Schicksal in Deutschland im 11. bis 13. Jahrhundert," *Central Verein Zeitung,* June 28, 1934; Wera-Rahel Levin, "Zur Zeit ausgehenden Mittelalters," *Central Verein Zeitung,* July 12, 1934; Rosy Bodenheimer, "Im Zietalter Luthers," *Central Verein Zeitung,* July 26, 1934; A. Cohen, "Im 17. und 18. Jahrhundert," *Central Verein Zeitung,* August 9, 1934; and Fritz Friedländer, "Jüdische Assimilation im Zeitalter der Emanzipation," *Central Verein Zeitung,* August 30, 1934.

4. Ismar Elbogen, *Geschichte der Juden in Deutschland* (Berlin, 1935).

5. Meyer, *"Without Wissenschaft There Is No Judaism,"* 28. Along with Elbogen can also be mentioned Ismar Freund, Elbogen's colleague at the Berlin liberal Hochschule für die Wissenschaft des Judentums (high school for Jewish studies), as well as the younger historian Selma Stern-Täubler. Freund, whose main research field—the history of emancipation in Prussia—became highly relevant after 1933, turned to publishing popular articles in defense of the historical path of Prussian Jewry and to rehabilitating its historical heroes. See Ismar Freund, "Grundlagen der Emanzipation," *Central Verein Zeitung,* November 7, 1935, and Ismar Freund, "David Friedländer und die politische Emanzipation der Juden in Preussen," *Zeitschrift für die Geschichte der Juden in Deutschland* 6 (1935): 77–87. Stern, the author of

the biography *Jud Süss* (1929) as well as the research about the Prussian state and the Jews (1925), also turned in the 1930s to more popular writing, dealing primarily with the legacy of the Enlightenment and the emancipation. Stern's biographer, Marina Sassenberg, asserted that Stern's publications from the first years of the Nazi regime—including a biographical discussion about Mendelssohn and a review of the legacy of the Enlightenment and the emancipation—expressed a growing ambivalent tendency concerning the German Jewish synthesis. See Marina Sassenberg, *Selma Stern (1890–1981), Das Eigene in der Geschichte* (London, 2004), 188–95.

6. The presence of historical scholarship in the German Jewish public sphere of the 1930s, primarily in the liberal sector, was also expressed by the insertion of detailed bibliographical lists of research publications in the *Central Verein Zeitung*. These lists, which were published from October 1935 partly in order to guide the development of the communal libraries, at first included a few dozen general books about Jewish history. Later they presented the wide research literature about German Jewish history on the communal level and eventually also included a variety of books about the history of various Jewish communities outside of Germany. See "Bibliographie jüdischer Werke," *Central Verein Zeitung*, October 24, October 31, November 7, November 14, November 28, December 12, and December 24, 1935, and Jaunary 9, Jaunary 23, and Jaunary 30, 1936, and "Bibliographie der Geschichte der jüdischen Diaspora," *Central Verein Zeitung*, April 2, April 30, May 14, and June 4, 1936.

7. For basic literature about places of memory, see Pierre Nora, ed., *Les Lieux de mémoire* (Paris, 1997); Etienne Francois and Hagen Schulze, eds., *Deutsche Erinnerungsorte* (München, 2001); and Aleida Assmann, *Erinnerungsräume: Formen und Wandlungen des kulturellen Gedächtnisses* (München, 1999).

8. R. Lacher, "100 Jahre Judenordnung in Posen," *Israelitisches Familienblatt*, June 8, 1933.

9. Dr. W., "125 Jahre Badischer Oberrat der Israeliten," *Central Verein Zeitung*, February 22, 1934, and Dr. W., "125 Jahre Oberrat der Israeliten Badens," *Israelitisches Familienblatt*, March 1, 1934.

10. See, for example, Jacob Jacobson, "Das Emanzipationsedikt von 1812," *Gemeindeblatt der Jüdischen Gemeinde zu Berlin*, December 29, 1934; "Jüdisches Leben und jüdischer Geist, Aus den Vortragssälen," *Central Verein Zeitung*, November 7, 1935; Ismar Freund, "Die deutsche Judenfrage vor 100 Jahren," *Zeitschrift für die Geschichte der Juden in Deutschland* 5 (1934): 34–42; and Ismar Freund, "Erste Kämpfe um die Emanzipation nach 1812," *Central Verein Zeitung*, December 5, 1935.

11. On the concept of the homemaking myth, see Orm Øverland, *Immigrant Minds, American Identities: Making the United States Home, 1870–1930* (Urbana, IL, 2000), 7–8, 175.

12. Ismar Elbogen, "Seit wann leben Juden in Deutschland?," *Jüdische Rundschau*, July 13, 1934, and Ismar Elbogen, "Die Anfänge des deutschen Judentums," *Central Verein Zeitung*, February 28, 1935.

13. Raphael Straus, *Die Judengemeinde Regensburg im ausgehenden Mittelalter* (Heidelberg, 1932); Fr., "Regensburg im Mittelalter," *Central Verein Zeitung*, July 19, 1934; and L. F. [Ludwig Feuchtwanger], "Die deutsche Judenheit des Spätmit-

telalters," *Israelitisches Familienblatt,* November 15, 1934. It is noteworthy that the last article was a Jewish reaction to the book by the Nazi historian Wilhelm Grau about medieval Jewish Regensburg: Wilhelm Grau, *Antisemitismus im späten Mittelalter; Das Ende der Regensburger Judengemeinde, 1450–1519* (München, 1934).

14. On the unique place of Worms in the German Jewish culture of memory as well as in German Jewish tourism, see Nils Roemer, *German City, Jewish Memory: The Story of Worms* (Waltham, MA, 2010), 71–141, and Nils Roemer, "Provincializing the Past: Worms and the Making of a German-Jewish Cultural Heritage," *Jewish Studies Quarterly* 12, no. 1 (2005): 80–100. On the tension between the integration of a general German Jewish memory to communal local memories such as that of Worms, see Nils Roemer, "Between the Provinces and the City: Mapping German-Jewish Memories," *Leo Baeck Institute Year Book* 51 (2006): 61–77.

15. Roemer, *German City, Jewish Memory,* 120–23.

16. "Glückwünsche an die Wormser Gemeinde," *Central Verein Zeitung,* May 31, 1934. For a report about the central ceremony and the speeches, see "Die Neunhundertjahrfeier der Wormser Synagoge," *Israelitisches Familienblatt,* June 7, 1934.

17. Der Vorstand der israelitischen Religionsgemeinde Worms, "Zum Geleit," *Zeitschrift für die Geschichte der Juden in Deutschland* 5 (1934): 85.

18. Alfred Hirschberg, "900 Jahre Wormser Synagoge," *Central Verein Zeitung,* May 31, 1934. Hirschberg was active during the Weimar era in the field of legal defense of Jewish rights, and this made him especially close to the judicial issue.

19. For "faith and motherland," see Eugen Fuchs, "Glaube und Heimat," *Im Deutschen Reich,* September 1917, 338–51.

20. S. F., "Die Rechtsstellung der Wormser Juden im Mittelalter," *Central Verein Zeitung,* March 29, 1934; Ismar Elbogen, "Neunhundert Jahre Wormser Synagoge (1034–1934)," *Gemeindeblatt der Jüdischen Gemeinde zu Berlin,* June 2, 1934; and S. K., "Haus des Schicksals, Die Wormser Synagoge im Wandel der Zeiten," *Central Verein Zeitung,* May 31, 1934.

21. Max Dienermann, "Die Geschichte der Einzelgemeinde als Spiegel der Gesamtgeschichte," *Zeitschrift für die Geschichte der Juden in Deutschland* 5 (1934): 115–21.

22. Kurt Loewenstein, "Das Judengespenst. Vor 900 Jahren und heute," *Jüdische Rundschau,* June 1, 1934.

23. On the Zionist desire to fix the status of Germany's Jews as a minority with rights, see Avraham Margaliot, *Between Rescue and Annihilation: Studies in the History of German Jewry, 1932–1938* [in Hebrew] (Jerusalem, 1990), 232–43. It is noteworthy that a more scholarly contribution to the same *Jüdische Rundschau* issue referred to the Jews of thirteenth- and fourteenth-century Worms as "citizens"; see Guido Kisch, "Zur Geschichte der Wormser Juden," *Jüdische Rundschau,* June 1, 1934.

24. On the idea of *Distanz,* which was developed by the Zionist leader Kurt Blumenfeld, see Jehuda Reinharz, *Fatherland or Promised Land* (Ann Arbor, MI, 1975), 156.

25. M. Spitzer, "Die 900-Jahr-Feier in Worms," *Jüdische Rundschau,* June 8, 1934.

26. On the pantheon of heroes of the German Jewish Enlightenment move-

ment, see Shmuel Feiner, *Haskalah and History: The Emergence of a Modern Jewish Historical Consciousness* (Oxford, UK, 2002), 50–60. On the trend of writing biographies of rabbis and Jewish sages as cultural heroes within Central European Jewry, see Andreas Brämer, "Rabbinical Scholars as the Object of Biographical Interest: An Aspect of Jewish Historiography in the German-Speaking Countries of Europe (1780–1871)," *Leo Baeck Institute Year Book* 45 (2000): 51–79.

27. For an overview on the development of Mendelssohn's image as an icon, see David Sorkin, *Moses Mendelssohn and the Religious Enlightenment* (Berkeley, 1996), 148–55. On the history of Mendelssohn's anniversaries, see Christhard Hoffmann, "Constructing Jewish Modernity: Mendelssohn Jubilee Celebrations within German Jewry, 1829–1929," in *Towards Normality? Acculturation and Modern German Jewry,* edited by Rainer Liedtke and David Rechter, 27–52 (Tübingen, 2003). For a more comprehensive discussion on Mendelssohn's anniversaries in the 1920s and 1930s, see Guy Miron, "The Emancipation Heroes' Pantheon in German-Jewish Public Memory of the 1930s," *German History* 21, no. 4 (2003): 476–504.

28. See, for example, articles in *Central Verein Zeitung,* August 30, 1929; *Der Morgen,* August 1929; *Zeitschrift für die Geschichte der Juden in Deutschland* 1 (October 1929). See also Christhard Hoffmann, "Constructing Jewish Modernity," 48–50; Guy Miron, "Between History and a 'Useful Image of the Past': Representations of the Jewish and the German Past in the Liberal-Jewish Historical Discourse in Weimar Germany" [in Hebrew], *Zion* 66, no. 3 (2001): 309–13. See also in this context Elizabeth Petuchowski, "Zur Lessing-Rezeption in der deutsch-jüdischen Presse: Lessings 200. Geburtstag (22. Januar 1929)," *Lessing Yearbook* 14 (1982): 43–59.

29. Aron Gurwitsch, "Zum Problem der Judenemanzipation," *Frankfurter Israelitisches Gemeindeblatt,* September 1929, 9.

30. Israel Auerbach, "Moses Mendelssohn, Zur Wiederkehr seines Geburtstages am 6. September 1929," *Jüdische Rundschau,* September 6, 1929.

31. Heinz Kellermann, "Ende der Emanzipation," *Der Morgen,* August 1933, 173–77. It is interesting to point out the resonance of the phrase "internal emancipation" with the phrase "inner emigration" that was used by certain non-Jewish Germans regarding this period.

32. For such a position, see Alfred Hirschberg, "Sammeln und Richtung nehmen," *Central Verein Zeitung,* July 13, 1933.

33. Ignaz Maybaum, "Die jüdische Geschichte des deutschen Judentums," *Der Morgen,* November 1934, 336–44.

34. Ibid., 338–39.

35. Joachim Prinz, *Wir Juden* (Berlin, 1934), 23, 55. See more in the section "The Zionist Challenge" in chapter 1 of the present volume.

36. Bruno Weil, *Der Weg der deutschen Juden* (Berlin, 1934), 24.

37. Elsa Nathan, "Dokumente einer Freundschaft, Mendelssohn und Lessing," *Jüdische Rundschau,* January 19, 1934.

38. Joseph Carlebach, *Das gesetzestreue Judentum* (Berlin, 1936), 15–16.

39. Ibid., 27.

40. Ibid., 28–34. For a similar view, see "Samson Raphael Hirsch und unsere Zeit," Part 1, *Der Israelit,* May 5, 1938.

41. "Zum 150. Todestag Moses Mendelssohns am 4.1.1936, Was hat Mendelssohn uns zu sagen?," *Der Schild,* January 3, 1936.

42. Fritz Bamberger, "Moses Mendelssohn, Zur 150. Wiederkehr seines Todestages," *Central Verein Zeitung,* January 3, 1936.

43. For another article that presented Mendelssohn's Bible translation as his central initiative, see Rahel Wischnizer-Bernstein, "Eine Mendelssohnbibel mit Kupfern," *Gemeindeblatt der Jüdischen Gemeinde zu Berlin,* January 12, 1936.

44. Fritz Bamberger, "Moses Mendelssohn, Zur 150. Wiederkehr seines Todestages," *Central Verein Zeitung,* January 3, 1936.

45. "150 Jahre nach Mendelssohns Tod, 1786–4 January 1936," *Israelitisches Familienblatt,* January 2, 1936.

46. See, for example, Ludwig Feuchtwanger, "Der Streit um den Geist Moses Mendelssohns," *Jüdische Rundschau,* January 3, 1936.

47. See also in J. Bergmann, "Moses Mendelssohn und die Berliner jüdische Gemeinde," *Gemeindeblatt der Jüdischen Gemeinde zu Berlin,* January 12, 1936, and Ernst Fraenkel, "Moses Mendelssohn, der Jude. Zu seinem 150. Todestag am 4. Januar," *Gemeindeblatt für die Jüdischen Gemeinde Preussens, Verwaltungsblatt,* January 1, 1936.

48. Selma Stern-Täubler, "Die Judenfrage in der Ideologie der Aufklärung und Romantik," *Der Morgen,* November 1935, 339–48.

49. Ibid., 341–42.

50. The Jüdischer Kulturbund, which was established in Nazi Germany in 1933, was an institution created by unemployed Jewish performers. With the approval of the Nazi authorities, the Kulturbund offered a variety of theatrical performances, concerts, exhibitions, operas, and lectures all over Germany.

51. Arthur Eloesser, *Vom Ghetto nach Europa: Das Judentum im geistigen Leben des 19. Jahrhunderts* (Berlin, 1936), 54–55.

52. Abraham Goldthal, "Blick durch die Jahrtausende, Wendepunkte und Sinn jüdischer Geschichte (III)," *Israelitisches Familienblatt,* February 20, 1936.

53. Ismar Freund, "Grundlagen der Emanzipation," *Central Verein Zeitung,* November 7, 1935.

54. R. Lacher, "Ein Vorkämpfer der Emanzipation, Zum hundertsten Todestag David Friedländers am 25. Dezember 1934," *Israelitisches Familienblatt,* December 20, 1934, and Reinhold Lewin, "David Friedländer, Zur 100. Wiederkehr seines Todestages (25 Dezember 1834)," *Gemeindeblatt der Jüdischen Gemeinde zu Berlin,* December 29, 1934.

55. Leo Hirsch, "Im Angesicht der Totenmaske, Zu Heinrich Heines 80. Geburtstag," *Gemeindeblatt für die Jüdischen Gemeinden Preussens, Verwaltungsblatt,* February 1, 1936. There is an error in the original title, which refers to the anniversary of his birth rather than his death.

56. Kurt Pinthus, review article on Arthur Eloesser, *Vom Ghetto nach Europa, Central Verein Zeitung,* February 6, 1936.

57. Eloesser, *Vom Ghetto nach Europa,* 10, 130. About the prominent place that Eloesser devoted to Heine in his book, see the review articles Ludwig Feuchtwanger, "Vom Ghetto nach Europa," *Jüdische Rundschau,* April 10, 1936, and Hugo Lach-

mannski, "Der Weg aus dem Ghetto," *Gemeindeblatt der Jüdischen Gemeinde zu Berlin,* April 26, 1936. The two reviews relate positively to the choice of Heine as the representative of the emancipation period.

58. Eloesser, *Vom Ghetto nach Europa,* 103–4.

59. Ibid., 145, 153.

60. Ibid., 153.

61. Ibid., 118–19, 224–25.

62. Ibid., 125.

63. Even Kurt Pinthus, Eloesser's liberal critic, agreed in his review to the principle that the nineteenth century was in fact more tragic than it was considered in the past.

64. About Rahel Varnhagen, see Olga Bloch, "Rahel Varnhagen, Zu ihrem hundertsten Todestage," *Israelitisches Familienblatt,* February 9, 1933, and Hannah Arendt, "Originale Assimilation, Ein Nachwort zu Rahel Varnhagens 100. Todestag," *Jüdische Rundschau,* April 7, 1933. About Riesser, see Fritz Friedländer, "Eine Idee und ihre Zeit, 2 April 1806—Gabriel Riesser—2 April 1936," *Central Verein Zeitung,* April 2, 1936, and Eloesser, *Vom Ghetto nach Europa,* 237–49. For a more detailed discussion about the representations of Varnhagen and Riesser, see Miron, "The Emancipation Heroes' Pantheon in German-Jewish Public Memory of the 1930s," 492–96, 498–500. About Zunz's anniversary, see Gerhardt Neumann, "Leopold Zunz," *Jüdische Rundschau,* March 17, 1936, and Ismar Elbogen, "Der Schöpfer der 'Wissenschaft des Judentums', Zum 50. Todestag von Leopold Zunz am 17. März," *Frankfurter Israelitisches Gemeindeblatt,* April 1936. See also about Zunz in Guy Miron, "History, Science and Social Consciousness in the German-Jewish Public Discourse in the First Years of the Nazi Regime," in *Historiography and the Science of Judaism,* edited by Michael F. Mach and Yoram Jacobson, 246–49 [in Hebrew] (Tel Aviv, 2005).

65. Miron, "Between History and a 'Useful Image of the Past,'" 321–26.

66. Fritz Friedländer, "Wilhelm v. Humboldt, Zum 100. Todestag am 8. April 1935," *Central Verein Zeitung,* April 4, 1935.

67. Friedländer related again to Humboldt a few months later in a critical review of Wilhelm Grau's book about Humboldt and the Jewish problem; see Fritz Friedländer, "Ein Charakterbild in der Geschichte, Zu Wilhelm Grau: 'Wilhelm v. Humboldt,'" *Central Verein Zeitung,* November 7, 1935. See also in this context Hans Liebeschütz, "Zur Frage des jüdischen Geschichtsbildes von heute," *Gemeindeblatt der Deutsch-Israelitischen Gemeinde zu Hamburg,* June 12, 1936.

68. Ludwig Feuchtwanger, "Wandel eines Geschichtsbildes, Zum 100. Todestag Wilhelm von Humboldts," *Jüdische Rundschau,* April 5, 1935.

69. Feiner, *Haskalah and History,* 53–55, and Ismar Schorsch, "The Myth of Sephardic Supremacy," *Leo Baeck Institute Year Book* 34 (1989): 47–66.

70. For a report about the events in Spain and in other countries, see "Die Maimonides-Staatfeier eröffnet," *Jüdische Rundschau,* March 29, 1935. About the memorial events in Berlin, see Günther Looser, "Die Maimonidesfeiern der Gemeinde," *Gemeindeblatt der Jüdischen Gemeinde zu Berlin,* March 31, 1935, and Gerhardt Neumann, "Die Maimonides-Feiern der Gemeinde," *Jüdische Rundschau,*

April 2, 1935.

71. Fritz Bamberger, "Sinn des Maimonides-Jubiläums," *Central Verein Zeitung,* March 28, 1935. For Bamberger's scholarly book on Maimonides, see Fritz Bamberger, *Das System des Maimonides: Eine Analyse des More Newuchim vom Gottesbegriff aus* (Berlin, 1935).

72. "Den Andenken das Rabbi Mosche Ben Maimon, in der Überlieferung RAMBAM genannt, Achthundert Jahre nach seiner Geburt," *Jüdische Rundschau,* April 9, 1935. The presentation of Maimonides' life story in terms that included emigration was explicit in an article of the Frankfurt liberal rabbi Caesar Seligman. Seligman depicted Maimonides as carrying the "wandering stick" (*Wanderstab*) and stated that the persecutions had made his family lose its motherland (become *Heimatlos*); see C. Seligmann, "Zum 800. Geburtstag des Moses ben Maimon, Das Leben des Maimonides," *Frankfurter Israelitisches Gemeindeblatt,* April 1935.

73. S. Schachnowitz, *Rabbi Mosche Ben Maimun: Ein Lebenswerk für Gott, Israel und Thora* (Frankfurt am Main, 1935). For additional books about Maimonides that were published in 1935, see Leo Straus, *Philosophie und Gesetz, Beiträge zum Verständnis Maimunis und seiner Vorläufer* (Berlin, 1935), and Abraham Heschel, *Maimonides, Eine Biographie* (Berlin, 1935).

74. For a general discussion about Abravanel's multifaceted role in the twentieth-century Jewish memory culture, see Jean-Christophe Attias, "Isaac Abravanel: Between Ethnic Memory and National Memory," *Jewish Social Studies* 2, no. 3 (1996): 137–55.

75. On the exhibition, see Jüdisches Museum Berlin, *Gedenkausstellung Don Jizchaq Abarbanel, Seine Welt, Sein Werk* (Berlin, 1937), and Rahel Wischnitzer-Bernstein, "Die Welt der Abarbanel," *Gemeindeblatt der Jüdischen Gemeinde zu Berlin,* June 20, 1937.

76. Ismar Elbogen, "Don Jsaak Abarbanel," *Gemeindeblatt der Jüdischen Gemeinde zu Berlin,* February 7, 1937. For an assessment of Abravanel that focused on his dual life, torn between theological devotion and intensive political activity, see Abraham Heschel, "Staatsmann und Theologe," *Gemeindeblatt der Jüdischen Gemeinde zu Berlin,* February 7, 1937.

77. Max Nussbaum, "Abarbanel—Der Politiker und der Schriftsteller, Zu seinem 500. Geburtstag," *Jüdische Rundschau,* February 5, 1937.

78. Hans Wollenberg, ed., *Heroische Gestalten jüdischen Stammes* (Berlin, 1937), 14–22.

79. See some twenty articles under the title "Jüdische Gestalten und ihre Zeit" that were published in *Central Verein Zeitung* from February 21, 1935, to the summer of 1936.

80. See the articles written by Abraham Heschel in the section "Persönlichkeiten der jüdischen Geschichte"; for example, in *Gemeindeblatt der Jüdischen Gemeinde zu Berlin,* March 8, March 29, April 12, April 26, and May 17, 1936, and in *Frankfurter Israelitisches Gemeindeblatt,* January, February, March, June, and November 1938.

81. For an overview of the debates in the Jewish press as to whether German Jews should leave or stay, see Herbert Freeden, *The Jewish Press in the Third Reich* (Providence, RI, 1992), 49–74.

82. Fritz Friedländer, "Hemmung und Ziel jüdischer Geschichtsforschung," *Central Verein Zeitung,* September 6, 1934.

83. B. Weinryb, "Deutsch-jüdische Wanderungen im 19. Jahrhundert," *Der Morgen,* April 1934, 4–10.

84. On the centrality of Palestine as an immigration destination in the years 1933–35, see Daniel Fraenkel, *On the Edge of the Abyss: Zionist Policy and the Plight of the German Jews, 1933–1938* [in Hebrew] (Jerusalem, 1994), 97–100. For a previous discussion on the concept of Diaspora in the German Jewish discourse of this period, see Jacob Boas, "Germany or Diaspora? German Jewry's Shifting Perceptions in the Nazi Era (1933–1938)," *Leo Baeck Institute Year Book* 27 (1982): 123–25.

85. Eva Reichmann-Jungmann, "Diaspora als Aufgabe," *Der Morgen,* June 1934, 97–98.

86. Ibid., 98.

87. Ignaz Maybaum, "Raum und Grenze der Diaspora," *Der Morgen,* June 1934, 100, emphasis in original.

88. Grigori Landau, "Die Gewalt der Geschichte," *Der Morgen,* June 1934, 106–7.

89. Ibid., 110–13.

90. Franz Rosenthal. "Die Frage der Diaspora, Weg des Gesetzes," *Central Verein Zeitung,* Special issue, *Seite der Jugend,* February 21, 1935.

91. Ignaz Maybaum, "Der jüdische Sinn des deutschen Judentums," *Der Morgen,* January 1934, 407–10.

92. Ignaz Maybaum, "Die jüdische Geschichte des deutschen Judentums," *Der Morgen,* November 1934, 344.

93. About the change in the German Jewish public discourse after the Nuremberg Laws, see Abraham Margaliot, "The Reaction of the Jewish Public in Germany to the Nuremberg Laws," *Yad Vashem Studies* 12 (1977): 75–107.

94. Fritz Friedländer, "Ein Charakterbild in der Geschichte, Zu Wilhelm Grau: 'Wilhelm v. Humboldt,'" *Central Verein Zeitung,* November 7, 1935.

95. A. H. [Hirschberg], "Mikrokosmos der Weltgeschichte," *Der Morgen,* January 1936, 427. Hirschberg relates to Ahasuerus the wandering Jew and not to the ancient Persian king.

96. Adolf Altmann, *Volk im Aufbruch, Diaspora in Bewegung: Reflexionen zur jüdischen Zeitgeschichte* (Frankfurt am Main, 1936), 7–9.

97. Ibid., 36.

98. L. K. "Gedenktage," *Gemeindeblatt der Jüdischen Gemeinde zu Berlin,* February 7, 1937. For an additional article about Abravanel in this context, see Rabbiner Dr. Bergmann, "Ein Tisch'a b'aw im Jahre 1492," *Gemeindeblatt der Jüdischen Gemeinde zu Berlin,* July 18, 1937.

99. Hanns Reissner, "Auswanderung—Hundert Jahre später," *Der Morgen,* October 1937, 287.

100. Ibid., 287–93. See also Hanns Reissner, *Familie auf Wanderschaft* (Berlin, 1938).

101. Dr. Herzfeld, "Jüdischer Central Verein," *Central Verein Zeitung,* August 13, 1936.

102. Ernst Herzfeld, "Assimilation, Dissimilation, Auswanderung," *Central Verein Zeitung,* February 25, 1937. On this discussion, see Guy Miron, "Emancipation and Assimilation in the German Jewish Discourse of the 1930s," *Leo Baeck Institute Year Book* 48 (2003): 165–89.

103. H. F., "Assimilation, Dissimilation und neue Assimilation, Eine Erwiderung," *Jüdische Rundschau,* March 12, 1937. See also in this context Anon., "Assimilierbarkeit," *Jüdische Rundschau,* February 12, 1937, and Hans Pomeranz, "Erneuerung der jüdischen Begriffsbildung, Mut zur Entwicklung," *Jüdische Rundschau,* May 13, 1938.

104. Manfred Swarsensky, "Pessach, Das Fest der Erinnerung," *Gemeindeblatt der Jüdischen Gemeinde zu Berlin,* April 17, 1938.

105. Ignaz Maybaum, "Ruf an Juden im Aufbruch," *Central Verein Zeitung,* April 7, 1938.

106. Ibid.

107. Günter Looser, "Die jüdische Wissenschaft, Von der historischen Entwicklung und Zukunft," *Gemeindeblatt der Jüdischen Gemeinde zu Berlin,* July 31, 1938.

108. Ernst Fraenkel, "Geschichte im Kreise," *Jüdisches Gemeindeblatt für die Synagogen in Preussen und Norddeutschland,* October 1, 1938.

109. *Kristallnacht,* also known as the pogrom of November (Novemberpogrom), was a series of attacks against Jews throughout Nazi Germany and parts of Austria during November 9–10, 1938. Jewish homes and shops were attacked, more than ninety Jews were killed, and much damage was made to Jewish property. Following the pogrom, around thirty thousand Jewish men were taken to concentration camps. *Kristallnacht* signifies the peak of the radical turning point in the Nazi anti-Jewish policy in 1938.

Chapter 3

1. Paule E. Hyman, *The Jews of Modern France* (Berkeley, 1998), 137; see chap. 8 for an overview of French Jewry in the interwar period.

2. Often cited is this context is Maurice Barrès's statement that the sacrifice of French Jews in World War I made them part of the "spiritual Family of France" (*Les Familles spirituelles de la France*) and the "scacred union" (*l'union sacrée*). This statement, which was in fact an expression of the total mobilization of French society to the war effort at the time, was presented later by French Jewish spokespeople as proof of their acceptance by French society, especially because Barrès had previously tended toward right-wing anti-Semitic views; see Annette Becker, "Les Juifs de France et Verdun, 1916–1940," *Archives Juives* 33, no. 1 (2000): 72.

3. Michael Marrus, *The Politics of Assimilation: A Study of the French Jewish Community at the Time of the Dreyfus Affair* (Oxford, UK, 1971), 86–121.

4. For a general discussion about the development of the Jewish community in France and the tensions between the local and immigrant communities, see Paula Hyman, *From Dreyfus to Vichy: The Remaking of French Jewry, 1906–1939* (New York, 1979), 115–52, and Nadia Malinovich, *French and Jewish: Culture and the Politics of Identity of Early Twentieth-Century Jewish France* (Oxford, UK, 2008).

5. Nancy L. Green, "La révolution dans l'imaginaire des immigrants juifs," in *Histoire politique des Juifs de France,* edited by Pierre Birnbaum, 153–62 (Paris, 1990).

6. This description of the 1930s' Paris Jewish community is based on David H. Weinberg, *A Community on Trial: The Jews of Paris in the 1930s* (Chicago, 1977), 22.

7. Eugen Weber, *The Hollow Years: France in the 1930s* (London, 1995), 6–7. For other basic overviews of the French history in this decade, see Olivier Dard, *Les années trente: Le choix impossible* (Paris, 1999), and Serge Berstein, *La France des années 30* (Paris, 2001).

8. Weber, *The Hollow Years,* chap. 1.

9. Berstein opens his book about the 1930s with data about this demographic decline; see Berstein, *La France des années 30,* 5–7.

10. The Maginot Line, named after French minister of defense André Maginot, was a defensive military line that France constructed along its borders with Germany and Italy in light of France's experience during World War I. The Maginot Line became a metaphor for the French defensive mentality during the interwar period.

11. Daniel J. Sherman, *The Construction of Memory in Interwar France* (Chicago, 1999), 311–14, and Mona L. Siegel, "'History Is the Opposite of Forgetting': The Limits of Memory and the Lessons of History in Interwar France," *Journal of Modern History* 74, no. 4 (December 2002): 770–800. See especially pp. 784–89 concerning turning November 11 into a key date in the French public consciousness.

12. Weber, *The Hollow Years,* 26–54; Berstein, *La France des années 30,* 25–52; and Dard, *Les années trente,* 21–25.

13. Weber, *The Hollow Years,* 87–110. Weber claims that the Jews were viewed by the French Right in this period as the ultimate foreigners (103). See also in this context Clifford Rosenberg, *Policing Paris: The Origins of Modern Immigration Control between the Wars* (Ithaca, NY, 2006).

14. Julian Jackson, *The Popular Front in France: Defending Democracy, 1934–38* (Cambridge, UK, 1988), 1–3.

15. Jackson, *The Popular Front in France,* 4–6; Weber, *The Hollow Years,* 139–40; Dard, *Les années trente,* 71–81; and Rod Kedward, *La vie en bleu: France and the French since 1900* (London, 2006), 167–76.

16. Julian Jackson, *France: The Dark Years, 1940–1944* (Oxford, UK, 2001), 65–80.

17. Christian Amalvi, "Le 14-Juillet, Du dies irae à jour de fête," in *Les Lieux de mémoire,* edited by Pierre Nora, 413–15 (Paris, 1997), and Jackson, *The Popular Front in France,* 6–10, 36–51.

18. Jackson, *The Popular Front in France,* 189–208, and Weber, *The Hollow Years,* 166–69.

19. Paul Farmer, *France Reviews Its Revolutionary Origins: Social Politics and Historical Opinion in the Third Republic* (New York, 1963), 86–109, 114–15. Concerning the interpretations of the great Revolution during the Third Republic, see in general Robert Gildea, *The Past in French History* (New Haven, CT, 1994), chap. 7.

20. David Carroll, *French Literary Fascism: Nationalism, Anti-Semitism, and the Ideology of Culture* (Princeton, NJ, 1995), 71–96; see also Jackson, *France,* 59.

21. Raymond-Raoul Lambert, "Hitler au pouvoir," *L'Univers Israélite,* February 10, 1933.

22. For a discussion about the reaction of the general French press to the anti-Jewish policy of the Nazi regime in its first year, see Haim Shamir, "French Press Reaction in 1933 to Hitler's Anti-Jewish Policies," *Wiener Library Bulletin* 25, nos. 1–2 (1971): 23–32.

23. H. Prague, "De Torquemada à Hitler," *Archives Israélites,* February 18, 1932.

24. Nina Gourfinkel, "Revue des livres: Sur les chemins de l'exil," *L'Univers Israélite,* December 28, 1934.

25. Edmund Cahen, "La vérité sur les Juifs," *L'Univers Israélite,* April 5, 1935. See also in this context the description of the German Jewish refugees in Paris as the modern manifestation of the ancient Ahasuerus the wanderer in W. Strauss, "Le Juif errant à Paris, impressions d'un réfugié," *L'Univers Israélite,* June 9, 1933.

26. L. D. [Lucien Dreyfus], "L'Histoire est notre juge," *La Tribune juive,* May 22, 1936.

27. H. Prague, "Le 9 Ab, la mémoire du coeur," *Archives Israélites,* July 19, 1934.

28. H. Prague, "Une anomalie fondamentale," *Archives Israélites,* February 16, 1933; Judaeus, "La persecution des Juifs en Allemange et le devoir des Juifs français," *L'Univers Israélite,* March 31, 1933; and Henri-Théophile Blanc, "La destinée des Juifs allemands," *L'Univers Israélite,* May 19, 1933. See also Jay Berkovitz, *The Shaping of Jewish Identity in Nineteenth-century France* (Detroit, 1989), 190.

29. Rabbin Mathieu Wolff, "A propos du jeûne d'Ab," *L'Univers Israélite,* July 28, 1933.

30. Robert Loewel, "Une enquête sur l'antisémitisme en France, il y a trente-cinq ans," *L'Univers Israélite,* November 10, 1933.

31. Joachim Prinz, *Wir Juden* (Berlin, 1934), 54.

32. E. Laurence, "Revue des livres: Nous autres Juifs (Wir Juden), Joachim Prinz," *L'Univers Israélite,* February 16, 1934.

33. Frédéric Sternthal, "L'Emancipation des Juifs en Prusse, A propos du 125e anniversaire de cet évènement," *L'Univers Israélite,* September 17, 1937.

34. Baruch Hagani, *L'Emancipation des juifs* (Paris, 1928), 85–116. About Hagani and his milieu, see Malinovich, *French and Jewish,* 215–19.

35. Hagani, *L'Emancipation des juifs,* 116–48. See especially his harsh critique of the "salon women" (136–37). For a later French Jewish discussion about Mendelssohn's heritage and the gap between him and his disciples, see H. Schilli, "Un anniversaire, Mendelssohn 'Juif de combat,'" *Le Journal Juif,* March 6, 1936.

36. Hagani, *L'Emancipation des juifs,* 153–54.

37. Ibid., 170–72, 190–217.

38. Ibid., 206.

39. Ibid., 218–60.

40. Ibid., 256.

41. Meyerskey, "L'émancipation a-t-elle fait faillite? Conférence faite par M. le grand-rabbin Liber," *L'Univers Israélite,* February 16, 1934.

42. Ibid.

43. Ibid.

44. For another discussion of Liber's position about assimilation and emancipation, see Robert Sommer, "La doctrine politique et l'action religieuse du grand-rabbin Maurice Liber," *Revue de Études Juives Historia Judaica,* 125 (1966): 9–20.

45. "Le Dilema," *La Tribune juive,* December 9, 1932, and "La tribut de l'assimilation," *La Tribune juive,* February 17, 1933.

46. "Was heisst Assimilation: Ausspracheabend der Luxemburger Jugend," *La Tribune juive,* December 22, 1933. For a further discussion in "La page de Luxemburg" about the ghetto concept and its renewed meaning in German Jewish life, see "Die seelischen Wirkungen des Ghettos/Vortrag von Rabbiner Dr. Rülf-Saarbrücken," *La Tribune juive,* January 26, 1934.

47. Marcel Greilsammer, "L'exclusivisme juif," *Chalom,* April 1934, 1–3.

48. See, for example, Noel Parker, *Portrayals of the Revolution: Images, Debates and Patterns of Thought on the French Revolution* (Carbondale, IL, 1990), and Gildea, *The Past in French History,* chap. 7.

49. Jay R. Berkovitz, *Rites and Passages: The Beginnings of Modern Jewish Culture in France, 1650–1860* (Philadelphia, 2004), 10, 89. Berkovitz has sought to reconstruct the complicated French Jewish experience of the revolutionary and Napoleonic eras in a more balanced way.

50. On the celebration of the one hundredth anniversary of the Revolution by the French Jews, see Pierre Birnbaum, *The Jews of the Republic: A Political History of State Jews in France from Gambetta to Vichy* (Stanford, CA, 1996), 115–16; Hyman, *The Jews of Modern France,* 91–92; and Marrus, *The Politics of Assimilation,* 91.

51. Weinberg, *A Community on Trial,* 46. The French Jewish press reported every year about the ceremonies and celebrations marking July 14 in the various communities; see, for example, "Fête du 14 Juillet à la Synagogue," *La Tribune juive,* July 21, 1933.

52. Green, "La révolution dans l'imaginaire des immigrants juifs," 153–62. About the interest of east European Jewish intellectuals in the legacy of the Revolution, see Shmuel Feiner, "'Rebellious French' and 'Jewish Freedom'—The French Revolution in the East European *Haskalah*'s Image of the Past," in *The French Revolution and Its Impact,* 215–47, edited by Richard I. Cohen [in Hebrew] (Jerusalem, 1991).

53. For possible connotations on contemporary conditions in a sermon given by the chief rabbi of Strasbourg to mark July 14, see "Le quatorze juillet au temple consistorial/Un émouvant sermon de Mr. Le Grand-Rabbin," *La Tribune juive,* July 17, 1936.

54. Becker, "Les Juifs de France et Verdun, 1916–1940," 74–75. The Battle of Verdun was one of the major battles during World War I on the Western Front. The battle became a myth (known as the myth of Verdun) of French determination to hold the ground and then roll back the enemy, even with the price of great human loss.

55. Weinberg, *A Community on Trial,* 78–81, and David Shapira, "Crises et mutations de la communauté juive française sous l'influence du grand-rabbin de France Jacob Kaplan" (PhD dissertation [Hebrew with French abstract], Hebrew University of Jerusalem, 2005), 79–82, 87–96, 102–8.

56. Jacob Kaplan, "L'antisémitisme, campagne antifrançaise," *L'Univers Israélite,* June 14, 1935.

57. For a critical discussion of this political strategy, which exposes the tensions within the local French Jewish community, see Raymond-Raoul Lambert, "Israël au-dessus des parties," *L'Univers Israélite,* June 19, 1936. About this topic, see also Shapira, "Crises et mutations de la communaté juive française sous l'influence du grand-rabbin de France Jacob Kaplan," 102–7.

58. S. Posener, "L'immigration des Juifs allemands en France sous le Premier Empire," *L'Univers Israélite,* March 9, 16, and 23, 1934.

59. Léon Berman, *Histoire des Juifs de France des origines a nos jours* (Paris, 1937), 7–8.

60. Ibid., 207. For another example of the representation of the Jewish past in France as a multigenerational continuity of Jewish presence and thus contrary to the anti-Semitic depiction of the foreigners who penetrated France from the East, see Jean Davray, "Un antisémite qui s'ignore," *L'Univers Israélite,* February 25, 1938.

61. Ibid. On French politics and public opinion as well as the dilemma of French Jewish leaders with regard to the question of Jewish immigration to France in those years, see Vicki Caron, *Uneasy Asylum: France and the Jewish Refugee Crisis, 1933–1942* (Stanford, CA, 1999), especially chaps. 4, 5, and 6. See also Posener's review article on Berman's book: S. Posener, "Revue des livres: Histoire des Juifs de France," *L'Univers Israélite,* March 18, 1938.

62. Robert Lévy-Dreyfus, "Le judaisme français devant sa propre histoire," *La Terre Retrouvée,* October 25, 1932.

63. The Damascus Affair was an 1840 incident in which the accusation of ritual murder was brought against members of the Jewish community of Damascus. The incident developed into an international scandal that involved several European powers as well as Jewish organizations and public activists, among them the young Adolph Crémieux.

64. H. Prague, "Une histoire qui recommence," *Archives Israélites,* March 16, 1933.

65. M. Vichniac, "Le problème des apatrides," *L'Univers Israélite,* July 17, 1936.

66. A. S. Lirik, "Moyshe mendelson," *Pariser Haynt,* January 12, 1936. For another article that indicates an essential connection between German history and Nazi anti-Semitism, see Sh. Rozenfeld, "Nirenberg in undzer geshikhte," *Pariser Haynt,* December 6, 1935.

67. A. Ginzburg, "Der hitlerism un undzere asimilatoren," *Pariser Haynt,* March 11, 1934.

68. A. Ginzburg, "Di eybike sine tsum yidishn folk," *Parizer Haynt,* September 20, 1935.

69. A. S. Lirik, "Tsurik in geto," *Pariser Haynt,* September 27, 1935.

70. A. S. Lirik, "Fun paro biz hitler," *Pariser Haynt,* April 10, 1936.

71. About the Yiddish press in Paris at that time, including the *Pariser Haynt,* see Shmuel Bunim, "La presse yiddish parisienne dans l'entre-deux guerres; un miroir du monde du travail," *Archives Juives* 33, no. 2 (2000): 47–66.

72. Y. Gotlib, "Der galgal-hahozer," *Pariser Haynt,* July 1, 1934.

73. See also in this context the publication of an article written by a German Jewish refugee with a critical comment by a French Jewish writer: Irwin Levy, "Eloge de l'assimilation," and Guy Cohen, "Commentaire," *Chalom,* October 1933, 12–14.

74. Y. Gotlib, "Der galgal-hahozer," *Pariser Haynt,* July 1, 1934.

75. M. Jarblum, "Der politisher krizis in frankraykh," *Pariser Haynt,* February 9, 1934. The Action Française is a French counterrevolutionary movement that was founded during the Dreyfus Affair in 1898 and became a prominent representative of French radical Right integral nationalism, which regarded the nation as an organic entity and was associated with xenophobia.

76. On the events in Paris on that day, see Weber, *The Hollow Years,* 140, and Jackson, *The Popular Front in France,* 7.

77. M. Jarblum, "Tsvey manifestatsies—tsvey lagern," *Pariser Haynt,* July 14, 1935. See also news reports about this day's events in Paris: "Haynt der 14 yuli," *Pariser Haynt,* July 14, 1935, and "Impozanter 14 yuli in pariz," *Pariser Haynt,* July 15, 1935.

78. M. Jarblum, "Tsvey manifestatsies—tsvey lagern," *Pariser Haynt,* July 14, 1935.

79. Weber, *The Hollow Years,* 140, and "Di levaye fun kapitan Dreyfus," *Pariser Haynt,* July 14, 1935.

80. Y. Chomsky, "Di levaye fun kapitan Dreyfus iz forgekumen nekhtn in groys geheymnish," *Pariser Haynt,* July 15, 1935.

81. A. Gelernter, "Di geshikhte fun di yidn in frankraykh," *Pariser Haynt,* 1935–36.

82. Joseph Hollander, "Yidn in elzas-lotringen," *Pariser Haynt,* March 30, 1937.

83. N. Frank, "Marselieze un 'Hatikva,'" *Pariser Haynt,* March 11, 1938.

84. Jackson, *The Popular Front in France,* 39–40, 120–21.

85. Weinberg, *A Community on Trial,* 131–32.

86. A. Raiski, "A groyse date," *Naye Presse,* July 14, 1937. For another Jewish Communist representation of the French Revolution as a French anti-Fascist legacy, which was under dispute in French society in the 1930s, see A. Lerman, "Nokhn kongres in ARL, di historie misiefun folks-front-frankraykh," *Naye Presse,* January 8, 1938.

87. See in this context another article dealing with the involvement of Jews in the revolutionary committees that ruled France during the Jacobin regime: Z. Szajokowski, "A yidisher yakobiner-klub beys der groyser frantsozisher revolutsie," *Naye Presse,* July 14 and 15, 1937.

88. Alyssa Sepinwall, *The Abbé Grégoire and the French Revolution: The Making of Modern Universalism* (Berkeley, 2005), 221–22. See also in this context Pierre Birnbaum, *Jewish Destinies: Citizenship, State and Community in Modern France* (New York, 2000), 13.

89. Sepinwall, *The Abbé Grégoire and the French Revolution,* 222–23. For an overview of the ceremonies in various Jewish communities in France, see "La célébration du centenaire de la mort de l'abbé Grégoire," *L'Univers Israélite,* June 5 and 12, 1931; "L'abbé Grégoire," *La Tribune juive,* June 5, 1931; and "Le Centenaire de l'Abbé Grégoire," *La Terre Retrouvée,* May 25, 1931. For a report on the ceremonies held to

mark the anniversary in all of the Alliance Israélite Universelle schools in the Middle East and northern Africa, see "En l'honneur de l'abbé Grégoire," *Paix et Droit,* September 1931, 8.

90. Pierre Paraf, "Français . . . Juif . . . Israélite," *L'Univers Israélite,* May 29, 1931.

91. Alfred Berl, "L'abbé Grégoire et l'émancipation des Juif," *Paix et Droit,* May 1931, 1–3.

92. Sepinwall, *The Abbé Grégoire and the French Revolution,* 226–29. For one comment on these revisionist attitudes, see "Revue de la Presse, L'Abbé Grégoire," *La Tribune juive,* March 11, 1932.

93. "A la Mémoire de l'Abbé Grégoire," *Samedi,* June 19, 1937.

94. N. Frank, "Tsvery frantsoyzishe galokhim: abe greguar un abe lamber," *Pariser Haynt,* July 17, 1936.

95. Ibid.

96. M. Liber, "Grégoire et Crémieux," *Paix et Droit,* May 1931, 4–5.

97. See also, for example, "L' Alliance Israélite et l'abbé Grégoire," *L'Univers Israélite,* June 5, 1931.

98. See Andrea Hopp, "Das Jahr 1929: Erinnerung und Selbstverständnis im deutschen Judentum," *Trumah* 7 (1998): 113–34, and Guy Miron, "Between History and a 'Useful Image of the Past': Representations of the Jewish and the German Past in the Liberal-Jewish Historical Discourse in Weimar Germany" [in Hebrew], *Zion* 66, no. 3 (2001): 309–10.

99. S. [Solomon Vladimirovich] Posener, *Adolphe Cremieux (1796–1880),* 2 vols. (Paris, 1933–34).

100. Bernard Dorset, "Crémieux et l'Alsace," *L'Univers Israélite,* December 29, 1933.

101. G. Bernard, "Une noble intervention de Crémieux en faveur de Chrétiens massacrés," *L'Univers Israélite,* November 24, 1933.

102. "Un professeur de patriotisme Adolph Crémieux," *La Tribune juive,* May 25, 1934.

103. Ida R. See, "L'action politique des juifs au XIX siècle," *Samedi,* October 30, 1936.

104. H. Sliosberg, "Adolphe Crémieux," *Le Journal Juif,* February 8, 1935.

105. Maurice Leven, "l'Alliance Israélite Universelle," *L'Univers Israélite,* June 22, 1934.

106. A. Alperin, "Alians izraelit universel—75 yor, di geshikhte fun der antshteyung fun der ershter yiddisher veltorganizatsie," (2 parts), *Pariser Haynt,* June 14 and 16, 1935.

107. Ibid., pt. 2.

108. For a discussion about the way French Jews treated Gambetta during the fiftieth anniversary of his death, see Robert Anchel, "La Judaisme et Gambetta," *L'Univers Israélite,* February 7, 1933.

109. Joseph Milner, "Leon gambeta," *Pariser Haynt,* April 1, 1938, and Y. Gotlib, "Leon gambeta," *Pariser Haynt,* April 12, 1938. For an article published a few months earlier to mark the sixty-seventh anniversary of the Third Republic, see Ben-Yehuda, "67 yor drite repulbik," *Pariser Haynt,* September 5, 1937.

110. S. Posener, "Gambetta et Crémieux," *La Terre Retrouvée,* June 15, 1938.

111. Poyl Held, "Der ershter etap, tsum 64tn yortog fun der parizer komune," *Naye Presse,* March 17, 1935.

112. Y. Lerman, "Haynt—manifestatsie tsu komunaru-vant," *Naye Presse,* May 30, 1937. For an additional presentation of the Jewish involvement in the commune, see Y. Shay Aves, "Der yid frenkel, arbet-komisar fun der komune," *Naye Presse,* May 30, 1937.

113. Y. Spera, "Di parizer komune, geshtalt fun frantsoyzishn folk," *Naye Presse,* May 30, 1937.

114. Y. Spera, "Di komune fun 1871 un frankraykh frun 1938," *Naye Presse,* March 18, 1938.

Chapter 4

1. For a general discussion about this period, see Olivier Dard, *Les années trente: Le choix impossible* (Paris, 1999), 159–211. See also Eugen Weber, *The Hollow Years: France in the 1930s* (London, 1995), 174–78, and Robert J. Young, *France and the Origins of the Second World War* (London, 1996), 28–30.

2. Julian Jackson, *France: The Dark Years, 1940–1944* (Oxford, UK, 2001), 104–7.

3. Vicki Caron, *Uneasy Asylum: France and the Jewish Refugee Crisis, 1933–1942* (Stanford, CA, 1999), 171–205, 268–95.

4. David H. Weinberg, *A Community on Trial: The Jews of Paris in the 1930s* (Chicago, 1977), 171–88.

5. J. Milner, "KIR'H," *Pariser Haynt,* March 16, 1938. For another article that mourned the past of Jewish Vienna while facing its present destruction, see Y. Chomsky, "Vin on yidn . . . ," *Pariser Haynt,* July 10, 1938.

6. J. Milner, "1848," *Pariser Haynt,* March 18, 1938.

7. For an additional reference to the turning point in the status of the Jews in Europe as heralding a new Middle Ages, see "Au vingtième siécle vers un nouveau moyen-âge," *La Tribune juive,* February 18, 1938.

8. Y. Gotlib, "Ven di geshikhte khazrt zikh iber, tsum rasizm in italien," *Pariser Haynt,* August 2, 1938. For another reference to the anti-Semitic developments in Italy in historical perspective, see Yeshaye Uger, "Musolini un dos yidishe geto," *Pariser Haynt,* October 21, 1938.

9. See in this context an interesting attempt to link Christian principles to the 1789 legacy in Alfred Berl, "Les juifs parmi les nations," *Paix et Droit,* March 1938, 1–3.

10. Similar arguments were also evident in Jewish appeals to the Vatican in the wake of the November pogrom and during the first months of the war.

11. For the presentation of the repression of the Jews in Germany as a return of German history to medieval despotism, see J. Hollander, "Der untergang fun daytshn yidntum," *Pariser Haynt,* September 9, 1938.

12. Moris Shvarts, "Vi ikh hob gezen frankraykh un di frantsoyzn," *Pariser Haynt,* July 24, 1938.

13. W. Weviorka, "Panik . . . ," *Pariser Haynt,* October 23, 1938.

14. K. Nekhemiezon, "Es zenen shoyn amol geven hitlers," *Pariser Haynt,* November 25, 1938.

15. Y. Gotlib, "Der emes-protest," *Pariser Haynt,* November 22, 1938.

16. Young, *France and the Origins of the Second World War,* 117–18; Daniel J. Sherman, *The Construction of Memory in Interwar France* (Chicago, 1999), 314; and Janine Bourdin, "Les anciens combattants et la célébration du 11 novembre 1938," in *La France et les Français 1938 en 1939,* edited by René Rémond and Janine Bourdin, 95–114 (Paris, 1978).

17. For a discussion on how the Jews in France coped with these problems in 1938, see Weinberg, *A Community on Trial,* 171–88.

18. See, for example, "Le 15e anniversaire de l'Armistice," *L'Univers Israélite,* November 17 and 24, 1933.

19. "Le 11 Novembre à Strasbourg," *L'Univers Israélite,* November 24, 1933.

20. Y. Chomsky, "17 yor nokh der armistis . . . ," *Pariser Haynt,* November 10, 1935.

21. Raymond-Raoul Lambert, "11 Novembre, où sont tes joies et tes espoirs?," *L'Univers Israélite,* November 5, 1937.

22. Raymond-Raoul Lambert, "L'Heure du Salut Public," *L'Univers Israélite,* March 18, 1938. See also Raymond-Raoul Lambert, "France d'abord," *L'Univers Israélite,* May 27, 1938.

23. Mark Jarblum, "In 1914 un itst," *Pariser Haynt,* September 25, 1938. See also N. Frank, "Pariz in di letste sholem-teg fun 1914," *Pariser Haynt,* July 31, 1938, and W. Weviorka, "Tishebov 1914," *Pariser Haynt,* August 7, 1938.

24. N. Frank, "In di vegn fun 1914," *Pariser Haynt,* October 2, 1938. See also Frank's article marking the twentieth anniversary of the cease-fire: "Der man mit der oysgeshnitener tsung," *Pariser Haynt,* November 13, 1938.

25. Weber claims that French spokespeople attacked the Jewish press in late 1938, stating that it created a war psychosis; see Weber, *The Hollow Years,* 22–23.

26. Raymond-Raoul Lambert, "Vingt ans aprés," *L'Univers Israélite,* November 11, 1938. For additional statements by French Jewish spokespeople marking the twentieth anniversary of the cease-fire, see "Onze Novembre," *L'Univers Israélite,* November 11, 1938, and "Le celebration du 20 anniversaire de l'Armistice," *L'Univers Israélite,* November 18, 1938.

27. Jacob Kaplan, *Témoignages sur Israël dans la littérature française* (Paris, 1938). Kaplan referred to this book in an interview forty years later, stating that he had published it in order to raise the confidence of French Jews in light of the violent anti-Semitic campaign that was then going on in France; see Pierre Pierrard, *Justice pour la foi juive: Pierre Pierrard interroge le Grand Rabbin Kaplan* (Paris, 1977), 58–60. See also David Shapira, "Crises et mutations de la communauté juive française sous l'influence du grand-rabbin de France Jacob Kaplan" (PhD dissertation [Hebrew with French abstract], Hebrew University of Jerusalem, 2005), 126–30.

28. A similar German Jewish project was Arthur Eloesser, *Vom Ghetto nach Europa: Das Judentum im geistigen Leben des 19. Jahrhunderts* (Berlin, 1936). For a discussion about such anthologies, which were complied by Hungarian Jews in this pe-

riod, see Anna Szalai, "Will the Past Protect Hungarian Jewry? The Response of Jewish Intellectuals to Anti-Jewish Legislation," *Yad Vashem Studies* 32 (2004): 179–85.

29. Kaplan, *Témoignages sur Israël dans la littérature française,* 4–7.

30. Ibid., 7–9.

31. Ibid., 15–16. See also sources throughout Kaplan's book that recognize the significant Jewish contribution to European and world civilization.

32. Raymond-Raoul Lambert, "La thèse d'Israël dans la symphonie française," *L'Univers Israélite,* April 8, 1938.

33. Nathan Netter, *Vingt siècles d'histoire d'une communauté juive (Metz et son grand passé)* (Paris, 1938). Metz was a model Jewish community for other Alsatian communities in the seventeenth and eighteenth centuries; see Jay R. Berkovitz, *Rites and Passages: The Beginnings of Modern Jewish Culture in France, 1650–1860* (Philadelphia, 2004), 19.

34. Georges Samuel, "Préface," in Netter, *Vingt siècles d'histoire d'une communauté juive,* xii.

35. Netter, *Vingt siècles d'histoire d'une communauté juive,* 3–13.

36. Ibid., 152–83.

37. L. D., "Vingt siècles d'histoire d'une communauté juive," *La Tribune juive,* December 30, 1938. For additional reviews, see U U.I., "Un bastion de l'Est," *L'Univers Israélite,* March 3, 1939, and S. Posener, "L'histoire de la communuté juive de Metz," *La Terre Retrouvée,* April 15, 1939.

38. J. Bielinky, "A travers l'Histoire juive," *Affirmation,* February 10, 1939.

39. "Dos heylike rekht fun umgliklekhe," *Naye Presse,* March 21, 1938.

40. A. Raiski, "Yidishe aynvanderungen keyn frankraykh, fun der ershter legende biz dem hayntikn tog," *Naye Presse, Yubiley-oysgabe,* February 1939.

41. A clearer expression of the tendency to present continuity in the Jewish history in France can be found in a series of articles about the history of the Jews in France in a small journal that was published only four times: "Di yidn in frankraykh," *Di Naye Parizher Yidishe Tsaytung,* June 13, 1938; May 1939; June 1939; and July–August 1939. The anonymous writer discusses French Jewish history since the Jewish settlement in ancient Gaul through the consolidation of the Jewish community in the early Middle Ages until the postrevolutionary era but without even mentioning the expulsion of the Jews from France in the fourteenth century.

42. M. M., "Conférences de 'Chema Israël,' Les plus belles pages du judaïsme durant le haut moyen-âge," *L'Univers Israélite,* January 27, 1939.

43. M. M., "Les Conférences de Chema Israël, Le Judaïsme français au moyen-âge," *L'Univers Israélite,* March 24, 1939.

44. For the concept of the homemaking myth, see Orm Øverland, *Immigrant Minds, American Identities: Making the United States Home, 1870–1930* (Urbana, IL, 2000), 7–8, 175.

45. About Lecache and LICA, see Emmanuel Debono, "Le visage de l'anti-France dans la France des années trente: L'exemple de la Ligue internationale contre l'antisémitisme (LICA)," *Revue d'Histoire de la Shoah,* no. 173 (September–December 2001): 113–36, and Emmanuel Debono, "Bernard Abraham Lecache, président fondateur de la Ligue internationale contre l'antisémitisme," *Archives Juives* 40, no.

1 (2007): 140–44.

46. Bernard Lecache, "14 yuli—dos aynnemen di bastilie," *Pariser Haynt,* July 14, 1938.

47. Lecache tried here to mobilize his readers to support the campaign initiated by LICA for overall French Jewish unity against anti-Semitism. About these efforts and about the difficulties of creating such a unity during 1934–38, see Weinberg, *A Community on Trial,* 148–70.

48. W. Weviorka, "Yidn in der frantsoyzisher revolutsie," Part 1, *Pariser Haynt,* April 8, 1938.

49. W. Weviorka, "Yidn in der frantsoyzisher revolutsie," Part 3, "Der kamf far emantsipatsie," *Pariser Haynt,* April 17, 1938, and Part 8, "Parizer komune shikt a delegatsie tsu der natsional farzamlung," *Pariser Haynt,* May 13, 1938.

50. W. Weviorka, "Yidn in der frantsoyzisher revolutsie," Part 11, "Vi azoy di yidishe galykhbarekhtikung iz opgenumen gevorn," *Pariser Haynt,* June 7, 1938.

51. For various references to the negative phenomena, see W. Weviorka, "Yidn in der frantsoyzisher revolutsie," Part 14, "Der religiezer terror," *Pariser Haynt,* June 24, 1938; Part 15, "Yidn in der 'kult fun seykhl,'" *Pariser Haynt,* July 1, 1938; and Part 17, "Ekonominsher terror," *Pariser Haynt,* July 26, 1938. For the closing article of the series, see Part 20, "Nokhn termidor," *Pariser Haynt,* August 12, 1938.

52. Sh. Rozenfeld, "Fun khmelnitskin biz itst . . . ," *Pariser Haynt,* January 18, 1938.

53. Joseph Ben Aron, "Entretien sur Blum, le ghetto, l'antisémitisme et l'assimilation," *La Terre Retrouvée,* May 1, 1938.

54. Paul Mendes-Flohr and Jehuda Reinharz, eds., *The Jew in the Modern World: A Documentary History* (New York, 1995), 115.

55. For a previous scholarly discussion about the return-to-the-ghetto polemic in the Yiddish press in Paris, see Weinberg, *A Community on Trial,* 189–97.

56. This article was also published in Paris; see Y. Grinboym, "Geto," *Pariser Haynt,* March 29–30, 1937.

57. For an overview of the debate in the Yiddish press, mostly in the United States, concerning the return to the ghetto, see E. Tcherikower, "Yiddisher gaystiker krizis in shayn fun der prese (iberblik)," *Oyfn Shaydveg* 1 (April 1939): 201–17. The citation from Glatshteyn's article is on 201.

58. A. M. Fuks, "A brokhe-levatole," *Pariser Haynt,* July 3, 1938.

59. For another discussion of those questions from a less pessimistic point of view, see A. Kremer, "Tsurik in geto?," *Pariser Haynt,* July 12, 1938. Fuks's and Kremer's articles are also discussed by Weinberg, *A Community on Trial,* 189–90.

60. See in this context a report about an alleged German decision to establish ghettos for the Jews followed by a discussion about the history of the ghettos: A. Gelernter, "Dos aynfirn getos in daytshland," *Pariser Haynt,* December 13, 1938.

61. "Tsurik in geto?," *Pariser Haynt,* December 21–22, 1938. For further biographical details about Efroykin as well as some of the other participants in the debate, see Joshua M. Karlip, "At the Crossroads between War and Genocide: A Reassessment of Jewish Ideology in 1940," *Jewish Social Studies* 11, no. 2 (Winter 2005): 171–74.

62. "Tsurik in geto?," *Pariser Haynt,* December 22, 1938.

63. W. Weviorka, "Tsurik in geto, diskusie-artikl," *Pariser Haynt,* December 23, 1938. This article was not the first time that Weviorka related to the ghetto debate; see also W. Weviorka, "Undzere yomim-toyvim," *Pariser Haynt,* September 25, 1938.

64. A. Kremer, "Mitn ponim tsu zikh," *Pariser Haynt,* December 27, 1938.

65. Y. Lerman, "Tsurik in geto? Neyn!," *Naye Presse,* January 8, 1939.

66. Y. Shie, "Tsurik tsum geto," *Undzer Shtime,* October 8, 1938. See also the article of a Bundist spokesman in Warsaw that was also published in Paris: Sh. Mendelson, "Tsurik in geto," *Undzer Shtime,* February 18 and 25, 1939.

67. See, for example, "Amerike af der shvel fun fashizm?," *Pariser Haynt,* October 10, 1935, and Joseph Milner, "Amerike," *Pariser Haynt,* March 29, 1938.

68. Y. Gotlib, "Amerike kegn eyrope," *Pariser Haynt,* January 17, 1939.

69. Ibid.

70. A third volume of the journal was prepared in early 1940, but its editors could not publish it because of the Nazi occupation of France. See Karlip, "At the Crossroads between War and Genocide," 170–201.

71. Redaktsie [Editorial Board, E. Tcherikower and Y. Efroykin], "A vort tsu di leyener," *Oyfn Shaydveg* 1 (April 1939): 4.

72. E. Tcherikower, "Di tragedie fun a shvakhn dor," *Oyfn Shaydveg* 1 (April 1939): 5–28, and E. Tcherikower, "Yidisher gaystiker krizis in shayn fun der prese (iberblik)," *Oyfn Shaydveg* 1 (April 1939): 201–17.

73. About Tcherikower, see Joshua M. Karlip, "Between Martyrology and Historiography: Elias Tcherikower and the Making of a Pogrom Historian," *East European Jewish Affairs* 38, no. 3 (2008): 257–80.

74. E. Tcherikower, "Di tragedie fun a shvakhn dor," *Oyfn Shaydveg* 1 (April 1939): 5–6.

75. Ibid., 6–10; quotations from pp. 8 and 10.

76. Ibid., 20.

77. Ibid., 26–27.

78. For a basically similar position, see A. Menes, "Undzer veg un undzer goyrl," *Oyfn Shaydveg* 1 (April 1939): 53–72. For a discussion of this position, see Karlip, "At the Crossroads between War and Genocide," 172–73, 176–77.

79. Weinberg, *A Community on Trial,* 195–96.

80. L. D. [Lucien Dreyfus], "Au carrefour," *La Tribune juive,* December 23, 1938. For a slightly revised German version, see L. D., "Am Scheideweg," *La Tribune juive,* January 6, 1939.

81. L. D., "Pouvons-nous échapper à notre collectivité," *La Tribune juive,* January 27, 1939.

82. A few months later Dreyfus again expressed his identification with the positive narrative of Jewish emancipation in France in several articles that he published relating to the 150th anniversary of the French Revolution. See L. D., "Le cent cinquantième anniversaire de la Révolution française," *La Tribune juive,* May 12, 1939, and L. D., "Quatorze juillet 1939," *La Tribune juive,* July 14, 1939. Dreyfus's historical views and the tension between his firm belief in Jewish integration in France and his deep disappointment from the emancipation in Europe continued to

develop in the next few years in the diary that he wrote during World War II until he was murdered by the Nazis; see Alexandra Garbarini, *Numbered Days: Diaries and the Holocaust* (New Haven, CT, 2006), 22–57.

83. This attitude was expressed in the opening editorials of the first volume: "Aujourd'hui," *Affirmation,* January 13, 1939, and David Knout, "Nous unir ou périr," *Affirmation,* January 13, 1939.

84. Also about *Affirmation,* see Weinberg, *A Community on Trial,* 191–92; see there note 66 on p. 208 concerning the ideological development of Mandel as a young man.

85. Arnold Mandel, "Prendre conscience," *Affirmation,* February 3, 1939.

86. Arnold Mandel, "D'une révision nécessaire," *Affirmation,* March 17, 1939.

87. Ibid.

88. Ibid.

89. See, for example, Dard, *Les années trente,* 213–36.

90. Young, *France and the Origins of the Second World War,* 114, 122–25. For a discussion concerning the various voices in France relating to the anniversary of the Revolution, see Pascal Ory, "La commémoration révolutionnaire en 1939," in *La France et les Français 1938 en 1939,* edited by René Rémond and Janine Bourdin, 115–36 (Paris, 1978).

91. Yoysef Milner, "89 . . . , 150 yor frantsoyzishe revolutsie," *Pariser Haynt,* January 13, 1939.

92. P. Geismar, "Cent cinquante ans," *L'Univers Israélite,* February 3, 1939; Edouard Herriot, "La Révolution et le Racisme," *L'Univers Israélite,* April 21, 1939; and L. D., "Le cent cinquantième anniversaire de la Révolution française," *La Tribune juive,* May 12, 1939.

93. Raoul Mourgues, "Un décret . . . ," *Affirmation,* February 3, 1939.

94. Sh. Niger, "150 yor yidishe emansipatsie," *Pariser Haynt,* March 19, 1939.

95. J. Bielinky, "1789–1939 Eternel recommencement," *Affirmation,* May 12, 1939.

96. Ibid.

97. J. Biélinky, "Le 150e anniversaire de la Révolution Française, deux manifestations," *L'Univers Israélite,* June 23, 1939; "Le 150e anniversaire de la Révolution française," *Affirmation,* June 23, 1939; and J. B., "Cent cinquante ans après . . . ," *Samedi,* June 24, 1939. See also Philippe Boukara, "Commémorations juives de la Révolution française; le cas du cent cinquantenaire (1939) vu par les Juifs de Paris immigrés en particulier," in *Les Juifs et la Révolution française: Histoire et mentalités,* edited by Mireille Hadas-Lebel and Evelyne Oliel-Grausz, 333–41 (Louvain, 1992).

98. Y. Panin, "Frantsoyzishe revolutsie git yidn glaykhbarekhtikung," *Naye Presse, Yubiley-oysgabe,* February 1939.

99. "Echos du 14 juillet et la commémoration du 150e anniversaire de la Révolution française dans nos communautés: Metz," *La Tribune juive,* July 21, 1939.

100. Y. Chomsky, "Frankraykh hot tsurikgefunen ir koyekh," *Pariser Haynt,* July 16, 1939, and Yoysef Kruk, "150 yor nokh der frantsoyzisher revolutsie," *Pariser Haynt,* July 16, 1939. See also in this context similar opinions by Bundist interpreters: Zh. Sl., "Di simbolishe mil in valmi," *Undzer Shtime,* June 30, 1939; Y. Goles,

"Di yerushe fun demy or 1789," *Undzer Shtime,* June 23, 1939; and Dovid Ayn-horn, "Der 14ter yuli, gedanken un shtimungen," *Undzer Shtime,* July 21, 1939.

101. Shimen Dubnov, "Vos darf men ton in homens tsaytn? A briv tsu der redak-tsie fun 'Sheydveg,'" *Oyfn Shaydveg* 2 (August 1939): 3–7.

102. A. Tcherikower, "Vegn sheydveg un shlakhtfeld, a frayndlekher entfer af a frayndlekher kritik," *Oyfn Shaydveg* 2 (August 1939): 8–13, mainly 12–13. For a more detailed analysis of this debate, see Karlip, "At the Crossroads between War and Genocide," 174–84.

103. William Oualid, "Le cent-cinquantième anniversaire de la Révolution fran-çaise," *L'Univers Israélite,* August 25–September 1, 1939.

104. Robert Anchel, "L'affranchissement des Juifs en France de 1789 à 1831," *L'Univers Israélite,* August 25–September 1, 1939.

105. See especially P. Geismar, "Recherche d'une conclusion," *L'Univers Israélite,* August 25–September 1, 1939.

106. Maurice Liber, "La Révolution, Les Juifs et le Judaisme," *L'Univers Israélite,* August 25–September 1, 1939.

107. Ibid.

108. "Vive la France!," *Pariser Haynt,* September 2, 1939, and A. Kremer, "Di yidishe frayvilike in frankraykh" *Pariser Haynt,* October 13, 1939.

109. Zola's struggle against anti-Semitism during the Dreyfus Affair was also men-tioned in the Jewish press during the harsh days of 1938, when the fortieth anni-versary of his open letter "J'Accuse" was marked. See Moris Mayer, "40 yor nokh *J'Accuse*—vu nemt men itst a nayem Emil Zola?," *Pariser Haynt,* January 16, 1938; A. Raiski, "40 yor zint Zola hot gezogt *J'Accuse*," *Naye Presse,* January 16, 1938; and Jean Tild, "A la memoire d'Emile Zola," *L'Univers Israélite,* November 4, 1938.

110. Pierre Geismar, "Zola et l'Affaire," *L'Univers Israélite,* April 5–12, 1940; N. Frank, "Vu nemt men itst a Zola?," *Pariser Haynt,* April 2, 1940; and Yoysef Milner, "Der kemfer far gerekhtikayt," *Pariser Haynt,* April 2 and 3, 1940.

111. W. Weviorka, "Ikh gloyb in frankraykh," *Pariser Haynt,* May 27, 1940.

112. Ibid.

Chapter 5

1. For the identity of emancipated Jewry in Hungary, see, for example, Jacob Katz, "The Identity of Post Emancipatory Hungarian Jewry," in *A Social and Economic History of Central European Jewry,* edited by Jehuda Don and Victor Karady, 13–31 (New Brunswick, NJ, 1990). For a detailed social historical research on the develop-ment of the Trends sectors in Hungary, see Kinga Frojimovics, *The Religious Trends of the Jewry in Hungary (Orthodox, Neolog, Status Quo Ante) between 1868/1869–1950: Socio-Economic, Demographic, and Organizational Characteristics* (PhD dissertation [in Hebrew], Bar Ilan University, Ramat Gan, Israel, 2002). For a historical overview of Jewish emancipation in Hungary, see, for example, Guy Miron, "Between 'Center' and 'East'—The Special Way of Jewish Emancipation in Hungary," *Jewish Studies at the CEU* 4 (2004–5): 111–38.

2. For a general overview on Hungarian historiography, see István Deák, "Histo-

riography of the Countries of Eastern Europe: Hungary," *American Historical Review* 97, no. 4 (1992): 1041–63; Steven Béla Várdy, *Modern Hungarian Historiography* (New York, 1976); and Steven Béla Várdy, *Clio's Art in Hungary and in Hungarian-America* (New York, 1985).

3. Nathaniel Katzburg, "Jewish Historiography in Hungary" [in Hebrew], *Sinai* 40, nos. 2–3 (1956–57): 113–26, 164–76. See also in this context Kinga Frojimovics, "A 'doktor-rabbik' nagy nemzedéke Magyarországon: A neológ identitás kialakítása a történetíráson keresztül," in *Széfer Jószéf*, edited by József Zsengellér, 221–39 (Budapest, 2002).

4. This chapter is partly based on my article: Guy Miron, "History, Remembrance, and a 'Useful Past' in the Public Thought of Hungarian Jewry, 1938–1939," *Yad Vashem Studies* 32 (2004): 131–70.

5. Ignác Romsics, *Hungary in the Twentieth Century* (Budapest, 1999), 117–25. For the immense effect that the refugee problem had on the extreme swing to the right of Hungarian politics, among other things as regards the Jews, see István I. Mócsy, *The Effects of World War I: The Uprooted; Hungarians, Refugees, and Their Impact on Hungary's Domestic Politics, 1918–1921* (New York, 1983).

6. On the liberal character of Hungarian nationalism before World War I and the emphasis placed on cultural and linguistic foundations, see Vera Ranki, *The Politics of Inclusion and Exclusion: Jews and Nationalism in Hungary* (London, 1999), 37–44. On the turn of Hungarian political culture following World War I, see Paul A. Hanebrink, *In Defense of Christian Hungary: Religion, Nationalism, and Antisemitism, 1890–1944* (Ithaca, NY, 2006), 108–36. For a critical discussion of the various historical interpretations concerning the Jewish emancipation in pre–World War I Hungary, see Kati Vörös, "A Unique Contract: Interpretations of Modern Hungarian Jewish History," *Jewish Studies at the CEU* 3 (2002–3): 229–55.

7. For a discussion on the nature of the Jews' involvement in the Hungarian capitalist economy, see Michael K. Silber, "A Jewish Minority in a Backward Economy: An Introduction," in *Jews in the Hungarian Economy, 1760–1945,* edited Michael K. Silber, 3–22 (Jerusalem, 1992), and János Gyurgyák, *A zsidókérdés Magyarországon* (Budapest, 2001), 80–87.

8. Gyurgyák, *A zsidókérdés Magyarországon,* 117–23, and Nathaniel Katzburg, *Hungary and the Jews: Policy and Legislation, 1920–1943* (Ramat Gan, Israel, 1981), 60–79.

9. Romsics, *Hungary in the Twentieth Century,* 149. See also Rolf Fischer, *Entwicklungsstufen des Antisemitismus in Ungarn 1867–1939: Die Zerstörung der magyarisch-jüdischen Symbiose* (München, 1988), 124–80, and Ranki, *The Politics of Inclusion and Exclusion,* 83–132.

10. For a political biography of Bethlen, who was the most influential political figure in Hungary in the 1920s, see Ignác Romsics, *István Bethlen: A Great Conservative Statesman of Hungary, 1874–1946* (New York, 1995).

11. On the Gömbös era and the rise of the Hungarian extreme Right after his death, see Randolph L. Braham, *The Politics of Genocide: The Holocaust in Hungary,* Vol. 1 (New York, 1994), 45–70. On the influence of Nazi Germany on Hungary at that time, see Claudia Papp, *Ungarn im Schatten nationalsozialistischer Bündnis- und*

Hegemonialpolitik, 1933–1941, CD ROM (Marburg, 1999), 66–86.

12. Frojimovics, *The Religious Trends of the Jewry in Hungary,* chap. 4; see primarily 188–91, 220–21.

13. About Hungarian Zionism at that time, see Hava Eichler, "The Uniqueness of the Zionist Movement in Hungary between the World Wars" [in Hebrew], *Yahadut Zemanenu* 5 (1989): 91–114.

14. About Thaly's activities, see Ágnes R. Várkonyi, *Thaly Kálmán és történetírása* (Budapest, 1961), and Péter Gunst, "A tudományos történetírás kibontakozása Magyarországon (1867–1918)," *Debreceni Szemle* 3, no. 1 (1995): 69–78. About the institutionalization of the cult of 1848 in pre–World War I Hungary, see Árpád von Klimó, *Nation, Konfession, Geschichte: Zur nationalen Geschichtskultur Ungarns im europäischen Kontext (1860–1948)* (München, 2003), 55–91.

15. Hanebrink, *In Defense of Christian Hungary,* 10–46, and von Klimó, *Nation, Konfession, Geschichte,* 137–52. See also Katalin Sinkó, "Árpád versus Saint István: Competing Heroes and Competing Interests in the Figurative Representation of Hungarian History," *Ethnologia Europaea: Journal of European Ethnology* 19, no. 1 (1989): 67–94.

16. Gyula Szekfű, *Három nemzedék: Egy hanyatló kor története* (Budapest, 1920). The book was published again in 1934 with a new fifth part in which Szekfű related to the events in postwar Hungary; see Gyula Szekfű, *Három nemzedék és ami utána következik* (Budapest, 1934). About Szekfű and his impact on the Hungarian political culture, see Irena Raab Epstein, *Gyula Szekfű: A Study in the Political Basis of Hungarian Historiography* (New York and London, 1987). About the culture of defeat concept, see Wolfgang Schivelbusch, *The Culture of Defeat: On National Trauma, Mourning, and Recovery* (New York, 2003).

17. Várdy, *Modern Hungarian Historiography,* 47.

18. Epstein, *Gyula Szekfű,* 128–33, 146–77. In spite of his anti-Jewish bias, Szekfű did not present the defeat in the Battle of Mohács and the post–World War I disintegration as two national catastrophes caused by the Jews (167). Still, this position was quite popular in Hungary at that time.

19. On the Hungarian political culture in the interwar period, see Steven Béla Várdy, "The Impact of Trianon upon the Hungarian Mind: Irredentism and Hungary's Path to War," in *Hungary in the Age of Total War (1938–1948),* edited by Nándor Dreisziger, 27–48 (New York, 1998). For a comprehensive view of Hungarian historiography between the two world wars, see Domokos Kosáry, "A magyar történetírás a két világháború között," in Kosáry, *A történelem veszedelem* (Budapest, 1987), 321–55, and Vilmos Erős, "A magyar történetírás a két világháború közötti időszakban," in *Magyarország a XX. században,* Vol. 5, 292–304 (Szekszárd, 2000). For the polemic between Szekfű and his critics, see Várdy, *Modern Hungarian Historiography,* 121–28, and Vilmos Erős, "Szekfű és Mályusz vitája a magyar történet'-ről," *Századok* 131, no. 2 (1997): 453–76.

20. Guy Miron and Anna Szalai, eds., *Jews at the Crossroads: The Discourse on Jewish Identity in Hungary between Crisis and Innovation, 1908–1926* [in Hebrew] (Ramat Gan, Israel, 2008). See also in English: Guy Miron, "Conversations on the Jewish Question in Hungary, 1925–1926" (translated and annotated text), *Jewish*

History and Culture 7 (Winter 2004), no. 3, 93–109.

21. Katzburg, "Jewish Historiography in Hungary," 316–20.

22. Pál Sándor, "A magyar zsidóság és a német események," *Egyenlőség,* June 3, 1933.

23. Ernő Ballagi, "Párbeszéd 1933 nyarán," *Egyenlőség,* July 22, 1933.

24. For the article relating to the first anniversary of the Nazi regime, see Ernő Ballagi, "Goethe és Hitler," *Egyenlőség,* February 3, 1934. For his criticism on the positions of Zionist spokespeople in Germany regarding assimilation and dissimilation, see Ernő Ballagi, "Disszimiláció," *Egyenlőség,* May 19, 1934, and Ernő Ballagi, "Cséplő és jégverés (Válasz a cionista sajtónak)," *Egyenlőség,* June 9, 1934. It is noteworthy that Ballagi did not link this discussion explicitly to the problems of emancipation and assimilation in Hungary.

25. Sámuel Löwinger, "Hitlerizmus és bojkottmozgalom a XVI. század második felében," *Magyar Zsidó Szemle* 51 (1934): 295–329; citation from p. 329.

26. "Új antiszemitizmus felé?," *Zsidó Élet,* January 5, 1935.

27. Ede Iszák, "A németországi tanulság," *Zsidó Szemle,* May 5, 1933.

28. Fülöp Grünwald, "A magyar zsidó múlt histórikusai," in *IMIT [Izraelita Magyar Irodalmi Társulat] Évkönyv* (1934): 208–25.

29. For articles from these series, see, for example, "Deák Ferenc és a zsidóság," *Egyenlőség,* October 12, 1935; "Bethlen Gábor és a zsidók," *Egyenlőség,* December 21, 1935; "Habsburgok és zsidók," *Egyenlőség,* January 1, 1936; and "Különös világ Európában 140 év előtt," *Egyenlőség,* February 27, 1936.

30. For an Orthodox example, see "Ha Kossuth ma élne . . . ," *Zsidó Újság,* January 15, 1937. For a Zionist example, see Ármin Beregi, "Petőfi és a zsidók, március 15-re," *Zsidó Szemle,* March 9, 1934.

31. See, for example, Dezső Korein, *Mi az oka a zsidógyűlöletnek* (Budapest, 1935), and György Kecskeméti, "Az antiszemitizmus szociológiája," *Libanon* 1, no. 1 (1936): 13–16.

32. György Kecskeméti, "Liberializmus, zsidóság és magyar nemzeti szellem," *Zsidó Élet,* February 3, 1934.

33. György Kecskeméti, "Világproblémák sodrában," *Múlt és Jövő,* September 1936, 228–29.

34. Ernő Munkácsi, "Az emancipációs törvény története," *Libanon* 2 (1937): 190, reprinted in Ernő Munkácsi, *Küzdelmes évek . . . , Cikkek és tanulmányok a magyar zsidóság elmúlt évtizedéből* (Budapest, 1943), 54–61.

35. See, for example, Munkácsi, "Az emancipációs törvény története," 190–94. See also Zsigmond Groszmann, "Hetvenéves a magyar zsidók emancipációja!," *Egyenlőség,* November 25, 1937.

36. "Az emancipáció," *Egyenlőség,* January 20, 1938.

37. "Nemzetgyalázás!, A Királyi Kúria a nyilaskeresztes izgatás ellen," *Egyenlőség,* January 14, 1937.

38. István Virág, "A magyar zsidó történettudomány célkitűzéseihez," *Libanon* 2 (1937): 145–48.

39. On the political process that led to the enactment of this law and the public discourse around it, see Katzburg, *Hungary and the Jews,* 94–113, and Gyurgyák, *A*

zsidókérdés Magyarországon, 135–42.

40. Arthur Stein, "A zsidók emancipációja Magyarországon," *Zsidó Élet,* March 16, 1938.

41. "Március 15.," *Zsidó Élet,* March 16, 1938.

42. Von Klimó, *Nation, Konfession, Geschichte,* 311–15.

43. Lajos Szabolcsi, "Gyászolunk . . . ," *Egyenlőség,* April 14, 1938.

44. Ibid.

45. Samu Stern, *A zsidókérdés Magyarországon* (Budapest, 1938). For a brief discussion of Stern's pamphlet, see Nathaniel Katzburg, "Zionist Reactions to Hungarian Anti-Jewish Legislation, 1939–1942," *Yad Vashem Studies* 16 (1984): 162.

46. Stern, *A zsidókérdés Magyarországon,* 6.

47. Similarly, Endre Sós maintained in 1937 in reference to the Nuremberg Laws that the disseminators of anti-Semitic propaganda in Hungary, from Istóczy in the nineteenth century to the Hungarian Fascists, were merely "peddlers of imported ideas"; Endre Sós, "A nürnbergi tölcsér," *Egyenlőség,* September 1, 1937.

48. Stern, *A zsidókérdés Magyarországon,* 5–6. For a similar approach that attributes the heritage of Jewish equality to the ancient national Hungarian spirit, which began during the first dynasty, and asserts that the situation of the Jews in Hungary deteriorated later following the infiltration of German influence through the Habsburgs, see Ernő Munkácsi, "A magyar zsidóság és a zsidó vallású magyarok jogi helyzete az 1938: XV. T.C. után," *Ararát* (1939): 17–25. Munkácsi's article was written in 1938 in response to the First Jewish Law.

49. Epstein, *Gyula Szekfű,* 181–82.

50. Stern, *A zsidókérdés Magyarországon,* 15.

51. See, for example, Ernő Munkácsi, "A magyar zsidóság lelkivilága a zsidótörvény után," *Egyenlőség,* September 22, 1938. Munkácsi depicts the period when Jews were being expelled at the end of the Middle Ages as being worse than his own time and claims that a historical examination of that period could give the Jews of Hungary a historical perspective on the period in which they were living.

52. Katzburg, "Zionist Reactions to Hungarian Anti-Jewish Legislation, 1939–1942," 163.

53. Endre Sós, *Becsapott ajtók előtt* (Budapest, 1938).

54. Ibid., 18.

55. Ibid., 21–29.

56. József Patai, "Gyónás a zsidó törvény előtt," *Múlt és Jövő,* May 1938, 131. See also remarks about the article in Katzburg, "Zionist Reactions to Hungarian Anti-Jewish Legislation, 1939–1942," 146. About the monthly and its editor, see Heidemarie Petersen, "Die Assimilationsidee überwinden: Die ungarisch-jüdische Zeitschrift Múlt és Jövő (1911–1944)," in *Die jüdische Presse im europäischen Kontext (1686–1990),* edited by Susanne Marten-Finnis and Markus Winkler, 179–89 (Bremen, Germany, 2006).

57. Lajos Fodor, "A zsidótörvény és a cionisták," *Múlt és Jövő,* June–July 1938, 163–64.

58. "A magyar zsidóság tiltakozása a 'zsidótörvény' javaslat ellen," *Zsidó Újság,* April 19, 1938.

59. "A miniszterelnök és a hercegprímás szava," *Zsidó Újság*, March 9, 1938.

60. See von Klimó, *Nation, Konfession, Geschichte*, 244–77, and Árpád von Klimó, "Die gespaltene Vergangenheit, Die grossen christlichen Kirchen im Kampf um die Nationalgeschichte Ungarns 1920–1948," *Zeitschrift für Geschichtswissenschaft* 47, no. 10 (1999): 876–84.

61. Hanebrink, *In Defense of Christian Hungary*, 137–44.

62. Von Klimó, *Nation, Konfession, Geschichte*, 273–77, and Hanebrink, *In Defense of Christian Hungary*, 148–54. Both von Klimó and Hanebrink provide extensive discussion of the Catholic and Protestant discourse on the subject and the different meanings attributed to the persona of Saint Stephen.

63. "Szent István éve," *Egyenlőség*, January 20, 1938.

64. "A mi napos oldalunk," *Zsidó Újság*, April 1, 1938.

65. Ödön Gerő, "A Szent István év," *Zsidó Élet*, June 4, 1938.

66. Dezső Korein, "Ünnepek után," *Zsidó Újság*, June 17, 1938.

67. Bernát Heller, "Szent István éve," *Zsidó Élet*, July 9, 1938.

68. Ernő Munkácsi, "Szent István," *Egyenlőség*, August 11, 1938.

69. Ibid. The distinction between the Hungarian nation (*nemzetiség*) as a basic political and cultural unit, to which affiliation is derived from a voluntary decision by individuals, and ethnic identities (*népiség*) was developed at the time by the outstanding Hungarian historian Elemér Mályusz, who portrayed Hungarian history as one thousand years of shared existence of Magyars and non-Magyars; see Várdy, *Modern Hungarian Historiography*, 102–7.

70. For a historical survey of the status of the Jews in Saint Stephen's Hungary, expressed in a similar if more academic vein, see Artur Stein, "Szent István és a zsidók," *Zsidó Élet*, September 10, 1938.

71. On the shaping of the Hungarian view of history in the liberal era in the late nineteenth century, including the secularization that occurred at the time in the perception of King Stephen's holy crown, see Gabor Vermes, *István Tisza: The Liberal Vision and Conservative Statecraft of a Magyar Nationalist* (New York, 1985), 44–45.

72. Ernő Munkácsi, "A pápa beszédes," *Egyenlőség*, August 25, 1938.

73. Dezső Korein, "Megszólalt a Vatikán," *Zsidó Újság*, January 11, 1938.

74. In regard to Szekfű's change of heart and the spiritual national defense activity, see Epstein, *Gyula Szekfű*, 230–38, and Várdy, *Modern Hungarian Historiography*, 114–15. In the new edition of his book *Three Generations*, published in 1934, Szekfű addressed himself to the possibility of the integration of longtime Hungarian Jews (as opposed to recent immigrants from eastern Europe) in the Christian Hungarian state and to an easing of tension between them and Christian Hungarians; see Gyula Szekfű, *Három nemzedék és ami utána következik* (Budapest, 1934), 443–44. A eulogy by Szekfű in June 1943 at the grave of the Jewish historian Henrik Marczali was regarded at the time as a demonstrative act against the anti-Jewish policy of the regime. In this matter, see Nathaniel Katzburg, *History of the Holocaust: Hungary* [in Hebrew] (Jerusalem, 1992), 139. For an explicit Jewish reference to Szekfű's position on these issues, see "Szekfű Gyula súlyos megállapításai a faji kérdésben," *Egyenlőség*, October 7, 1937.

75. Henrik Guttman, "Adalékok a magyar zsidók történetéhez a tizenhatodik

században," *IMIT [Izraelita Magyar Irodalmi Társulat] Évkönyv* (1939): 154–70.

76. With regard to the law and its enactment process and implications, see Katzburg, *Hungary and the Jews*, 114–57, and Gyurgyák, *A zsidókérdés Magyarországon*, 143–52. The German Hungarian alliance in foreign policy was gathering strength at that time because in late 1938, pursuant to the Munich Pact, Hungary had received some of the territories that it had lost after World War I. For the connection between these two facts, see Braham, *The Politics of Genocide*, 1:135; for the official responses of the Hungarian Jewish organizations to the law, see ibid., 153–54.

77. For a discussion of the change that occurred in the Hungarian Jewish press during these years, see Guy Miron, "Confronting Evil: How the Jewish Press in Hungary Dealt with Anti-Semitism from the Late 1930s until 1944" [in Hebrew], *Kesher* 33 (May 2003): 100–107.

78. "Átment a felsőház retortáján" and "Egy fővárosi falragasz előtt," *Orthodox Zsidó Újság*, April 20, 1939.

79. G. G., "Megható látogatás a zsidó-múzeumba," *Magyar Zsidók Lapja*, May 4, 1939.

80. For Munkácsi's response to the First Jewish Law, written in June 1938, see Ernő Munkácsi, "A magyar zsidóság és a zsidó vallású magyarok jogi helyzete az 1939: XV. T.C.után," *Ararát* (1939): 17–25. For his response to the Second Jewish Law, see "A zsidótörvény után (I), A legsúlyosabb vád," *Magyar Zsidók Lapja*, April 20, 1939.

81. Ernő Munkácsi, "A zsidótörvény után (II), Csak a kikeresztelkedett zsidó asszimilált!?," *Magyar Zsidók Lapja*, May 4, 1939, and Ernő Munkácsi "A faji teória," *Magyar Zsidók Lapja*, May 11, 1939.

82. Ernő Munkácsi, "Milyen polgárokra van szükség?," *Magyar Zsidók Lapja*, May 19, 1939. On this matter, see his previous article: Ernő Munkácsi, "A mi feleletünk," *Egyenlőség*, December 1, 1938.

83. Lipót Sás, "Mit jelentsen emancipációnk?," *Zsidó Szemle*, August 8, 1938.

84. Dezső Korein, "Asszimiláció és zsidótörvény," *Zsidó Újság*, December 30, 1938.

85. Jenő Groszberg, "IV. Kelementől XII. Piusig," *Orthodox Zsidó Újság*, March 10, 1939.

86. Endre Sós, "Bevezetője," in *Magyar zsidó írók dekameronja*, edited by Endre Sós, 5–14 (Budapest, 1939).

87. Ibid., 7–8.

88. Ibid., 13.

89. Yehiel Michael [Mihály] Hacohen Guttmann, introduction to Rabbi Joseph Judah Gattinara, "The Talmud and Freedom," in *Jubilee Volume in Honor of Dr. Hayyim Zvi Kisch* [in Hebrew], edited by Mihály Guttmann, Simon Hevesi, and Sámuel Lőwinger (Budapest, 1939), 3.

90. Ibid., 4.

91. Ibid., 5.

92. On the origins of the schisms among Hungarian Jewish religious currents, see Jacob Katz, *A House Divided: Orthodoxy and Schism in Nineteenth-Century Central European Jewry* (Waltham, MA, 1998).

93. About this, see János Bak, "Die Mediävisierung der Politik im Ungarn des 19. und 20. Jahrhunderts," in *Umkämpfte Vergangenheit: Geschichtsbilder, Erinnerung und Vergangenheitspolitik im internationalen Vergleich,* edited by Petra Bock and Edgar Wolfrum, 103–13 (Göttingen, 1999).

94. In this context, see, for example, Arnold Kiss, "Sabosz Nachamu," *Egyenlőség,* August 11, 1938, and Anon., "Mi maradt meg nekünk?," *Magyar Zsidók Lapja,* May 4, 1939.

95. Zoltán Kohn, "A fiatalság megmentése," in "Mi a teendő, Válaszok a magyar zsidóság sorskérdéseire," *Magyar Zsidók Lapja,* February 16, 1939.

96. Victor Karády, "Identity strategies under Duress before and after the Shoah," in *The Holocaust in Hungary Fifty Years Later,* edited by Randolph L. Braham and Attila Pók, 159–60 (New York, 1997).

Chapter 6

1. On these territorial changes, see Ignác Romsics, *Hungary in the Twentieth Century* (Budapest, 1999), 198–204.

2. On the Jewish life in these areas and the transformation of Jewish political culture, see Raphael Vago, "The Jews of Transylvania: Between Integration and Segregation," in *The History of the Jews in Romania,* Vol. 3, *Between the Two World Wars,* edited by Liviu Rotman and Raphael Vago, 235–66 (Tel Aviv, 2005); Robert Büchler, "The Jewish Community in Slovakia before World War II," in *The Tragedy of Slovak Jews,* edited by Wacław Długoborski et al., 16–23 (Banská Bystrica, 1992), 16–23; and Zvi Hartman, "A Jewish Minority in a Multiethnic Society during a Change of Governments: The Jews of Transylvania in the Interwar Period," *Shvut* 9, no. 25 (2001): 162–82.

3. On the summer of 1941 expulsion and mass murder, see Randolph L. Braham, *The Politics of Genocide: The Holocaust in Hungary,* Vol. 1 (New York, 1994), 205–14; Klaus-Michael Mallmann, "Der qualitative Sprung im Vernichtungsprozess: Das Massaker von Kamenez-Podolsk Ende August 1941," *Jahrbuch für Antisemitismusforschung* 10 (2001): 239–64; and Nathaniel Katzburg, *Hungary and the Jews: Policy and Legislation, 1920–1943* (Ramat Gan, Israel, 1981), 201–11.

4. About the new legislation, see Katzburg, *Hungary and the Jews,* 158–200, and János Gyurgyák, *A zsidókérdés Magyarországon* (Budapest, 2001), 153–58.

5. For an overview of the Jewish policy of the Hungarian governments since the beginning of World War II until Hungary's conquest by the Nazis, see Braham, *The Politics of Genocide,* 1:144–261. On the social and political attitudes toward the Jewish problem in Hungary in the early 1940s, see Paul A. Hanebrink, *In Defense of Christian Hungary: Religion, Nationalism, and Antisemitism, 1890–1944* (Ithaca, NY, 2006), 164–91.

6. On Jewish refugees in Hungary in this period, see Kinga Frojimovics, *I Have Been a Stranger in a Strange Land: The Hungarian State and Jewish Refugees in Hungary, 1933–1945* (Jerusalem, 2007).

7. On the Hungarian Jewish press in these years, see Guy Miron, "Confronting Evil: How the Jewish Press in Hungary Dealt with Anti-Semitism from the Late

1930s until 1944" [in Hebrew], *Kesher* 33 (May 2003): 100–107. Also in the non-Jewish society there was a certain freedom of speech, and there were critical voices vis-à-vis Hungarian policy and, even more so, against the Nazi racial policy; see Mario D. Fenyo, "Did Hungarian Intellectuals Resist of Betray?," in *Hungary in the Age of Total War (1938–1948),* edited by Nándor Dreisziger, 123–32 (New York, 1998), and Romsics, *Hungary in the Twentieth Century,* 208–9.

8. "Most száz éve Pozsonyban megszületett az első zsidótörvény," *Magyar Zsidók Lapja,* February 1, 1940.

9. Ernő Ballagi, "A Magyar zsidóság harca az emancipációért," *IMIT [Izraelita Magyar Irodalmi Társulat] Évkönyv* (1940): 141.

10. "Március idusán . . . ," *Magyar Zsidók Lapja,* March 14, 1940; "Március 15-ének ünneplése a budapesti izr. templombam," *Magyar Zsidók Lapja,* March 21, 1940; "A szabadság napját," *Magyar Zsidók Lapja,* March 12, 1942; "Március 15," *Képes Családi Lapok,* March 15, 1942; and "Március tizenötödikét," *Magyar Zsidók Lapja,* March 9, 1944. On the importance of March 15 as a cultural symbol in the struggle of Hungarian intellectuals against the Nazi influence, see Árpád von Klimó, *Nation, Konfession, Geschichte: Zur nationalen Geschichtskultur Ungarns im europäischen Kontext (1860–1948)* (München, 2003), 313–14.

11. "Trianon," *Képes Családi Lapok,* June 9, 1940.

12. Benmose Junger, "A szentistváni gondolat és a zsidók," *Képes Családi Lapok,* September 8, 1940.

13. Jacob Katz, *From Prejudice to Destruction: Anti-Semitism, 1700–1933* (Cambridge, MA, 1980), 232–35.

14. "Gróf Széchenyi István és a zsidóság," *Magyar Zsidók Lapja,* August 14, 1941.

15. See, for example, "Kossuth válaszol . . . ," *Képes Családi Lapok,* August 3, 1941.

16. "Kossuth," *Magyar Zsidók Lapja,* March 16, 1944.

17. Ernő Ballagi, "Egy eszme és könyv centennáriuma, Báró Eötvös József: A zsidók emancipációja [1840]," *Magyar Zsidók Lapja,* August 1, 1940.

18. "Báró Eötvös József beszél . . . ," *Magyar Zsidók Lapja* February 13, 1941.

19. "A negyvenes évek," *Magyar Zsidók Lapja,* March 5, 1942.

20. Emma Lederer, "A magyar zsidók gazdasági jelentősége Mátyás korában," *IMIT [Izraelita Magyar Irodalmi Társulat] Évkönyv* (1940): 233–45.

21. "Szent István hetében," *Magyar Zsidók Lapja,* August 21, 1941.

22. Another statement by Neolog spokespeople that expressed a similar view was made in a comment regarding the abolishment of the Law of Reception in the summer of 1942; see "1895–1942," *Magyar Zsidók Lapja,* July 30, 1942.

23. Ernő Ballagi, "A magyarországi zsidóemancipáció előzményei," *Magyar Zsidó Szemle* 58 (1941): 61.

24. Ibid., 63.

25. Ernő Ballagi, "A százötvenéves európai emancipáció," *Ararát* (1942): 31–35.

26. Ernő Ballagi, ed., *A magyar zsidóság útja: Vezércikkek és beszédek tükrében (1840–1940)* (Budapest, 1940).

27. József Turóczi-Trostler and Jenő Zsoldos, eds., *Száz év előtt: Az első magyar-zsidó írónemzedék* (Budapest, 1940), and Jenő Zsoldos, ed., *Magyar irodalom és*

zsidóság: Költői és prózai szemelvények (Budapest, 1943). For a more detailed discussion, see Anna Szalai, "Will the Past Protect Hungarian Jewry? The Response of Jewish Intellectuals to Anti-Jewish Legislation," *Yad Vashem Studies* 32 (2004): 179–82, 193–207.

28. "Nem új jelenség," *Magyar Zsidók Lapja,* April 18, 1943.

29. Ernő Munkácsi, "Elmulasztott alkalmak (megjelent az 1940 évi OMZSA-naptárban)," in Ernő Munkácsi, *Küzdelmes évek . . . , Cikkek és tanulmányok a magyar zsidóság elmúlt évtizedéből* (Budapest, 1943), 127–28.

30. Ernő Munkácsi, "A magyar zsidóság jövője," *OMZSA Évkönyv* 5702 (1941–1942): 61–62.

31. Ernő Munkácsi, "Dr. Kohn Sámuel történeti munkáinak jelentősége napjainkban," *Magyar Zsidó Szemle* 58 (1941): 16–26.

32. Munkácsi, *Küzdelmes évek,* 5–9. For a comprehensive review article on this collection, see Ernő Ballagi, "A zsidóság nagy kérdései a történelemszemlélet tükrében," *Magyar Zsidók Lapja,* February 17, 1944.

33. Hugó Csergő, "Három magyar zsidó nemzedék," *OMZSA Évkönyv* 5703 (1942–1943): 135–43. For Szekfű's book, see Gyula Szekfű, *Három nemzedék és ami utána következik* (Budapest, 1934), and also chapter 5 in the present volume.

34. Hugó Csergő, "Három magyar zsidó nemzedék," *OMZSA Évkönyv* 5703 (1942–1943): 143.

35. Sámuel Kandel, "A mai zsidó útja," *Libanon* 7, no. 2 (1942): 41.

36. Ibid., 44–45.

37. Endre Sós, *Zsidók a magyar városokban: Történelmi tanulmány* (Budapest, 1940). These positions were also expressed in his article about the Jewish merchant; see Endre Sós, "A zsidó kereskedő," *Magyar Zsidók Lapja,* February 20, 1941.

38. Endre Sós, "Asszimiláció vagy cionizmus," *Múlt és Jövő,* June 1941, 85–86.

39. Ibid., 86.

40. Ibid.

41. Ibid.

42. Álmos Koral [Aladár Komlós], *Zsidók a válaszúton* (Presov, Slovakia, 1921).

43. Aladár Komlós, "Az 'asszimiláció kora,' a magyar irodalom és a zsidok," *IMIT [Izraelita Magyar Irodalmi Társulat] Évkönyv* (1940): 170–201.

44. Ibid., 199.

45. Ibid., 201.

46. On Komlós's editorial policy, see Szalai, "Will the Past Protect Hungarian Jewry?," 190–93.

47. "Előszó," *Ararát* (1940): 5.

48. "Az Ararát ankétje a magyar zsidóság legfontosabb mai teendőiről és feladatairól," *Ararát* (1941): 12–26, and "Miért vagyok zsidó?," *Ararát* (1944): 74–94.

49. Aladár Komlós, "Zsidó költők a magyar irodalomban," *Ararát* (1942): 166.

50. Aladár Komlós, "Zsidóság, Magyarság, Európa," *Ararát* (1943): 24–27. For an earlier formation of these ideas, see the editorial that Komlós published two years earlier: "Előszó," *Ararát* (1941): 6–8.

51. Aladár Komlós, "Zsidóság, Magyarság, Európa," *Ararát* (1943), 25.

52. Ibid., 25–26.

53. The journal *Huszadik Század,* which was founded in 1900, was associated with left-wing Hungarian intellectuals who criticized the conservative character of Hungarian society and called for democratization. Many of its writers and its editor Oszkár Jászi were Jewish; see Gábor Vermes, *István Tisza: The Liberal Vision and Conservative Statecraft of a Magyar Nationalist* (New York, 1985), 150–60, and Baruch Yaron, *Jewish Assimilation and Radicalism in Hungary* [in Hebrew] (Jerusalem, 1985), esp. 16–28, 42–138.

54. Aladár Komlós, "A magyar zsidó író útjai," *Ararát* (1939): 132, and "Előszó," *Ararát* (1941): 7. For a fundamentally similar position to that of Komlós, see László Bakonyi, "Zsidó gondok és remények," *Ararát* (1942): 24–30.

55. On the distinction between Western and Eastern Orthodoxy within Hungarian Jewry, see Viktor Karády, "Religious Divisions, Socio-Economic Scarification and the Modernization of Hungarian Jewry after the Emancipation," in *Jews in the Hungarian Economy, 1760–1945,* edited by Michael K. Silber, 161–84 (Jerusalem, 1992).

56. The positions taken by the Eastern (mostly Hasidic) Orthodoxy require separate research. An interesting although not representative rabbinical figure in this context is Rabbi Yissakhar Shlomo Teichthal; see Pesach Schindler, "'Tikkun' as Response to Tragedy: 'Em habanim smeha' of Rabbi Yissakhar Shlomo Teichthal-Budapest, 1943," *Holocaust and Genocide Studies* 4, no. 4 (1989): 413–33.

57. Regarding the Jewish contribution to the Hungarian economy, see, for example, Dezső Korein, "Jóval a számarányon felül," *Orthodox Zsidó Újság,* October 31, 1940. About Kossuth's relation to anti-Semitism and the Jews, see "Kossuth Lajos az antiszemitizmus ellen," *Orthodox Zsidó Újság,* March 10, 1940. Similar ideas were raised in an article that marked the twenty-fifth anniversary of the death of Franz Joseph; see "I. Ferenc József és az orthodoxia," *Orthodox Zsidó Újság,* November 20, 1941.

58. Dezső Korein, "Trianon felszámolása," *Orthodox Zsidó Újság,* September 10, 1940.

59. "A hetvenéves magyar orthodoxia," *Orthodox Zsidó Újság,* March 20, 1940.

60. Nathaniel Katzburg, *History of the Holocaust: Hungary* [in Hebrew] (Jerusalem, 1992), 124.

61. Dezső Korein, "Történelmi dokumentum," *Orthodox Zsidó Újság,* May 17, 1940.

62. "Zsidó törvény és zsidótörvény," *Orthodox Zsidó Újság,* June 10, 1941.

63. Dezső Korein, "A francia zsidók emancipációja," *Orthodox Zsidó Újság,* March 10, 1940.

64. Salamon Stern, "Az Ararát ankétje a magyar zsidóság legfontosabb mai teendőiről és feladatairól," *Ararát* (1941): 20–26.

65. See Imre Reiner, "A hetvenéves orthodoxia," *Orthodox Zsidó Újság,* December 20, 1941.

66. "A szefira napjaiban," *Orthodox Zsidó Újság,* April 17, 1942.

67. Ibid.

68. "Az országokról elhatároztatik . . . ," *Orthodox Zsidó Újság,* September 29, 1943.

69. Salamon Stern, "Új kor, új nevelés," *Orthodox Zsidó Újság,* February 1, 1943.

70. Dezső Korein, "Az asszimiláció csődbe jutott," *Orthodox Zsidó Újság,* October 29, 1943.

71. See also "A háromhét," *Orthodox Zsidó Újság,* July 20, 1943.

72. György Kecskeméti, "A zsidóság mai problémái," *Ararát* (1940): 97–100.

73. Lajos Fodor, "A zsidó élet útjai," *Múlt és Jövő,* May 1940, 67.

74. József Junger, "Szellemtörténeti szempontok az asszimiláció problémájához," *Múlt és Jövő,* February 1941, 17–18.

75. József Junger, "Generációs problémák a magyar zsidóságban," *Múlt és Jövő,* June 1941, 81–82.

76. József Junger, "Magyarság és zsidóság," *Múlt és Jövő,* September 1941, 131–32.

77. Ibid., 132.

78. József Junger, "A magyar zsidóság és a zsidó népi politika," *Múlt és Jövő,* November 1941, 161–62.

79. On the attempts to realize the vision of the national community (*Volksgemeinde*) by Zionist groups in Weimar Germany, see Michael Brenner, *The Renaissance of Jewish Culture in Weimar Germany* (New Haven, CT, 1996), 49–65.

80. József Junger, "A magyar zsidóság és a zsidó népi politika," *Múlt és Jövő,* November 1941, 162.

81. About Marton's life story, see Moses Gartner, "Dr. Yeheskel (Ernst) Marton, His Life Story" [in Hebrew], Marton collection, 1.2., Documentation Center, Strochlitz Institute of University of Haifa, Israel.

82. Ernő Marton, *A magyar zsidóság családfája* (Kolozsvár, 1941), 3–4.

83. Ibid., 6.

84. About Dubnow, his historical views, and his impact, see Sophie Dubnov-Erlich, *The Life and Work of S. M. Dubnov: Diaspora Nationalism and Jewish History* (Bloomington, IN, 1991); David H. Weinberg, *Between Tradition and Modernity: Haim Zhitlowski, Simon Dubnow, Ahad Ha-Am and the Shaping of Modern Jewish Identity* (New York, 1996), 145–216; and Marcos Silber, "S. Dubnow: The Idea of Diaspora Nationalism and Its Dissemination" [in Hebrew], *Studies in Zionism, the Yishuv and the State of Israel* 15 (2005): 83–101.

85. Marton, *A magyar zsidóság családfájs,* 10.

86. Ibid., 24 and (more detailed) 42–62.

87. Ibid., 69–70.

88. Ibid., 11, 28–32.

89. Ernő Marton, *A zsidó nép jövője (a népi asszimiláció törvényszerűségei)* (Kolozsvár, 1941), 3–11. In the second book, which was published in August 1941 two months after the Nazi invasion of the Soviet Union, Marton anticipated the uprooting of millions of Jews from Europe in the wake of the war; see Ernő Marton, *A zsidó nép világhelyzete 1941-ben* (Kolozsvár, 1941), 23. In a later essay Marton proposed a summary of the life of the Jews in Europe as they neared their decline; see Ernő Marton, "Europa és a zsidóság," *Múlt és Jövő,* October 1943, 149–50.

90. Marton, *A zsidó nép jövője,* 18.

91. Ibid., 19–25.

92. In this period Marton devoted another book to an analysis of the new Jewish settlement in Palestine and its significance for future world Jewry; see Ernő Marton, *Mit nyújthat Palesztina a világ zsidóságának?* (Kolozsvár, [1941/1942]).

93. Ernő Marton, "Az első emancipáció a történelem mérlegén," in Ernő Marton, Rezső Kasztner, Siegfried Róth, and József Junger, *Az emancipáció multja és jövője, Negy tanulmány* (Kolozsvár, 1942), 46, emphasis in original.

94. See also the other three articles in Marton, Kasztner, Róth, and Junger, *Az emancipáció múltja és jövője,* and see Miklós Buk, *A kétezeréves út, A zsidókérdés történetszociológiája* (Budapest, 1943). About Buk and his book, see the interview with Dr. Moshe (Miklós) Buk, April 1958, 03/1007, Yad Vashem Archives, Jerusalem.

95. See "Az emancipáció múltja és jövője," *Magyar Zsidók Lapja,* July 16, 1942, and "Tisztázzuk a fogalmakat!," *Magyar Zsidók Lapja,* January 13, 1944.

Conclusion

1. About the forms of the various Jewish camps in modern Jewish politics, see Ezra Mendelssohn, *On Modern Jewish Politics* (New York, 1993).

2. Ismar Elbogen, *Geschichte der Juden in Deutschland* (Berlin, 1935); see my chapter 2 for a discussion of Elbogen's book. Jacob Kaplan, *Témoignages sur Israël dans la littérature française* (Paris, 1938); see my chapter 4 for a discussion of Kaplan's book. Ernő Ballagi, ed., *A magyar zsidóság útja: Vezércikkek és beszédek tükrében (1840–1940)* (Budapest, 1940); see my chapter 6 for a discussion of Ballagi's book.

3. On the development of the idea of progress as a dominant idea in the Western world from the mid-eighteenth century until the late nineteenth century, see Robert A. Nisbet, *History of the Idea of Progress* (New York, 1980), 171–316. On the optimistic tendencies and the belief in historical progress in German national liberalism, see, for example, Jörn Echternkamp, *Der Aufstieg des deutschen Nationalismus (1770–1840)* (Frankfurt am Main, 1998), chap. 7; Dieter Langewiesche, *Nation, Nationalismus, Nationalstaat in Deutschland und Europa* (München, 2000), 191–209; and Marc-Wilhelm Kohfink, *Für Freiheit und Vaterland: Eine sozialwissenschaftliche Studie über den liberalen Nationalismus 1890–1933 in Deutschland* (Konstanz, 2002), 277–310. In Hungary this position was associated with the radical historical view that concentrated on the commemoration of the Hungarian Revolution of 1848–49; see Árpád von Klimó, *Nation, Konfession, Geschichte: Zur nationalen Geschichtskultur Ungarns im europäischen Kontext (1860–1948)* (München, 2003), 55–91.

4. Heinz Warschauer, "Innere Wandlung," *Central Verein Zeitung,* September 20, 1933.

5. Friedrich Brodnitz, "Um eine neue Emanzipation," *Central Verein Zeitung,* January 25, 1934.

6. Endre Sós, "Bevezetője," in *Magyar zsidó írók dekameronja,* edited by Endre Sós, 5–14 (Budapest, 1939), and Endre Sós, "Asszimiláció vagy cionizmus," *Múlt és Jövő,* June 1941.

7. For Liber's positions, see Meyerskey, "L'émancipation a-t-elle fait faillite? Conférence faite par M. le grand-rabbin Liber," *L'Univers Israélite,* February 16,

1934, and Maurice Liber, "La Révolution, Les Juifs et le Judaisme," *L'Univers Israélite,* August 25–September 1, 1939. See also my chapters 3 and 4.

8. A. S. Lirik, "Zurik in Ghetta," *Pariser Haynt,* September 27, 1935; A. S. Lirik, "Moses Mendelssohn," *Pariser Haynt,* January 12, 1936; and A. S. Lirik, "Fon Paroa biz Hitler," *Pariser Haynt,* April 10, 1936.

9. Joseph Ben Aron, "Entretien sur Blum, le ghetto, l'antisémitisme et l'assimilation," *La Terra Retrouvée,* May 1, 1938.

10. About this, see Jacob Katz, *A House Divided: Orthodoxy and Schism in Nineteenth-Century Central European Jewry* (Hanover, NH, 1998).

11. For an overview on the phenomenon of modern rabbinical seminaries in Europe, see Guy Miron, ed., *From Breslau to Jerusalem: Rabbinical Seminaries Past, Present and Future* [in Hebrew] (Jerusalem, 2009).

12. Victor Karády, "Identity Strategies under Duress before and after the Shoah," in *The Holocaust in Hungary Fifty Years Later,* edited by Randolph L. Braham and Attila Pók, 159–60 (New York, 1997).

13. Natalia Aleksiun, "Narratives under Siege: Polish-Jewish Relations and Jewish Historical Writings in Interwar Poland," in *Anti-Semitism Worldwide, 2003–2004* (Tel Aviv, 2005), 29–50, and Katrin Steffen, *Jüdische Polonität: Ethnizität und Nation im Spiegel der polnischsprachigen jüdischen Presse 1918–1939* (Göttingen, 2004), 92–151.

14. Havi Dreifuss (Ben-Sasson), *"We Polish Jews"? The Relations between Jews and Poles during the Holocaust; The Jewish Perspective* [in Hebrew] (Jerusalem, 2009).

BIBLIOGRAPHY

PRIMARY SOURCES

Germany

PERIODICALS

Central Verein Zeitung
Der Israelit
Der Morgen
Der Schild
Frankfurter Israelitisches Gemeindeblatt
Gemeindeblatt der Deutsch-Israelitischen Gemeinde zu Hamburg
Gemeindeblatt der Jüdischen Gemeinde zu Berlin
Gemeindeblatt für die Jüdischen Gemeinden Preussens
Israelitisches Familienblatt
Jüdische Rundschau
Jüdisch-liberale Zeitung
Zeitschrift für die Geschichte der Juden in Deutschland

BOOKS

Altmann, Adolf. *Volk im Aufbruch, Diaspora in Bewegung: Reflexionen zur jüdischen Zeitgeschichte*. Frankfurt am Main, 1936.
Bamberger, Fritz. *Das System des Maimonides: Eine Analyse des More Newuchim vom Gottesbegriff aus*. Berlin, 1935.
Carlebach, Joseph. *Das gesetzestreue Judentum*. Berlin, 1936.
Elbogen, Ismar. *Geschichte der Juden in Deutschland*. Berlin, 1935.
Eloesser, Arthur. *Vom Ghetto nach Europa: Das Judentum im geistigen Leben des 19. Jahrhunderts*. Berlin, 1936.
Friedländer, Fritz. *Das Leben Gabriel Riessers*. Berlin, 1926.
Jüdisches Museum in Berlin. *Gedenkausstellung Don Jizchaq Abarbanel, Seine Welt, Sein Werk*. Berlin, 1937.
Kastein, Josef. *Eine Geschichte der Juden*. Berlin, 1931.
Krojanker, Gustav. *Zum Problem des neuen deutschen Nationalismus*. Berlin, 1932.
Prinz, Joachim. *Jüdische Geschichte*. Berlin, 1931.
———. "A Rabbi under the Hitler Regime." In *Gegenwart im Rückblick,* edited by

Herbert A. Strauss and Kurt R. Grossmann, 231–38. Heidelberg, 1970.

———. *Rebellious Rabbi, an Autobiography: The German and Early American Years.* Edited by Michael A. Meyer. Bloomington, IN, 2007.

———. *Wir Juden.* Berlin, 1934.

Reissner, Hanns, *Familie auf Wanderschaft.* Berlin, 1938.

Schachnowitz, Selig, *Rabbi Mosche Ben Maimun: Ein Lebenswerk für Gott, Israel und Thora.* Frankfurt am Main, 1935.

Schoeps, Hans Joachim. *Wir deutschen Juden.* Berlin, 1934.

Schwab, Simon. *Heimkehr ins Judentum.* Frankfurt am Main, 1934.

Stern, Selma. *Jud Süss.* Berlin, 1929.

Stern-Täubler, Selma. *Der preussische Staat und die Juden,* Vol. 1. Berlin, 1925.

Straus, Raphael. *Die Judengemeinde Regensburg im ausgehenden Mittelalter.* Heidelberg, 1932.

Weil, Bruno. *Der Weg der deutschen Juden.* Berlin, 1934.

Wille und Weg des deutschen Judentums. Berlin, 1935.

Wollenberg, Hans, ed. *Heroische Gestalten jüdischen Stammes.* Berlin, 1937.

ARCHIVES

Neue Tendenzen im jüdischen Schrifttum, Yad Vashem Archives, Jerusalem, 051/OSOBI/52.

France

PERIODICALS

Affirmation
Archives Israélites
Chalom
Die Naye Parisisher Yidishe tsytung (Yiddish)
La Terre Retrouvée
La Tribune juive
Le Journal Juif
L'Univers Israélite
Naye Presse (Yiddish)
Oyfn Shaydveg (Yiddish)
Paix et Droit
Pariser Haynt (Yiddish)
Samedi
Unzer Shtime (Yiddish)

BOOKS

Berman, Léon. *Histoire des Juifs de France des origines a nos jours.* Paris, 1937.

Hagani, Baruch. *L'Emancipation des juifs.* Paris, 1928.

Kaplan, Jacob. *Témoignages sur Israël dans la littérature française.* Paris, 1938.

Netter, Nathan. *Vingt siècles d'histoire d'une communauté juive (Metz et son grand passé)*. Paris, 1938.

Pierrard, Pierre. *Justice pour la foi juive: Pierre Pierrard interroge le Grand Rabbin Kaplan*. Paris, 1977.

Posener, Solomon Vladimirovich. *Adolphe Cremieux (1796–1880)*. 2 vols. Paris, 1933–34.

Hungary

PERIODICALS

Ararát
Egyenlőség
IMIT [Izraelita Magyar Irodalmi Társulat] Évkönyv
Képes Családi Lapok
Libanon
Magyar Zsidók Lapja
Magyar Zsidó Szemle
Múlt és Jövő
OMZSA Évkönyv
Orthodox Zsidó Újság
Zsidó Élet
Zsidó Szemle
Zsidó Újság

BOOKS

Ballagi, Ernő, ed. *A magyar zsidóság útja: Vezércikkek és beszédek tükrében (1840–1940)*. Budapest, 1940.

Buk, Miklós. *A kétezeréves út, A zsidókérdés történetszociológiája*. Budapest, 1943.

Guttmann, Yehiel Michael [Mihály] Hacohen. Introduction to Rabbi Joseph Judah Gattinara, "The Talmud and Freedom." In *Jubilee Volume in Honor of Dr. Hayyim Zvi Kisch* [in Hebrew], edited by Mihály Guttmann, Simon Hevesi, and Sámuel Lőwinger, 3–8. Budapest, 1939.

Korein, Dezső. *Mi az oka a zsidógyűlöletnek*. Budapest, 1935.

Marton, Ernő. *A magyar zsidóság családfája*. Kolozsvár, 1941.

———. *A zsidó nép jövője (a népi asszimiláció törvényszerűségei)*. Kolozsvár, 1941.

———. *A zsidó nép világhelyzete 1941-ben*. Kolozsvár, 1941.

———. *Mit nyújthat Palesztina a világ zsidóságának?* (Kolozsvár, [1941/1942]).

Marton Ernő, Rezső Kasztner, Siegfried Róth, and József Junger. *Az emancipáció multja és jövője, Negy tanulmány*. Kolozsvár, 1942.

Munkácsi Ernő. *Küzdelmes évek . . . , Cikkek és tanulmányok a magyar zsidóság elmúlt évtizedéből*. Budapest, 1943.

Sós, Endre. *Becsapott ajtók előtt*. Budapest, 1938.

———. *Zsidók a magyar városokban: Történelmi tanulmány*. Budapest, 1940.

———, ed. *Magyar zsidó írók dekameronja*. Budapest, 1939.

Stern, Samu. *A zsidókérdés Magyarországon.* Budapest, 1938.

Turóczi-Trostler, József, and Jenő Zsoldos, eds. *Száz év előtt: Az első magyar-zsidó írónemzedék.* Budapest, 1940.

Zsoldos, Jenő, ed. *Magyar irodalom és zsidóság: Költői és prózai szemelvények.* Budapest, 1943.

ARCHIVES

Marton Collection, 1.2. The Documentation Center, Strochlitz Institute of University of Haifa, Israel.

RESEARCH LITERATURE

Aleksiun, Natalia. "Narratives under Siege: Polish-Jewish Relations and Jewish Historical Writings in Interwar Poland." In *Anti-Semitism Worldwide, 2003–2004,* 29–50. Tel Aviv University, 2005. 29–50.

Alter, Peter, Claus-Ekkehard Baersch, and Peter Berghoff, eds. *Die Konstruktion der Nation gegen die Juden.* München, 1999.

Anderson, Benedict. *Imagined Communities: Reflections on the Origin and Spread of Nationalism.* London, 1993.

Aschheim, Steven E. "German History and German Jewry: Junctions, Boundaries, and Interdependencies." In *In Times of Crisis: Essays on European Culture, Germans, and Jews.* Madison, WI, 2001. 86–92.

Assmann, Aleida. *Erinnerungsräume: Formen und Wandlungen des kulturellen Gedächtnisses.* München, 1999.

Assmann, Jan. *Das kulturelle Gedächtnis.* München, 1992.

———. *Moses the Egyptian: The Memory of Egypt in Western Monotheism.* Cambridge, MA, 1997.

Attias, Jean-Christophe. "Isaac Abravanel: Between Ethnic Memory and National Memory." *Jewish Social Studies* 2, no. 3 (1996): 137–55.

Barkai, Avraham. *"Wehr Dich": Der Centralverein deutscher Staatsbürger jüdischen Glaubens, 1893–1938.* München, 2002.

Becker, Annette. "Les Juifs de France et Verdun, 1916–1940." *Archives Juives* 33, no. 1 (2000): 69–81.

Ben-Amos, Dan, and Liliane Weissberg, eds. *Cultural Memory and the Construction of Identity.* Detroit, 1999.

Ben-Ari, Nitsa. *Romance with the Past: The Nineteenth-Century German-Jewish Historical Novel and the Creation of a National Literature* [in Hebrew]. Tel Aviv, 1997.

Ben-Avner, Yehuda. *Vom orthodoxen Judentum in Deutschland zwischen zwei Weltkriegen.* Hildesheim, Germany, 1987.

Benz, Wolfgang. *Die deutschen Juden und der Nationalsozialismus, 1933–1939.* Bonn, 1988.

Berger, Stefan. *The Search for Normality: National Identity and Historical Consciousness in Germany since 1800.* Providence, RI, 1997.

Berkovitz, Jay R. *Rites and Passages: The Beginnings of Modern Jewish Culture in France, 1650–1860.* Philadelphia, 2004.

———. *The Shaping of Jewish Identity in Nineteenth-century France.* Detroit, 1989.

Berstein, Serge. *La France des années 30.* Paris, 2001.

Bialas, Wolfgang, and Gerard Raulet, eds. *Die Historismusdebatte in der Weimarer Republik.* Frankfurt am Main, 1996.

Birnbaum, Pierre, ed., *Histoire politique des Juifs de France.* Paris, 1990.

———. *Jewish Destinies: Citizenship, State and Community in Modern France.* New York, 2000.

———. *The Jews of the Republic: A Political History of State Jews in France from Gambetta to Vichy.* Stanford, CA, 1996.

Birnbaum, Pierre, and Ira Katznelson, eds. *Paths of Emancipation: Jews, States, and Citizenship.* Princeton, NJ, 1995.

Blackbourn, David. *The Long Nineteenth Century: A History of Germany, 1780–1918.* New York, 1998.

Boas, Jacob. "German-Jewish Internal Politics under Hitler, 1933–1938." *Leo Baeck Institute Year Book* 29 (1984): 3–25.

———. "Germany or Diaspora? German Jewry's Shifting Perceptions in the Nazi Era (1933–1938)." *Leo Baeck Institute Year Book* 27 (1982): 109–26.

———. "The Shrinking World of German Jewry: 1933–1938." *Leo Baeck Institute Year Book* 31 (1986): 241–66.

Bock, Petra, and Edgar Wolfrum, eds. *Umkämpfte Vergangenheit: Geschichtsbilder, Erinnerung und Vergangenheitspolitik im internationalen Vergleich.* Göttingen, 1999. 103–13.

Bonnell, Victoria E., and Lynn Hunt, eds. *Beyond the Cultural Turn: New Directions in the Study of Society and Culture.* Berkeley, 1999.

Borut, Jacob. *"A New Spirit among our Brethren in Ashkenaz": German Jewry's Change in Dierction at the End of the 19th Century* [in Hebrew]. Jerusalem, 1999.

Boukara, Philippe. "Commémorations juives de la Révolution française; le cas du cent cinquantenaire (1939) vu par les Juifs de Paris-immigrés en particulier." In *Les Juifs et la Révolution française: Histoire et mentalités,* edited by Mireille Hadas-Lebel and Evelyne Oliel-Grausz, 333–41. Louvain, 1992.

Braham, Randolph L. *The Politics of Genocide: The Holocaust in Hungary.* 2 vols. New York, 1994.

Brämer, Andreas. "Rabbinical Scholars as the Object of Biographical Interest: An aspect of Jewish Historiography in the German-speaking Countries of Europe (1780–1871)." *Leo Baeck Institute Year Book* 45 (2000): 51–79.

Brenner, Michael. *The Renaissance of Jewish Culture in Weimar Germany.* New Haven, CT, 1996.

Brenner, Michael, Vicki Caron, and Uri R. Kaufmann, eds. *Jewish Emancipation Reconsidered: The French and German Models.* Tübingen, 2003.

Breuer, Mordechai. *Modernity within Tradition: The Social History of Orthodox Jewry in Imperial Germany.* New York, 1992.

Büchler, Robert. "The Jewish Community in Slovakia before World War II." In *The*

Tragedy of Slovak Jews, edited by Wacław Długoborski et al., 16–23. Banská Bystrica, 1992.

Bunim, Shmuel. "La presse yiddish parisienne dans l'entre-deux-guerres; un miroir du monde du travail." *Archives Juives,* 33, no. 2 (2000): 47–66.

Caron, Vicki. *Uneasy Asylum: France and the Jewish Refugee Crisis, 1933–1942.* Stanford, CA, 1999.

Carroll, David. *French Literary Fascism: Nationalism, Anti-Semitism, and the Ideology of Culture.* Princeton, NJ, 1995.

Clark, Elizabeth A. *History, Theory, Text: Historians and the Linguistic Turn.* Cambridge, MA, 2004.

Cohen, Richard I. (Yerachmiel). "The Dreyfus Affair and the Jews." In *Antisemitism through the Ages,* edited by Shmuel Almog, 291–310. Oxford, UK, 1988.

Confino, Alon. *The Nation as a Local Metaphor: Württemberg, Imperial Germany, and National Memory, 1871–1918.* Chapel Hill, NC, 1997.

Dann, Otto. *Nation und Nationalismus in Deutschland, 1770–1990.* München, 1996.

Dard, Olivier. *Les années trente: Le choix impossible.* Paris, 1999.

Deák, István. "Historiography of the Countries of Eastern Europe: Hungary." *American Historical Review* 97, no. 4 (1992): 1041–63.

Debono, Emmanuel. "Bernard Abraham Lecache, président fondateur de la Ligue internationale contre l'antisémitisme," *Archives Juives* 40, no. 1 (2007): 140–44.

———. "Le visage de l'anti-France dans la France des années trente: L'exemple de la Ligue internationale contre l'antisémitisme (LICA)." *Revue d'Histoire de la Shoah,* no. 173 (September–December 2001): 113–36.

Diehl, Katrin. *Die jüdische Presse im Dritten Reich: Zwischen Selbstbehauptung und Fremdbestimmung.* Tübingen, 1997.

Dreifuss (Ben-Sasson), Havi. *"We Polish Jews"? The Relations between Jews and Poles during the Holocaust; The Jewish Perspective* [in Hebrew]. Jerusalem, 2009.

Dubnov-Erlich, Sophie. *The Life and Work of S. M. Dubnov: Diaspora Nationalism and Jewish History.* Bloomington, IN, 1991.

Echternkamp, Jörn. *Der Aufstieg des deutschen Nationalismus (1770–1840).* Frankfurt am Main, 1998.

Ehrenfreund, Jacques. "Citizenship and Acculturation: Some Relections on German Jews during the Second Empire and French Jews during the Third Republic." In *Jewish Emancipation Reconsidered: The French and German Models,* edited by Michael Brenner, Vicki Caron, and Uri R. Kaufmann, 155–63. Tübingen, 2003.

———. *Mémoire juive et nationalité allemanje: Les juifs berlinois à la belle époque.* Paris, 2000.

Eichler, Hava. "The Uniqueness of the Zionist Movement in Hungary between the World Wars" [in Hebrew]. *Yahadut Zemanenu* 5 (1989): 91–114.

Endelman, Todd M. "The Englishness of Jewish Modernity in England." In *Toward Modernity: The European Jewish Model,* edited by Jacob Katz, 225–46. New Brunswick, NJ, 1987.

———, ed. *Comparing Jewish Societies.* Ann Arbor, MI, 1997.

Epstein, Irena Raab. *Gyula Szekfü: A Study in the Political Basis of Hungarian Historiography.* New York, 1987.

Erős, Vilmos. "A Magyar történetírás a két világháború közötti időszakban." In *Magyarország a XX. században,* Vol. 5, 292–304. Szekszárd, 2000.

Farmer, Paul. *France Reviews Its Revolutionary Origins: Social Politics and Historical Opinion in the Third Republic.* New York, 1963.

Faulenbach, Bernd. *Ideologie des deutschen Weges: Die deutsche Geschichte in der Historiographie zwischen Kaiserreich und Nationalsozialismus.* München, 1980.

Feiner, Shmuel. *Haskalah and History: The Emergence of a Modern Jewish Historical Consciousness.* Oxford, UK, 2002.

———. "'Rebellious French' and 'Jewish Freedom': The French Revolution in the East European *Haskalah*'s Image of the Past." In *The French Revolution and Its Impact,* edited by Richard I. Cohen, 215–47 [in Hebrew]. Jerusalem, 1991.

Fenyo, Mario D. "Did Hungarian Intellectuals Resist of Betray?" In *Hungary in the Age of Total War (1938–1948),* edited by Nándor Dreisziger, 123–32. New York, 1998.

Fischer, Rolf. *Entwicklungsstufen des Antisemitismus in Ungarn 1867–1939: Die Zerstörung der magyarisch-jüdischen Symbiose.* München, 1988.

Fraenkel, Daniel. *On the Edge of the Abyss: Zionist Policy and the Plight of the German Jews, 1933–1938* [in Hebrew]. Jerusalem, 1994.

Frankel, Jonathan, and Steven J. Zipperstein, eds. *Assimilation and Community: The Jews in Nineteenth-Century Europe.* Cambridge, UK, 1992.

Fraiman, Sarah. "The Transformation of Jewish Consciousness in Nazi Germany as Reflected in the German Jewish Journal *Der Morgen,* 1925–1938." *Modern Judaism* 20, no. 1 (2000): 41–59.

Francois, Etienne, and Hagen Schulze, eds. *Deutsche Erinnerungsorte.* München, 2001.

Freeden, Herbert. *The Jewish Press in the Third Reich.* Providence, RI, 1992.

Freifeld, Alice. *Nationalism and the Crowd in Liberal Hungary, 1848–1914.* Washington, DC, 2000.

Friedländer, Fritz. "Trials and Tribulations of Jewish Education in Nazi Germany." *Leo Baeck Institute Year Book* 3 (1958): 187–201.

Friedlander, Saul. *Nazi Germany and the Jews.* New York, 1997.

Frojimovics, Kinga. "A 'doktor-rabbik' nagy nemzedéke Magyarországon: A neológ identitás kialakítása a történetíráson keresztül." In *Széfer Józséf,* edited by József Zsengellér, 221–39. Budapest, 2002.

———. *I Have Been a Stranger in a Strange Land: The Hungarian State and Jewish Refugees in Hungary, 1933–1945.* Jerusalem, 2007.

———. *The Religious Trends of the Jewry in Hungary (Orthodox, Neolog, Status Quo Ante) between 1868/1869–1950, Socio-Economic, Demographic, and Organizational Characteristics* [in Hebrew]. PhD dissertation, Bar Ilan University, Ramat Gan, Israel, 2002.

———. "Who Were They? Characteristics of the Religious Streams within Hungarian Jewry on the Eve of the Community's extermination." *Yad Vashem Studies* 35 no. 1 (2007): 143–77.

Funkenstein, Amos. "Collective Memory and Historical Consciousness." *History and Memory* 1, no. 1 (1989): 5–26.

Garbarini, Alexandra. *Numbered Days: Diaries and the Holocaust.* New Haven, CT, 2006.

Gebhardt, Miriam. *Das Familiengedächtnis: Erinnerungen im deutsch-jüdischen Bürgertum 1890 bis 1932.* Stuttgart, 1999.

Gellner, Ernest. *Nations and Nationalism.* Ithaca, NY, 1983.

Gerwarth, Robert. "The Past in Weimar History." *Contemporary European History* 15, no. 1 (2006): 1–22.

Gildea, Robert. *The Past in French History.* New Haven, CT, 1994.

Gillis, John R., ed. *Commemorations: The Politics of National Identity.* Princeton, NJ, 1994.

Grameley, Hedda. *Propheten des deutschen Nationalismus: Theologen, Historiker und Nationalökonomen, 1848–1880.* Frankfurt, 2001.

Green, Nancy L. "La révolution dans l'imaginaire des immigrants juifs." In *Histoire politique des Juifs de France,* edited by Pierre Birnbaum, 153–62. Paris, 1990.

Gunst, Péter. "A tudományos történetírás kibontakozása Magyarországon (1867–1918)." *Debreceni Szemle* 3, no. 1 (1995): 69–78.

Gyurgyák, János. *A zsidókérdés Magyarországon.* Budapest, 2001.

Haar, Ingo. *Historiker im Nationalsozialismus: Die deutsche Geschichte und der "Volkstumskampf" im Osten.* Göttingen, 2000.

Hanebrink, Paul A. *In Defense of Christian Hungary: Religion, Nationalism, and Antisemitism, 1890–1944.* Ithaca, NY, 2006.

Hartman, Zvi. "A Jewish Minority in a Multiethnic Society during a Change of Governments: The Jews of Transylvania in the Interwar Period." *Shvut* 9, no. 25 (2001): 162–82.

Hecht, Cornelia. *Deutsche Juden und Antisemitismus in der Weimarer Republik.* Bonn, 2003.

Heiber, Helmut. *Walter Frank und sein Reichsinstitut für Geschichte des neuen Deutschlands.* Stuttgart, 1966.

Hobsbawm, Eric J., and Terence Ranger, eds. *The Invention of Tradition.* Cambridge, UK, 1983.

Hoffmann, Christhard. "Constructing Jewish Modernity: Mendelssohn Jubilee Celebrations within German Jewry, 1829–1929." In *Towards Normality? Acculturation and Modern German Jewry,* edited by Rainer Liedtke and David Rechter, 27–52. Tübingen, 2003.

———. "Die Verbürgerlichung der jüdischen Vergangenheit: Formen, Inhalte, Kritik." In *Judentum und Historismus: Zur Entstehung der jüdischen Geschichtswissenschaft in Europa,* edited by Ulrich Wyrwa, 149–71. Frankfurt am Main, 2003.

———. "Jüdische Geschichtswissenschaft in Deutschland: 1918–1938, Konzepte, Schwerpunkte, Ergebnisse." In *Wissenschaft des Judentums: Anfänge der Judaistik in Europa,* edited by Julius Carlebach, 132–52. Darmstadt, 1992.

Hopp, Andrea. "Das Jahr 1929: Erinnerung und Selbstverständnis im deutschen

Judentum." *Trumah* 7 (1998): 113–34.

Hyman, Paula E. *The Jews of Modern France.* Berkeley, 1998.

Iggers, Georg G. *The German Conception of History: The National Tradition of Historical Thought from Herder to the Present.* Middletown, CT, 1983.

Irvine, William D. *Between Justice and Politics: The Ligue des droits de l'homme, 1898–1945.* Stanford, CA, 2007.

Jackson, Julian, *France: The Dark Years, 1940–1944.* Oxford, UK, 2001.

———. *The Popular Front in France: Defending Democracy, 1934–38.* Cambridge, UK, 1988.

Kaplan, Marion A. *Between Dignity and Despair: Jewish Life in Nazi Germany.* New York, 1998.

Karády, Victor. "Identity Strategies under Duress before and after the Shoah." In *The Holocaust in Hungary Fifty Years Later,* edited by Randolph L. Braham and Attila Pók, 147–78. New York, 1997.

———. "Religious Divisions, Socio-Economic Stratification and the Modernization of Hungarian Jewry after the Emancipation." In *Jews in the Hungarian Economy, 1760–1945,* edited by Michael K. Silber, 161–84. Jerusalem, 1992.

Karlip, Joshua M. "At the Crossroads between War and Genocide: A Reassessment of Jewish Ideology in 1940." *Jewish Social Studies* 11, no. 2 (2005): 170–201.

———. "Between Martyrology and Historiography: Elias Tcherikower and the Making of a Pogrom Historian." *East European Jewish Affairs* 38, no. 3 (2008): 257–80.

Katz, Jacob. *A House Divided: Orthodoxy and Schism in Nineteenth-Century Central European Jewry.* Hanover, NH, 1998.

———. *From Prejudice to Destruction: Anti-Semitism, 1700–1933.* Cambridge, MA, 1980.

———. "The Identity of Post Emancipatory Hungarian Jewry." In *A Social and Economic History of Central European Jewry,* edited by Jehuda Don and Victor Karady, 13–31. New Brunswick, NJ, 1990.

———. *Out of the Ghetto: The Social Background of Jewish Emancipation, 1770–1870.* Cambridge, MA, 1973.

———, ed. *Toward Modernity: The European Jewish Model.* New Brunswick, NJ, 1987.

Katzburg, Nathaniel. *Antisemitism in Hungary, 1867–1944* [in Hebrew]. Jerusalem, 1993.

———. *History of the Holocaust: Hungary* [in Hebrew]. Jerusalem, 1992.

———. *Hungary and the Jews: Policy and Legislation, 1920–1943.* Ramat Gan, Israel, 1981.

———. "Jewish Historiography in Hungary" [in Hebrew]. *Sinai* 40, nos. 2–3 (1956–57): 113–26, 164–76.

———. "Zionist Reactions to Hungarian Anti-Jewish Legislation, 1939–1942." *Yad Vashem Studies* 16 (1984): 161–76.

Kauders, Anthony. *German Politics and the Jews: Duesseldorf and Nuremberg, 1910–1933.* Oxford, UK, 1996.

Kedward, Rod. *La vie en bleu: France and the French since 1900*. London, 2006.

Klimó, Árpád von. "Die gespaltene Vergangenheit, Die grossen christlichen Kirchen im Kampf um die Nationalgeschichte Ungarns 1920–1948." *Zeitschrift für Geschichtswissenschaft* 47, no. 10 (1999): 876–84.

———. *Nation, Konfession, Geschichte: Zur nationalen Geschichtskultur Ungarns im europäischen Kontext (1860–1948)*. München, 2003.

Kohfink, Marc-Wilhelm. *Für Freiheit und Vaterland: Eine sozialwissenschaftliche Studie über den liberalen Nationalismus 1890–1933 in Deutschland*. Konstanz, 2002.

Kolb, Eberhard. *The Weimar Republic*. London, 1988.

Koshar, Rudy. *From Monuments to Traces: Artifacts of German Memory, 1870–1990*. Berkeley, 2000.

Kosáry, Domokos. "A magyar történetírás a két világháború között." In *A történelem veszedelem,* 351–55. Budapest, 1987.

Koselleck, Reinhart. "The Limits of Emancipation: A Conceptual-Historical Sketch." In *The Practice of Conceptual History: Timing History, Spacing Concepts,* 248–64. Stanford, CA, 2002.

Krieger, Leonard. *Ranke: The Meaning of History*. Chicago, 1977.

Kroll, Frank-Lothar. *Utopie als Ideologie: Geschichtsdenken und politisches Handeln im Dritten Reich*. Paderborn, 1998.

Kulka, Otto Dov, ed. *Deutsches Judentum unter dem Nationalsozialismus,* Vol. 1. Tübingen, 1997.

Langewiesche, Dieter. *Nation, Nationalismus, Nationalstaat in Deutschland und Europa*. München, 2000.

Lässig, Simone. *Jüdische Wege ins Bürgertum: Kulturelles Kapital und sozialer Aufstieg im 19. Jahrhundert*. Göttingen, 2004.

Lavsky, Hagit. *Before Catastrophe: The Distinctive Path of German Zionism*. Detroit, 1996.

Mócsy, István I. *The Effects of World War I: The Uprooted; Hungarians, Refugees, and Their Impact on Hungary's Domestic Politics, 1918–1921*. New York, 1983.

Malino, Frances, and Bernard Wasserstein, eds. *The Jews in Modern France*. Hanover, NH, 1985.

Malinovich, Nadia. *French and Jewish: Culture and the Politics of Identity of Early Twentieth-Century Jewish France*. Oxford, UK, 2008.

Mallmann, Klaus-Michael. "Der qualitative Sprung im Vernichtungsprozess: Das Massaker von Kamenez-Podolsk Ende August 1941." *Jahrbuch für Antisemitismusforschung* 10 (2001): 239–64.

Margaliot, Abraham. *Between Rescue and Annihilation: Studies in the History of German Jewry, 1932–1938* [in Hebrew]. Jerusalem, 1990.

Marrus, Michael. *The Politics of Assimilation: A Study of the French Jewish Community at the Time of the Dreyfus Affair*. Oxford, UK, 1971.

Matsuda, Matt K. *The Memory of the Modern*. New York, 1996.

Mendelsohn, Ezra. *The Jews of East Central Europe between the World Wars*. Bloomington, IN, 1987.

Mendes-Flohr, Paul, and Jehuda Reinharz, eds. *The Jew in the Modern World: A Documentary History.* New York, 1995.

Meyer, Michael A. "The Emergence of Jewish Historiography: Motives and Motifs." In *Judaism within Modernity: Essays on Modern Jewish History and Religion,* 44–63. Detroit, 2001.

———. "Liberal Judaism in Nazi Germany." In *On Germans and Jews under Nazi Germany: Essays by Three Generations of Historians,* edited by Moshe Zimmermann, 281–95. Jerusalem, 2006.

———. "*Without Wissenschaft There Is No Judaism*": The Life and Thought of the Jewish Historian Ismar Elbogen. Braun Lectures in the History of the Jews in Prussia. Ramat Gan, Israel, 2004.

———, ed. *German-Jewish History in Modern Times.* New York, 1996–98.

Miron, Guy. "Between 'Center' and 'East': The Special Way of Jewish Emancipation in Hungary." *Jewish Studies at the CEU* 4 (2004–5): 111–38.

———. "Between History and a 'Useful Image of the Past': Representations of the Jewish and the German Past in the Liberal-Jewish Historical Discourse in Weimar Germany" [in Hebrew]. *Zion* 66, no. 3 (2001): 297–330.

———. "Confronting Evil: How the Jewish Press in Hungary Dealt with Anti-Semitism from the Late 1930s until 1944" [in Hebrew]. *Kesher* 33 (May 2003): 100–107.

———. "Conversations on the Jewish Question in Hungary, 1925-1926" (translated and annotated text), *Jewish History and Culture* 7, no. 3 (2004): 93–109.

———. "Emancipation and Assimilation in the German Jewish Discourse of the 1930s." *Leo Baeck Institute Year Book* 48 (2003): 165–89.

———. "The Emancipation Heroes' Pantheon in German-Jewish Public Memory of the 1930s." *German History* 21, no. 4 (2003): 476–504.

———. "History, Remembrance, and a 'Useful Past' in the Public Thought of Hungarian Jewry, 1938–1939." *Yad Vashem Studies* 32 (2004): 131–70.

———. "History, Science and Social Consciousness in the German-Jewish Public Discourse in the First Years of the Nazi Regime." In *Historiography and the Science of Judaism,* edited by Michael F. Mach and Yoram Jacobson, 231–52 [in Hebrew]. Tel Aviv, 2005.

Miron, Guy, ed., *From Breslau to Jerusalem: Rabbinical Seminaries Past, Present and Future* [in Hebrew]. Jerusalem, 2009.

Miron, Guy, and Anna Szalai, eds. *Jews at the Crossroads: The Discourse on Jewish Identity in Hungary between Crisis and Innovation, 1908–1926* [in Hebrew]. Ramat Gan, Israel, 2008.

Mosse, George L. *The Crisis of German Ideology: Intellectual Origins of the Third Reich.* New York, 1964.

Mosse, Werner E., and Arnold Paucker, eds. *Entscheidungsjahr 1932: Zur Judenfrage in der Endphase der Weimarer Republik.* Tübingen, 1965.

Myers, David N. *Re-Inventing the Jewish Past: European Jewish Intellectuals and the Zionist Return to History.* New York, 1995.

———. *Resisting History: Historicism and Its Discontents in German Jewish Thought.* Princeton, NJ, 2003.

Niewyk, Donald. *The Jews in Weimar Germany.* Baton Rouge, 1980.

Nisbet, Robert A. *History of the Idea of Progress.* New York, 1980.

Nora, Pierre, ed. *Les Lieux de mémoire.* Paris, 1997.

Nord, Philip. *The Republican Moment: Struggles for Democracy in Nineteenth-Century France.* Cambridge, MA, 1995.

Øverland, Orm. *Immigrant Minds, American Identities: Making the United States Home, 1870–1930.* Urbana, IL, 2000.

Papp, Claudia. *Ungarn im Schatten nationalsozialistischer Bündnis- und Hegemonialpolitik, 1933–1941.* CD ROM. Marburg, 1999.

Parker, Noel. *Portrayals of the Revolution: Images, Debates and Patterns of Thought on the French Revolution.* Carbondale, IL, 1990.

Paucker, Arnold, ed. *The Jews in Nazi Germany, 1933–1943.* Tübingen, 1986.

Petersen, Heidemarie. "Die Assimilationsidee überwinden: Die ungarisch-jüdische Zeitschrift Múlt és Jövő (1911–1944)." In *Die jüdische Presse im europäischen Kontext (1686–1990),* edited by Susanne Marten-Finnis and Markus Winkler, 179–89. Bremen, Germany, 2006.

Petuchowski, Elizabeth. "Zur Lessing-Rezeption in der deutsch-jüdischen Presse: Lessings 200. Geburtstag (22. Januar 1929)." *Lessing Yearbook* 14 (1982): 43–59.

Peukert, Detlev K. *The Weimar Republic: The Crisis of Classical Modernity.* London, 1991.

Pulzer, Peter. *Jews and the German State.* Cambridge, MA, 1992.

———. *The Rise of Political Anti-Semitism in Germany and Austria.* Cambridge, MA, 1988.

Puschner, Uwe. *Die völkische Bewegung im wilhelminischen Kaiserreich: Sprache-Rasse-Religion.* Darmstadt, 2001.

Ragins, Sanford. *Jewish Responses to Anti-Semitism in Germany, 1870–1914: A Study in the History of Ideas.* Cincinnati, 1980.

Ranki, Vera. *The Politics of Inclusion and Exclusion: Jews and Nationalism in Hungary.* London, 1999.

Reinharz, Jehuda. *Fatherland or Promised Land: The Dilemma of the German Jew, 1893–1914.* Ann Arbor, MI, 1975.

Rémond, René, and Janine Bourdin, eds. *La France et les Français 1938 en 1939.* Paris, 1978.

Rheins, Carl J. "Deutscher Vortrupp, Gefolgschaft deutscher Juden, 1933–1935." *Leo Baeck Institute Year Book* 26 (1981): 207–30.

Roemer, Nils. "Between the Provinces and the City: Mapping German-Jewish Memories." *Leo Baeck Institute Year Book* 51 (2006): 61–77.

———. "The City of Worms in Modern Jewish Traveling Cultures of Remembrance." *Jewish Social Studies* 11, no. 3 (2005): 67–91.

———. *German City, Jewish Memory: The Story of Worms.* Waltham, MA, 2010.

———. *Jewish Scholarship and Culture in Nineteenth-Century Germany: Between History and Faith.* Madison, WI, 2005.

———. "Provincializing the Past: Worms and the Making of a German-Jewish Cultural Heritage." *Jewish Studies Quarterly* 12, no. 1 (2005): 80–100.

Romsics, Ignác. *Hungary in the Twentieth Century.* Budapest, 1999.

———. *István Bethlen: A Great Conservative Statesman of Hungary, 1874–1946.* New York, 1995.

Rosenberg, Clifford. *Policing Paris: The Origins of Modern Immigration Control between the Wars.* Ithaca, NY, 2006.

Rosenthal, Erwin. "Ismar Elbogen and the New Jewish Learning." *Leo Baeck Institute Year Book* 8 (1963): 3–28.

Rosman, Moshe. "Jewish History across Borders." In *Rethinking European Jewish History,* edited by Jeremy Cohen and Moshe Rosman, 15–29. Oxford, UK, 2009.

Rürup, Reinhard. "The Tortuous and Thorny Path to Legal Equality: 'Jew Laws' and Emancipatory Legislation in Germany from the Late Eighteenth Century." *Leo Baeck Institute Year Book* 31 (1986): 3–33.

Rüsen, Jörn. *History: Narration, Interpretation, Orientation.* New York, 2004.

Sassenberg, Marina. *Selma Stern (1890–1981), Das Eigene in der Geschichte.* Tübingen, 2004.

Schindler, Pesach. "'Tikkun' as Response to Tragedy: 'Em habanim smeha' of Rabbi Yissakhar Shlomo Teichthal-Budapest, 1943." *Holocaust and Genocide Studies* 4, no. 4 (1989): 413–33.

Schirmer, Dietmar. *Mythos-Heilshoffnung-Modernität, Politisch-kulturelle Deutungscodes in der Weimarer Republik.* Opladen, 1992.

———. "Politisch-Kulturelle Deutungsmuster: Vorstellungen von der Welt der Politik in der Weimarer Republik." In *Politische Identität und Nationale Gedenktage: Zur politischen Kultur in der Weimarer Republik,* edited by Detlef Lehnert and Klaus Megerle, 31–60. Opladen, 1989.

Schivelbusch, Wolfgang. *The Culture of Defeat: On National Trauma, Mourning, and Recovery.* New York, 2003.

Schleier, Hans. *Die bürgerliche deutsche Geschichtsschreibung der Weimarer Republik.* Köln, 1975.

Schönwälder, Karen. *Historiker und Politik: Geschichtswissenschaft im Nationalsozialismus.* Frankfurt am Main, 1992.

Schorsch, Ismar. *From Text to Context: The Turn to History in Modern Judaism.* Hanover, NH, 1994.

———. *Jewish Reactions to German Anti-Semitism, 1870–1914.* New York, 1972.

———. "The Myth of Sephardic Supremacy." *Leo Baeck Institute Year Book* 34 (1989): 47–66.

Schöttler, Peter, ed. *Geschichtsschreibung als Legitimationswissenschaft, 1918–1945.* Frankfurt am Main, 1999.

Schulin, Ernst. "Doppel-Nationalität? Die Integration der Juden in die deutsche Kulturnation und die neue Konstruktion der jüdischen Geschichte." In *Die Konstruktion der Nation gegen die Juden,* edited by Peter Alter, Claus-Ekkehard Baersch, and Peter Berghoff, 243–59. München, 1999.

Schulz, Petra Maria. *Ästhetisierung von Gewalt in der Weimarer Republik.* Münster, 2004.

Schulze, Winfried, and Otto Gerhard Oexle, eds. *Deutsche Historiker im Nationalsozialismus.* Frankfurt am Main, 1999.

Sepinwall, Alyssa. *The Abbé Grégoire and the French Revolution: The Making of Modern Universalism.* Berkeley, 2005.

Shamir, Haim. "French Press Reaction in 1933 to Hitler's Anti-Jewish Policies." *Wiener Library Bulletin* 25, nos. 1–2 (1971): 23–32.

Shapira, David. "Crises et mutations de la communaté juive française sous l'influence du grand-rabbin de France Jacob Kaplan." PhD dissertation (Hebrew with French abstract), Hebrew University of Jerusalem, 2005.

Sherman, Daniel J. *The Construction of Memory in Interwar France.* Chicago, 1999.

Siegel, Mona L. "'History Is the Opposite of Forgetting': The Limits of Memory and the Lessons of History in Interwar France." *Journal of Modern History* 74, no. 4 (December 2002): 770–800.

Silber, Marcos. "S. Dubnow: The Idea of Diaspora Nationalism and Its Dissemination" [in Hebrew]. *Studies in Zionism, the Yishuv and the State of Israel* 15 (2005): 83–101.

Silber, Michael K., ed. *Jews in the Hungarian Economy, 1760–1945.* Jerusalem, 1992.

Simon-Nahum, Perrine. "Jüdische Historiographie im Frankreich des 19. Jahrhunderts." In *Judentum und Historismus: Zur Entstehung der jüdischen Geschichtswissenschaft in Europa,* edited by Ulrich Wyrwa, 91–116. Frankfurt am Main, 2003.

Sinkó, Katalin. "Árpád versus Saint István: Competing Heroes and Competing Interests in the Figurative Representation of Hungarian History." *Ethnologia Europaea: Journal of European Ethnology* 19, no. 1 (1989): 67–94.

Smith, Anthony D. *The Nation in History: Historiographical Debates about Ethnicity and Nationalism.* Hanover, NH, 2000.

Sommer, Robert. "La doctrine politique et l'action religieuse du grand-rabbin Maurice Liber." *Revue de Études Juives Historia Judaica* 125 (1966): 9–20.

Sorkin, David. *Moses Mendelssohn and the Religious Enlightenment.* Berkeley, 1996.

Sowerwine, Charles. *France since 1870: Culture, Politics and Society.* New York, 2001.

Steffen, Katrin. *Jüdische Polonität: Ethnizität und Nation im Spiegel der polnischsprachigen jüdischen Presse, 1918–1939.* Göttingen, 2004.

Sternhell, Zeev. *Neither Right nor Left: Fascist Ideology in France.* Berkeley, 1986.

Sugar, Peter F., ed. *A History of Hungary.* Bloomington, IN, 1994.

Szalai, Anna. "Will the Past Protect Hungarian Jewry? The Response of Jewish Intellectuals to Anti-Jewish Legislation." *Yad Vashem Studies* 32 (2004): 171–208.

Szekfű, Gyula. *Három nemzedék és ami utána következik.* Budapest, 1934.

Teichert, Carsten. *Chasak! Zionismus im nationalsozialistischen Deutschland, 1933–1938.* Köln, 2000.

Várdy, Steven Béla. "The Impact of Trianon upon the Hungarian Mind: Irredentism and Hungary's Path to War." In *Hungary in the Age of Total War (1938–1948),* edited by Nándor Dreisziger, 27–48. New York, 1998.

Várkonyi, Ágnes R. *Thaly Kálmán és történetírása.* Budapest, 1961.

Vago, Raphael. "The Jews of Transylvania: Between Integration and Segregation." In *The History of the Jews in Romania,* Vol. 3, *Between the Two World Wars,* edited by Liviu Rotman and Raphael Vago, 235–66. Tel Aviv, 2005.

van Rahden, Till. "Germans of the Jewish *Stamm:* Visions of Community between Nationalism and Particularism, 1850 to 1933." In *German History from the Margins,* edited by Neil Gregor, Nils Roemer, and Mark Roseman, 27–48. Bloomington, IN, 2006.

Várdy, Steven Béla. *Clio's Art in Hungary and in Hungarian-America.* New York, 1985.

———. *Modern Hungarian Historiography.* New York, 1976.

Vermes, Gabor. *István Tisza: The Liberal Vision and Conservative Statecraft of a Magyar Nationalist.* New York, 1985.

Volkov, Shulamit. *Die Juden in Deutschland, 1780–1918.* München, 1994.

———. *Germans, Jews, and Antisemites: Trials in Emancipation.* Cambridge, UK, 2006.

———. "Inventing Tradition: On the Formation of Modern Jewish Culture." *Jewish Studies at the CEU* 3 (2002–3): 211–27.

———. "Jews among the Nations: A Unique National Narrative or a Chapter in National Historiographies" [in Hebrew]. *Zion* 61, no. 1 (1996): 91–112.

von Papen, Patricia. *"Scholarly" Antisemitism during the Third Reich: The Reichsinstitut's Research on the "Jewish Question" 1935–1945.* PhD dissertation, Columbia University, 1999.

Vörös, Kati. "A Unique Contract: Interpretations of Modern Hungarian Jewish History." *Jewish Studies at the CEU* 3 (2002–3): 229–55.

Walter, Dirk. *Antisemitische Kriminalität und Gewalt: Judenfeindschaft in der Weimarer Republik.* Bonn, 1999.

Wassermann, Henry. Review of *Zwischen Selbstbehauptung und Verfolgung: Deutschjüdische Zeitungen und Zeitschriften von der Aufklärung bis zum Nationalsozialismus,* edited by Michael Nagel (Hildesheim, Germany, 2002), *Zion* 71, no. 1 (2006): 112–16 [in Hebrew].

Weber, Eugen. *The Hollow Years: France in the 1930s.* London, 1995.

Weinberg, David H. *Between Tradition and Modernity: Haim Zhitlowski, Simon Dubnow, Ahad Ha-Am and the Shaping of Modern Jewish Identity.* New York, 1996.

———. *A Community on Trial: The Jews of Paris in the 1930s.* Chicago, 1977.

Werner, Karl Ferdinand. *Das NS-Geschichtsbild und die deutsche Geschichtswissenschaft.* Stuttgart, 1967.

Wiese, Christian. "Modern Antisemitism and Jewish Responses in Germany and France, 1880–1914." In *Jewish Emancipation Reconsidered: The French and German Models,* edited by Michael Brenner, Vicki Caron, and Uri R. Kaufmann, 129–47. Tübingen, 2003.

Wilson, Stephen. "The Dreyfus Affair and French Jews." *Wiener Library Bulletin* 26, no. 1 (1972): 32–40.

Winock, Michel. *La France et le juifs.* Paris, 2004.

———. *Nationalism, Anti-Semitism, and Fascism in France.* Stanford, CA, 1998.

Wittenberg, Erich. *Geschichte und Tradition von 1918–1933 im Bismarckbild der deutschen Weimarer Republik.* Lund, Sweden, 1969.

Yaron, Baruch. *Jewish Assimilation and Radicalism in Hungary* [in Hebrew]. Jerusalem, 1985.

Yerushalmi, Yosef Hayim. *Zakhor: Jewish History and Jewish Memory.* Seattle, 1982.

Young, Robert J. *France and the Origins of the Second World War.* London, 1996.

Zur, Yaakov. "Orthodox Jewry in Germany during the Nazi Regime." [in Hebrew] In *History of the Holocaust: Germany,* Vol. 2, edited by Abraham Margaliot and Yehoyakim Cochavi, 839–910. Jerusalem, 1998.

Subject Index

Action Française, 104, 261n75
Alexandria, 74. *See also* exile
Algerian Jews, 113
Alliance Israélite Universelle, 8, 95, 100, 113, 114–15, 262n89
Alsace, Alsace-Lorraine, 93, 106, 113, 124, 145
America, 78, 101, 136–37. *See also* United States
Anschluss, 119, 131, 166, 172
anti-Semitism, 35, 38, 101–2, 121, 135, 219; in America, 101; in France, 86, 91, 98, 120, 122, 257n13; in Germany, 21, 30, 39, 90–92, 114, 118, 121, 123, 161; in Hungary, 131, 156–58, 160–62, 167–68, 171, 185–86, 191, 197–98, 214; in Poland, 132, 135, 232
appeasement policy, 119–20, 123, 150
archaic-mythic discourse, 24, 27, 35, 38, 39–40, 45, 52, 65, 160. *See also* cyclical view of history
Arrow Cross Party (Hungary), 158, 165, 172, 186, 190
Asia, 136
assimilation, 34–35, 39, 42–50, 92–97, 118, 143, 178–82, 198–202, 215, 228–230; active, 50; bankruptcy of, failure of, 132–133, 207, 215, 217, 227; continuous, 201–202; external, 32; false understanding of, 42, 180, 198, 211, 225; full, 141, 196; hyperassimilation, overassimilation, 179, 199; "melting in" (*összeolvadás*), 197; national, 179; natural, 180;

Orthoprax, 49; "old assimilatory Jewish shadow-life," 34, 225; partial, 48; radical, 59, 202; realistic, 180; religious, 179; swallowing, 107; total, 209–210; unhealthy, 179; unrestrained, 227
Austerlitz, 45, 220
Austria, Austrians, Austrian, 92, 131, 156, 169, 188, 190, 213. See also *Anschluss*
Australia, 78

Babylon, 74, 78. *See also* Babylonian exile
Baden, 56
Bar Kokhba Revolt, 59
Battle of Mohács (1526), 156, 159, 167–68, 175, 182, 188, 191, 214, 271n18
Battle of Valmy (1792), 145–46, 150, 222
Bavaria, 76
Bavarian Jewish law (1813), 72
Berlin, 37, 51, 66
Berlin-Rome axis, 150
Bildung, 33, 61–62; Judaism of, 62, 75
Black Death, 90, 215
bolshevism, 160, 172
Bordeaux, 145
Boulanger coup d'état (France), 91
bourgeoisie, bourgeois culture, bourgeois values, 25, 26, 28, 58, 135–36, 210–11
Brazil, 77
Budapest, Pest, 155, 158, 172, 202
Bund, Bundists, 84, 135–36, 221

NAME INDEX

Abravanel, Don Isaac, 69–71, 76, 79–80
Akiva ben Yosef, 59
Alperin, Aharon, 114–15
Altman, Adolf, 76
Anchel, Robert, 147
Anderson, Benedict, 6–7
Árpád (king), 159
Assmann, Jan, 235n18
Auerbach, Israel, 61
Auerbach, Moses, 47, 230

Baeck, Leo, 57
Ballagi, Ernö, 161, 188, 190–92, 223, 272n24
Bamberger, Fritz, 63–64, 69
Bárdossy, László, 185
Baron, Salo, 4
Barrès, Maurice, 256n2
Béla IV (king), 171
Ben Aron, Joseph, 131–32, 227
Bergel, Joseph, 233n9
Bergel-Gronemann, Elfride, 35
Berl, Alfred, 110–11
Berman, Léon, 99, 129, 230
Berr Isaac Berr, 93
Bethlen, István, 157, 270n10
Bielinky, Jacques, 128, 144–45
Bismarck, Otto von, 24, 47, 116
Blum, Leon, 87, 114, 119
Blumenfeld, Kurt, 29, 250n24
Bonnet, Georges-Étienne, 119
Börne, Ludwig, 67
Brodnitz, Friedrich, 244–45n62
Buber, Martin, 211

Carlebach, Joseph, 63
Casimir the Great, 171
Charlemagne (emperor), 174
Chautemps, Camille, 119
Chomsky, Yitzhak, 105, 108, 124, 146
Clermont-Tonnerre, Stanislas de, 37, 131, 145, 245n79
Cohen, Raphael, 48
Crémieux, Adolph, 112–14, 116, 121, 260n63
Csergö, Hugó, 196–97

Daladier, Édouard, 86, 119–20, 137, 143
Danton, Georges Jacques, 88
Darányi, Kálmán, 165, 171
Dienermann, Max, 58, 230
Dreyfus, Alfred, 105
Dreyfus, Lucien, 140–41, 267n82
Dubnow, Simon, 79, 138, 146, 213, 214, 216

Efroykin, Israel (Jacques), 133, 137
Elbogen, Ismar, 25, 54–55, 56, 58, 70, 71, 223
Eloesser, Arthur, 65–67
Eötvös, József, 190, 223
Eschelbacher, Max, 30–31, 230

Faulenbach, Bernd, 23, 24
Feuchtwanger, Ludwig, 69, 71
Flietzer, Karl-Heinz, 39
Fodor, Lajos, 170, 209
Fraenkel, Ernst, 78–79
Frank, Nissen, 106–7, 111–12, 125
Freund, Ismar, 25, 66, 248n5

Liber, Maurice, 94–95, 99, 112, 147–48, 225, 230
Lirik, A. S. (Aaron Levi Riklis), 101–2
Loewel, Robert, 91
Loewenstein, Kurt, 58–60, 62
Louis XIV (king), 128
Louis XVI (king), 144
Löwinger, Sámuel, 162, 230

Maimon, Solomon, 36
Maimonides (Rabbi Moses ben Maimon, RAMBAM), 69–71, 79, 254n72
Mályusz, Elemér, 274n69
Mandel, Arnold, 141–43, 227, 231
Marczali, Henrik, 274n74
Markus, Elias, 46, 50–51
Marton, Ernö,14, 211–16, 218, 227–28
Mátyás Hunyadi (king), 191
Maybaum, Ignaz, 61–62, 73, 74–75, 78
Meinecke, Friedrich, 24, 45
Mendelssohn, Moses, 15, 27, 33, 36–37, 48–49, 51, 60–65, 79, 93, 101, 110, 113, 205, 225, 226, 228, 251n27
Menes, Avraham, 133
Meyer, Michael, 55
Milner, Joseph, 120–21, 144
Mirabeau (Honoré-Gabriel Riqueti), 145
Molcho, Solomon, 74
Montesquieu (Charles-Louis de Secondat), 110
Munkácsi, Ernö,174–75, 176, 178, 195–96, 273n51

Nahmanides (Moses ben Nahman, RAMBAN), 74
Napoleon (emperor), 45, 93, 204, 220
Nechunia Ben Hakana, 247n123
Netter, Nathan, 127–28, 145, 150, 193, 230
Niger, Sh., 148
Nora, Pierre, 55
Nordau, Max, 92
Nussbaum, Max, 70–71

Panin, Y., 145
Patai, József, 169–70, 227
Petöfi, Sándor, 163, 165

Pinthus, Kurt, 253n63
Posener, S. (Solomon Vladimirovich Pozner), 98–99, 113–14
Prague, Hippolyte, 90, 100
Prinz, Joachim, 14, 25, 35–38, 39–42, 51, 52–53, 62, 80, 91, 181, 226, 231

Rabbenu Gershom (the "Light of the Exile"), 128
Rabbenu, Tam, 128
Raiski, A. (Adam Raigadski), 108, 128–29
Ranke, Leopold von, 44,
Rapaport, Charles, 133
Rashi (Rabbi Shlomo Yitzhaki), 55, 94, 99, 128
Rath, Ernst vom 120, 125
Reichmann-Jungmann, Eva, 73
Reissner, Hanns, 76–77
Riesser, Gabriel, 33, 43, 45, 68, 121
Robespierre, Maximilien, 88
Rosenthal, Franz, 74
Rosenthal, Hugo, 34, 226
Rousseau, Jean-Jacques, 110

Saint Stephen (Szent István, King Stephen), 159, 171–76, 182, 189, 191, 222, 228
Saint-Just, Louis-Anton-Léon de, 88
Samson, 37
Samuel, Georges, 127
Sándor, Pál, 161
Sás, Lipót, 179
Sassenberg, Marina, 249n5
Schach, Fabius, 31–32
Schachnowitz, Selig, 70, 71
Schiller, Friedrich, 161
Schirmer, Dietmar, 24, 35
Schoemann, Eugen, 95–96
Schoeps, Hans Joachim, 42–43
Schwab, Simon (Nechunia), 47–51, 52–53, 80, 207, 228, 231, 247n123
Schwarz, Moris, 121–22
Seligmann, Caesar, 32, 230, 254n72
Sieyès, Emmanuel-Joseph, 145
Singalovski, Aaron, 133–34
Smith, Anthony D., 7